# The Magazine Publishing Industry

WITHDRAWN

## Charles P. Daly
Formerly, CEO, Thomson Business Information

## Patrick Henry
Editorial Director, Printing News East

## Ellen Ryder
Ellen Ryder Communications

**Allyn and Bac**

Boston    London    Toronto    Sydney

D1044366

*Vice President, Humanities:* Joseph Opiela
*Editorial Assistant:* Kate Tolini
*Marketing Manager:* Karen Bowers
*Editorial Production Service:* Chestnut Hill Enterprises, Inc.
*Composition/Prepress Buyer:* Linda Cox
*Manufacturing Buyer:* Suzanne Lareau
*Cover Administrator:* Suzanne Harbison

**Library of Congress Cataloging-in-Publication Data**

Daly, Charles P.
    The magazine publishing industry / by Charles P. Daly, Patrick
Henry, Ellen Ryder.
        p.    cm.
    Includes bibliographical references and index.
    ISBN 0-205-16612-1
    1. Periodicals, Publishing of—United States.    I. Title. Henry,
Patrick T.,    II. Ryder, Ellen,    III. Title
Z479.D34   1996
070.5'72—dc20                                   96-32138
                                                CIP

Printed in the United States of America

10 9 8 7 6 5 4        01  00

# Contents

# 5    Circulation Principles    85

# 6    Advertising Sales    113

# 8   How Magazines Are Made   206

# 9   The Magazine of The Future— and *Your* Future in Magazines   235

# Preface

"A magazine is not just a pound of paper. A magazine is a bunch of people with special interests and ideas communicating with a larger group who share the dedication to those interests. That equation promises permanence."
                                                            –John Mack Carter (1981)

On more than one occasion in the past 250 years or so, someone has sounded the death knell for the American magazine. Improvements in the printing press and mail distribution in the late 1800s enabled some magazines to increase their circulations dramatically. That was bad news for one editor, who gloomily predicted that magazines wouldn't be worth reading anymore because large circulations could only mean mediocrity and conservatism.

When Model T's began rolling off the assembly line and families took to the highways in great numbers, magazine publishers noisily fretted that no one would have spare time to read; that driving around would be more exciting than magazine reading for Americans.

A similar chorus was heard when talking pictures came to movie theaters and then when families found hours of entertainment around the radio. With new amusements, Americans began allocating their leisure time differently—but they never stopped reading or buying magazines.

Television truly did change the magazine industry in dramatic ways. But the magazine industry didn't succumb. Instead, it adapted to the new competition. At the same time *Life, Saturday Evening Post,* and other giants of the magazine industry were overwhelmed by television's ability to reach tens of millions of households; hundreds of new magazines were launched to appeal to specialized audiences, that is, to targeted groups of readers with special interests that the mass market of television couldn't reach. Editors and publishers reshaped magazines for the times—and for their readers.

The opinion expressed by longtime magazine editor John Mack Carter back in 1981 still holds firm. His words also serve as a steadying perspective as many magazine executives break out in a cold sweat at the thought of the World Wide Web snaring the leisure time of their readers, swallowing up advertisers' budgets, and keeping magazine buyers away from the newsstand. This book has been written to demonstrate the importance of the magazine industry in our culture and in the current marketplace. It's also been written to help keep things in perspective.

As you'll read, one of the themes throughout this book is the interdependence of functions at a magazine. The disciplines of advertising, circulation, and editorial compose a sturdy "three-legged stool" upon which the business of a magazine rests. Carter, who has edited some of the largest American magazines, including *Good Housekeeping*, rightly points out that magazines are essentially "a bunch of people"—a team of individuals, talented and highly skilled, who work together to create a product. Their ideas end up on ink and paper in a most powerful, influential tool of communication. This book explores in detail this collaborative and technical process—as well as the advertising and circulation principles of the contemporary magazine industry.

In the nine chapters that follow, we'll examine the current state of the industry, along with the inner workings of magazines—for example, how magazines are actually made, how their advertising pages are sold, how ideas progress from concept to cover story. Chapter 1 outlines the history and development of the magazine in America, and attempts—as many other books about this industry have done before—to craft a contemporary definition of magazines. Composing that definition is an increasingly complicated job. Magazines take many forms and serve many purposes and constituencies today. What kind of ownership does the industry have of the term when television programs and World Wide Web sites so often appropriate the word *magazine* for themselves? Chapter 2 explores the state of the magazine business domestically and internationally. Chapter 3 dissects the work and responsibilities of the magazine publisher. Chapter 4 explains the role of the editor in chief and the editorial function, and summarizes contemporary intellectual property issues. Chapter 5 looks at the distinctive, complex function of magazine circulation. Chapter 6 surveys the goals, objectives, and challenges inherent in the magazine's advertising department. The three-legged stool analogy used throughout this text sparked the creation of the case studies at the end of Chapters 3, 4, 5, and 6. They've been positioned here and written expressly to help you further explore the interconnectedness of the advertising-editorial-circulation relationship—as well as the fundamental issues you'll inevitably encounter in a magazine career. Chapters 7 and 8 provide a comprehensive overview of the production function at magazines—that is, the magic of how magazines get made. Chapter 9 considers the magazine of the future and includes a few collegial words of advice for readers considering—or advancing in—a career in publishing. A glossary provides a road map to key terms in the field, and a complete bibliography of references cited in this book is also included.

The historical and cultural influences of magazines in America are undeniable. So are the changes to come in this industry. This book, we hope, will provide you with resources and background to assess and critique this vibrant, influential segment of the publishing industry.

# ACKNOWLEDGMENTS

We wish to acknowledge the support and advice we received during the course of our work from Joseph Opiela and the editors at Allyn & Bacon; Albert N. Greco, general series editor; and our colleagues and students at New York University's Gallatin School of Individualized Study and School of Continuing Education. Several reviewers provided invaluable criticism and commentary on early drafts of this book, and we thank them for their time and effort: Charles Higginson, University of Kansas; Peter P. Jacobi, Indiana University; Nancy Roberts, University of Minnesota; Michael Bugeja, EW Scripps School of Journalism, University of Ohio; Maureen Croteau, University of Connecticut; James Franklin, Northwestern University; Robert V. Hudson, Michigan State University. In addition, Charles P. Daly wishes to thank Martha Pryor and Marie Salerno for their invaluable research assistance, and Carroll Dowden, Thomas McGill, Stephen Sorkenn, Robert Doll, William O'Brien, Brian Beckwith, and Bruce White for their guidance and generous sharing of expertise. Patrick Henry thanks Marilyn Matty for her unfailing editorial support; and his coauthors for theirs. Ellen Ryder is most grateful to Soomie Ahn for her research assistance, as well as to Suzanne Ball, Mary Schjeldahl, Paul Keegan, Lynn Carlson, Lisa Newman, Joseph Nocera, Daniel Okrent, and Robert and Kit Nylen for their professional advice, counsel, support, and kindness all along the way.

# About the Authors

Charles P. Daly most recently was chief executive officer at Thompson Business Information, publishers of magazines, books, directories, and audiovisual products in the automotive, communications, and electronics industries. He began his career as an advertising sales representative at Medical Economics and ultimately became that company's CEO. He has served as chairman of the American Business Press and as a member of the American Business Publishers Audit. He is currently an adjunct professor at New York University.

Patrick Henry is editorial director of PTN Publishing Company's Graphic Arts Network (Printing News/East, Printing News/Midwest, Southern Graphics, and Quick Printing). A former director of publications for the National Association of Printers and Lithographers, he has taught editing and publishing courses at New York University since 1987.

Ellen Ryder is owner of Ellen Ryder Communications, a public relations and marketing firm specializing in work for publishers and authors. Formerly a publicity and promotion specialist at New England Monthly, Harper's Magazine, and GQ, she has taught consumer magazine publishing courses at New York University and has lectured in the publishing programs at Radcliffe, Rice University, and University of Chicago. She is a graduate of Wellesley College and the Medill School of Journalism at Northwestern University.

# Overview of
# Magazine Publishing

## A FINE ROMANCE

It's not unusual on a weekday lunch hour to witness a whole range of human emotion at Eastern Lobby Shop, the biggest and perhaps busiest of the newsstands in the Metropolitan Life Building over Grand Central Station in midtown Manhattan. More than 3,800 magazines are on sale in less than 900 square feet. Customers squeeze by each other, stand on tiptoe, raise chins, and angle for a good view of the new titles, displayed on racks reaching from floor to ceiling and in stacks in front of the cashiers. Impatient businesspeople looking for an edge on the competition elbow each other to scan the headlines in *Variety*, *Advertising Age*, *Economist*, *Publishers Weekly*. Oblivious to clerks unpacking and stocking the new issues, an engaged couple stops gazing into each other's eyes for a moment and gathers up bridal magazines for ideas and advice. Deskbound travelers stoke their dreams by checking out destinations in *Islands*, *Condé Nast Traveler*, *Travel & Leisure*, and any of the dozens of city and regional magazines on display. One customer is brought up short by the cover photograph on the new issue of *Newsweek*, strategically positioned by the cash register. Another picks up five computer magazines for help with a purchasing decision. Frantic for reading material on the train ride home, a commuter grabs one of the few remaining copies of *People*. A student enlists a clerk in a search for the new issue of a respected foreign policy magazine, which her professor mentioned in class the other night. A few customers furtively leaf through magazines with photographs of nude women.

This single urban spot attracts scores of browsers, researchers, news gatherers, romantics, business executives, travelers, cooks, gardeners, teachers, students, parents, and teenagers, and every magazine on display caters to a special interest they might have. Because of its size, this isn't a typical newsstand—just as midtown Manhattan isn't a typical American community. But the Eastern Lobby Shop scene—repeated hour after hour as an estimated 125,000 purchases are made each day—is indicative of American magazine publishing today. The activity at Eastern Lobby Shop represents the vitality, diversity, intense competition, and concerns inherent in this industry. The frenetic pace here is clear evidence of why publishers and editors *must* have a passion for the magazines they produce. In a marketplace crowded with choices and competition, it is creative and energetic work that gets noticed and attracts new readers.

As exemplified by a busy Manhattan retail outlet, magazine publishing in America is a thriving business and a snapshot of our culture. That means there's a big story waiting to be told. How then can we even begin to describe our relationship with the beautiful, dazzling array of words and images in print that we call magazines?

We might start by considering this: As a nation of magazine consumers, we're engaged in a serious and complicated romance. For generations, Americans as diverse as Frank Munsey, Fletcher Harper, Malcolm Forbes, Eric Utne, Grace Mirabella, and Martha Stewart have all experienced the thrill of seeing their name in a magazine title. As readers, we're variously challenged, informed, outraged, and transported to new places by magazines. Advertisers understand and depend on the appeal of magazines to sell their products and services; yet they also often struggle to justify the money spent to appear in their pages, requiring publishers to produce extensive research and employ sophisticated marketing techniques. Marketers and promoters of magazines—including editors and advertising and circulation executives—are preoccupied with mushrooming production and manufacturing costs as well as with aggressive competition everywhere from the corner newsstand all the way to cyberspace.

Nearly everyone reads magazines. Some magazines are pure entertainment, others are required on-the-job reading, still others are used to fill time—waiting in doctors' offices and in grocery store lines. Some people treat magazines like part of the family, loyally subscribing year after year. The tactile pleasure of turning pages, the portability, photography, design, and authority of the published word all contribute to the distinctive appeal of magazines.

Magazines have been described as a reflection of a nation's political, social, and cultural life. Our magazines tell us about ourselves. The articles and artwork published in the pages of a magazine, the launch of a new magazine, the demise of an established title are all windows on the lives of a reading public—and a buying public. In the 1860s, a bicycle craze swept America. The novelty and new availability of bicycles sparked a spate of new magazines into existence.[1] Bicycle owners and would-be bicycle owners were eager to learn everything about the new contraption, and magazines filled a need. More than a century later, in the mid-1990s, several large publishing companies began testing and launching magazines devoted to home renovation and remodeling—based on industry projections that in the coming decade families would spend billions of dollars on renovating their homes, rather than building new ones.[2] With magazines as a record of our special interests, it's understandable why historians find the study of them a rich resource.

A magazine is also a powerful vehicle for extending discussion and debate on a topic among interested, motivated readers. Without the constraints of regular news reporting of newspapers, magazines have been freer to publish analysis and opinion. Magazines have given voice to new views on current issues on a local, regional, and national level. The abolitionist movement and women's suffrage movement provided the editorial direction for scores of magazines. From 1858 to 1863, Frederick Douglass published *Douglass' Monthly*, containing his own work and argument, as well as reports on legislation, speeches, and the activities of abolitionist societies and individuals. It became the most influential African-American magazine of the period.[3] Before she edited her own magazine, *Revolution*, reformer and feminist Elizabeth Cady Stanton's first writing on women's rights appeared in the popular periodical *Lily, A Ladies Journal Devoted to Temperance and Literature*, which was published from 1849 to 1856.[4] In 1972, the great-great-great granddaughters of *Lily*'s readers were introduced to new perspectives on feminism when Gloria Steinem founded *Ms.*

While magazines help promulgate common interests, they are also commercial ventures and quickly respond to changes in the economy. Editors and publishers must constantly evaluate their magazines' position in the marketplace. In the early 1990s, Time Inc. Magazines, publisher of *Life*—the magazine that gave prestige and glamour to photojournalism—was considering closing the historic, now money-losing title. The magazine, which had become a monthly in 1972, was suffering from the defection of both subscribers and advertisers, not in small part because it was competing for readers and advertisers with dozens of new entertainment and general interest magazines. But instead of closing the magazine, the company decided to make its business operations leaner by cutting staff and the magazine's page size, and by refocusing the magazine's editorial offerings on "softer" features and photography. In 1994, commenting on the redesign of *Life*, managing editor Daniel Okrent told a *New York Times* reporter: "*Life* is a window, not a mirror. We use pictures to create a sense of community. We do essays on people and we do much less celebrity coverage than we used to."[5] These editorial changes at *Life* were seen as one reason the magazine's issues in 1994 had advertising page increases of up to 78 percent over the same issues published in the previous year.[6]

Discovering the right combination for editorial and commercial success in a competitive, quickly changing marketplace is not the exclusive domain of big, mass market consumer magazines like *Life*. In a study of music magazines launched in the 1980s, researchers found that in addition to serving a community of readers dispersed throughout the country, these primarily small-circulation magazines were "the most economical means for advertisers to reach a market for their products."[7] Advertisers of guitars, sound systems, and other music services found these magazines the best way to reach a buyer in their small, highly specialized and widely dispersed market.

Because no good romance endures without clear-eyed understanding of the other forces at work, these chapters have been written to provide structure, history, and background to help you understand and critique magazines within both the publishing industry and our culture. Through the years, the advent of automobiles, motion pictures, radio, and television all affected—or threatened to affect— American magazine publishing. Today, magazines are being profoundly shaped by developments in communications technology as well as the explosive growth in computer usage at home and work. In addition, developments in interactive media will continue to affect how we conduct business and obtain information, entertainment, and news—requiring magazines to adapt to new competition.

Change is inevitable in the magazine publishing industry. What won't change is the industry's continuing need for informed analysis, evaluation, and new ideas.

## TOWARD A DEFINITION

What is a magazine anyway? Easy, you might say. Simply go to any newsstand or coffee table—and point. A magazine is 8 1/2 inches by 11 inches with articles and colorful pages. It has photographs. Ads. Subscribers. Letters to the editor. But *must* it have subscribers to be called a magazine? Must it be printed on glossy paper? Must it even have pages? Must it be published more than once a year? Must it have advertising? What if it only has one or two readers? Where do magazines on CD-ROM fit? Magazines that look like newspapers? The magazine in your Sunday newspaper? 'Zines? Comic books?

Just what makes a magazine a magazine? The word itself comes from the Arabic word *makhazhin*, meaning a place where goods or supplies (especially ammunitions) were stored. In 1731, the British publishers of the *London Gentleman's Magazine* were most likely the first to use the word in a publication title, deriving it from the French *magasin*.[8] So, with such linguistic roots, today's magazines hold and dispense information.

Here's a most basic definition, adapted from dictionaries. A magazine is published periodically on paper with a collection of any or all of the following: articles, reportage, essays, fiction, artwork, photography, other editorial features. But that definition doesn't help much when so many other words to describe magazines are used, seemingly interchangeably. *Journal, review, periodical, house organ* can all refer to what we commonly know as magazines. Further compounding the confusion, in industry jargon magazines are called *books*. *Vogue* is a fashion book, *House Beautiful*, a shelter book. Even the U.S. Postal Service, which has never been accused of being stingy with *its* definitions, doesn't include a definition of *magazine*. A second-class mailing permit (which most magazines have) can be given to a publication that is bound or unbound. (The Pulitzer Prize–winning magazine historian Frank Luther Mott contended in 1943 that a magazine must be bound to be a true magazine.[9]) Neither is the post office picky about the type of stock a magazine is printed on. The Postal Service manual says that an approved publication can be printed on sheets that "may be die cut or deckle-edged and may be made of paper, cellophane, foil...."[10]

Magazines are usually referred to as *periodicals*, especially in official definitions. In its Census of Manufacturers, the U.S. Department of Commerce says "publications are classified as periodicals rather than newspapers if their news and editorial presentations do not appear to be directed to the public at large."[11] This government definition hits on an important distinction: a magazine is a regularly published periodical that targets a select audience, a group of readers defined by their demographics or interests. And, because most magazines need advertising dollars to support the costs of publishing, a publisher will also identify categories of businesses that want to sell products and services to those same readers. Newsletters and some newspapers could conceivably elbow their way into this definition, and many even have all the above-mentioned characteristics of a typical magazine. Many have color photography, a regular publication schedule, contributing writers, and a targeted audience. Most newsletters, though, contain *highly* specialized information and reporting and are geared to an audience even more select than that of magazines. For instance, a single newsletter could be successfully marketed to music festival organizers, attorneys who represent adoptive parents, or food service managers at colleges. Newsletter subscription costs can be in the hundreds of dollars—out of reach for the average magazine reader. There's also a difference in *style*—which is difficult to describe in a tidy way. Magazines as a group have more sophisticated art direction, more personality, more flair, and more entertainment value than their newsletter cousins. As we'll explore in later chapters, magazines also have unique requirements in the areas of circulation marketing, advertising, staffing, and production that set them apart from newsletters, newspapers, and, of course, the cyberspace versions of magazines appearing on computer screens. While their production and distribution are unique, magazine supplements in newspapers are usually considered magazines because their editorial and advertising standards are similar.[12]

For the purposes of this book, we will consider comic books and 'Zines (the independently produced, small circulation, mostly literary magazines that burst onto the publishing scene in the 1990s with the advances in desktop publishing) in separate publishing categories. As single titles, comics, puzzle books, and other theme publications are not large enough to generate significant revenue. But as a group, they contribute significantly to revenues for their parent companies. Dell

Puzzle Magazine Group's 30 puzzle magazines generated about $40 million in revenue in 1995, and the *Ellery Queen's Mystery Magazine* and *Alfred Hitchcock Mystery Magazine* generated about $12 million.[13] Comic books have a long, colorful publishing history, and many do have sophisticated circulation and advertising goals. But neither comic books nor 'Zines—which typically have print runs of 200 copies and production costs of only about $500[14]—account for significant revenues or impact in the periodical publishing world.

Here are the basic points to remember as we begin our exploration of magazines:

- A magazine has a defined audience.
- A magazine need not have subscribers. It can be sold exclusively on newsstands or given away.
- A magazine can be printed on paper of any quality, but it must have pages.
- A magazine can be published in any frequency—from a one-time test issue to once a week.
- A magazine needn't publish the advertising of other companies. In 1994 the 10-year-old *Garbage Magazine* joined a list of consumer magazines—including *Consumer Reports* and *Ms.*—when its publishers decided to discontinue advertising and rely solely on circulation revenue.

A magazine can be classified as either a *consumer* or a *specialized business* (or *trade*) title. Within the consumer classification, literally hundreds of publishing categories and niches exist. Name a hobby, sport, major city, cultural activity, computer system, and chances are very good there's a magazine (or two or three) devoted to the subject. Consumer magazines appeal directly to an audience of readers who are targeted as potential readers by virtue of where they live, their interest in a specific topic, or their demographics—age, sex, profession, income level, race, religion, or nationality. *Esquire, Redbook, Atlantic Monthly, Field & Stream, Texas Monthly, Premiere, Seventeen,* and *Modern Maturity* are all examples of national consumer magazines and all have markedly different core audiences. *Esquire's* editor and publisher have designed their magazine for men aged 18–49 with an interest in fashion, sports, and politics. *Redbook* seeks out women readers who are most likely married with children. *Atlantic Monthly* readers are mostly professional, well-educated men and women with an interest in politics, business, and the arts. *Field & Stream* appeals to outdoor enthusiasts, *Texas Monthly* to residents of that state, *Premiere* to movie buffs, *Seventeen* to teenage girls, and *Modern Maturity* to men and women over 55. When the potential number of readers and advertisers can support publication of a magazine, the categories within the major niches can become even narrower. There are magazines for residents of particular neighborhoods of a city, for women who play volleyball, for people who like to smoke cigars, for expectant parents, for teenagers who skateboard.

Consumer magazines have two other things in common besides targeting a specific group of readers: advertising and availability. Most consumer magazines sell pages of advertising, and the income from advertising is essential to their survival. Some consumer magazines *can* be viable without advertising income, but, as we'll explore in later chapters, it is the exception in today's marketplace. For many readers, too, the advertising in consumer magazines is part of their enjoyment of the magazine. Readers of *Vogue* pore over fashion advertising. *Philadelphia* magazine's restaurant and entertainment advertising is a resource for city residents and visitors. Readers of *Crafts Magazine* turn to its advertising pages to find new techniques, tools, and materials. Consumer magazines are easy for readers to find. In most cases, the publisher works hard to identify potential readers through direct mail marketing techniques. Consumer magazines are readily available and accessible to readers by subscription or on the newsstand, at a friend's house or in doctors' waiting rooms.

The other major classification of magazines is specialized business magazines. We'll refer to these throughout this text with the commonly used term *trade publications.* Contrary to what some people think, trade magazines are not limited to those about construction, plumbing, refrigeration, or other jobs where hands-on work is involved. Trade magazines are written and edited for readers who have a need for more information about their particular job, industry, or profession. They can be devoted to technical, scientific, professional, or marketing subjects. The editorial contained in trade magazines may include information on products, applications, technological changes, industry news and statistics, government regulations and political news, personnel changes, and new techniques in marketing and production.

Trade magazines usually do not directly compete (for either readers or advertisers) with consumer magazines. In comparison to a typical consumer magazine, the circulation of the typical trade magazine is smaller and much more specialized. A trade magazine may or may not publish advertising, but most do. In comparison to the consumer field, the total revenue generated by trade magazines is limited. Each year, *Folio:* compiles its *Folio:*500 list, ranking magazines in terms of revenue. In 1993, the magazines on this list had $18.8 billion in cumulative revenues, with trade publications accounting for only about one-sixth of that total.[15] Not readily available on newsstands, trade magazines may have a comparatively high subscription price. For example, in 1995 *Publishers Weekly*, directed to people working in the book publishing industry, had an annual subscription rate of $139, compared to *Newsweek*'s basic annual subscription rate of $41.08. A trade magazine is often office or "homework" reading for many professionals. Other trade magazines are sent free to eligible readers. In order to get the magazine delivered to them, readers must hold specific job titles or responsibilities. Such a defined audience of readers makes the magazine very attractive to advertisers. This kind of distribution is known as *controlled circulation* and is explored in detail in Chapter 5.

There is yet another category of magazines known collectively as *public relations magazines*. Clubs, corporations, colleges, manufacturers, institutions, and other entities can all publish bound, glossy, high-quality magazines that are designed to appeal to a group of readers with very specific interests and information needs. Magazine expert James Click outlined six different categories of public relations magazines: those for employees, customers, stockholders (or corporation members), salespeople, dealers, and technical service providers.[16] While numerous, public relations magazines are in a separate category from the two broad classifications—trade and consumer—because their marketing and circulation objectives are extremely narrow. They exist to communicate to small, self-defined audiences: graduates of a colleges, salespeople at an international company, employees at a health management organization. These publications may, of course, have high editorial standards, but as a group they stand apart from those based on many of the principles we'll be exploring in these chapters.

## MAJOR NICHES

The variety of experiences and subject matter addressed by magazines—as well developments in how we sell and market goods and services— has created identifiable categories of magazines or *niches*. *Bacon's* publishes an annual directory of magazines, organized into 225 "market classifications"—from advertising to woodworking.

Here are the major niches—but remember, it's only a partial list. These are collected here because of their high proportion of readers and advertisers.

*Automotive.* Magazines such as *Car & Driver* and *Motor Trend* are often referred to as "buff books" because they're read—with a special voraciousness—by car enthusiasts.

*Boating.* Examples include *Sail*, *Boating*, *Yachting*, and *WoodenBoat*.

*Associations, clubs, and institutions.* Organizations big and small publish magazines: *Harvard Alumni Magazine*, *Audubon*, *Smithsonian*, *Modern Maturity* are all examples. Civic and fraternal magazines—published by groups such as Elks, Kiwanis, VFW—are also included in this category.

*Epicurean.* Magazines about food, restaurants, cooking, and wine. In the 1980s, new titles featuring lean cuisine and quick recipes were launched by publishers to capitalize on Americans' new interest in healthy eating.

*General interest.* If magazines had college diplomas, the publications in this niche would hold liberal arts degrees. These contain a little bit of everything for readers who are curious about ideas, people, news, and trends (both serious and not-so-serious). Examples are: *Harper's Magazine*, the *New Yorker*, *Reader's Digest*, *Utne Reader*, *Vanity Fair*.

**Home.** This category includes magazines focusing on decorating, renovation, and gardening, such as *House Beautiful, Martha Stewart Living, Condé Nast House and Garden*. In publishing industry jargon, these magazines are sometimes referred to as "shelter books."

***Inflight, in-hotel, and other passenger magazines.*** Distributed free to hotel guests or passengers on airlines or trains, containing subject matter on the transportation company, its services, and articles of interest to the traveler or visitor.

***Men's.*** For example: *GQ, Esquire, Playboy, Details, Men's Journal.*

***Women's.*** A category with a long history and many titles, ranging from how-to service magazines to the more fashion-oriented *Vogue, Harper's Bazaar*, and *Elle*, to magazines with various levels of emphasis on women's health, fitness, relationships, family, and work. The largest-circulation women's titles are known as the "Seven Sisters" (*Better Homes and Gardens, Family Circle, Good Housekeeping, Ladies' Home Journal, McCall's, Redbook*, and *Woman's Day*).

***Music/entertainment.*** Magazines in this category range from magazines for rock musicians, opera fans, moviegoers, and people-watchers.

***Outdoor/sport.*** Name the sport and there's most likely a magazine (or two): From the generalist's *Outside* and *Sports Illustrated* to the particular enthusiast's *Triathlete, Volleyball Monthly, Windsurfing.*

***Parenting and family.*** Magazines for every stage of a family: *American Baby, Child, Family Fun, Parenting.*

***Photography.*** Ranging from magazines for the specialist (*News Photographer* and *Industrial Photography*) to the consumer enthusiast, professional, and aspiring amateur (*American Photo* and *Popular Photography*).

***Science/technology.*** Magazines focusing on the natural and technological sciences, including computer magazines, and the more generalist publications such as *Scientific American, Sciences, Discover.*

***Ethnic.*** Magazines that are directed to readers sharing a racial, ethnic, or ancestral characteristic. Examples range from *Essence* and *Ebony* (which have been publishing since 1970 and 1945, respectively) to relative newcomers such as *A.* (for Asian Americans) launched in 1990.

*Youth*. For young men and women there is a teen category (*Seventeen,
American Girl, YM, Boy's Life*) and for even younger readers: *Sports
Illustrated for Kids* and *Highlights for Children*. The Cricket Magazine Group
in Peru, Illinois, publishes four titles targeting children from toddlers
(*Babybug*) to early teens.

*Regional*. A category that has its own association, the City and Regional
Magazine Association, and includes magazines that target readers and advertising in a city, region, state, or section of the country. Editorial focus may be
either on personalities, news, and lifestyle or on business in that region. *South
Florida, Utah Business, Oregon Business, New Orleans, Arizona Highways*,
and *Midwest Life* are all examples.

*Political*. Those magazines with a stated political point of view and usually a
devoted, loyal readership. Examples are *American Spectator* (monthly,
300,000 circulation); *Commentary* (monthly, 30,000), *The Nation* (weekly,
86,000), *National Review* (bi-weekly, 262,000).

*Farm*. *Farm Journal* (circulation 815,000), *Successful Farming* (500,000) and
*Progressive Farmer* (450,000) are distributed nationally throughout the U.S.
farm belt. Smaller-circulation farm magazines focus on regions of the country
and on varieties of growing, chemicals, and fertilizers. Standard Rate and Data
Service lists 256 farm titles in 12 categories.

*Medical*. As with the agricultural magazines, the significance of this category
of publishing is often underestimated. For instance, *JAMA: Journal of the
American Medical Association* is ranked number 104 in the *Folio: 500*, with
revenues of $43 million. Consider the range of disciplines (nursing, radiology,
pediatrics, psychology, cardiology, surgery) and you'll understand why
*Bacon's* lists more than 757 magazines in the medical category. It's been estimated that there is a total of more than 3,500 medical periodicals.[17]

## COUNTING MAGAZINES

How many magazines are there? The short answer: No one really knows. But we
can make an educated guess.

Magazine historian John Tebbel estimates that 22,000 magazines are published
in the United States. He includes in his figure all manner of magazines—from the
2,000 magazines that have the most visiblity and significance in the marketplace
(*TV Guide, Farm Journal, Modern Bride, Business Week*, etc.) to the numerous
public relations magazines published by colleges, hospitals, corporations, and other
entities exclusively for constituents.[18] In 1995 Gale Directory of Publications
reported the number of U.S. periodicals at 11,239[19]—but that figure includes schol-

arly journals, comics, yearbooks, and other periodicals. The Standard Rate and Data Service listed 2,276 consumer and farm magazines that sold advertising, about 750 more than a decade earlier.[20] Each year Samir A. Husni of the University of Mississippi counts up the number of new consumer magazines (whether they sell advertising or not), and in 1994 he found that 832 new magazines were launched. (The number that fold is too difficult to monitor.) His estimate: 4,000 consumer magazines.[21] Estimates of the number of trade magazines published today vary widely. One observer estimates 12,000[22] but most listings range from 2,400 to 3,200. The Association of Business Publishers listed 689 active member magazines in 1995,[23] but acknowledges there are many more individual titles, many published by multi-title publishers. There's simply no accurate way to count public relations magazines, especially because very few sell advertising space and are not eligible for second-class mailing privileges. There may be as many as 10,000. Tebbel's estimate of 22,000 magazines seems right if we project that there are 4,000 consumer, 8,000 trade, and 10,000 public relations magazines.

An international code is used to help count the number of magazines in the world. Most publications with a regular publication schedule—which, in addition to magazines, includes journals, yearbooks, and comics—have an assigned International Standard Serials Number. This is the internationally accepted, concise, unique, unambiguous code of identification of serial publications, consisting of seven numbers with an eighth "check" digit used to verify the number in computer processing. A hyphen is printed after the fourth digit, as a visual aid. The acronym ISSN precedes the number. The number is assigned by one of the more than 50 national centers worldwide. The centers form a network coordinated by the ISSN International Centre in Paris. The ISSN aids in ordering, billing, inventory control, abstracting and indexes. There's no charge to get an ISSN, but a publisher must supply bibliographic evidence of the serial, including a copy of the title page and cover.

Where are magazines published? For the past decade, four states—New York, Illinois, California, and Pennsylvania—have been home to more than half the publishing companies in the U.S.[24] New York City is the headquarters of most multi-title magazine publishers, but isn't—and wasn't always—the only address for a successful magazine business. In 1885, William Dean Howells (who, four years earlier, had left his editor's desk at the *Atlantic Monthly* to devote more time to his own writing[25]) moved from Boston to take an editorial post at *Harper's*, and a great uproar ensued about how the center of publishing was moving from "literary" Boston to "commercial" New York.

*Time* and *Newsweek* have headquarters in New York; their primary competitor, *U.S. News and World Report* is based in Washington, D.C. All three news weeklies also have editorial branch offices all over the world. Meredith Corporation—which publishes about 60 titles, including *Better Homes and Gardens*—has its corporate headquarters in Des Moines. *Outside* magazine moved from Chicago to Santa Fe in 1994. Northampton, Massachusetts (population 30,000), is the home of two national magazines, *FamilyFun* and *Family PC*. The National Magazine Award–winner *Wired* magazine set up shop in San Francisco in 1994. Public relations magazines are published everywhere—from major metropolitan areas to rural communities.

## A BASIC TENET: THE THREE-LEGGED STOOL

American publishing is big business. Multi-title companies dominate the consumer market. The "top tier" of the nation's big circulation magazines are published by large media companies—Condé Nast, Hearst, Meredith, Hachette Fillipachi, and Time Warner among them. Only about 160 magazines are responsible for 85 percent of the industry's total revenues. With an estimated 22,000 magazines, that means magazine publishing is a *small* business, too. Magazine publishing has always been an appealing venture for entrepreneurs, for men and women with a cause, for editors with ideas.

What the giants of the industry today share with titles having a fraction of their circulation, revenue, and resources is a basic tenet of magazine publishing: Success rests on the three-legged stool of editorial, advertising, and circulation. The three-legged stool is a commonly used metaphor for magazine publishing because weakness or shortcoming in any "leg" affects the others—as well as the stability of the entire venture. What happens with editorial decisions affects how many copies are sold on the newsstand—which in turn affects how many new subscribers a magazine can expect. Advertisers make their decisions based on how many people buy the magazine. The three functions are intimately entwined.

Here's an example. Most magazines sell advertising pages to outside companies. For a magazine to sell the pages, the title's advertising director must be able to tell advertisers exactly who's buying and reading the title. Without that information, few companies will hand over the money it costs to advertise. Advertisers must be assured that a certain number of readers buy the magazine, either through subscription or on the newsstand; and that this number won't fluctuate wildly from month to month. The magazine's circulation department, for its part, must have both faith and knowledge that the editor and the editorial department will maintain their implicit promise to readers (and advertisers) to deliver a consistent editorial message. Imagine, for instance, a gardening magazine treasured by readers for its beautiful photography of flowers and practical information on how to create the best garden. Imagine this magazine's suddenly arriving one month in homes and on newsstands featuring a cover story on a world-famous supermodel giving a behind-the-scenes guided tour of her fabulous backyard garden in the Hollywood Hills. You'd expect longtime readers to object by canceling subscriptions. "This isn't the magazine I decided to buy!" they'd complain. Of course, some readers—new to gardening or fans of supermodels—might be thrilled at the celebrity turn the magazine had taken. Most of the established, core audience, however, would probably find reason to stop subscribing. Advertisers who had signed on to reach readers interested in buying tools for the garden wouldn't find any value in trying to reach movie star watchers. Who can prove celebrity watchers are also spending time in their gardens? This editorial decision would affect circulation and advertising. Celebrity gardening is not what readers or advertisers were promised. An editorial move would result in a loss of core customers and income—a detrimental effect on both the advertising and circulation effort.

Three functions—advertising, circulation, and editorial—must work in concert. Along with principles of production and finance, they are the keys to publishing a successful magazine. To have a fuller understanding of contemporary trends in magazine publishing and in these three critical functions, let's look at how we got where we are today.

## AMERICA'S MAGAZINE HISTORY: WHERE TODAY'S TRENDS TOOK ROOT

The story of America's first magazine is more important for the trends it established than for a particular literary or journalistic milestone. In a foreshadowing of decades of competition, rival Philadelphia printers Andrew Bradford and Benjamin Franklin engaged in a race to be the first magazine publishers in the colonies. Bradford won, publishing *American Magazine, or A Monthly View of the Political State of the British Colonies* on February 13, 1741, beating Franklin's *General Magazine, and Historical Chronicle, for All the British Plantations in America* by three days. Six months later, both magazines were out of business—due, some historians say, to lack of reader interest.[26]

In addition to the elements of competition and business risk, the early attempts at magazine publishing in America also tell the story of how distinctly American magazines began to evolve. In the emerging democracy, a cacophony of voices and opinions found a home in periodicals. Many of these early magazines were conceived and published by an individual with strong political views, eager to let the world know of his philosophies and beliefs.

But not all the early titles were publishing brash, revolutionary reading. Up until the early 1800s, many of America's early magazines were indistinguishable from their British counterparts. Lax copyright practices and a lack of access to original writing meant that entire pages of British magazines could be reproduced—without compensation to either the author or original publisher—in American magazines. Some magazines were launched not because of a publisher's burning need to get his ideas to a wide audience, but because he (and the publisher then was most likely a *he*) saw a way to make money. *Harper's Magazine* started life in New York City because the industrious Harper brothers—whose successful book business was thriving—realized that idle presses could be put to use during downtime. They began publishing a "new monthly magazine" in 1850 and soon thereafter a weekly magazine. Fletcher Harper himself referred to the beginnings of the magazine that would make news and influence national opinion for well over a century as "a tender to our business,"[27] serving to extend the already purchased work of their book authors to an even wider audience. *Collier's*, the *Atlantic Monthly*, and *Putnam's New Monthly Magazine* (the magazine historian Frank Luther Mott called "the first genuinely civilized magazine in America"[28]) were also spun off successful book businesses. In 1888, Peter Collier founded a periodical called *Once a Week* (later renamed *Collier's Weekly*), which was sold in conjunction with his low-priced library sets. These popular "instant libraries" were sold on the installment plan by book agents. *McCall's* started life in 1873 because the tailor and pattern maker James McCall saw a way to promote his dress-making designs.[29]

As the population in American cities grew and businesses began thriving, literacy increased. With the reading public and buying public growing, new magazines were born. Americans were interested in reading magazines, talking about them, and having them in their home libraries. Soon it became acceptable to be a professional writer or editor. Bylined articles appeared. The *North American Review* and *Saturday Evening Post* led the way with hiring regular staff writers and paying livable salaries. Editors' personalities and points of view became known.

Author and feminist Sarah Josepha Hale was at the forefront of shaping women's magazines in the nineteenth century. Widowed in 1822 with five children, she began publishing her writing to support her family. Publisher Louis Godey hired her in 1837, by buying the magazine she was editing, *Ladies' Magazine*, and made her editor of his *Godey's Ladies Book*—a post she held for more than 40 years. Her great cause was women's education, and she pushed Godey into publishing articles on history, travel, music, art, famous women, healthy care of children, cooking—along with the popular color illustrations of fashion. Under her leadership, the magazine's circulation grew to a stunning 150,000.[30]

A most important milestone for American magazine publishing occurred in 1879 when Congress passed the first of two acts that lowered postal rates for magazines. The second decrease occurred in 1885, followed by the creation of a rural free-delivery system in the 1890s. It became less expensive to mail and distribute magazines to a mass audience. That led to stunning growth. In 1885, there were 3,300 periodicals in the United States. Less than 20 years later, the list had doubled. More than 7,000 magazines were founded in a 20-year period. While half that number eventually folded or merged, this is considered the Golden Age of Magazines, with magazines attaining an important place in shaping public opinion and providing a forum for new ideas. The importance of the magazine's cover image was realized during this period. It was a trade magazine—*Inland Printer*—that became the first to change the cover illustration from issue to issue. Soon after, magazines began changing the cover images, enlisting the newly popular illustrators of the day to help create the magazine's particular personality."

But not everyone was thrilled with this unleashing of reading material on the public. Francis Browne, editor of *Dial*, believed that mass readership of the early

1890s "great circulation" magazines (the ones that boasted circulations of up to 200,000) led to mediocrity, saying that such magazines were "bound to be conservative because they cannot afford to offend."[31]

A distinct difference began to emerge between the journalism in magazines and the reporting in newspapers. Newspapers recounted stories and events. Magazines assimilated information and brought the perspective and opinion of the author to the forefront. *Harper's*, *Nation*, *Scribner's*, *Atlantic Monthly*, and other journals established a new level of sophistication in magazines. Emphasis was placed on public affairs and what editors believed the public needed to know. In the pages of these "thought leader" magazines some of the most memorable opinion and essays of the age were published. Commentary and reports on labor problems, income tax, direct election of senators, child labor laws, and women's suffrage all appeared in magazines. *McClure's* became known for publishing reports chronicling abuses in employment, food packaging, and false advertising claims. *Leslie's* from its beginning published crusading articles; especially noteworthy was its series on the unsanitary conditions of dairies supplying New York and corruption among milk producers and distributors. *McClure's* and its crusade against the patent medicine business helped push Congress to establish the Food and Drug Administration. *Collier's* lobbied for the repeal of prohibition.

Magazines also began marking newsworthy, world-shaking events with commemorative issues—another trend that continues today. *Collier's* might have been the first with its "special number" dated May 5, 1906, published two weeks after the San Francisco earthquake, complete with Jack London's article and 16 pages of pictures.[32] Today, big sports and entertainment news, the end of a year, beginning of a decade, or death of a celebrity prompt a magazine publisher to bring out a special issue. Even war can get the presses rolling. When the United States entered the Gulf War in 1991, *Life* for several months produced an unusual weekly devoted to patriotic news and feature stories about America's role in the conflict.

Illustration and photography became increasingly important to magazines. The invention of halftones and advances in printing technology in the 1880s enabled printers to make even more attractive, readable magazines. By the 1890s, high-speed rotary presses were perfected. The low-priced, illustrated magazines especially benefited from this development. Instead of expensive fine line engravings in wood, photographs and illustrations could be printed for a fraction of the cost. *Century* magazine, for instance, paid $300 for a page-size woodcut—but less than $20 for a halftone.[33] Color reproduction was rare before 1900. After 1910, photography played an important role in magazine publishing. Jimmy Hare's photographs in *Collier's* were popular, leading *Life* to offer him a lucrative, exclusive contract to lure him to its pages.[34] Illustrators such as Charles Dana Gibson (the "darling of the 1890s"), Maxfield Parrish, Edward Penfield, Frederic Remington, and Jessie Wilcox Smith were also sought-after contributors to magazines.

Premiums (the gifts given by magazine publishers to encourage subscriptions and renewals) were instituted during this period. *McCall's* used patterns for premiums in the 1900s. Color photographs, calendars, bookmarks, and other items also made appearances. In one extravagant plan, a magazine publisher offered new subscribers free life insurance.

It would be a long time before mass mail solicitations by a publisher to new and renewing subscribers became widespread. Sophisticated direct mail techniques were still a hundred years away; yet magazine publishers early on realized the importance of trying to bring lapsed subscribers back into the fold and often encouraged them to renew with a personal letter.

From just before the Civil War up to the early 1900s, the nation experienced explosive political, social, and economic changes. New manufacturing technologies along with changes in how goods were marketed and advertised helped magazines prosper. Advertising in magazines grew in importance. What first seemed tawdry and demeaning to some publishers (Fletcher Harper turned down Singer's $18,000 bid to advertise sewing machines in *Harper's Magazine* because he believed it would lower the quality of the publication[35]), quickly became an essential part of the business of publishing. Families were buying goods such as cameras, typewriters, and sewing machines directly from manufacturers who recognized magazines as a way to get their messages to this purchasing public. By the 1890s, a national railroad system was operating, to bring these goods directly to retail establishments and families across the country. Automobile manufacturers started advertising in magazines other than trade publications in the early 1900s. Advertising agencies were established to handle manufacturers' needs to create and place ads. Magazines began seeing their editorial distinctiveness as attractive to advertisers—as salable. The *Ladies' Home Journal* was probably the first magazine to offer an advertiser an "adjacency"—the opportunity to place an advertisement at the end of a piece of fiction—at an added cost. Publishers became sophisticated about soliciting advertising, engaging their own salespeople to work with agencies and manufacturers.

Publishers made no effort to account for their magazines' circulation until advertising became important. Before advertisers demanded proof of the number of readers that publishers were claiming, creative guesswork and outright lying were the rules in magazine circulation. In 1914, to bring order to this state of affairs, a group of advertisers and publishers established the Audit Bureau of Circulations to monitor publishers' circulation. The ABC and its counterpart for trade magazines—Business Publications Audit, Inc. (BPA)—are still the two auditing bodies for magazine publishing today.

After World War I, the news and picture magazines—*Life*, *Time*, *Newsweek*, and others—made their mark on the culture. By the 1930s and 1940s, a handful of magazines were reaching record-breaking circulation numbers. George Horace Lorimer is considered by some to be the first great contemporary magazine editor. He held the top job at the *Saturday Evening Post* for 38 years and made that magazine an intrinsic part of the American cultural landscape. Lorimer's *Post* and the popular *Ladies' Home Journal* were the first magazines to reach a circulation of one million.

With television on the horizon, such stunning readership numbers wouldn't last, however. By the 1960s, advertisers of cars, soap, cereal, tobacco, and other products could easily reach 100 million American households with a commercial on *The Ed Sullivan Show*. *Life*, even with its record-breaking 8.5 million readers, couldn't compete with the audience numbers television offered. General interest magazines such as *Life*, *Look*, and the *Saturday Evening Post* suffered the most from the sea change in marketing goods and the defection of advertisers. But while television had captured audience and advertiser attention with huge numbers, hundreds of new magazines and new magazine companies were able to define a slice of the mass market and serve up a magazine to appeal to a specific group of readers. Magazines did what television couldn't do: reach targeted audiences with special interests.

## THE PEOPLE BEHIND THE IDEAS

Successful magazines today are not merely the result of a marketing formula concocted to reach a specific group of readers. America's recent magazine history is rich with the stories of men and women who helped shape the publishing industry and our culture with their editorial vision and inventions. Helen Gurley Brown's eternal "Cosmo Girl," Harold Hayes's shepherding of the spirited "New Journalism" into the pages of *Esquire*, young Jann Wenner's idea for *Rolling Stone*, Lewis Lapham's often-imitated "Harper's Index"—to name just a few. Ideas still drive magazines. Many contemporary magazines owe their success to editors whose editorial inventions as well as entrepreneurial spirit not only have been inspirations for scores of magazine editors and publishers, but also have sparked some of today's biggest magazine publishing businesses into existence. Here's a look at three such stories.

Twenty-eight-year-old DeWitt Wallace refined his magazine idea while recuperating in a French army hospital from wounds he received during the Meuse-Argonne offensive in 1918. Impatient with what he considered the needless length of articles in copies of the *Saturday Evening Post*, *Vanity Fair,* and *Scribner's* sent to soldiers, he practiced a technique he had already formulated: condensing articles so that the "practical articles" of "lasting interest" could be cut to a quarter of their original size and still retain "their essence."[36] Returning to the United States, Wallace, in partnership with his wife, Lila Acheson, borrowed $5,000 and began publishing the *Reader's Digest* in 1922 in a Greenwich Village apartment. He selected the articles for his conveniently sized, inexpensive magazine on the basis of three criteria: applicability, lasting interest, and constructiveness.[37] The combination struck a chord with the postwar middle class interested in self-improvement, information, and good reading when time was at a premium. Circulation grew to record-breaking levels. Originally, the Wallaces wanted their magazine to be free of advertising, but in 1955 they decided not only to accept advertising but also to sell advertising at higher rates than any other magazine. The magazine grew richer and diversified into other areas, including book publishing and record distribution. In the late 1990s the international publishing company based in Pleasantville, New York, had revenues of more than $500 million and the flagship magazine is second only to the Bible in worldwide readership.[38]

For Condé Nast, the way to publishing success was through "quality circulation," not amassing high numbers of subscribers. The St. Louis–born Nast was a lawyer by training but found the work uninspiring. When his college friend Robert Collier asked him to work for his family's weekly, he discovered advertising as a second career. As advertising director of *Collier's* he quickly revitalized the circulation of the magazine and engaged in strategic marketing by showing individual advertisers how they could benefit from advertising in *Collier's*. He spent ten years at *Collier's* and during that time became exposed to the opportunities offered by *Collier's* fashion and home pattern market divisions. Under his direction, advertising revenue at the *Quarterly Style Book* grew from $1,500 in 1907 to $180,000 in 1908.[39] With this background, he decided he wanted a magazine of his own and purchased a small, highly regarded but struggling society and fashion magazine called *Vogue* in 1909. He worked feverishly and successfully with editor Edna Woolman Chase to bring the magazine to the attention of the elite, rich, and stylish. Chase and Nast pioneered charity fashion shows of exclusively American designers, and gained the respect and admiration of the social leaders of the day.[40] Nast subsequently purchased *Vanity Fair* and *House & Garden* and incorporated his holdings as Condé Nast Publications in 1922. He saw his task thusly: "To bait the editorial pages in such a way as to lift out of all the millions of Americans just the 100,000 cultivated people who can buy these quality goods." [41] Today, the Condé Nast Publications is part of Advance Publications, the Newhouse family–owned company, which includes the *New Yorker*, newspaper and cable operations, and book publishing houses. *Vogue* has a circulation of 1.2 million and nine international editions.

It has been said that modern magazine publishing began with Henry Luce and Briton Hadden.[42] In their early 20s, the Yale graduates decided that Americans were woefully uninformed about the world and needed a publication that gave them facts, in an easy-to-read, summarized format. An initial 7,000-piece mail solicitation sent in 1922 describing the magazine they wanted to publish got an extraordinary response. Well over 6 percent of the households receiving their letter responded positively.[43] Buoyed by the popular interest in a magazine focusing on news, not comment, the partners launched *Time* in 1923 by raising money from family and friends. They were both listed as editors on the masthead, and devoted themselves to developing an identifiable style and creating a news magazine that could be read in less than an hour. Circulation rose quickly (more than doubling to 70,000 within only two years) and advertisers followed. The publishers quickly began exploring other magazine opportunities. They recognized the early potential of *Saturday*

*Review of Literature* and started a monthly digest of advertising news. In addition to their entrepreneurial skills, Luce and Hadden excelled at identifying *audiences* for their magazines. Hadden died unexpectedly in 1929 at the age of 31. Luce went on to start *Fortune*—a revolutionary business magazine—just before the Depression hit. When he launched *Life* in 1936, it was "the most remarkable instant success in the history of magazine publishing."[44] After merging with Warner Communications in 1989, Time Inc. Magazines became part of a mammoth communications and entertainment conglomerate. Because he also had direct editorial involvement in the startup of *Sports Illustrated*, a total of four of the company's core magazines owe their existence to Henry Luce.

## NOTES

[1] John Tebbel and Mary Ellen Zuckerman, *The Magazine in America, 1741–1990* (New York: Oxford University Press, 1991), 64.

[2] Deirdre Carmody, "Sensing Trend Toward Renovation and Remodeling, Home Magazines Are Adding Up," *The New York Times*, June 8, 1995.

[3] Tebbel and Zuckerman, *The Magazine in America 1741–1990*, 44.

[4] Frank Luther Mott, *A History of American Magazines.* vol. 2, 1850–1865 (Cambridge: Harvard University Press, 1938), 50–51.

[5] Deirdre Carmody, "A Rejuvenated Life Magazine Bounces Back," *The New York Times*, September 26, 1994.

[6] Carmody. "A Rejuvenated Life Magazine Bounces Back."

[7] P. Theberge, "Musician Magazines in the 1980s, the Creation of a Community and Consumer Market," in *Cultural Studies*, October 1991, 5(3): 270–293.

[8] William H. Taft, *American Magazines for the 1980s.* (New York: Hastings House, 1982), 19.

[9] Mott, *A History of American Magazines*, vol. 2, 69.

[10] U.S. Postal Service, Domestic Mail Manual, 44 9-1-95, 3.0, E211.2.7.

[11] Census of Manufacturers, 1992.

[12] The Commerce Department includes magazines distributed as newspaper supplements in their statistics on U.S. periodical publishing.

[13] "The Ad Age 300," *Advertising Age*, June 19, 1995, 5–17. In March 1996, Penny Press, Inc., a privately owned business, acquired all of the approximately three dozen Dell Magazines.

[14] David M. Gross, "Zine Dreams," *The New York Times Sunday Magazine*, December 17, 1995, 72–74.

[15] "Folio: 500," *Folio:*, July 1, 1994, 51.

[16] J. William Click and Russell N. Baird, *Magazine Editing and Production.* (Dubuque, Iowa: William C. Brown, 1990), 23–24.

[17] Click, *Magazine Editing and Production,* 25.

[18] Tebbel and Zuckerman, *The Magazine in America,* 44.

[19] Gale Directory of Publications.

[20] SRDS, February 1995.

[21] Deirdre Carmody, "On the Annual Scoreboard of Magazines, It's Sports 67, Sex 44," *The New York Times,* June 12, 1995.

[22] Carmody, "On the Annual Scoreboard of Magazines."

[23] Telephone interview with Nancy Schlick, Director of Communications, ABP, June 7, 1995.

[24] Census of Manufacturers, 1992.

[25] Mott, *A History of American Magazines,* 510.

[26] Tebbel and Zuckerman, *The Magazine in America,* 4.

[27] Tebbel and Zuckerman, *The Magazine in America,* 21.

[28] Mott, *A History of American Magazines,* 320.

[29] Tebbel and Zuckerman, *The Magazine in America,* 99.

[30] Tebbel and Zuckerman, *The Magazine in America,* 33.

[31] Mott, *A History of American Magazines,* 632.

[32] Mott, *A History of American Magazines,* 458.

[33] Mott, *A History of American Magazines,* 710.

[34] Deirdre Carmody, *The New York Times,* September 26, 1994.

[35] Tebbel and Zuckerman, *The Magazine in America,* 143.

[36] John Heidenry, *Theirs Was the Kingdom, Lila and DeWitt Wallace and the Story of the Reader's Digest,* (New York: W. W. Norton, 1993), 40.

[37] Tebbel and Zuckerman, *The Magazine in America,* 185.

[38] Heidenry, *Theirs Was the Kingdom,* 224.

[39] Tebbel and Zuckerman, *The Magazine in America,* 105.

[40] Tebbel and Zuckerman, *The Magazine in America,* 106.

[41] Amy Janello and Brennon Jones for Magazine Publishers of America and American Society of Magazine Editors, *The American Magazine* (New York: Harry N. Abrams, Inc., 1991), 72.

[42] Tebbel and Zuckerman, *The Magazine in America,* 158.

[43] Tebbel and Zuckerman, *The Magazine in America,* 161.

[44] Tebbel and Zuckerman, *The Magazine in America,* 169.

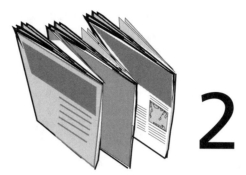

2

# The Business of Magazine Publishing

## TYPICAL STRUCTURE OF A MAGAZINE COMPANY

A student immersed in the history of American magazines and the strong impact entrepreneurs and independent publishers have had in this industry over two centuries, must do an abrupt about-face when considering the current structure of publishing. Name a popular, widely sold magazine and it's likely to be published by a huge conglomerate with holdings in businesses having little or nothing to do with print publishing, such as real estate, cable television, or moviemaking. Making headlines in the 1980s and 1990s were big deals, big mergers, and big acquisitions that created huge companies. Time and Warner merged in 1989. Six years later, the new company announced an $8 billion stock acquisition of Turner Broadcasting System. ABC and Capital Cities merged in 1986. Then Capital Cities/ABC merged with the Walt Disney Company in 1995 to create a company with $16.4 billion in revenues. Magazines are but one slice of this rich and diverse media pie. Magazine holdings in large media companies usually account for less revenue than its other revenue streams. For instance, Time Warner's magazine holdings account for about one-third of its total media revenue—and media revenue only accounts for 45 percent of total corporate revenue. Figure 2.1 illustrates how almost one-half of the top media companies have *no* magazine holdings.

In spite of the headlines these huge companies generate, the vast majority of magazines are still published by smaller companies that are not traded on the stock

**TABLE 2.1 Magazine holdings of the 25 top media companies, by net revenue, in millions of dollars.**

| Rank | Company | HQ | Total media revenue | Magazine revenue |
|------|---------|-----|------|------|
| 1. | Capital Cities/ABC | NY | 6,257.7 | 365.3 |
| 2. | Time Warner | NY | 6,036.6 | 2,281.6 |
| 3. | Tele-Communications Inc. | CO | 4,247.0 | — |
| 4. | CBS Inc. | NY | 3,711.9 | — |
| 5. | Gannett Co. | VA | 3,650.1 | — |
| 6. | Advance Publications | NJ | 3,460.0 | 1,008.0 |
| 7. | General Electric Co. | CT | 3,361.0 | — |
| 8. | News Corp. | Sydney | 2,914.0 | 635.0 |
| 9. | New York Times Co. | NY | 2,357.6 | 280.1 |
| 10. | Times Mirror Co. | CA | 2,300.2 | 237.2 |
| 11. | Hearst Corp. | NY | 2,298.7 | 1,236.0 |
| 12. | Viacom | NY | 2,292.2 | — |
| 13. | Knight-Ridder | FL | 2,194.5 | — |
| 14. | Cox Enterprises | GA | 2,069.6 | .4 |
| 15. | Turner Broadcasting System | GA | 2,047.4 | — |
| 16. | Tribune Co. | IL | 1,960.0 | 9.5 |
| 17. | Thomson Corp. | Canada | 1,631.0 | 900.0 |
| 18. | Washington Post Co. | DC | 1,497.3 | 337.6 |
| 19. | Continental Cablevision | MA | 1,200.0 | — |
| 20. | E.W Scripps | OH | 1,146.5 | — |
| 21. | Dow Jones & Co. | NY | 1,114.0 | — |
| 22. | Comcast Corp. | PA | 1,065.3 | — |
| 23. | Reed Elsevier | MA | 1045.0 | 1,045.0 |
| 24. | Advo | CT | 975.5 | — |
| 25. | International Data Group | MA | 912.0 | 912.0 |

Source: *Advertising Age*, August 14, 1995.

exchange. An estimated 22,000 consumer and business magazines are published in America—and only about 160 of them have a circulation over 500,000 and revenues of over $1 million. Magazine-only companies can indeed prosper with as few as a half-dozen employees. But the road for independent publishers is littered with economic hazards, due primarily to ever-increasing costs of postage, paper, and manufacturing. As you'll read in Chapter 3, most magazine publishers actively explore other revenue streams to support their business. In the mid-1990s, paper costs soared by almost 50 percent.[1] Substantial hikes in postage rates have caused the demise of many magazines in recent years, because publishers are dependent on the mail for both distribution of their magazines and direct mail marketing. Big companies that publish several magazines can buy paper in bulk and command

**TABLE 2.2  Top 15 media companies, ranked by net magazine revenues, in millions of dollars.**

| Company | Revenues |
|---|---|
| 1.  Time Warner | 2,281.6 |
| 2.  Hearst Corporation | 1,236 |
| 3.  Reed Elsevier | 1,045.0 |
| 4.  Advance Publications | 1,008.0 |
| 5.  International Data Group | 912.0 |
| 6.  Thomson Corp. | 900.0 |
| 7.  Ziff Davis Publishing | 821.0 |
| 8.  Reader's Digest Association | 780.0 |
| 9.  News Corp. | 635.0 |
| 10.  Meredith Corporation | 494.3 |
| 11.  Hachette Filipacchi Magazines | 455.0 |
| 12.  United News & Media | 442.8 |
| 13.  McGraw-Hill | 418.1 |
| 14.  Bertelsmann AG | 377.0 |
| 15.  Capital Cities/ABC | 365.3 |

Source: *Advertising Age*, August 14, 1995. United News & Media revenue is U.S. total for subsidiary, Miller Freeman. Bertelsmann revenue is U.S. total for Gruner & Jahr USA.

good newsstand placement because of their contracts with distributors. They are at a distinct advantage in today's marketplace.

Any kind of company or organization can publish a magazine. Religious groups are in the magazine business. So are banks, colleges, libraries, museums, fashion designers, lobbying groups, department stores, and airlines. Prisoners at the Louisiana State Penitentiary publish a magazine called the *Angolite*—which has been a finalist for the coveted National Magazine Award.

Consider, too, that a contemporary magazine can be the product of a business that has decided a print vehicle is the best way to reach its target customer. This kind of "custom publishing" is another kind of public relations magazine discussed in Chapter 1; in recent years, it has been employed by financial institutions, credit card companies, and many other businesses without traditional experience in magazine publishing. For instance, in the early 1990s, Federal Express launched a 350,000-circulation quarterly magazine for office support staff called *Via FedEx*, and in 1992 IBM brought out two bimonthly titles, *Profit* and *Beyond Computing*, which were sent to 200,000 information technology executives and small businesses.[2] The liquor company Schieffelin and Somerset in 1995 launched *Dewar's Magazine*, a twice-a-year lifestyle title. The 24-page magazine was sent to 175,000 people whose names had been entered in a database after attending Dewar's-sponsored events at bars. The magazine included eight pages of ads and a toll-free phone number for more information on upcoming bar nights. The magazine "gives us a way of reaching consumers between events," a Dewar's executive told a reporter.[3] When magazines like the one published by Dewar's are sent directly to existing and potential customers, all the advertisements are the company's advertisements; all the editorial relates to the company and doing business with it. Such titles might look like typical magazines, but they aren't. The same sophisticated editorial, circulation, and advertising strategies that preoccupy publishers of consumer and trade magazines do not pertain. In most cases, the company publishing the custom magazine has entered into a partnership with another firm with direct experience in print production to actually publish the magazine. Schieffelin and Somerset, for instance, hired an outside marketing firm to handle both bar nights and production and distribution of the magazine.[4]

With major corporations publishing magazines for marketing purposes, with conglomerates run by real estate moguls and entertainment lawyers publishing some of the biggest-selling magazines today, and with so many different kinds of companies—from mom and pop operations to a giant like Disney—publishing quality, money-making titles, how can there possibly be a *typical* structure to a magazine publishing concern?

Clearly, there isn't one. But there are disciplines common to all magazines, as well as systems that have been proved successful. Most magazines have a bifurcate structure, one side operating the creative engine (editorial and art) and the other the business function (advertising, circulation, production, and general management). Within these two functions are areas that are best handled by experts and professionals with skill and specialized training. Like any other business operation, a magazine company will have office support staff, computer experts, accounting personnel, and perhaps a public relations staff. And, naturally, these jobs require skills specific to magazine publishing. But several key positions are in place at any magazine company no matter what the size or wealth of the business. These are the jobs unique to the magazine publishing industry.

> ***President or chief executive officer.*** The person with this job may or may not have risen through the ranks of publishing. In the case of large, multifaceted media companies that have varied concerns and holdings, the president/CEO might never have managed a subscription campaign, sold advertising, or edited a cover story. At other companies, the president may be a magazine veteran, with many years of hands-on experience at individual magazines. At smaller companies, the president and publisher (see below) responsibilities may be combined. In most cases, someone who is president or CEO of a magazine reports to the chairman of the board and board of directors of the company and is responsible for the profit and loss of the company, direction, strategy, and reputation. The job requires a person with exceptionally strong management and leadership skills. Depending on the size and type of company, the president might be charged with identifying and soliciting investors, developing

new product lines, setting personnel policy, and other high-level management and financial duties.

***Publisher***. The publisher is usually the senior sales executive for the magazine and is responsible for ensuring the magazine's visibility in the marketplace. Since most magazines sell advertising and depend on it as a principal source of revenue, the publisher's responsibilities have historically been centered around advertising. Therefore, the publisher has typically come to his or her position through the sales ranks. But with circulation gaining in importance as a revenue stream and with many magazines depending on circulation funds, publishers are also getting their training in circulation departments. In terms of the publisher's business relationship with the company, he or she may be an owner, partner, or employee. Chapter 3 contains a detailed discussion of the role and responsibilities of a magazine publisher.

***Advertising director***. At any other company, a person with the title *advertising director* is usually responsible for handling the image and sales message of the company and helping promote and sell the company's products or services through advertising placements. For instance, the advertising director at a book publisher makes decisions regarding how each book will be advertised. He or she will determine which books will get advertised in the *New York Times Book Review* and which books will get radio, television, or subway advertising. The ad director will also set advertising budgets for each book, deciding how many advertisements will appear, when they will appear, and what kind of language will be used to describe the book. At a magazine, however, the advertising director is responsible for convincing other companies to buy advertising in the magazine. Instead of *spending* money like their counterparts at other companies, magazine ad directors are always looking for people to *give* them money. Magazines, of course, do advertise themselves in a variety of media, and sometimes the advertising director becomes involved in this process. However, the primary responsibility of the magazine ad director is to sell advertising and to direct the selling effort of the magazine. The advertising director's job is discussed in detail in Chapter 6.

***Circulation director***. The circulation director identifies the people who are likely readers of the magazine. This is a complex, involved process, and, depending on the kind of magazine, the circulation director's responsibilities will change. At magazines that sell advertising pages (and, remember, not all magazines do), the circulation director is responsible for managing and maintaining the magazine's rate base. Rate base is the number of readers that the magazine guarantees advertisers will reach and the number on which it sets advertising rates. As you'll read in Chapter 5, magazines can have paid or unpaid circulation—sometimes they have both. Paid circulation is the number of copies that readers pay money for and obtain either through a subscription or by a single-copy purchase on the newsstand. The circulation director manages the process involved in these newsstand and subscription purchases. Unpaid circulation includes copies given away for promotional reasons, office copies, and other distribution that isn't purchased. Many magazines have unpaid circulation limited to people with a specific job or work responsibilities. This is known as qualified circulation.

***Production director.*** The production director is responsible for the manufacturing and distribution of the magazine. He or she ensures that ads and editorial pages come together. At many magazines, the production director is also responsible for the purchase and inventory of paper and for negotiating printing contracts. Chapters 7 and 8 detail the intricacies of this function.

***Administrative director.*** This position—which can also be titled *general manager* or *controller*—has financial responsibilities for the magazine. He or she oversees planning and accounting policies. The magazine world has its own set of requirements and accounting. For instance, a magazine subscription is entered as income as soon as the subscriber indicates an intent to subscribe by checking "Yes" on the business reply card received in a direct mail package. If the subscriber ends up canceling a subscription, the circulation department must be charged with a "bad debt"—noted on the books in the same way as someone who doesn't pay for a subscription. Advertisers can be "short rated"—that is, charged more if they fail to buy advertisements in the specified frequency. The administrator and staff provide the regulatory, operational, and statistical information necessary to satisfy both internal and external reporting requirements.

***Editor-in-chief.*** This is the magazine job that combines creativity and strong management skills. The editor of a magazine must generate ideas (and hire people who can generate ideas) that will become the stories, reports, articles, surveys, and essays we read, as well as the artwork and photographs in a magazine's pages. The generation of compelling ideas, as well as the actual visual presentation of the editorial pages, is the editor's job. As you'll read in Chapter 4, editors and their staffs must bring skills in journalism, editing, design, and production that are unique to magazines.

Editor, advertising director, circulation director, administrator, and production director all report to the publisher or president. The basic magazine structure is the same whether a magazine is a consumer or a trade title, or has a paid or unpaid circulation. The key functions described above are usually always in place whatever the size and complexity of a magazine. Of course, if a magazine doesn't accept advertising from outside companies, there isn't a need for an ad director as described above, and the publisher's responsibilities will vary accordingly.

# REVENUE

Most magazines are designed as profit-making businesses. There is a small number of nonprofit magazines. The great advantage of a magazine being a nonprofit is that it receives a reduction in mailing costs. In order to be considered a nonprofit business and receive these mailing privileges, a magazine must prove to the government that it is published for the social and educational welfare of the country. Whether a profit-making business or not, magazines must have money coming in to operate. Magazines make money by selling copies on the newsstand and by subscription and by selling advertising pages. The total income from these sources is reduced by all the expected usual expenses—the cost of printing, staff salaries, promotion dollars spent to get subscribers, the money it costs to convince an advertiser around the corner or around the world to buy a page of advertising, postage, administrative staff, insurance, taxes, computers, leasing a photocopier, electricity, desks, pens, and paper clips. To expand its business, a magazine can also build revenue from other sources beyond advertising and circulation. *Old Farmer's Almanac*, for instance, collects 15 percent of its gross revenue from licensing, mail order, and premium and specialty advertising.[5]

A magazine with advertising as a revenue base is affected by changes in consumer demand. In the fall of 1994, the *Wall Street Journal* reported that a surge in consumer demand for home goods (furniture, renovation materials, etc.) helped increase advertising at home-related magazines such as *Country Home*, *Home,* and *House Beautiful*.[6] But fashion and beauty magazines lagged in the same period, because there were fewer fragrance launches in 1995 and cosmetic and apparel retailers tightened ad spending following weak sales and industry consolidation.[7]

When corporate profits grow, advertisers want to reach the targeted consumer markets magazines can provide. In a healthy economy, magazine advertising benefits. Similarly, when personal income and personal consumption expenditures grow, magazine circulation benefits—though many experts believe that circulation is less likely than ad pages to suffer from swings in the economy.[8] In the recession years of the 1980s, publishers suffered large losses in advertising receipts, and they learned not to depend solely on advertising revenues. As a result, in recent years, publishers have given significantly more attention to revenues derived from their circulation base and ancillary products.

As we'll explore in more detail in Chapter 6, if a magazine publishes advertising, the number of editorial pages is related in some way to its ad pages. (If a magazine does not publish advertising, the number of editorial pages usually does not fluctuate; the publisher has already determined how many editorial pages he or she can afford to print based on cost of printing, distribution, and circulation revenue.) Advertising also affects how much color can appear and where in the magazine it can appear. This relationship between editorial pages and advertising pages can be a fixed number or a ratio. Most often it is a combination of the two, with a minimum number of editorial pages added when advertising goes above some critical number. For example, a magazine might aim to publish 55 ad pages and 35 editorial pages each month, for an ad-to-edit ratio of 60:40. Then, when the advertising department of this magazine sells two additional pages, the editor can add one editorial page. Each magazine works out the best formula, based on its unique set of costs and revenues.

## CPM: A BASIC MEASUREMENT

The challenge for publishers and editors is discovering whether the special audience they want to reach can support a magazine. To do so, a magazine first must have a critical mass of support. As one publisher told an interviewer: "If you want a magazine for butterfly collectors, you must first measure the universe, its interest, and what butterfly collectors will pay for a magazine…. There may be 15,000 butterfly collectors who would appreciate a high-quality magazine on butterfly collecting, but these numbers won't justify that kind of magazine."[9] The cost of creating and producing such a high-quality magazine would far outweigh the revenue the potential publisher could hope to receive from either subscription fees or advertising in a market of only 15,000. The publisher might be better off publishing a special interest newsletter with a higher subscription price and lower production costs—or a definitive book on butterfly collecting.

One of the ways a would-be butterfly magazine publisher—or any publisher—might begin to evaluate how a new magazine could fit in the market amid existing competition is to make use of the key measurements in the business of magazine publishing: CPM or cost-per-thousand. It is simply the cost of reaching an audience of 1,000 and is used by advertising directors, circulation directors, and production directors to gauge the efficiency of an advertising medium. The cost of a page of advertising divided by that magazine's circulation in thousands provides the CPM. If a black-and-white page of advertising in a magazine with a circulation of 750,000 costs $26,250, the black-and-white page CPM is $35. ($26,250 ÷ 750 = $35). CPM is used by advertisers to compare competing magazines as a measure of efficiency. In most categories, the CPM will not be markedly different from one magazine to another and is an important tool in positioning competing magazines. Consider the following invented magazines:

> *Gourmet Meals at Home* is written and edited for people who love to cook and serve complicated, involved recipes for their families and friends. *Gourmet Meals* features extensive menu ideas, timetables for planning, shopping hints, decorating tips, and entertaining ideas. It's for people who have a good deal of time and money to spend on cooking. *Budget Time* is designed for people who don't have the same luxury of time and money and want to cut their grocery bills dramatically. It contains practical infor-

mation and tips on coupon cutting, comparison shopping, budget-minded recipes and menus, as well as advice on seasonal specials. With those two magazines on either end of the spectrum, the publisher of a newly launched magazine—*Take Out/Eat In*—wants to enter the category of food shopping and advice magazines squarely in the middle. The publisher believes there is a large number of people who are interested in serving meals in a way that neither of the existing competition provides. *Take Out/Eat In* is designed for people who are busy and cost-conscious but who like to cook occasional special, more elaborate meals. It contains information and tips on incorporating prepared food into an evening meal and entertaining stylishly. Here's how the three titles compare:

|  | Circulation | 1 Page B/W | CPM |
|---|---|---|---|
| Gourmet Meals | 100,000 | $4,250 | $42.50 |
| Take Out/Eat In | 250,000 | $8,500 | $34.00 |
| Budget Time | 120,000 | $3,600 | $30.00 |

You'll see that even though the cost of an advertisement in *Take Out/Eat In* is the most expensive of the three, its CPM is in the middle because its circulation is much higher. This kind of comparison is one of the methods a publisher will use to set advertising rates and position a magazine within a category.

## LAUNCHING A MAGAZINE

If *Take Out/Eat In* really were to launch, most experts would recommend that the publishers have $5-$20 million on hand.[10] Despite the extraordinary cost, risk, and competition, magazine publishing is still a compelling business option for many. But it's a long, pothole-filled road. The University of Mississippi's Samir Husni, who has been collecting data since the mid-1980s on individuals and companies publishing magazines, contends that it takes five years for the average startup to make money.[11] But, he adds, it's the lucky few who make it that far: half of all new consumer magazines die before their first anniversary, and only two in ten survive the first four years.[12]

A new magazine can begin life in any of several ways. Sometimes big magazine companies will test a magazine idea by distributing a limited number of copies on newsstands and study buyer response. If copies move quickly off the newsstand, the publishers may suspect that they have a hit on their hands and will roll out the publication with a regular frequency and a bigger distribution. Individuals with an idea for a magazine launch will typically either raise the necessary millions of dollars on their own, or propose that a publishing partner, in exchange for an investment in funds or support, join in the endeavor. A young copywriter from Los Angeles who had just written *Sex and the Single Girl* approached executives at Hearst Magazines in the 1960s with an idea for a magazine. The Hearst executives didn't like her idea, but they liked Helen Gurley Brown enough to offer her the job of reinventing their faltering general interest magazine, *Cosmopolitan*. Brown reinvented and relaunched *Cosmopolitan* in 1965 for a new audience of young women readers.

Whether it's an individual or a corporation that is launching a consumer or trade magazine, the universal warning is: Don't imagine you can create your own market. The market for readers and advertisers must be defined and cohesive. A publisher of a new trade magazine would carefully explore government or industry estimates of how sales in that industry will increase or decrease in the next five years. Experts usually recommend that would-be-publishers develop editorial ideas for at least a year of issues, as well as a graphic presentation and cover design. Direct mail tests are usually conducted, describing the magazine to likely subscribers. If the results of the direct mail test are positive (that is, if 3 to 5 percent of the people to whom you mailed the initial solicitation say they'll subscribe), the nascent publishers will write a comprehensive three-to-five-year business plan. This plan (which can be 20 to 30 pages in length) will project cash flow and all circulation and advertising scenarios. Experienced help with the business plan is critical for a successful launch. Usually a prototype issue is created to present to potential advertisers and investors. Finance, circulation planning, and advertising consultants specialize in all areas of the business, and a would-be publisher who doesn't have access to such people within his or her company would be wise to seek them out through industry resources such as the *Folio: Source Book* and trade associations such as the Magazine Publishers of America and Business Publishers Association.

## INTERNATIONAL PUBLISHING

Magazine publishing, of course, is not exclusive to New York City or 50 states. Or even to North America. While American companies do have a significant presence in global publishing (U.S.-based companies publish an estimated 1,500 magazines overseas), magazine publishing is not restricted by international borders. *Reader's Digest* pioneered international print editions with its 1938 British edition. Soon after, the company began publishing foreign language editions in South America and Central America—and now publishes 47 international editions in 18 languages with a total circulation of 13 million. Nearly all operate through wholly owned foreign subsidiaries. Condé Nast International publishes 31 magazines through wholly owned companies in Europe and Australia. Hearst publishes 64 foreign language editions of eight magazines.

With publishers experiencing a slowdown in advertising and circulation revenues in the 1990s, many looked to overseas markets for new sources of revenue. U.S. periodical exports were up an estimated 6 percent in 1992 over the 1991 level—to $747 million in current dollars. Consumer and farm publications accounted for most of this increase. But keep in mind that many U.S. business and professional publications are requested individually by foreign subscribers and are not reported in government trade data. Major markets for U.S. magazine exports in 1991 were Canada, accounting for 78 percent of the total; the United Kingdom with 6 percent, Mexico 4 percent and the Netherlands 3 percent.[13]

Subsidiaries, joint venture operations, and licensing magazines are the predominant forms of global expansion for U.S. magazine publishers. Eastern European and Asian markets became particularly attractive to publishers in the late 1990s. Magazines either publish editions overseas or circulate the same American edition via subscriptions and newsstand sales. California-based *Surfing Magazine* reported in 1993 that its circulation had doubled in the previous five years in Australia—due to Australia's prominence as a surfing mecca—and had grown by 50 percent in the United Kingdom and France during the same period. The same edition of *Surfing* circulates everywhere, and most of its foreign circulation is sold on newsstands.[14] At many other publishing companies—from giant corporations to small technical magazines—publishers find a licensee who pays to use the name of the magazine. The licensee may or may not use the content from the original magazine. The local publisher is responsible for selling advertising, producing editorial content, and arranging distribution. Typically, this relationship is a happy, profitable one. Exceptions are notable, however. In 1995, *Forbes* withdrew its five-year-old publishing license from Burda Holding, which was publishing an unprofitable edition of the magazine. *Forbes* said the German publisher "failed to match *Forbes*'s U.S. quality" after officials said it published questionable rankings of executive salaries and offered "dubious" investment advice.[15]

Top European publishers, especially German and French firms, have invested heavily in foreign editions of their publications both in the United States and other European countries during the past five years.[16] In one of the most noteworthy examples, in 1995 the London-based publisher Time Out Group Ltd joined with a group of private investors to launch a New York City version of *Time Out*, the London weekly magazine of arts and entertainment. It was the first American venture by the publishing group, which also publishes magazine guides in Paris and Amsterdam. Foreign *direct* investment in the U.S. magazine industry has been declining in recent years. In 1991 other countries spent an estimated $70 million in U.S. companies, far below the levels of previous years. British and French firms accounted for much of this investment.

## NOTES

[1] Lorra Manly, "Launch Log." *Folio:*, January 15, 1995, 12.

[2] Ann Marie Kerwin, "Custom Publishing Heats Up," *Inside Media*, March 15, 1995, 32.

[3] Lambeth Hochwald, "Have Database, Will Publish," in *Folio:*, November 15, 1995, 69.

[4] Hochwald, "Have Database, Will Publish."

[5] The Ad Age 300," *Advertising Age*, June 19, 1995, 5–17.

[6] *The Wall Street Journal*, "Magazine Firms Celebrate Ad Page Gains," October 24, 1995.

[7] *Women's Wear Daily*, November 15, 1994, special supplement.

[8] U.S. Industrial Outlook, 1993.

[9] Jim Mann, ed. *Magazine Editing: Its Art and Practice*. (New Canaan, CT: Folio Magazine Publishing Corp., 1985) 8–9.

[10] Deirdre Carmody, "Magazines Find Green Pastures Abroad," *The New York Times*, March 20, 1995.

[11] *Women's Wear Daily*, November 15, 1994.

[12] *Women's Wear Daily*, November 15, 1994.

[13] U.S. Industrial Outlook, 1993.

[14] *Folio:*, "Away From Home," June 15, 1993, 42.

[15] *Folio:*, "Away From Home."

[16] *U.S. Industrial Outlook*, 1993.

# Publishers and Their Magazines

## INTRODUCTION

Without taxing our imaginations, we can usually come up with a pretty good idea of how people spend their workdays when we hear their job titles. But when you hear that someone is a publisher, what images come to mind? What exactly does a magazine publisher *do* all day? The secondary dictionary definition describes a publisher as "the business head of a newspaper organization or publishing house, commonly the owner or the representative of the owner."[1] In the first half of the twentieth century, more often than not, the owner of the magazine business was the publisher. To build a business, magazine publishers realized they needed to add new magazine titles. As publishers created or acquired magazines, additional management was needed to run the operation effectively. The result is that the title of publisher was and is still bestowed on the person responsible for the general management of a single magazine—even in a multiple publication house. Therefore, the dictionary definition is still operative.

A publisher is responsible for all activities that are necessary to maintain and grow the magazine. The publisher of a title in a multiple publication house represents the owner. Consider the example of Rodale Press, Inc., based in Pennsylvania. Rodale publishes several magazines including *American Woodworker*, *Backpacker*, *Men's Health,* and *Prevention*. Each of these publications is under the direction of an individual publisher. As we've seen at smaller companies, the publisher might report directly to the chief operating officer, who may also be the company's owner.

There are, of course, exceptions to the simple definition. The title of publisher carries a significant level of prestige, especially for well-known magazines. This can result in muddied waters. Some publishing companies may decide that their sales manager or advertising director would appear more important to advertisers if he or she had the title of publisher. So, in some instances the "publisher" of a magazine may not be responsible for activities outside the sales realm. Time Inc. complicated matters further in 1994 when the company decided to call the head of each magazine the "president" of the particular magazine enterprise. Each magazine still has a publisher, but it is the president who is responsible for the health of the business. The publisher title still exists at individual magazines, but the president is the general manager of the enterprise. Therefore, in some situations, even though an individual may hold the title of publisher, he or she may not be responsible for all the areas we'll discuss in this chapter. In some instances, in other words, the title of publisher has lost significance or has diminished in clarity.

## THE ROLE OF THE PUBLISHER

For our purposes we will consider the publisher to be the general manager who has overall profit and loss responsibility for a magazine. This means the publisher is responsible for all operations: editorial, advertising, circulation, production, manufacturing, and administration, including finance. The editor, ad director, circulation director, and production director all report to the publisher. The publisher must be a strategist, setting challenging but achievable short- and long-term goals for each department. The publisher must be well-versed in both the economics of publishing and the state of the economy. To create a strategy, the publisher must know the magazine inside and out. He or she must know the readers and how they rate the service performed by the magazine. The publisher must also know which advertisers are most likely to be interested in reaching readers with the demographics and lifestyle attributes (or psychographics) that the publication offers. The publisher needs to keep abreast of short- and long-term economic and market changes that can force a change in the primary strategy. The publisher must live and breathe the magazine. He or she needs to use every possible resource—personal experience, market research, the current economic and business press—to keep up with and stay ahead of the many factors that can affect the business, either positively or negatively.

As we'll explore in Chapter 4, fundamental to every magazine is its editorial and marketing reasons for being—that is, its mission. The publisher needs to have a perfectly clear understanding of this and must be capable of communicating the mission to every person who is associated with the publication. In a multiple magazine house, it is important that the publisher be in agreement with management on the mission of the magazine. In fact, from time to time, the publisher might need to remind corporate management of the magazine's mission. Corporate management has been known to put on pressure for improved financial performance, pushing a publisher to make changes that would alter the magazine's mission in the short term—to the longer-term detriment of the publication.

The publisher is also the prime mover in the development of new products that can be developed from the primary business. For example, the publisher of a general interest cooking magazine might see the opportunity to introduce an annual special issue on outdoor cooking. Most publishers view his or her magazine as the nucleus of a finely tuned marketing machine. The publisher is responsible for making the decision to add something new to the marketing arsenal. While the publisher cannot be expected to generate and execute all the ideas for new revenue streams, he or she must create a climate in which new ideas are encouraged and flow freely. Knowledge of the reader as well as the advertiser's marketing goals and challenges will help develop a sense of what new product idea is likely to be successful. How much revenue can such ancillary programs generate? It is the responsibility of the publisher to decide, carefully weighing the cost of development against projected long- and short-term revenues.

In the 1990s, the popular sources of revenue for magazines include:

- *List rentals*. Subscriber lists can be desirable for many direct mail marketers.
- *Reprints or books*. Editorial originally published in the magazine can be repackaged and sold on the newsstand, in bookstores, or by direct mail.
- *Custom publishing*. A custom publication can be an occasional magazine or newsletter produced for one advertiser.
- *Advertorials*. Many magazines sell advertorials. These are multiple-page sections dedicated to one or more advertisers with a special interest. The advertising department supervises the creation of these sections, which usually are accompanied by text relevant to the advertiser. The Magazine Publishers of America and the American Society of Magazine Editors have issued guidelines for the creation and publication of such sections, one of the most obvious being that such sections should carry a banner at the top of the page, indicating that the section is an advertisement.
- *Cable television*. The number of television channels added by cable has dramatically increased demand for program content. For example, cooking magazines can be a source of first-class content for the TV Food Network. Many magazine publishers and cable programmers have collaborated on the creation of programming that promotes a title to a targeted audience.
- *Card decks and sample packs*. Advertisers purchase a postcard that is pack-

aged with others and mailed to the subscriber list, or have a sample of their product distributed with others to a specific demographic market. Brides-to-be and families expecting a baby are examples of markets that are especially attractive because they are likely to be buying products in which they have not had a prior interest.

- *Special issues or one-shots*. These stand-alone issues are especially popular in the home market, with kitchen and bathroom issues.
- *Out-of-field distribution*. Some trade magazines have profitable paid circulation outside their target audience. *Medical Economics*, a publication for physicians, has had success in selling subscriptions to accountants and lawyers who have physician clients.
- *Market data*. Usually generated for the magazine editorial and sales efforts, some hard-to-find market data can be successfully sold to outside companies or consultants who are not advertising prospects.
- *Buyers' guides, catalogs, and directories*. These are popular in many trade markets. These publications can be useful as directories of product descriptions, key personnel in the market, and other uses peculiar to individual markets. Where job opportunities exceed the supply of qualified people, an annual or semiannual recruitment directory can be successful. Computer magazines have had notable success in developing these product lines.
- *Global markets*. Some markets are sufficiently universal that a publication can simply solicit overseas subscribers. Others need to change their editorial or need to be translated and are best published by a separate company abroad. Licensing can also be used to generate revenue and measure the appeal of a magazine in foreign markets.
- *Conferences and seminars*. These gatherings can be used both to enhance the reputation of a magazine and provide additional revenue.
- *Trade shows*. A big and profitable business, these major events are commonly planned and produced in conjunction with firms that specialize in trade show management.

All of the above are tried-and-true methods to parlay the magazine's many resources into increased revenue and importance to both readers and advertisers. Many publishers are also exploring opportunities on the Internet and its World Wide Web. There is extraordinary hype about new media, particularly the Internet. Any good publisher has a sensible level of paranoia about the future of print. This does not mean the publisher should react immediately every time a threat to print appears, but it is wise to put a toe in the water as long as the cost of doing so makes sense. That is, there is a reasonable opportunity to extend the magazine product profitably. As you'll read in Chapter 8, up to now none of the new media have proved to be sufficiently portable and readable to replace a magazine in print. CD-ROM has great utility for reference works and presentations that demand TV-like graphics and sound, neither of which are important to a magazine reader. In 1995, the signs were already apparent that CD-ROM magazines weren't the hot commodity once imagined. *Medio Magazine,* a CD-ROM magazine, announced a reduction in frequency, and *Newsweek* dropped its CD-ROM quarterly to concentrate on its venture on Prodigy, an on-line service.[2]

## DEPARTMENT MANAGEMENT

If the publisher is responsible for all the diverse areas of a magazine, how much day-to-day involvement can he or she realistically have in each? It would be unusual for a publisher to be steeped in knowledge about every department of the magazine. Successful publishers have gained their magazine experience in both the business and editorial sides of a publication. If a publisher came up through the ranks of advertising sales or circulation, he or she will have much to learn about editorial; publishers who have been editors will need to concentrate on learning the business side of the operation. In an ideal situation, a publisher will have strong, knowledgeable, experienced personnel heading up each department

In a single-title publishing operation, the publisher is directly in charge of these various functions. Multiple-title publishers will centralize some departments. Centralized departments are organized to serve more than one publication. Rarely are editorial, advertising, and publishing management centralized. Candidates for centralization are departments where most functions can be considered generic to the operation of any magazine. For example, basic accounting and financial planning is the same from one publication to another. So is the circulation fulfillment function. Centralization can take advantage of efficiencies that can be had with personnel and office equipment. Smaller single magazines are not likely to be able to afford the services of a high-powered director of finance or circulation director, but spreading the cost of the person among numerous magazines can make it possible. Even when there are centralized functions, a larger magazine in the stable may have its own circulation director or business manager as the day-to-day contact with the central department.

A hazard of centralization is the possibility that the publisher feels that he or she does not have sufficient control of the centralized function. This can result in some silly politics and in the worst case, the publisher abrogating responsibility for all or part of an important function. Professionals with a singleness of purpose are capable of working together effectively and efficiently, so that centralization does indeed produce the anticipated benefits. The bottom line is that centralization of a function does not remove the publisher's responsibility for the function. It does demand that the head of the centralized department and the publisher accept and respect each other as peers. They must not let the control issue get in the way of efficiency and effectiveness of the separate functions. With this in mind, let's look at the basics that publishers must know or learn about their various departments. A warning: In some cases in the following discussion, technical terms might be used to describe the relationship between the publisher and department head. These terms are fully defined in the glossary and extensively discussed in the chapters devoted to that particular function.

## Editorial

With a few exceptions, the editorial pages of the magazine are the key to business success or failure. The exceptions are those publications that are read as much for their advertising as their editorial. Some publications exist solely to showcase products. Some fashion magazines and computer magazines are read purely for information on the new, improved, or "hot" products advertised. For the majority of magazines in which editorial is the principal offering, the most important requirement is a skilled editor, one who knows the needs and tastes of the audience and can manage communications to that audience with on-target articles and departments, superb writing, and appealing graphics. If a publisher has all this in the editor, what is there to manage? First of all, the publisher and editor must agree on a clear statement of the editorial purpose of the magazine. The statement should paint a clear picture of why the magazine exists and how it will serve its readers. Some formal statements of purpose go further, elaborating on the way the editorial will meet the need, including comments on the subject areas to be covered, length of articles, types of departments, and the general graphic approach. The time a publisher spends on the editorial area will vary depending on numerous factors such as the experience of the editor, the health of the magazine, and economic conditions. The editorial is so critical to the success of the publication that publishers cannot afford to be aloof about their dealings with the editor. Most publishers who gain their experience on the business side are not accomplished writers but they can be accomplished readers. Reading every issue while putting oneself in the mindset of the average reader can uncover many items for discussion with, and amplification by, the editor.

Every magazine should conduct regular formal and informal research to keep up with the changing needs of the audience. One of the keys to keeping editorial current with readers' needs is objectivity. Too frequently, magazines conduct self-serving research, exploring areas of strength for the sole purpose of self-congratulation. Obviously, it is important to know the magazine's strengths, but equally important to know where it misses the mark. The publication must ensure that there is constant feedback from readers demonstrating how well it is meeting their needs. A publisher's review and discussion of this data with the editor can be fruitful and can ensure that regular feedback from the audience is a priority.

One of the many balancing acts in which a publisher engages is the relationship between editorial and advertising. Every magazine that sells advertising struggles with how stringently the editorial department should be protected from the influence and expectations of advertisers. You may hear this referred to as "separation between church and state"—the church being the purity and objectivity of the editorial effort and the state being the commercial goals of the business side. The obvious fear is that the credibility the magazine has with its readers might be tarnished if editors are influenced—or appear to be influenced—by advertisers. One can separate editorial and advertising completely, assuring no undue influence, or establish protocols to avoid conflict. Harold Ross, the founding editor of *The New Yorker*, was an ardent believer of this strict separation, relegating salespeople and editors to different floors and forbidding "fraternization."[3] Most magazine publishers take a less extreme approach and have established an advertising/editorial policy. Such a policy might include the dictum that if an advertiser is mentioned or is the subject of reporting in an article, the publisher will be alerted and have the opportunity to read the article before it is published. The publisher would then make a determination about advising the advertiser to reschedule—or reposition—its advertising placement. The most important aspect of this difficult balance is for the publisher to establish a policy and then be consistent in its implementation.

The publisher is also responsible for overseeing the legal policy that affects the editorial department and the magazine. If the publication is part of a multiple-title house, there will usually be a policy under which the publisher will be required to get legal department counsel, and in some instances approval, for matters that could create the threat of legal action. There must be a policy regarding the publisher's role and responsibility in approving or rejecting an article that might give rise to a libel action. Legal advice on such an article must be part of the consideration.

Many editors gather their staff of editors and key art personnel to critique the strengths and weaknesses of each issue as soon as it is in print. Periodically, editors will also convene major editorial planning meetings. The publisher's attendance during these meetings can provide the opportunity to stay abreast of developments in the editorial area of the magazine.

At least annually, the publisher will work with the editor to develop the budget for the coming year. The publisher should seize this opportunity to encourage the editor to look further ahead on broad editorial issues. In times of economic hardship the publisher must consult with the editor regarding cost reduction measures. Care must be taken to reduce costs without damaging the quality of the editorial product. Many magazines have a long life cycle. Invariably such publications will have changed with the times in subject area coverage and graphic design. The publisher is the conscience of the magazine who can help assure such longevity.

## Advertising

Advertising sales is an area of broad and deep involvement for most publishers because it is the key to the financial success of the publication. For smaller magazines the publisher is likely to double as the ad sales director, especially if he or she came to the job through the sales ranks. In a multiple-magazine company, a corporate policy is established regarding advertising sales. Such policies might address the relationship of the editorial and sales departments, rates and discounts, employee compensation and evaluation, and employee promotions. Publishers of some magazines seek out or are offered products and services in exchange for advertising space, called bartered space. Hotels and airlines commonly are open to such arrangements. Company policy can help avoid misunderstandings on which advertising barters can be pursued and negotiated.

Whether a single-title or multi-title operation, most magazines serving a market will have unique characteristics that will call for the establishment of advertising sales policies for the individual magazine. For example, a publication dependent on only a few advertisers may have a policy under which it would not offer preferred positions other than the inside front, inside back, and the back covers. Another publication in the same company may serve an advertising market in which it would be at a competitive disadvantage if it did not sell preferred positions.

Publishers have day-to-day contact with the advertising sales director. Few weeks will pass without some activity that will demand the publisher's advice, decision, or involvement. Among the issues that arise regularly in the advertising sales category are:

- New ad programs being developed for products
- New product introductions
- Demands for special treatment, like the acceptance of an insert (inserts are ads provided by the advertiser, usually on heavier paper, and are placed between pages in the magazine at the bindery) that does not conform to the magazine's policy
- Competitive activity threatening the status of current advertisers
- Alleged rate cutting by the competition
- Circulation changes by the competition
- Competitors' announcement offering new marketing services
- Management of sales personnel

A goal of every publisher should be to become an "industry figure." Essential to this role is knowing the market extremely well and being able to establish strong working relationships with the key people in the ad market. Often the publisher title can help gain entrance to key decision makers at agencies and advertiser companies that would be more difficult for a sales representative or advertising sales director to reach. Attendance at the industry meetings held primarily for the top executives is an important route to developing such relationships. These relationships are usually not to sell advertising space directly, but rather to create a favorable view of the magazine. They are extremely important when there is a major problem with an account, one that can be resolved with the involvement of higher level corporate management. Often a problem situation can be defused simply because the publisher is friendly with the president of the company and the two can discuss the problem. A publisher comes to know the market through enthusiastic interest in its workings. A high level of interest will make the job of keeping up-to-date via personal contact, market research, and reading business publications more fun than work.

The publisher will also actively participate in the development of the sales budget or plan and strategy for the magazine. In the final analysis he or she is responsible for the success of the publication, which is directly connected to the sales effort. Additionally, it would be a rare publisher who was not involved in solving sales problems related to important accounts and problems that arise as a result of competitive activity.

## Circulation

As you will see in Chapter 5, circulation comprises at least three distinct functions: subscriber acquisition and renewal; management of single-copy sales; and list maintenance and fulfillment. The publisher's involvement in circulation varies according to the size of the magazine and status of these functions. Regardless of the size of the magazine, circulation is so critical to its success that the publisher must play an active role in the strategy and tactics used by the circulation department to maintain the all-important rate base—the number of buyers of the magazine on which advertising rates are set.

With a few exceptions such as *Woman's Day* and *TV Guide*, where the largest percent of the circulation is through newsstands, paid circulation magazines rely heavily on subscription sales to maintain rate base. Subscription sales are based on a sophisticated direct mail sales operation. Newsstand sales are made through national distributors and their local wholesalers. Both efforts require skill in tracking sales to develop the optimum number of copies in circulation.

Controlled circulation publications—distributed free to qualified readers—don't have the same need for a sophisticated direct mail effort. Nevertheless, to be eligible for lower, second-class postage rates, postal regulations demand that the publication be able to prove it was directly requested by at least 50 percent of the recipients. A magazine with a high direct request rate will use its direct response ratio as a selling tool.

The circulation department is centralized in most multiple-magazine companies and most use vendors for many, if not all, of the fulfillment functions. A variation is to have a circulation director for an individual magazine who is the strategist for subscriber and newsstand sales. He or she will also be the liaison with the centralized department. In a single-title company there will be a circulation director who is the strategist and also oversees a small staff. At smaller companies, consultants and vendors will be hired to perform many of the circulation functions.

Publishers will be active in circulation planning, budgeting, and strategy. An annual circulation plan can generally be executed with minimum variation, if the magazine has been in business for several years and can benefit from data about how their subscribers and newsstand buyers have behaved over the years. A newer magazine that is still developing data will require more constant attention from the publisher. On a regular schedule, the publisher will expect to be informed of subscription acquisition and renewal results, and analysis of the sell-through (number of copies sold of all those distributed) result of newsstand sales efforts. Involvement with fulfillment is necessary when contracts with vendors are up for renegotiation and on a problem solving basis.

## Production and Manufacturing

For most magazines, production (including prepress preparation, printing, paper, and binding) is the largest or second-largest cost of publication. Salaries and benefits are usually number one. While much of the department operation is methodical, several functions demand the publisher's close attention. This department is one that is usually centralized in multiple-title publishing companies. Printing and paper contract pricing and conditions benefit from volume purchasing. In the production area, technology has been advancing rapidly. Desktop publishing, relatively unknown in the early 1980s, is now commonplace. Publishers can now assume in-house control of numerous production steps that were previously provided by vendors. With these advances has come the cost of sophisticated and expensive equipment, making centralization of the functions all the more sensible.

Large-circulation magazines such as the news weeklies or *TV Guide* have exceptionally complicated production challenges. Each week there are geographic and demographic editions that require complex planning and execution. Often printing is done at numerous locations, and the use of satellite transmission of editorial and art to printers has become routine.

Publishers need to be conversant with the prices of paper and printing. Changing printers can be a major transition for a magazine. Doing business with a quality printer who demonstrates care for the job at hand can be worth a premium. Paper prices are cyclical. The capacity of paper mills tends to be low in good times and too high in poor economic times, thus the wild swings in price from one cycle to the next. Indeed, a shortage of paper can be a significant problem when economic conditions are buoyant. Printers will supply paper or publishers can purchase their own from a paper merchant or directly from the mill. Paper quality, which affects reproduction quality, can sometimes be a factor in an advertiser's decision to buy space in some magazines. A publisher, in consultation with his or her production director, needs to evaluate the economics of inventorying paper and the assurance of supply at competitive prices.

A publisher must monitor developments in the production or prepress function. Production managers range from those who want to be on the cutting edge of technology to those who are very conservative about its use. Somewhere near the center of the spectrum is the place to be. There is no question that quality and efficiency can be enhanced by technological advances such as desktop publishing, computer-generated art, and four-color separations. However, in some areas the technology changes so rapidly that a publisher can find the software and hardware out-of-date in short order. When the rapid advances occur, a publisher needs to weigh the current cost of the hardware and software, and the cost of almost continuous upgrades and equipment replacement against the value provided by vendors.

## Financial Management

The publisher is responsible for the financial health of a magazine. A publisher of a single title is often the owner in part or in full, and, as such, will be far more involved with matters related to balance sheet accounts (debt, cash, and capital) than a publisher in a multiple-title company—who most likely is an employee of the company. In addition to the profit or loss from operations, a regular activity for the single-title publisher will be the management of investors and cash. Multiple-title publishers benefit from corporate services that manage these functions, so he or she will be primarily interested in the profit or loss from operations.

A publisher must be continually equipped for the annual planning and budgeting cycle by assessing economic and marketing signs from field trips, economic prognostications in the business and economic press, and day-to-day intelligence from sales activity. A recession does not happen on a moment's notice. More than one ex-publisher or ex-business manager has seen the signs of trouble but ignored them or wished them away. Attention must be paid to danger signals in order to minimize or avoid expense reductions that are forced by unanticipated business conditions after a new business year is under way. If there are strong signals that an economic downturn is likely in the year ahead, expenses should be budgeted very conservatively. The decision to freeze the hiring and replacement of personnel might be made to mitigate against the disruption that would accompany the need to downsize later. On the other hand, if signals are ignored and after three months revenues are ten or twenty percent below budget, drastic and disrupting expense reductions will be necessary to make a profit or avoid a loss for the full year. The construction of the annual budget begins with the publisher's assumptions about general conditions that are likely to affect the magazine's financial performance and continues with careful assumptions on some basics of the operation.

***Budgetary elements and assumptions for a magazine publisher***    To start this process, a publisher will project the following for each issue published in the coming year:

1. Number of issues per year
2. Makeup of issues:
   A.   Number of paid display ad pages. This is the number of display advertising pages (as distinguished from classified advertising) that are inserted and paid for by advertisers.
   B.   Other advertising pages:
      • Classified. Some publications offer classified advertising similar to that in a newspaper. Most often it is printed toward the back of the magazine.
      • House and subscription ads. These are ads for products and services provided by the publisher. Some magazine companies publish books based on information in the magazine and will offer those books for sale in a house ad. Many publications use ads in their own magazine offering the opportunity to subscribe or extend the subscription to the publication itself. Other ads in this category are those run without charge for charitable causes, like The Partnership for a Drug Free America.
   C. Total advertising pages. The count of all advertising pages for the year being budgeted.
   D. Editorial pages. This is the number of all editorial pages anticipated for the year.
   E. Total pages. This, then, would be the total number of pages expected to be published.

3. Advertising page:Editorial page ratio. This ratio is the percentage of pages of editorial to the percentage carrying advertising. A 60-40 percent ratio would mean that 60 percent of the pages were dedicated to editorial and 40 percent to advertising. A magazine will have a target ratio. It is important because of its effect on the profit or loss: 1 percent more in advertising is revenue and 1 percent more in editorial is a cost.

4. Average print run per issue. This figure represents the average number of copies printed for each issue. A magazine with 12 issues and an annual print run of 12 million has an average print run per issue of 1 million.

5. Average net revenue per paid advertising page. This figure takes into consideration discounts offered for volume purchasing, prompt payment, in

some cases the varying income from different page sizes (single page, spread, half page, et al.), and advertising agency commissions. The actual total net revenue derived from advertising is divided by the actual number of paid advertising pages. A magazine with revenue of $10 million carrying 1,000 ad pages would have an average net of $10,000 per paid advertising page.

Figure 3.1 on pages 46 and 47 shows the accounts that most magazine publishers use to track their operating income or loss. Many of these items will be described in detail in later chapters.

Individual departmental expenses are even more detailed than is shown in Figure 3.1. For example, circulation fulfillment costs would have numerous sub-accounts, so the department head would be able to track the cost of additions, deletions, and other changes to the mailing list. There would also be accounts for newsstand sales.

The budgeting process includes creating a profit and loss (P&L) statement for the coming year based on sales and expense estimates. Once the budget is approved, the annual budget is broken down into monthly P&Ls. This is not simply dividing the annual figures by twelve. Seasonal and other variables are weighted so that each month's budgeted revenue and expense come as close to reality as possible. This, then, becomes the benchmark against which progress is measured month by month in the coming business year.

One problem with profit and loss statements is that variable expenses are provided without consideration for normal variances that occur. Therefore, the business manager will be asked to develop additional information, often in a more statistical form. Total mechanical costs may be up five or ten percent from one issue to the next, but this might be the result of more advertising pages being sold, which results in more advertising and editorial pages per copy. This is, of course, a positive situation. A better measure the publisher would use is mechanical cost per 1,000 pages, so a valid comparison can be made from one month to the other. Some of the thumbnail measures permits a publisher to compare with cost surveys conducted and reported on by the magazine associations.

Here are some of the calculations among many that help the publisher manage the business:

- *Cost per thousand (m) printed pages*
  This measure is designed to compare relatively like circumstances. As mentioned above, printing costs for an individual issue can be affected by an increase in ad pages sold. However, cost per thousand printed pages should not vary significantly from one issue to the next. If it does, investigation of the cause is in order.
- *Average mechanical cost per copy*
  This is the average cost to print a copy of the magazine. It can vary based on

## FIGURE 3.1    Major accounts used by magazine publishers to track operating profits and loss

| REVENUE | EXPENSE |
|---|---|
| Advertising | Mechanical costs |
|    Paid display advertising revenue |    Internal expenses |
|    Classified advertising revenue |       Production staff salaries |
|    Advertising supplement revenue |       Benefits |
| Circulation |    External expenses |
|    Subscription revenue |       Composition |
|    Single copy sales revenue |       Printing and binding |
| |       Paper |
| |       Postage |
| |       Shipping |
| | Circulation costs |
| |    Circulation staff salaries |
| |    Benefits |
| |    Fulfillment |
| |    Circulation promotion |
| |       New subscriptions |
| |       Conversions |
| |       Renewals |
| |       Audit |
| | Marketing costs |
| |    Direct sales costs |
| |       Staff salaries |
| |       Benefits |
| |       Commissions |
| |       Independent representatives' commissions |
| |       Travel and entertainment |
| |       Automobile |
| |       Sales meetings |
| |       Conventions/exhibitions |
| |    Indirect sales costs |
| |       Staff salaries |
| |       Benefits |
| |       Market research |
| |       Reader service |
| |    Sales promotion costs |
| |       Staff salaries |
| |       Benefits |
| |       Consulting |
| |       Advertising |
| |       Direct mail |
| |       Sakes materials |

(continued)

**FIGURE 3.1   (continued )**

| REVENUE | EXPENSE |
|---------|---------|
| | Editorial costs |
| |     Editorial staff salaries and benefits |
| |     Art staff salaries and benefits |
| |     Freelance articles |
| |     Freelance art, photos |
| |     Separations |
| |     Travel and entertainment |
| |     Research/surveys |
| |     Dues/subscriptions |
| |     Equipment rental |
| | **Administrative and overhead costs** |
| |     Staff salaries |
| |     Benefits |
| |     Incentive |
| |     Travel and entertainment |
| |     Automobile |
| |     Insurance |
| |     Dues/subscriptions |
| |     Board meetings |
| |     Bank charges |
| |     Donations |
| |     Data processing |
| |     Depreciation |
| |     Rent |
| |     Utilities |
| |     Telephone |
| |     Professional fees |
| |     Postage, freight, delivery |
| |     Repairs and maintenance |
| |     Supplies |

REVENUE – EXPENSES = OPERATING PROFIT

the number of pages in an issue, so is simply a comprehensive figure that provides a ballpark figure on production, paper, and printing and binding costs against which to compare the cost of a copy from a specific issue.

- *Average prepress cost per editorial page*
  The cost to prepare a page for printing is affected by the words and graphics

on a page and can help determine the allocation of dollars to art and photography. Industry associations will include this measure in statistics they gather from member magazines.

The circulation department of a subscriber-based magazine will use a myriad of figures to assess the success of its efforts to acquire and renew subscriptions. The publisher must be familiar with these calculations to keep abreast of the circulation effort. For example:

- *Cost per thousand (m) circulation*
  This is a broad benchmark measure of the cost to acquire and maintain the circulation of the publication. The total circulation is divided by 1,000 and the total cost is divided by the result of the first calculation.
- *Cost per acquisition*—of a new subscriber
  This figure is calculated by dividing the number of new subscribers into the cost of new-subscriber promotion. This and the next two categories provide a benchmark figure a publisher uses for comparison with current promotional efforts.
- *Cost per acquisition*—of a conversion
  This figure is calculated by dividing the number of subscribers who renew for the first time by the cost of renewal promotion to this group.
- *Cost per acquisition*—of a renewal
  This figure is calculated by dividing the number of renewal subscribers into the cost of renewal promotion.

Useful measures to the publisher for the editorial and advertising functions are:

- *Editorial cost per page*
  Editorial department costs are divided by the number of editorial pages published to arrive at this figure. Industry associations commonly use this measure in statistics they gather from member magazines.
- *Direct sales cost per ad page*
  Generally this is the cost attributed to the salesforce, such as salary, commissions, and travel and entertainment expense divided by the number of paid advertising pages.

A monthly review of the financial status of the magazine is essential. The monthly P&L will compare the month's results against the monthly budget and year-to-date results against the year-to-date budget. The meeting provides an opportunity to gather department heads for interdepartmental communication. It is sometimes referred to as the monthly operations or management meeting. It is an important vehicle for reemphasizing the magazine's longer term strategy. Besides keeping departments alert to expense control, many ideas for new products and spin-offs can be generated at an organized and well run monthly P&L review. These meetings are not for detailed review of a departmental operation. This is better done at supplementary meetings with individual department heads.

## Administration

In a multiple-title publishing company, a publisher will be supported with considerable help from corporate headquarters on administrative matters. The single-title publisher will be responsible for handling many of these chores on his or her own. Some, like relations with the insurance agent, accounting firm, and legal firm, can be a once- or twice-a-year event unless problems arise. Often the single-title publisher will report to a board of directors. This will mean preparing for and leading board meetings a few times each year. Personnel matters will always consume more time than anticipated. In the smallest of organizations there will be employees who need special attention. A star salesperson may be wooed by a competitor. Others may be performing poorly or suffering personal difficulties. Interpersonal conflicts with colleagues and supervisors often require the attention of the publisher. Beyond everyday problems in this area there are the extraordinary difficulties that arise because of federal and local laws and regulations regarding employer and employee rights. Even companies rated "best to work for" find themselves defending against legal actions based on age, sex, or ethnic discrimination charges. Charges of sexual harassment in the workplace have increased in recent years. Every publisher should know the procedures that must be followed to avoid time-consuming legal activity in the personnel area. The smallest publication needs to be sure that all managers and supervisors know what they can and cannot do regarding employee evaluation, as well as the hiring and firing process.

Overall, the publisher's job is an exciting, challenging, and rewarding position. Above all, the publisher needs to create enthusiasm for the service the magazine performs and pride in accomplishment and build esprit de corps that radiates excitement and personal fulfillment throughout the magazine's organization. Where and when to spend time to get the most significant result cannot be overemphasized. There will always be a feeling of satisfaction despite the problems that the publisher needs to face almost week by week. The best-managed publications keep the problems to a minimum so that management can dedicate most of its time to building a profitable, prestigious publishing enterprise.

### CASE STUDIES
#### Video Rental Retailer

In 1990, as video rental stores began to proliferate, Bill Doll was hired by Consumer Publishing Company to create a monthly controlled circulation magazine for video store retailers. The magazine would be named *Video Rental Retailer*. The editorial mission of the magazine was to provide retailers with information that would help them to advertise, promote, and manage their businesses. The magazine would also include charts with information on the most popular video rentals.

The advertising was primarily from national companies such as Fox, Columbia, and Sony. These advertisers were anxious to have retailers aware of their new film releases. New releases were promoted heavily to retailers two weeks prior to and eight weeks following the release. The industry had learned that this was the time period that a new release remained hot. Thereafter, sales slowed dramatically.

The video rental business was booming. In its first three years *Video Rental Retailer* circulation also grew as more video stores were opened but then stabilized at 25,000. Because this market was growing rapidly, other publishers took notice. Having had a single competing magazine in its first year, in its fourth year of publication *Video Rental Retailer* had three competitors. All were controlled circulation monthlies with similar advertising rates.

Editorial fare was also similar. Despite new competition, *Video Rental Retailer* had built a credible position with readers, but it was second in share of ad dollars and pages. In this small market for advertising sales, differences in share of market among the four magazines were negligible.

In the fifth year of operation *Video Rental Retailer* advertising dollars and pages declined. Ad pages went from 950 to 800. The number of ad pages in the market was just about flat at 4,200. Doll's intelligence network suggested that regional video distributors might be taking ad pages away from the national magazines. Bill investigated the situation. Regional distributors printed weekly sheets that featured new releases. Some had discovered the 10-week pattern of promotion that the national advertisers wanted. They then decided to transform their weekly sheets to glossy, four-color product-promotion vehicles and sold advertising to the national companies. Since the national magazines were all monthlies, they could not satisfy the advertisers' desire for a weekly promotional vehicle.

Doll decided that the growth of *Video Rental Retailer* would be stunted if he did not change the frequency to weekly. This would be a high-risk change. His production costs would escalate dramatically when he produced 52 issues annually, 40 more than the current frequency. Merely to maintain its current level of profit, *Video Rental Retailer* would need to sell more than 500 additional ad pages in a market showing no sign of growth. Paid circulation would need to be considered. The drawback was that a competitive disadvantage could be created if the magazine did not cover the total market. Besides, acquiring subscribers could be costly. Doll went on a tour of advertisers to test his theory that the frequency was the problem. By and large his assumption was confirmed. Some advertisers indicated that they would embrace a weekly publication. However, Bill knew that the national advertisers needed the regional distributors and would not want to abruptly drop their advertising in their weekly publications. The weekly national magazine would have to gamble that the national advertisers would add funds to their budgets to accommodate the opportunity for continual communication that *Video Rental Retailer* would make available. If advertisers did not respond by increasing their advertising in *Video Rental Retailer*, its market share of advertising pages would need to grow from slightly less than 20 percent to at least 30 percent, an unlikely scenario.

Overall, any decision to change is high risk. If it does not work, *Video Rental Retailer* might begin publishing at an intolerable loss. If Doll makes no change in frequency, he could find himself in a slow or no growth advertising market.

What should he do?

### Medical Business

HealthCare Press Inc. was a small family business publishing four magazines and two directories for health-care professionals. Randy Doerr Jr., the son of the deceased founder, had inherited the business and was the CEO for over ten years. Doerr was well known among the top executive levels of pharmaceutical companies and the major advertisers in the company's magazines and directories. All of the publications in the fields served by HealthCare Press were owned by associations, entrepreneurs, or families. It came as a surprise when Randy announced that the business was being sold to TAV Industries Inc., which was a large conglomerate with interests in numerous industrial and government markets. Doerr continued as CEO for five years after the sale, but TAV demanded that a line of succession be established. This led Doerr to name publishers for each of the company's publications.

Seton Beckwith was named publisher of the flagship magazine, *Medical Business*, a controlled circulation monthly. The magazine was directed at the non-clinical interests of physicians in the private practice of medicine. For many years *Medical Business* was the acknowledged leader in readership among magazines for doctors in private practice. However, among its six direct competitors it was never higher than second in share of advertising dollars. One of Beckwith's objectives was to become number one in market share. Although she knew it would take more than a few months or a year, another was to become an "industry figure."

Within two years of her reign as publisher, *Medical Business* was number one in market share for the first time in its history. During the same time period, Beckwith became better and better known throughout the health-care industry. In her third year she was regularly invited to speak as an industry expert before pharmaceutical company executives and physicians' regional associations about trends in private-practice medicine and how they would affect physicians, and marketing to physicians, in the future.

By the fourth year *Medical Business* was drawing almost twice the level of ad dollars as the second-nearest competitor. On a pleasant April day, Beckwith received a phone call from Luke Brindley, CEO of the Thatchex Pharmaceutical Group Inc., one of the top ten pharmaceutical companies in the United States. Thatchex had grown rapidly in recent years, in part from an aggressive acquisition program. Brindley said in a very angry tone, "HealthCare Press Inc. is not the company it was when Randy Doerr was in charge." He went on to say that his legal department had recommended a $15 million dollar suit against HealthCare Press Inc. because of an article that was published in the April issue. Effective immediately they were canceling all advertising in HealthCare Press Inc. publications, which amounted to over $2 million annually.

The article in question was entitled "The Cost of Losing Control." Beckwith remembered reading the article, and nothing in it had caused her to question it. She mentioned this to Brindley, who ranted that the article was not only illegal but unfair to their newly acquired company, Minno Manufacturing Inc. of Louisville, Kentucky. Beckwith promised to look into the matter and get back to Brindley within two hours.

The article reported on Dr. Robert Massey, who had invented and perfected a hip replacement prosthesis. He had hundreds of successful operations using the prosthesis and gained significant recognition for having invented the device. Dr. Massey sold his product to Minno Manufacturing Inc. A year later he claimed to have been receiving numerous complaints about unhappy patients who complained of pain after the prosthesis had been used. Dr. Massey investigated further and found that Minno had made a minute change in one of the measurements used in the manufacture of the device. He felt this was causing the problem and demanded that Minno Manufacturing change back to the original measurements. Minno executives disagreed and advised Jordan Minno, the CEO, to deny Massey's request, which he did. A few months later Dr. Massey filed a $2 million suit accusing Minno Manufacturing of bad manufacturing practices, and of tarnishing his good name.

Minno was so sure of its position that it decided to defend itself in court. The case was tried, and Dr. Massey was awarded $900,000. Minno Manufacturing continued to believe in its position and appealed the decision to a higher court.

A *Medical Business* midwest editor had heard of the case and the article was written. It accurately reported the circumstances but did not state that the case was under appeal. *Medical Business* had a policy regarding "separation of church and state" that was designed to keep editorial matters away from the influence of the advertising sales department. However, it was editorial policy that all facts were checked and that all articles were to be balanced with comment from representatives of both sides of an issue. Also, articles that mentioned companies in the health-care industry were to be brought to the attention of the publisher for review and comment. From the meeting Beckwith had with the editor and others associated with the article, it was clear that they did not solicit comment from Minno Manufacturing and did not bring it to her attention.

Beckwith called Brindley and told him that there was a breakdown in the editorial procedures. She emphasized that the article was factual. Nevertheless, Brindley made much of the fact that the impending appeal was not mentioned in the text of the article, which would cause the company to be damaged. She asked for the opportunity to meet with Minno to get more details and try to work toward a solution that might neutralize the problem. Brindley approved this request, subject to agreement by his legal counsel, which was forthcoming. Beckwith arranged the meeting in Louisville with Minno. She decided to bring her advertising sales director and research director along. Beckwith purposely did not bring her legal counsel, suggesting that HealthCare Press and *Medical Business* were not viewing the situation as one that demanded a legal solution. The HealthCare Press Marketing and Media Research Department had an enviable reputation for innovation and quality. Beckwith included the company research director, anticipating that some research might be offered as part of the solution.

Beckwith's position was that the article was accurate despite the missing reference to the appeal, but she knew any argument about this would be fruitless. *Medical Business* did not publish articles to correct information in a prior article, but from time to time would publish a letter to the editor to accommodate someone who had a reasonable complaint. She planned to offer this and also to conduct some market research for Minno Manufacturing as part of the solution. The offer of a free ad or two might be made even though Minno Manufacturing's product did not have a market among all physicians in the *Medical Business* audience.

Jordan Minno provided the conference room off his office for the meeting. In attendance he had his executive vice president and legal counsel from the parent company. Minno was clearly very angry. He felt that his business would "go to pot" because of the reputation and credibility of *Medical Business* among doctors. Beckwith began to realize that Minno's company was probably purchased for cash and an earn-out, a common practice in mergers and acquisitions. An earn-out is a formula based on the future performance of the company whereby the seller of the company can earn additional money. Such a provision might grant the seller 25 percent of the amount by which the profit in the three years succeeding the sale of the company exceeds the profit for the year in which the company was sold. This might explain Minno's extreme anger and irrationality, at least from Beckwith's point of view, about the problem.

Early in the discussion, Seton Beckwith mentioned the possibility of a letter from Minno that would be published in the letters to the editor department of the magazine. Minno brushed this idea off. Beckwith added that *Medical Business* would conduct research among orthopedic physicians to get a handle on the extent of their concern about the issue. This only fueled Minno's anger. Fortunately, Minno called for a caucus among his personnel, which gave the *Medical Business* delegation a chance to assess the reaction of the Minno delegation and come up with some ideas for appeasing Minno. They assumed that Luke Brindley, even though he was not attending the meeting, would be consulted about the outcome of the discussion. They felt any offer should be generous enough to appeal to Brindley, who was likely to moderate the situation. Among the possibilities they discussed were the letter to the editor, research among orthopedic physicians to test their reaction to the article, a letter to all orthopedic physicians explaining that the case was under appeal, and free advertising space.

What options would you choose to solve this problem without compromising the policies and reputation of *Medical Business*? Put yourself in Jordan Minno's place, who sees his business going up in smoke. What is the least you would expect to have happen were you he?

## NOTES

[1] *Random House Dictionary of the English Language*, 2nd ed. (New York: Random House Inc., 1987).

[2] Lorne Manly, "CD-ROM Titles Fail to Catch Fire," *Folio*: August 1, 1995, 26.

[3] Gigi Mahon, *The Last Days of the New Yorker.* (New York: New American Library, 1988), 14–16.

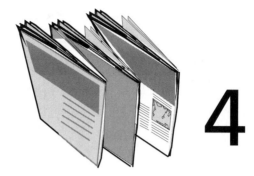

# Editorial Principles

## THE EDITORIAL MISSION: THE BACKBONE OF A MAGAZINE

Ann Shaughnessy leaves work at her Des Moines law office on Monday evening looking forward to picking up her mail when she gets home. Monday is the day *The New Yorker* arrives. She's been a subscriber for 15 years, since she graduated from Northwestern University and it is her favorite magazine for news and entertainment. During those years, she's kept track of the changes in the magazine, knows who the editor is, and remembers favorite articles from year to year. She is, in fact, one of the magazine's loyal readers. But she has never once considered whether the magazine was meeting its original mission statement, written in the prospectus to the new magazine in 1925 by founding editor Harold Ross:

> *The New Yorker* will be a reflection in word and picture of metropolitan life. It will not be what is commonly called radical or highbrow; it will be what is commonly called sophisticated, in that it will assume a reasonable degree of enlightenment on the part of its readers. It will hate bunk. *The New Yorker* will be the magazine which is not edited for the old lady in Dubuque. This not meant in disrespect, but *The New Yorker* is a magazine avowedly published for a metropolitan audience and thereby will escape an influence which hampers most national publications. It expects a considerable national circulation, but this will come from persons who have a metropolitan interest.[1]

As a magazine reader like Ann, you don't care—nor *should* you care—about the magazine's editorial mission statement. It's invisible to the average reader. It may not even be written down anywhere in the magazine's offices. But the editorial mission is essential to the management of a successful magazine and must be understood implicitly by the entire staff. Without a clear editorial mission, a magazine has no heart or soul. The editorial pages give life, focus, and direction to the magazine's other principal functions. When Harold Ross hammered out the famous description of the *New Yorker* in 1925, he certainly didn't have a lawyer living in Iowa at the end of the century in mind, but he knew exactly what kind of magazine he wanted.

Here are several examples of editorial mission statements written by editors and publishers over the years:

*Harper's New Monthly Magazine* was projected and commenced in the belief that it might be the means of bringing within reach of the American people an immense amount of useful and entertaining reading matter, to which, on account of the great number and expense of the books and periodicals in which it originally appears, they have hitherto had no access. (1850)[2]

The basic premise upon which [*Life*] is published is that people like to look. They like to look at everything including themselves in the mirror. They also like to look at pictures, and especially in these swift-changing days they like to look at pictures which show them what is going on in America and in the world. (1936)[3]

*Southerner* believes in a southern spirit...in a historical tradition of letters and lifestyle not derailed or defined by intellectual currents from the north and west. This magazine is for southerners—a document, a diary, an agenda. It is also for northerners and westerners—to foster understanding, not overreaction. Science and sex, love and labor, sin and cinema, dream and disaster, Atlantic to Ozark. We embrace it all. *Southerner* is a general interest magazine exclusively for the South. It will contain profiles of interesting southerners, ideas on contemporary southern issues, directions in Southern arts and letters, popular history, our folk culture and travel in the South. (1984)[4]

[*George*] will bring politics to life and make it useful...will cover the points where politics and popular culture converge...will demystify the political process and show readers how to get the most from their government while staying abreast of the issues that matter. [*George*] aims to make the political process a little hip and a lot more fun." (1995)[5]


# THE ROLE OF THE EDITOR

The responsibility for making sure the magazine follows its heart and reflects its mission statement falls to the person directing the editorial operation. This job usually carries the title editor-in-chief—or simply, and as we'll refer to it throughout this text, *editor.* The magazine's editor decides what will appear in the magazine's editorial pages. Editorial pages are everything in a magazine that isn't advertising. That includes captions, headlines, investigative reports, artwork, photographs, and the cover. But that doesn't mean the editor is actually composing or even editing all these items. The editor delegates to a staff of editors and writers that he or she has assembled, hired, and trusts. The editor keeps the words and images in the magazine consistent with the magazine's editorial mission and must satisfy its audience's needs and interests. Good editors have an abiding love of words and language. They understand that the printed word, art, and photography are all powerful communication tools. Good editors are also obsessed with detail. The attention they pay to their craft, to getting it *right*, to creating a magazine that speaks to their audience, is part of their love affair with language and communication.

As we've seen, readers turn to magazines for many reasons. For amusement, education, information, or breaking news; for cutting-edge ideas, topical analysis, or current fashion. With hundreds of thousands—sometimes millions—of readers, the editor's job is complicated. Editors know how important it is to meet the expectations of readers. To promise one kind of magazine and deliver another could lead to a canceled subscription or a decision not to buy at the newsstand. But at the same time, it's important to offer new, fresh, entertaining, or provocative material; to keep readers engaged and surprised. A successful editor must walk a difficult balance: offer more than what the reader expects, along with comfort and consistency.

Editing a magazine is a human activity, not purely the result of statistical research, opinion polls, and surveys. The editor's personality shapes the form and tone of the magazine. Human qualities— bias, playfulness, personal likes and dislikes—all get factored into decisions an editor makes. As Norman Cousins wrote in the final issue of *Saturday Review*: "The one thing I learned about editing over the years is that you have to edit and publish out of your own tastes, enthusiasms and concerns, and not out of notions or guesswork about what other people might like to read." [6]

Remember the three-legged-stool analogy—and the interrelationship between editorial and advertising. That relationship sometimes results in difficulty between the interests of the editor and the expectations of advertisers. Advertisers decide to buy space in a magazine based on their expectations of editorial coverage as well as on the numbers and kinds of readers buying the magazine. If an editor of a city business magazine publishes a cover story revealing corruption in the city's tax arrangement with a major hotel chain, there's a strong possibility that the hotel will refuse to advertise—which means a loss in revenue for the magazine. In such a case, the editor must balance the readers' needs and interests, journalistic ethics, and the realities of the marketplace.

Just as there are many kinds of magazines, there are many kinds of editors. While the responsibilities vary from magazine to magazine, the basic job of the editor is to oversee the editorial direction and content of the magazine, including text, artwork, and cover. Editors spend a majority of time managing staff and delegating assignments. They also manage the editorial department budget and have final approval on what appears in the magazine. The personal quirks and qualities of editors also enter into their management style. One editor may delegate work more than another; an editor of one magazine may prefer informal, one-on-one meetings instead of weekly meetings with the entire staff. One editor may be dictatorial in pronouncements and opinion, while another seeks input from staff up and down the masthead.

At large publishing companies, the editor of a single title may report to a corporate editorial director, who has responsibility for the direction and development of all the company's magazines, including content and graphic appearance. Editors are as unique as their magazines, and their responsibilities change, too, depending on the size and structure of the publishing company. Some magazine editors are intimately involved in the day-to-day operations of the editorial department. In the case of a small-circulation magazine (under 100,000), which publishes bimonthly and must produce about 50 editorial pages each issue, the entire editorial department might consist of five people. The editor at such a magazine would wear many hats: assigning articles to freelancers, writing articles, researching a story, rewriting a headline, proofreading. This editor's day—from 8 a.m. to late at night on deadline—would be consumed with the details and mechanics of readying each editorial page for publication. In addition to crafting the copy into publishable form, he or she might also be responsible for writing a regular column, covering news events, and even filling in as a photographer at an industry convention.

At a bigger monthly magazine—with a circulation above 200,000, and with 100 or more editorial pages per issue—the editor must have more people to call upon to create those editorial pages. The editor still might write a column and be involved and identified strongly with the editorial product. Yet the day-to-day editorial management and overseeing the flow of manuscripts to layout falls to the staff editors he or she has hired.

At some large consumer magazine publishing companies, the editors have a proved, well-known expertise in a certain area (such as fashion or high technology) that requires socializing, travel, and public appearances as part of their job. The educational experience of editors can range from no college education to advanced degrees in journalism or the subject area of the magazine. Trade magazines will frequently have a top editor who has extensive education or professional experience in the subject area. Scientific and technical magazines are other examples where this is often the case. Despite these differences in experience and job responsibility, successful editors-in-chief share several important attributes:

- *Overall vision*. The editor must be able to see clearly where his or her magazine is headed, who's reading it, and how it fits in the marketplace. He or she must be able to set the course for the magazine's editorial "voice" or "tone" to appeal to a group of readers. Some magazine editors use a quick trick of conjuring up an imaginary "typical" reader or newsstand buyer when faced with an editorial decision. Betsy Carter, editor in chief of *New Woman*, when considering photographs of cover models for her magazine (which has a circulation of 1.2 million and sells about 30 percent of that circulation on the newsstand) says she often asks herself: "Is she too scary to have lunch with?"[7] Devices like this help bring focus to the overall vision of who's reading the magazine. Equally important is the editor's ability to articulate that vision to staff and contributors.

- *Creativity and demonstrated editorial skill*. Many successful editors are exceptional writers. Others built their careers on their investigative reporting skills. Many others demonstrate their creativity through fashion, design, engineering, photography, computer programming, or any of scores of other fields. Magazine editors must be creative and must be able to recognize and nurture creative ability in others.

- *Graphic sensibility*. Because most magazines place a strong emphasis on quality graphic design, the editor must be comfortable imagining how a story will appear on the printed page, what kind of cover photograph will be most provocative, whether a story about a local politician should be illustrated with a light-hearted caricature or straightforward head-and-shoulders shot. The editor needn't be a skilled designer—most, in fact, are not. But the editor should have a well-developed sense of how type, photography, and artwork can be utilized in the magazine, and should be able to evaluate and appreciate the work of a publication designer.

- *Production knowledge*. Successful editors should also have an understanding of production and the other technical aspects of publishing. Without understanding and respect for matters such as computer imaging, film processing, paper quality, and printing, an editor won't recognize the possibilities—and limitations—for transforming ideas into words and images on a printed page.

- *Flair for promotion*. An editor must entice readers into reading, newsstand buyers into buying. To do so, the editor must be adept at "packaging" stories—writing eye-catching headlines, selecting a provocative photograph to illustrate an investigative report, deciding to publish the results of a city-wide poll as an attention-getting cover story, and composing captions and subheads to help a reader navigate a complex, technical story. Excitement is created in magazines not only by the choice of writer and subject but also by how information is treated and presented to readers.

## THE IMPORTANCE OF "THE MIX" AND PLANNING

If you study editorial mission statements—and business plans—you'll see that publishers and editors carefully point out to their constituencies (both readers and advertisers) exactly what editorial features will be published in their magazines. The mix of personality profiles, interviews, investigative reports, "softer" features, columns, photo essays, service journalism, opinion, events listings, and the like—all work together to give a magazine a distinctive personality and style. Most readers respond to a mix of voices, a combination of serious and playful articles. Assembling the right mix is critical for a successful magazine and requires careful planning as well as enthusiastic ideas and cooperation of the editor's staff. It's not unusual for editorial departments to plan issues a year or more in advance, sometimes even issuing an "editorial calendar" to assist the advertising and promotion departments in their own planning.

## EDITORIAL DEPARTMENT

The editorial department is composed of people who create and shepherd the text and artwork that appear on the editorial pages. The number of staff people varies, depending on the size of the magazine, its frequency, and the amount of original reporting it conducts. A magazine could be edited with as small as a two-person staff or might require a staff of 100. A look at the masthead (the listing of magazine staff and job titles, usually published in the front of the magazine) will tell a great deal about editorial organization. The size of the editorial staff is not merely a function of the circulation of the magazine but also of the complexity of the information and images it presents. A small-circulation business magazine that publishes many pages of technical information about products and trends would require an appropriate number of knowledgeable, trained reporters and editors. A weekly news magazine needs a staff of specialists in various areas such as politics, business, law, the arts. On the other hand, a staff of three or four can also edit quality annual, bimonthly, or monthly special interest magazines. Figures 4.1 and 4.2 show the editorial structure at two different magazines.

Editorial titles change in meaning from one magazine to another. The deputy editor at one magazine may have completely different responsibilities from the deputy editor at another magazine. For instance, at most magazines the managing editor is the second in command, charged with the smooth flow of copy. At Time

**FIGURE 4.1    Editorial department of a 750,000 paid
circulation monthly consumer magazine**

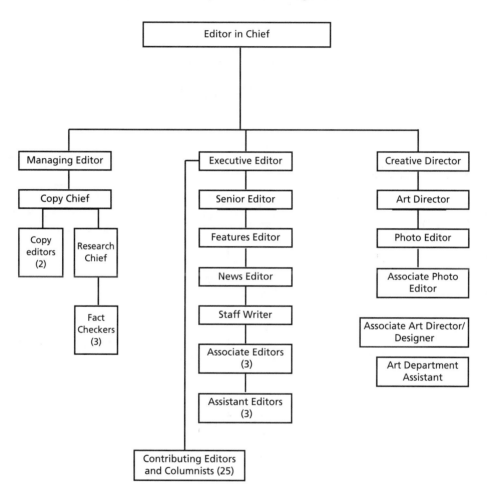

Inc. Magazines, however, the managing editor oversees editorial responsibilities for
each magazine—and is, in fact, the top editor of the publication, reporting only to
Time Inc.'s editor in chief, who serves as the corporate editorial director. Keeping
these differences in mind, what follows is a description of the various functions that
are most often needed in an editorial department.

**FIGURE 4.2    Editorial department of a 65,000 paid
circulation bimonthly trade magazine**

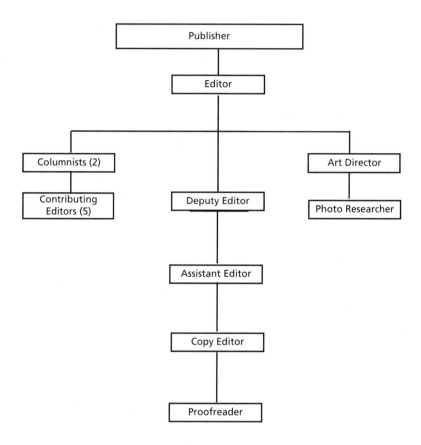

The people who are responsible for the text in a magazine include staff editors, staff writers, freelance writers, copyeditors, proofreaders, fact checkers, and researchers.

- *Managing editor*. The managing editor coordinates the editorial, art, and production departments to ensure that the current issue of the magazine is published on time and is in acceptable form. The managing editor also oversees copyediting and proofreading. While the editor in chief is preoccupied with planning issues six months or more ahead, the managing editor is the hands-on deputy, making sure that day-to-day operations proceed smoothly and deadlines are met. The managing editor is often the liaison with the magazine's legal counsel, and if a question about libel, copyright, or defamation arises in the development or writing of a story, the managing editor will usually be the first senior staff member to be consulted.

- *Staff editors*. The job of the staff editors will change depending on the size and scope of the magazine. Many magazines have staff editors who plan sections of the magazine, write and report stories, and assign articles to freelance writers. The staff editor (who might hold the title of articles editor, features editor, or senior editor) may head an editorial department (such as the travel section in a general interest magazine) and have supervisory responsibility for other staff members, freelancers, and designers.
- *Staff writers*. Just as the title implies, these are writers who are employed full time by the magazine. News weeklies will have dozens of staff writers, each assigned to a specific subject area or "beat." Trade magazines often require experts to follow technical developments in a field and will hire one or more staff writers devoted to monitoring and reporting the news. Unlike at newspapers, where many reporters are employed to spend their workdays reporting and writing, it's relatively rare for the typical magazine to devote one or two positions exclusively to writing. Most magazine staff members whose writing is published also do double duty as editors, developing sections of the magazine, working with freelance writers, and having other responsibilities.
- *Freelance writers*. The word itself hearkens back to medieval times when mercenary knights unattached to a particular lord would hire out themselves—and their lance—when extra help was needed on the battlefield. Freelance writers today are those men and women who are not employed full time by a magazine, but who write a single story under contract with a magazine. Many freelancers write for more than one magazine, although to work for some magazines, they might have to agree not to write for a direct competitor on the same subject. Some freelancers sign contracts with magazines to write more than one story over a period of time, thus assuring themselves—and the magazine—that their work will be published. For instance, a freelance writer under contract to write four stories a year for the *New York Times Sunday Magazine* might be prohibited from contributing to *The New Yorker* during that same period of time. Many editors have a stable of freelance writers to whom they turn again and again, writers who are familiar with the needs of the magazine. Many successful freelancers also develop a specialty: writing about the arts, or automotive news, or scientific topics, or computers. Making a living as a freelance writer has disadvantages. The pay can be low and the work irregular. Some magazines do not pay

more than 10 cents a word for freelance work. Also, steady freelance work can end when an editor leaves. Unlike their colleagues on staff, freelance writers do not have their health insurance or other benefits paid by the company, and they often suffer from the isolation of not working with a group of people. But there are advantages, too: career independence, freedom to develop their own style of writing, and a flexible schedule.

• *Copyeditors and proofreaders*. Before it goes to the printing press, every editorial page in a magazine is read, edited, reread, and checked by several people at several different stages. Writers will submit their work (or "copy") in one of several ways: on paper, on computer disk, or sent from their computer via modem directly to their editor's computer. After the assigning editor reads the work and makes any changes that are necessary, it will be read by a copyeditor who reads it very closely, correcting errors in spelling, grammar, usage, and making certain it conforms to the magazine's particular style. Some magazines issue their own stylesheet or stylebook, in which agreed-upon spelling and usage are described. Decisions as to how and when to use abbreviations, forms of address, foreign phrases, and other stylistic questions all will be described and will serve as an editorial reference for the magazine. For instance, one magazine might publish the cost of an item as "$11.00" while another might refer to the item as costing "eleven dollars." It's important that a magazine be consistent in usage, and the copyeditor is the check on consistency. Copyediting can be done either on paper or on computer. In the days before desktop publishing, when articles were re-keyboarded by typesetters after copyediting, another check on accuracy occurred. The typeset article would be printed on a page proof, and a proofreader would ensure that all the copyeditor's changes were made correctly, comparing the original document to the proof. Today, most page layouts are proofread either by the copyeditor or another editor, to make certain the editing changes were translated from manuscript to printed page. Proofreaders will also check that the elements on a page—captions, headlines, and page numbers—are correct and in the right position. Copyeditors and proofreaders must have a strong command of the language, work well under deadline pressure, and pay exceptionally careful attention to detail.

• *Fact checkers*. Many magazines have a fact-checking department with a staff devoted to confirming all statements of fact in an article. "Statements of fact" include the spelling of names and physical descriptions of people and places. If a writer states that an event happened under the light of a full moon, the fact-checker will refer to an almanac to confirm that the evening in question actually did have a full moon. At large magazines such as the news weeklies, there may be dozens of fact checkers (who are sometimes called researchers). At smaller magazines, an editor (in consultation with the writer) is responsible for confirming all statements of fact. This critical step in the editorial process is included not because writers can't be trusted to get things right. Instead, there's a twofold reason. Not only does fact checking serve to maintain the magazine's integrity and authority in the marketplace (a magazine that consistently makes little errors in description or reporting won't be trusted by readers on bigger issues); fact checking also minimizes the chances a magazine will be sued for libel. Without a fact checking process in place, a court may rule that a magazine showed "reckless disregard for the truth." In addition to being an essential part of the editorial process at a quality magazine, fact checking is a good, entry level job for many young people interested in magazine editorial work. It requires an inquisitive mind, thoroughness, strong journalistic instincts, and accuracy.

While these word people are creating, editing, accounting for, and checking the text in a magazine, there's another group responsible for the art that appears on editorial pages. Like the editorial department, the structure of the art staff will be shaped by the needs of the magazine; but many art departments consist of an art director, designer or designers, editorial production manager, and photo editor. Some magazines or groups of magazines have a creative director who oversees both the graphic presentation in the pages, as well as the conception and development of visually oriented sections such as fashion, travel, and food design. These staff members report to the editor in chief, but the art director will usually have budgetary responsibility for his or her department operations. Most magazines hire illustrators and photographers on a freelance or contract basis to produce work to accompany text—while some magazines employ staff artists and photographers.

To illustrate how a story appears in the pages of a magazines, let's explore the editorial process. A published magazine piece begins life as an idea. An editor might get a written query or a phone call from a freelance writer with an idea for a story. Or the idea may take shape during discussion at a regular editorial staff meeting. Or an editor might decide that a subject merits investigation. After consideration and discussion, the editor makes a formal assignment to the writer. On rare occasions a writer who sends a complete, unsolicited manuscript to an editor will see the story published. Busy editors don't usually look forward to reading unsolicited manuscripts; they send manuscripts to junior editors for review. Many prefer to hear the idea for a story first in query form, and some consumer magazines have a policy that they won't acknowledge or even return unsolicited manuscripts without a stamped, self-addressed envelope. In some cases, a query by a writer will result in an invitation by the editor to submit an article "on spec." The writer will be asked to complete the proposed article without a guarantee that it will be purchased or published.

At magazines with big circulations, big staff, and big budgets, this process is followed by editors at every level. Some staff editors are responsible for sections of the magazine consisting of short items, reviews, or recommendations. Senior editors typically work with a regular group of writers or have expertise in a certain

subject. The editor in chief oversees all this work and can make assignments directly to writers as well.

If an article is assigned to a freelance writer, a contract is written and is signed
by both the writer and the magazine's editor. The contract outlines payment, due
date, limitation on expenses, rights for republishing, and the kill fee. A kill fee is
the amount the publisher will pay the writer in the event the article submitted is
unacceptable or cannot be published for any number of reasons: the subject may no
longer be timely, news event may have changed, or the final article simply doesn't
measure up to the magazine's standards. The kill fee is considerably less than the
payment would be if the story were published—usually 20 to 25 percent of the
negotiated fee for the story. If the assignment goes to a writer on staff, a contract
usually is not written. One editor on staff is usually designated to work with the
writer.

Once the article is turned in, the editor either accepts it, sends it back to the
writer with instructions for rewriting, or "kills" it—that is, tells the writer the piece
will not appear. If and when the manuscript is ready for editing, the assigning editor
reads the article, editing it for structure, style, and sense. At many magazines, the
article then goes through the fact checking process. For magazines without fact
checkers, the editor (in consultation with the writer) is responsible for confirming
the accuracy of the article. After fact checking, the article is set in type as it will
appear in the magazine and edited again by a copyeditor, who checks the work of
the original editor and fact checker, paying special attention to style, grammar, and
usage. There is usually much back and forth exchange of copy between these people, as well as with the writer. While a fact checker is waiting for a call back from a
source, the copyeditor may be rephrasing a passage that was updated by the writer.
At smaller magazines, these functions are compressed, with editors doing many
jobs. The managing editor is responsible for the smooth flow of copy, and ensuring
that copy is where it is supposed to be by deadline. The importance of deadlines
can't be overemphasized. A writer who is late handing in a story or a fact checker
taking too long with research can slow down the entire editorial process and affect
everyone on the editorial and art team. Missed deadlines can affect a magazine's
printing schedule and even newsstand distribution.

After the writer's manuscript is approved by the assigning editor, the design
function begins. The art director or designer reads the article and confers with the
editor (and, sometimes, with the writer) about the art to accompany the text. If the
article is to be illustrated, the designer will assign an artist; if principals in the story
or a scene must be photographed, the art director or photo editor will assign a photographer. Editors will also work closely with the art department to develop charts,
tables, graphs, or any other explanatory material that must appear with the text.

Some magazines are more heavily edited than others. Occasionally, a freelance
writer will pick up a copy of the magazine and won't recognize his or her story

**FIGURE 4.3  Timeline and flow chart:  From assignment to publication (Based on the publication schedule of a consumer magazine for a 3,000-word feature article)**

**June 1**
Feature editor makes assignment to freelance writer for planned publication in October issue.

**June 15**
Contract signed, stipulating manuscript (ms) due date of July 30.

**July 28**
Freelancer submits article to assigning editor.

**August 5**
Editor suggests areas for additional reporting and requests rewrite.

**August 11**
Freelancer resubmits article.

**August 15**
Feature editor line edits manuscript. Submits to editor in chief for approval.

**August 16**
Editor-in-chief makes structural changes in article and suggests editing changes, requiring writer and assigning editor to cut 500 words.

**August 18**
Copies of edited, cut manuscript distributed to editor-in-chief, art director, managing editor.

**August 19–21**
Art director, in consultation with assigning editor, determines photography needs for story. Assigns photo editor to contract with freelance photographer to shoot characters in story. Assigns designer to consider story layout, incorporating 1 large opening photograph and 4-6 inset photos.

Managing editor distributes ms to copyediting and research departments. Copyeditor makes changes, corrections in consultation with assigning editor. Fact checker works with writer and editor to confirm all statements of fact.

**August 24**
Checked and copyedited story set in type, with direction from designer. Assigning editor writes headlines, subheads, pull quotes, as needed.

Photographer delivers slides from shoot. Art department and assigning editor review and make selection.

Assigning editor writes captions. Proofreading continues by copyediting.

**August 26**
Page layouts—with photographs and headlines in place—are prepared.

Reviewed by assigning editor and copy department. Changes ordered.

**August 27**
Final page layouts completed. Editor in chief and art director approve. Shipped along with other layouts in that issue for prepress preparation.

**September 2**
Blueline proofs delivered. Blues proofread, reviewed, and approved for publication.

**September 5**
Magazine printed.

**September 6**
The first copies of the October issue to come off the press are hand-bound and delivered to the magazine offices.

**September 8**
October issues shipped from the printer to subscribers and to newsstand distributors.

Freelance writer's payment check is issued.

**September 15**
October issue arrives in subscriber homes.

**September 20**
October issue on newsstands.

**FIGURE 4.4  Timeline and flow chart: A reporter's contribution to a biweekly business-to-business magazine.**

**June 1**
Deadline for all 250-word reports for June 15 issue.

**June 2**
News editor calls staff reporter seeking copy and discussing news developments on topic.

**June 4 10 a.m.**
Reporter submits copy, with several items missing, pending developments scheduled later that day.

**June 4 2 p.m.**
Report set in type. Editor proofreads, writes headlines. Calls reporter for missing facts.

**June 4 5 p.m.**
Page layouts due to be read by editor in chief.
Reporter returns to office with information. Enters the changes directly into typeset text.
News editor proofreads.

**June 4 9 p.m.**
News pages sent to printer.

**June 5 noon**
Blueline proofs delivered. Reporter needs to make substantial changes; word-by-word, character-by-character discussion of how to accommodate changes.

**June 5 3 p.m.**
Blueline changes made. Pages released for printing.

**June 6**
On press. 6 p.m. Unbound signatures delivered.

**June 7**
June 15 issue ships to subscribers.

---

because so many changes have been made. Most editors include writers in the process, discussing changes as they come up. Not only is this a courteous way to conduct business and work with a writer, but it also makes practical sense if an editor wants to work with this writer again. When a writer is aware of a magazine's style—and an editor's style—the editing process proceeds much more smoothly. On occasion, writers will review galleys with editors—especially if the story includes complex terms or narrative or sensitive legal language.

Editors write headlines and captions in consultation with the art department, which will give editors instructions on how much space is available. The copyeditor will do another reading of story as it appears in the layout, checking captions, headlines, and "pull quotes" or "call outs." A pull quote is a short selection of text from the story set in type larger than the body copy. It is usually a pithy, descriptive quote or statement from the article. A pull quote has a dual purpose: It breaks up the page of text and helps draw readers into the story. The copyeditor, assigning editor, editor in chief, and the art director will "sign off" on the pages, initialing the layouts to indicate that they are finally ready to be sent to the printer.

Usually there's one last opportunity for the editorial staff to make adjustments and check on accuracy. The printer will supply a "blueline" proof or "blueprint." This is a facsimile of the magazine, printed, folded, and bound the way the finished magazine will appear—except that all the colors are represented as a single shade of blue. The bluelines are from fully composed or "final" film—the same film from which the printing plates will be processed. Any change requested after the blueline is approved could require plate remake—a costly and time-consuming procedure.

Depending on the type of magazine, the editorial staff might have a need for other experts. Magazines offering readers specific, authoritative, original information or recommendations must also include a department of experts in the editorial structure. At fashion magazines, a staff of fashion editors directs selection of models and styling, clothing and sets. Similarly, at epicurean magazines, recipe testing and food styling is directed by the food department.

Consumer magazines often engage contributing editors to provide editorial assistance not available on staff. Investing in the cost of consulting or contract work can elevate a magazine's editorial offerings and standing without the expense of adding and training new staff members. Examples of editorial service a contributing editor might provide include: writing a regular column, offering objective criticism of editorial direction, assisting in attracting new writers, and even, simply, lending his or her name to the magazine for enhanced prestige among readers and in the publishing community. Often contributing editors are listed in the editorial masthead; other times their assistance is less formal or required only on a project basis, such as gathering information for a once-a-year editorial section.

Some consumer and business magazines assemble advisory editorial boards to offer expertise, criticism, and review of specialized information published in the magazine. *Family Circle* has an advisory board of experts in such areas as consumer affairs, medicine, and parenting. *Harvard Business Review* has an advisory board, as does *Scientific American*, and most medical journals. The editorial board may meet once or twice a year with editors to discuss coverage and direction. In some cases, the members are paid for their services; other magazines assemble voluntary boards. Allan Halcrow, editor of *Personnel Journal*, who has human-resource executives on his editorial board, sums up a board's value: People working in their fields every day, he says, "can provide the real-life context to a staff editor's hunches and brainstorms."[8]

# EDITORIAL EXPENSES

Editors and art directors must be creative—but that doesn't mean they can get away without being concerned with budgets and controlling costs. How much does it cost to create what appears on the editorial pages of a magazine? What kind of expenses must editors in chief manage?

## Salaries

Since ideas and talent control the success of the editorial function, it makes sense that this is usually the largest part of a magazine's editorial budget, accounting for up to one-third of the editorial department's total operation. *Folio:* publishes an annual survey of editorial salaries, examining trends in hiring, compensation, and benefits for editorial positions at consumer and business magazines. In its 1995 survey, *Folio:* found that the average annual salary for an editor in chief at a magazine with a circulation of 100,000 or more was $84,426.[9] *Folio:*'s recent findings, not surprisingly, have shown that editorial salaries are higher in the Northeast; editors with longer tenure make more money; salaries are also affected by the number of employees supervised, the size of the magazine (i.e., number of editorial pages), circulation, and frequency. *Folio:* has also consistently found that women make less than men in comparable editorial jobs—but in its 1995 survey, *Folio:* found that there was a much less pronounced difference between the sexes.[10] *Folio:* also found that the average salary for editors increased each decade of their working lives, except when they hit their fifties, when salaries dip or go flat.[11]

Senior editors responsible for themselves or one other staffer generally earn more than those supervising two to four others. *Folio:* suggests that this may reflect the nature of the job—responsible for producing a section including reporting and writing as well as editing. An art director's annual average salary was $46,386 in the 1995 survey.[12]

## Text

Editors buy articles written by freelancers for either an agreed-upon flat fee or a per-word basis. In the mid-1980s, when some large-circulation consumer magazines were battling for high profile contributions by a limited pool of well-known writers, the per-word fee paid to well-known freelancers quickly rose—in some cases up to $5 per word for a 3,000-word article. No industry standard exists for compensation, but each magazine's editorial management usually sets and maintains a policy for contributors that is in keeping with its editorial budget. One dollar a word for a 3,000 to 5,000-word article is a common standard for feature writers at 100,000-plus circulation magazines. Magazines publishing short items such as book or restaurant reviews will pay $50 to $100 per contribution. At magazines with smaller circulations, smaller budgets, and limited resources, compensation could average 10 cents per word. In the case of magazines with even more limited editorial budgets or a level of prestige associated with publication, freelance authors may receive only complimentary copies of the magazine in which their work is published.

Magazines sometimes buy the right to publish an excerpt of a forthcoming book because it will have great appeal to readers and can be promoted heavily. Many publishers want to be first with such publication, so a bidding war can occur. Costs vary from the stunning $250,000 *Life* agreed to pay McGraw Hill in 1971 for rights to a work that was thought to be Howard Hughes's autobiography to several thousand dollars for a chapter of a forthcoming book on a provocative subject by a first-time nonfiction author. The editor will negotiate the cost of buying this excerpt with the author's publisher or representative. (*Life* was "taken," by the way, in what turned out to be one of the most celebrated cases of a magazine's being defrauded.)[13]

## Research and Other Editorial Costs

In order to maintain a position of authority and gather current information, the editorial department subscribes to newspapers, newsletters, journals, other magazines, databases, on-line services, and other sources for information. If the magazine has a fact-checking department, it creates a library of reference materials that will be used regularly. Editors also attend trade shows and conferences in their field to be informed of trends, new products, and ideas.

## Reader Surveys

Editors of a magazine regularly decide they need to know more about what their readers like and dislike about the magazine. Some magazines engage in reader surveys on a regular basis, including questionnaires in the pages of the magazine that can be mailed or faxed back to the editors. Magazines can also hire a telephone polling company to call subscribers and ask questions about the magazine, including how much time they spend reading, which articles were memorable, what they liked most. Questions can be as simple as what parts of the magazine a reader likes best—or involve a complicated rating system of various sections of the magazine. Other magazines will fund "focus groups," in which an outside company will arrange to gather a group of subscribers and nonsubscribers together to talk about the magazine. Editors may or may not be present—on the other side of a two-way mirror—but do not engage with the participants so that they will speak freely about what they like and dislike. Focus group research is expensive and should be conducted only by an experienced firm. The cost of assembling such a gathering varies according to location (metropolitan areas are more expensive than small towns or suburbs) and type of participant required. It's usually more difficult for the contracted firm to find appropriate subscribers than nonsubscribers. Participants are usually paid a stipend for their time. One formal gathering can cost $5,000 to $10,000—and usually magazines will convene three or more focus groups in different locations. Definitive conclusions are rare. Focus groups can sometimes be more an exercise in group dynamics than a clear assessment of the magazine's editorial direction. Oftentimes, they are best used by a magazine company deciding to launch a new title and needing feedback from a specific group of target readers.

## Art and photography

The cost of purchasing art and photography for a magazine varies widely. Well-known photographers can command $10,000 and more to shoot a photograph of a celebrity for the cover of a magazine. Artwork to illustrate a regular department can be purchased for $100; some magazines purchase photographic contributions from readers for a token fee. Stock photography from libraries and archives can be acquired when an art director needs a generic image, such as a runner on a beach. Archival rates are set according to the magazine's circulation and the use of the photograph on the page. A 1-inch by 1-inch inset photo wouldn't cost as much as a full page illustrating a feature article. Some magazine editors choose to hire illustrators or cartoonists on contract. At Time Inc. Magazines, most freelance photographers in 1994 were paid $400 for a day's work, plus a fee for one-time rights for each photograph that is published.[14]

When a magazine is devoted to travel, architectural design, fashion or any other subject that requires the editors to send stylists, models, photographers, and writers to destinations around the country or around the world, costs naturally multiply. In these budget-conscious times, editors often try to limit expenses by doubling up assignments—arranging for a photographer to shoot film for two separate stories while in Europe, for instance—and by planning major trips well in advance.

## Editorial inventory

Good editors always buy more articles and stories than they will use. The amount of purchased articles in inventory—that is, scheduled for publication at a future date—is considered an editorial expense. It is critical for editors to maintain an inventory of articles available for publication in the event another writer misses a deadline or news events change dramatically, affecting planned coverage. For newly launched magazines, an investment in inventory is especially important because editorial lineups at new magazines are even more likely to change on a moment's notice. But editors don't want *too* much inventory either. Inventory can get out of control, as legend has it with *The New Yorker*. In 1978, it was estimated that editor William Shawn had 500 pieces in inventory—some purchased as far back as 1940.[15]

## EDITORIAL REVENUE

While the editorial department is a major "cost center" of a magazine, there are revenue opportunities within the editorial function, and many editors are encouraged to explore ways of producing income. Historically, editors have been spared the pressure of producing revenue for a magazine, but since the editorial product attracts readers and advertisers, many magazines are exploring new ways to turn editorial material into revenue. Among the methods: anthologies of short stories, books by authors closely associated with the magazine, guided tours led by editors, separate editions only available on newsstands, ancillary products such as calendars, videos, trade shows, lecture series, and clubs offering subscriber discounts. Like many companies, magazines are exploring revenue possibilities in on-line services and World Wide Web sites. And, with so few magazine-only companies today, coordinated tie-ins between magazines and the parent company's other divisions are more frequent.

Article reprints are one of the most popular revenue producers for many magazines. *IndustryWeek*—a 233,000-circulation trade magazine based in Cleveland—is one magazine that instituted an aggressive policy for selling reprints. In 1990, the magazine began a series called "America's Best Plants," and called the plants selected to see if they would be interested in purchasing reprints. The results were immediate and strong. One plant ordered 50,000 reprints of their profile. Revenue from *IW*'s reprint business was in the six figures in 1995, according to a source quoted in *Folio:* magazine, and the parent company, Penton Publishing, started a corporate reprint program based on *IW*'s success.[16]

## EDITORIAL PRESSURES

In 1985, on the eve of the finalization of its sale to the Newhouse family's publishing firm Advance Publications, William Shawn, the 77-year-old editor of *The New Yorker,* wrote in an unsigned piece in "Talk of the Town": "We re-assert our editorial independence…to publish what we want to publish…in defiance of commercial pressures or any other pressures…. We have never published anything in order to sell magazines, to cause a sensation, to be controversial, to be popular or fashionable, to be 'successful.'"[17] At the time of the sale to Advance, *The New Yorker* was rumored to be losing up to $10 million a year, with advertising and circulation figures declining.[18] Shawn stayed two more years until Robert Gottlieb succeeded him as editor. Then, in 1992, after the title experienced a circulation increase and other business improvements, S.I. Newhouse Jr. replaced Gottlieb with *Vanity Fair* editor Tina Brown. Since Brown's ascendancy, *The New Yorker* has published special Hollywood issues and issues totally devoted to fashion and to home design—all of which have attracted new advertisers to the magazine.

Like *The New Yorker*, all magazine publishers that do not rely solely on circulation revenue need to sell advertising pages and depend on advertisers to pay for them. Readers, of course, depend on the magazines they buy to report fairly, accurately, and provide substantive information. Advertisers looking to reach these same readers—advertisers that, in fact, most likely had been courted by the publisher and sometimes the editor—can get prickly when criticized in the pages of the magazine they are supporting. Randall Jones, a former publisher of *Esquire*, told a reporter from the *New York Times* that some of *Esquire*'s fashion advertisers would ask him: "Why haven't I had any editorial credit recently?"[19] Such questions can inevitably find their way to the editor's office. A direct threat from an advertiser to pull advertising over editorial coverage (or lack of it) is rare; the pressure usually comes in more subtle ways. An advertiser's suggestion to a salesperson can be passed on to the ad director or publisher, who might happen to mention it to the editor. Most quality magazines do everything in their power to avoid compromising their editorial integrity. Readers put trust in editors to give them real information and recommendations—not to read about someone simply because they've bought advertising space. Acknowledging the pressure from both advertisers and a publisher's own sales staff, Knight Kiplinger, the publisher and editor in chief of *Kiplinger's Personal Finance Magazine,* said that when advertisers are seeking out "supportive editorial atmosphere" for their products: "The only thing for a publisher to do is just say no."[20] The pressures are not limited to big magazines courting big-ticket consumer advertisers. One study surveyed the extent to which farm journalists came under advertiser pressure and showed that 62 percent of American Agricultural Editors Association members reported receiving threats of cancellation from advertisers displeased with editorial copy. More than one-third said that an advertiser had attempted to influence editorial copy.[21]

But at the same time, most magazines are commercial entities and need the support from the business community to survive. Some editors take an active interest and role in the sales effort. The editor may go along with salespeople on a critical sales call to a top client who needs to hear directly from the editor what is happening at the magazine or what the plans for a special issue might be. Editors also give speeches to groups of advertisers and make appearances at trade shows.

Another kind of editorial pressure related to journalistic ethics involves how magazines owned by large, multifaceted corporations report on business related to the company—or even the company itself. In 1995, *Time* magazine raised eyebrows and some corporate angst when it published a cover story on companies engaged in heavy promotion of records and films with violent and sexually degrading content. At the time, the music division of the magazine's corporate parent, Time Warner, was at the centerpiece of a storm of controversy over the release of gangsta rapper Ice T's "Cop Killer."[22] Again, such pressures are not limited to big companies. Around the same time as the *Time* controversy, the editor of the University of Pennsylvania alumni magazine came under attack by some members of the college community for publishing articles exploring lapses in campus security and harshly critical reviews of books written by Penn faculty members.[23]

## EDITORIAL REDESIGNS

On occasion, an editor and publisher will decide to change the look of an established magazine. Sometimes this redesign is as simple as a "tweaking" of logotype or reconfiguring of the front-of-the-book layout—and is sparked when there has been a personnel change among the top editorial or art department ranks. Other times, the redesign is significant and dramatic enough to intentionally attract a different audience or compete more directly in a new category. Such a redesign is usually the result of a studied evaluation of the magazine's fit in the marketplace.

It's a risky business, though. Condé Nast Publications, publishers of *Mademoiselle*, the magazine for young college and career women, decided in the early 1990s that a new editor, a new "hipper" design, and a shift in editorial emphasis to a grittier, more radical view of fashion, sexuality, and news would increase readership in its target market. The opposite proved true. Circulation and advertising fell dangerously low, until the company replaced editors once again and reverted to a more mainstream editorial style and look.

It may be that some magazines attempting a radical redesign don't recognize what media critic Edwin Diamond calls their "underlying character." Good magazines, he wrote, have "a DNA-like set of fingerprints—and last through the years and reinventions."[24] *Harper's Magazine* has been through six redesigns, but editor Lewis Lapham, who presided over the latest, in 1984, said: "I'm amazed at how remarkably consistent the magazine has been. In the 1850s, the editors wanted it to be a 'compendium,' and that's what we're still doing."[25]

## EDITORIAL PROMOTION AND PUBLICITY

You've seen how important it is for a successful editor to have a flair for promoting and "packaging" their magazines and stories. Many magazine editors take promotion to another degree, step from behind their desks, and become their magazine's best spokesperson. If the editor is comfortable answering questions in front of a television camera or on the radio, he or she may often be sought after as an expert commentator on a subject. Magazines have authority with readers, and their editors are seen as authorities in their own right. An editor who is effective in this role can help bring the magazine to the attention of an even wider audience.

Some editors are also comfortable with helping to market their title in an even more commercial way, by getting involved in reviewing the direct mail packages and ad campaigns planned for their magazines. This involvement can take the form of working behind the scenes to ensure that promotional copy and advertising messages are accurate and appropriate for the target audience or having a starring role in a television advertisement promoting the magazine.

# INTELLECTUAL PROPERTY

Magazine editors must have a thorough understanding of intellectual property—the original work, ideas, writing, and reporting created by a writer and then purchased and presented in the pages of a magazine. When an article is published in a magazine, three entities have entered into a partnership. The author, the publisher, and the reader who has purchased the magazine all have certain rights to the work published in a magazine. Additionally, the subject of an article published in the magazine has rights—which editors and publishers must understand, yet not exaggerate. The cost and frequency of lawsuits have crippled some publications and publishing companies in recent years. Delays and appeals can extend the duration of a libel suit up to 10 years. Yet a magazine's editorial responsibility should not be hindered by the threat of a lawsuit. Good, investigative journalism is required in both the trade and consumer press. Great magazines are made when editorial operations are conducted with a healthy respect for editors' rights to intellectual property and libel law. What follows is sketch of these contemporary issues and is not intended as a comprehensive guide. There's still no substitute for knowledgeable, experienced legal counsel. Seminars and workshops are frequently available for magazine professionals who want to learn more and stay current. One especially helpful guide is the newsletter, *Media & the Law*.[26]

## Copyright

> The Congress shall have Power...to promote the progress of Science and useful Arts, by securing for limited Time to Authors and Inventors Their Respective Writings and Discoveries..." Article I, Section 8.

As stated in the Constitution, the primary purpose of copyright is to promote the public welfare by the advancement of knowledge. Copyright is a form of protection provided by the laws of the United States (title 17, U.S. Code) to the authors of original works. A copyright gives the author limited exclusive rights to reproduce the work, create derivative works based on the original, distribute copies of the work, and perform or display the work in public. Both domestic copyright law and international copyright conventions respect this primary purpose. Magazines are considered "collective works" and are copyrighted as such. (Note that names of magazines cannot be copyrighted but can be registered as trademarks, signified by the letters *TM* in small capital letters.) Publishers have been temporarily assigned the copyright of written work by each contributor and have secured the rights from authors so those works can be included in their pages. In the fine print published in magazines (usually in the table of contents) you'll read that the contents of the magazine has a notice of copyright, with the letter © in a circle and the year of publication. Along with this notice, a magazine usually states restrictions on reproducing or publishing material from the magazine without permission of the publisher.

As mentioned, magazines are collective works. The copyright of each separate contribution in a magazine is distinct from the copyright in the collective work as a whole, and always belongs to the author of the contribution. The author usually owns the copyright automatically, unless he or she prepared the work as a "work for hire," in which case the publisher presumably owns the copyright. If the work is created by an employee within the "scope of employment"—that is, by someone on staff—the copyright automatically belongs to the publisher.

Copyright is completely divisible. When a freelance writer and a magazine editor enter into an agreement, a contract is written, spelling out that the magazine is buying first periodical rights to the writer's work. The writer—as creator—has temporarily assigned the copyright of his or her work to the publisher for the magazine's use. The author always retains control of the copyright. Even if there is no express transfer of rights (that is, no contract written and signed), "the owner of the collective work is presumed to have acquired only the privilege of reproducing and distributing the contribution as part of a particular collective work, any revision of that collective work, and any later collective work in the same series." [27]

It is the above distinction that allows magazines to publish anthologies or reprints of articles; to allow the magazine transferred to microfilm or microfiche; to grant permission to individuals or companies to reproduce portions of the magazine; and to use text and images from the magazine in publicity and promotional materials. When the author of a work makes temporary assignation of the copyright to a magazine publisher, all those conditions are delineated in a contract. The author, of course, has the right to refuse to any part of contract offered by the publisher.

Copyrights are not eternal. When a copyright expires, the work falls into the public domain, and anyone is free to use it without permission. Any work created on or after January 1, 1978, is automatically protected by copyright from the moment it was created. For these works, the copyright expires 50 years after the author's death. Works created and published or registered before January 1, 1978 and that were still under copyright protection on that date, are now copyrighted for a total of 75 years from the date they were created, published, or registered. Every editor—and freelance writer—should be aware of the basics of copyright law. Both parties need to pay attention to detail and keep careful records of what was published and when.

One area that is of increasing concern to authors and publishers—and is far from resolved—is the use of copyrighted editorial material in on-line databases, retrieval services, and interactive versions of the printed magazines to which consumers have access. Many magazines first exploring these technologies simply transferred print versions of articles to their on-line delivery systems. In 1993, 11 freelance writers filed suit in Federal District Court in Manhattan against six publishing companies seeking unspecified damages for work that was reproduced on electronic databases without permission or compensation.[28] Some magazine companies responded to the new technologies by rewriting contracts for freelance writers that include the publishers' right to include articles—without compensation to the writers—in any type of media and technology "whether now known or hereafter developed"… "in perpetuity throughout the universe."[29] When this book was being prepared, a handful of magazines had developed programs to pay freelancers additional fees for electronic rights. Among them: Time Inc.'s *Parenting*, Reader's Digest Association's *Travel Holiday*, and Times Mirror Magazines' two skiing titles, *Ski* and *Skiing*. The skiing magazines pay writers 10 percent of the original print-rights fee to use pieces on its World Wide Web site. The time limit on usage is one year.[30] In early 1996, *Harper's Magazine* and *Publishers Weekly* became the first magazines to pay writers royalties on the proceeds the company received from sales of CD-ROMs and other electronic services.[31]

## Rights and Permissions

When another party—a college professor, or the publisher of an anthology, or another magazine such as the *Utne Reader*—wishes to photocopy, publish, or distribute work (or a portion of such work) that appeared in the magazine, they must get permission from the copyright holder. While the copyright to the work is held by the author, many authors allow the magazine, through their contract, to negotiate the right to republish or permission to distribute the article. Many magazines have established a permissions department to handle these requests and negotiate fees. They will often have set up a fee structure for reprints, paying the author a percentage of the revenue. Some magazines charge for photocopy and reprint permissions, as well, and will subsequently send royalty checks to authors.

In some cases, a writer's work published in a magazine can be reproduced without permission. The "fair use doctrine" allows for this kind of copying, without permission, for such purposes as criticism, commentary, news reporting, teaching, scholarship, and research. Whether or not someone has "fair use" of written material is determined by four main factors: 1) Will the work be used for commercial or nonprofit purposes? 2) Was the original work published or unpublished? 3) What is the amount and importance of the portion used in relation to the original work as a whole? and 4) What's the impact on the original work's commercial value? If copying and reproducing an original work violates the rights of an author in any of these respects—or is not for educational purposes—you could be violating copyright. It's a good rule to always ask permission before you reproduce any written material. Editors and publishers should work to protect what is published in their magazines by establishing a system for reprint requests and permissions, and keeping careful records.

## Libel

Defamation is injury to a person's reputation. Both libel and slander are forms of defamation, with libel expressed by print, writing, pictures, cartoons, or signs; slander by spoken words. If a magazine publishes charges of crime, immorality, fraud, dishonesty, incompetence, or inefficiency the publisher is open to a libel charge. A publisher can also be charged with libel if he or she publishes a story that defames a subject professionally, causing financial loss either personally or to a business. Factual error or inexact language can lead to these situations, which is why fact checking is so important. But even accurate reporting of someone else's libelous assertions can generate a libel suit. Everyone associated with the publication—writer, editor, publisher—is at risk of being named in a libel suit. The only clear defense against libel is if the facts stated are *provably* true. It's not enough to quote someone correctly. A publisher must be prepared to prove the truth of the statement.

A second defense is *privilege*. Privilege can be one of two kinds: absolute and qualified. Certain people in some circumstances are given absolute privilege. They can state, without fear of being sued for libel, material that may be false, malicious, and damaging. The circumstances in which such remarks can be made include judicial, legislative, public, and official proceedings and the contents of most public records. Remarks by a member of a legislative body in the course of official duties are not actionable. Neither are libelous statements made in the course of legal proceedings. In qualified privilege, statements made outside the court by police, a prosecutor, or an attorney can be reported by the press because it's an important case and the public interest warrants doing so. But keep in mind that statutes vary widely from state to state over what is public and official discussion.

Several important legal decisions serve as the framework for our current understanding of libel law. In *New York Times vs. Sullivan,* the court reversed a $500,000 libel verdict returned in Alabama against the *New York Times* and four ministers in relation to what had been quoted about the work of a county sheriff. The court ruled that a public official cannot recover damages for a defamatory falsehood relating to his official conduct unless he proves that the statement was made with "actual malice"—that is, with knowledge that it was false or with reckless disregard of whether it was false or not.

Public officials and public figures have important constitutional protections extended by recent Supreme Court rulings. A public figure is a person who, though not a public official, is "involved in issues in which the public has a justified and important interest."[32] This can include artists, athletes, businesspeople, anyone who is famous or infamous because of who he is or what he has done. In order to recover for libel, a public figure must show by clear and convincing evidence that the defamation was done with malice. That is, he or she must prove that the writer or publisher knew the statement was false or was made with reckless disregard as to whether the statement was true or false.

In June 1967, the Supreme Court upheld an award granted Wallace Butts, former athletic director of the University of Georgia, against Curtis Publishing Co., publisher of the *Saturday Evening Post*. The suit was based on an article in the *Post* accusing Butts of giving his football team's strategy secrets to an opposing coach before a game between the two colleges. The court found that Butts was a "public figure," but said there was an important difference: The Butts story was in no sense "hot news" and the editors of the magazine should have recognized the need for a thorough investigation of the serious charges. Elementary precautions were, nevertheless, ignored. The court referred to "slipshod and sketchy investigatory techniques employed to check the veracity of the source."

Just who is a public figure is subject to definition and can change over time. *Time* magazine published an account of the divorce of Russell and Mary Alice Firestone. The magazine said she had been divorced on grounds of "extreme cruelty and adultery," but the court had made no finding of adultery. She sued. Even though she was a prominent Palm Beach social figure and held press conferences during the course of the trial, the court ruled she was not a public figure and found in her favor.

## Privacy Law

The right of privacy varies from state to state and is judged by the court in each case. This right protects four quite different types of interests:

- The appropriation of a person's name or likeness for business or commercial uses
- The disclosure of embarrassing private facts
- The placing of a false image of a person before the public
- Intrusion into a person's seclusion or private life

When newsworthiness can be proved, a person generally cannot collect damages for invasion of privacy. If a person becomes involved in a matter of legitimate public interest—even if it's not hot news—he or she can be written about.[33] But if the material in question was used without his or her consent for advertising or commercial purposes, a person's privacy is generally considered to have been invaded. Most invasion of privacy suits center around the use—or misuse—of a photograph. For instance, if a magazine published a photograph of a woman whose skirt tore while she was rescuing a child from a car accident, the woman can't sue. But if another magazine buys the photograph and publishes it as part of a "humorous" story about poorly designed clothing, the second magazine is open to an invasion of privacy suit. Many magazines require that models or anyone included in a non-news-related photograph sign a release form authorizing the magazine to use their likeness in an editorial context.

In 1955, *Life* magazine published a review of a play titled *The Desperate Hours*. To illustrate the review, the magazine posed actors in the house where a real family had been held captive. *Life* stated truthfully that three escaped convicts had imprisoned a suburban Philadelphia family for 19 hours, but it added fictional acts of violence and verbal sexual abuse. *Life* said the article was "basically truthful." The family, which had moved and sought obscurity, sued for invasion of privacy. The Supreme Court reversed a lower court's decision in favor of *Life*: "We create grave risk of serious impairment of the indispensable service of a free press in a free society if we saddle the press with the impossible burden of verifying to a certainty the facts associated in a news article with a person's name, picture or portrait, particularly as related to non-defamatory matter."

In another example, Betty Friedan's ex-husband sued *New York Magazine* after an article she wrote titled "The Year We Entered Modern Times" was published in the magazine. The article contained an illustrative photograph of her with her son and ex-husband. The court held that the former husband's right to privacy had not been violated because Betty Friedan had become a public figure and the course of her life 25 years before therefore was of public interest.

But not all privacy suits involve photographs. One of the most famous right-to-privacy cases in a magazine involved a child prodigy. William James Sidis, a mathematical whiz who graduated from Harvard at the age of 16 and attracted widespread attention, had disappeared from public sight. In 1937, 25 years after his youthful fame, a writer for *The New Yorker* published a profile of him without his cooperation, describing his current life. The court dismissed Sidis's suit because he "was once a public figure. As a child prodigy, he excited both admiration and curiosity. The question of whether he had fulfilled his early promise was still a matter of public concern." But the court warned that such revelations must be newsworthy. "Revelations may be so intimate and so unwarranted in view of the victim's position as to outrage the community's notions of decency."

Laws regarding libel, defamation, and privacy are constantly evolving. Editors and publishers should tread carefully but knowledgeably. The importance of good, experienced legal counsel cannot be overemphasized.

## CASE STUDY
### Northwest Monthly

In late 1983, after raising just over $3 million from a group of venture capitalists in the United States and Great Britain and after conducting a highly successful direct mail test (the prelaunch mailing received an astounding 4 percent response on a hard offer), Carl Van Brunt, 40, and Michael Elliott, 36, were prepared to publish the regional magazine they had planned for four years. All the elements were in place: a vigorous economic revival in an attractive, affluent, livable market; a compelling editorial idea; sufficient working capital, and experienced publishing executives. Van Brunt had spent 15 years in magazine publishing, most recently as associate publisher and advertising director at Los Angeles–based *Western Living*. He and Elliott (who was the executive editor at *Western*, after having written and edited books at some of Manhattan's largest book publishing companies) modeled their magazine on the success of *Western Living*. They planned a high-quality, regional magazine in the tradition of *Texas Monthly* and *New York Magazine*.

Elliott and Van Brunt assembled a young, talented, inexperienced, ambitious staff. With Elliott's publishing contacts and the promise of a sophisticated, quality new magazine *Northwest Monthly* attracted acclaimed writers and photographers. The new magazine premiered in May 1984 with a cover story by a noted landscape designer decrying the public parks in Seattle. Contributors in that premiere issue also included a Pulitzer Prize–winning biographer, noted humorists, well-known investigative reporters and essayists.

The publishing team positioned *Northwest Monthly* as the magazine for "the new Northwest"—not a chamber of commerce view of the region but a celebration of its physical beauty and real issues of concern—warts and all. Elliott himself wrote the initial direct mail letter, which became part of a winning package. Van Brunt organized the preparation of promotional material. A plan for contracting with a national sales force to represent the magazine fell apart just before the launch, and Van Brunt hurriedly set up the magazine's own New York sales staff. No prototype issue was prepared to show advertisers before the first issue. Van Brunt and Elliott had successfully sold the magazine's editorial concept to investors and charter subscribers on the basis of their own description. They were confident they could do the same with advertisers. The first issue attracted approximately 18 pages of advertising; the second, 14 pages, the third, 12, and the fourth, nine.

While Elliott's editorial staff had passion and a clear direction, the market of readers and advertisers was slow to respond. Critical articles about downtown Portland's seedy side, Mount Rainier's "ruination" by tourism, and even restaurant reviews were met with angry subscription cancellations and advertiser resistance. One major car advertiser canceled its 13-page advertising contract after a playful yet unflattering profile of its crash-car testing program was published.

The magazine had its best year in 1987: 650 pages of advertising were sold, producing $2.6 million in revenue. Circulation income brought the magazine's gross revenues to about $4 million. Circulation had risen slowly, but had inched over the "magic" number of 100,000. By that year, too, the magazine had won widespread critical acclaim in the journalism and publishing worlds, including an unprecedented number of journalism and design awards.

But by 1988, the magazine had yet to turn the expected profit—nor were there any serious buyers of the company. Elliott and Van Brunt had engaged in another round of raising money, had cut back on paper quality, and had secured additional bank loans to cover expenses, but they did not have the funds to increase circulation significantly.

In 1989, the magazine was purchased by Global Communications, Inc. Both Elliott and Van Brunt left the magazine. The debt to original investors and bank loans had increased to $6 million. Then a recession hit the once-booming Northwest region, and bank and retail advertising—the backbone of the magazine's advertising revenue—fell out. Global spent $5 million trying to rescue *Northwest Monthly*: consolidating billing and circulation departments with its other American magazines; opening new advertising offices in Los Angeles and New York; investing in an advertising campaign and new promotional materials; even laying off seven full-time staff people.

Eventually, Global closed *Northwest Monthly's* doors in September 1990, selling the magazine's 122,000 subscriber list for $500,000 to chief rival *Seattle Magazine*.

The reasons for *Northwest Monthly's* demise are complex. Elliott offered one explanation in the winter of 1990: "By mid-1986, we'd already made some long-term enemies. It's not enough simply to be good. Certain elements of my approach may have been wrong. I may have edited too much for the trade. It is useless to edit a magazine for one's peers, to focus on winning awards. I'd trade them [the awards] in for just one profitable year."

What would *you* have done differently?

# NOTES

[1] Gigi Mahon, *The Last Days of the New Yorker* (New York: McGraw-Hill, 1988), 14–15.

[2] *Cowles/SIMBA Media Daily*, November 18, 1994 (Stamford, CT: SIMBA Information Inc., 1994).

[3] Loudon Wainwright, *The Great American Magazine: An Inside History of Life* (New York: Knopf, 1986), 30. Note: Writing in the prospectus, the magazine was first called *Dime*—which caused many objections by the staff. "What if you want to raise the price?" asked one. "Sounds too much like *Time*," objected another.

[4] Click, *Magazine Editing and Production*, 49. Note: Renamed *Southern*, the magazine was acquired by a Time Inc. subsidiary in 1989 and was folded later that year.

[5] Media kit, *George* magazine.

[6] Norman Cousins, "Final Report to Readers," *Saturday Review*, November 27, 1971, 32.

[7] Address to American Society of Magazine Editors, March 1, 1995.

[8] Alan Halcrow, "Extending Your Reach with Editorial Boards," *Folio:*, July 1992, 67–70.

[9] "Editorial Salary Survey," *Folio:*, August 1, 1995, 59, 64–70.

[10] "Editorial Salary Survey," *Folio:*

[11] "Editorial Salary Survey," *Folio:*

[12] "Editorial Salary Survey," *Folio:*

[13]Wainwright, *The Great American Magazine,* 389.

[14] Deirdre Carmody, "Writers Fight for Electronic Rights," *The New York Times*, November 7, 1994.

[15] Mahon, *The Last Days of the New Yorker*, 239.

[16] *Folio:*, May 15, 1995.

[17] Mahon, *The Last Days of the New Yorker*, 109.

[18] *New York Magazine*, "Tina's Turn," July 2, 1992.

[19] Deirdre Carmody, "Where to Draw the Line When Helping Advertisers," *The New York Times*, July 1, 1991.

[20] Carmody, "Where to Draw the Line."

[21] *Journal of Communications Study.*

[22] Mark Landler, "Time Warner, Under Its Own Spotlight," *The New York Times,* June 12, 1995.

[23] Sabrina Rubin, "Another Fine Mess," *Philadelphia Magazine*, January 1996, 45.

[24] Edwin Diamond, "Can You Change a Magazine's DNA?" *New York Magazine*, July 20, 1992.

[25] Diamond, "Can You Change a Magazine's DNA?"

[26] *Media & the Law* is published by SIMBA Information Inc, (203) 834-0033.

[27] Donald M. Gilmore, *Power, Publicity, and the Abuse of Libel Law* (New York: Oxford University Press, 1992), 27.

[28] Deirdre Carmody, "Writers Fight for Electronic Rights," *The New York Times*, November 7, 1994.

[29] Carmody, "Writers Fight for Electronic Rights."

[30] *Folio: First Day*, "Times Mirror Unit Pays Freelancers for E-Rights," November 13, 1995.

[31] *The New York Times*, January 15, 1996.

[32] Gilmore, *Power, Publicity, and the Abuse of Libel Law*, 39.

[33] AP Stylebook and Libel Manual.

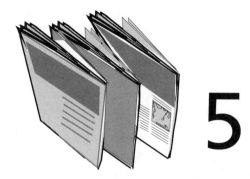

# Circulation Principles

Okay, so you have a great idea for a magazine. You've assembled a top-flight editorial staff. You've found out that there's a healthy advertising market and plenty of businesses will want to advertise in your magazine. What else do you need? Readers, of course. But not just any readers. To make your magazine a success, you need to identify the readers who will choose your magazine over others in the same category, who will open their wallets and spend money to keep getting your magazine, who are also likely buyers of the products and services your advertisers are offering. How do you find such people? And, once you find them, how do you get the magazine into their hands? On the face of it, the cards are stacked against you. Competition is fierce. Everyone's leisure time is valuable—who has time for another magazine? Printing, paper, and postal costs are forever rising, and you obviously can't afford to send free magazines to everyone you *think* might like it.

Good magazine circulation today is the epitome of efficiency and sophisticated marketing techniques. The second leg in our three-legged stool of magazine publishing is critical because it is the distribution system for a magazine, as well as second-largest source of income for many magazines, generating income from subscribers as well as the single-copy sales made via newsstands, supermarkets, convenience stores, bookstores, pharmacies, and specialty stores.

The basic duties of the circulation department are to identify potential magazine readers; to manage single-copy sales (at newsstands and other sites); to maintain the list of subscribers; to determine how many copies of the magazine need to be printed (known as the *print order*); and to provide the names of current subscribers to the printer so the magazine will be mailed to the right person. With such abundant and complex records to maintain, some of these duties are often performed by outside contractors under the direction of the in-house circulation department. The circulation function includes an almost endless number of details, and careful attention must be paid to every one of them. Circulators, as some who work in this arena call themselves, often delight in exchanging horror stories about what happened when details were overlooked. *Folio:* reported on the Direct Mail Marketing Council second annual "survivors" luncheon held in 1994. Dan Capell, a successful, well-known circulation consultant, told how he had neglected to obtain routine permission for a photograph of a famous football player that appeared in a full-page ad for one of his magazine clients. The football player sued and won. Others shared stories about glaring typographic errors in promotional material, address labels not sticking to magazine covers, double postcards falling apart, and scratch-off-and-win contests that would not scratch off.[1]

## PAID VERSUS CONTROLLED CIRCULATION

Magazines are circulated among people who have purchased multiple issues of a magazine for an agreed-upon period of time (subscribers), who buy individual copies of the magazine (single-copy sales), and who receive the magazine free because of who they are or where they work (controlled circulation). If a reader pays money for the magazine—either by buying a subscription or shelling out cash at the newsstand—the magazine counts those copies as *paid circulation*. Most consumer magazines are circulated on a paid-circulation basis. Most trade magazines are circulated on a controlled—or free—basis. The decision regarding which method to use for distribution of a magazine is usually based on the size of the potential audience, how readily the target audience can be identified, and the economics of creating a subscriber list.

The universe of potential readers for a consumer magazine usually is large. For example, even for a specialty magazine on photography the total universe of those interested in the editorial subject is in the millions. You could easily get the names and addresses of everyone who bought a particular kind of camera in the past year, but it would simply be uneconomic to send this many subscribers a free magazine. Additionally, there is a traditional view in the consumer advertising business that a paid subscriber is an actual reader of the magazine. A controlled circulation magazine does not have this indication of readership. As a result, controlled circulation magazines in the consumer segment generally have not been able to attract sufficient advertising to survive. Notable exceptions exist. *The Disney Channel Magazine* is delivered to more than five million people because they ordered the Disney Channel on cable television. Another exception is *American Baby*, with a controlled circulation of well over one million new mothers. Advertisers are eager to reach such an audience. In-flight magazines—published by the airlines and distributed in the seat pockets of planes—are another major exception. Seat-belted airline passengers are likely to read what's put in front of them. *Delta Sky* claims a controlled circulation of almost 500,000.

Figure 5.1 shows the top ten controlled circulation magazines in the United States. All have circulations over one million. You'll notice that *The Disney Channel Magazine* is not listed here because it did not file an audit report for the period. Most magazines that want to attract advertising to their pages submit their circulation records to one of two organizations that audit the circulation claims of magazines. The Audit Bureau of Circulations, Inc. (ABC) monitors most consumer magazines, and the Business Publication Audits of Circulation International, Inc. (BPA) checks trade magazines.

In most trade magazine markets, the potential audience is well under one million. For the few magazines with markets greater than one million, the likelihood is that the magazine will circulate on a paid subscription basis. The computer category yields extraordinarily high advertising revenues, even for those magazines that circulate only to businesses. *VARBusiness* circulates controlled to about 85,000 retailers in the computer hardware and software business, and enjoyed 1994 advertising revenue of more than $20 million. *Infoworld* and *PC Week* for the computer industry each have controlled circulation of over 200,000.

Except for the computer category, however, most trade magazines circulate among fewer than 200,000, with the vast majority circulating to less than 100,000. For example, *Successful Meetings,* with 1994 revenues of just over $19 million, has a controlled circulation of 75,000. *Food Engineering,* with revenues of $4.9 million, has a 60,000 controlled circulation. Magazines of this size operate on a controlled-circulation basis because the cost of identifying subscribers and then convincing them to pay for a subscription would far exceed the cost of compiling a subscriber list, and the cost of printing, binding and distributing the magazine. Thus, it can be more economical to send a magazine free to an audience with a pro-

### FIGURE 5.1    Top ten controlled circulation magazines in the United States (in thousands)

| | |
|---|---|
| Beyond the Wall | 2,500 |
| Lamaze Parents' Magazine | 2,215 |
| U–The National College Magazine | 1,550 |
| Compuserve Magazine | 1,318 |
| Baby Talk | 1,302 |
| Fantastic Flyer Magazine | 1,219 |
| Heartland USA | 1,093 |
| American Baby | 1,051 |
| Link, The College Magazine | 1,000 |

For the period July through December 1994. Source: *Advertising Age*, February 20, 1995.

fessional interest in the subject. Another important factor is the assurance that everyone in the target audience is, at the very least, receiving the publication, if not reading it. Very detailed information on readers of controlled circulation magazines can easily be obtained. In fact, it is part of the circulation verification process for most trade publications. This information collected on the audience can then, in turn, be shared with editors and advertisers. Figure 5.2 shows the top ten paid circulation magazines in 1994.

To summarize, the advantages of paid circulation are:

- Circulation revenue can make a substantial contribution to the financial health of the magazine.
- By paying for the magazine, the subscriber has indicated an intention to read the magazine regularly.
- Subscription records are likely to be more up-to-date because subscribers are conscious of the need to report changes of name and address.
- Advertisers will be more likely to consider the magazine's readers as loyal, attentive, and interested.

The advantages of controlled circulation are:

- Cost effective for magazines with a smaller target audience (less than 200,000).
- Advertisers can reach an entire target audience.
- Changes in the demographics of the market are easier to accommodate.
- Extensive demographic and job function information about the audience can be more readily obtained.

**FIGURE 5.2     Largest paid circulation magazines. All circulation figures are in millions.**

| | |
|---|---|
| Modern Maturity | 22,022 |
| Reader's Digest | 15,127 |
| TV Guide | 14,037 |
| National Geographic | 9,203 |
| Better Homes and Gardens | 7,614 |
| Good Housekeeping | 5,224 |
| Ladies' Home Journal | 5,048 |
| Family Circle | 5,005 |
| Consumer Reports | 4,866 |
| Woman's Day | 4,725 |

Source: *Folio: Special Sourcebook Issue,* 1994.

## CIRCULATION VERIFICATION

As mentioned earlier, the publishing industry relies on two major circulation auditing organizations, ABC and BPA. Both are nonprofit and are governed by a tripartite board of directors, consisting of representatives from magazine publishing companies, advertisers, and advertising agencies. Both organizations have specific rules regarding what conditions must be present to count a subscriber as paid, as a direct requester, or as a renewal. The rules and regulations are designed to provide uniformity and consistency so that advertisers and advertising agencies can rely on the information they receive from the many publishers with whom they do business. Both organizations audit magazines annually, and the audit report can be requested by advertisers who want to confirm circulation claims by the magazine. Because a year is a long time to wait for such information, every six months a publisher is permitted to publish a "Publisher's Statement," which is subject to corrections and adjustments based on the physical audit.

ABC audits most consumer magazines. The ABC Publisher's Statement (called "the pink sheet" in industry jargon because it is, in fact, printed on pink stock) is issued twice a year, in June and December, giving circulation information on the prior six months. The statement shows the magazine's average paid circulation and the magazine's *rate base*, the number of buyers of the magazine guaranteed by the publisher as well as the number on which the publisher bases the rates charged to advertisers. The rate base is an important number in the magazine business because advertisers use it as one of the key points in deciding whether to advertise in the magazine. The Publisher's Statement also indicates the percentage by which the magazine's circulation exceeded or fell under that rate base, and reports circulation on an issue-by-issue basis for a six-month period. The statement goes on to report on the number of subscriptions by price charged, by duration (one year, two years, etc.), sales channels, as well as how many subscriptions were acquired with the use of premiums—the free gifts publishers sometimes offer as an incentive to subscribe. Additional data is included on arrears—the number of subscriptions that a publisher continued to send, even though the reader's subscription expired—and the variance, if any, from the rate base for prior audit periods. A single issue during the audit period is analyzed geographically, showing state by state how many copies were sold by subscriptions and single copy sales. Finally, a five-year circulation trend report shows the average paid circulation as reported in the June and December Publisher's Statements.

A BPA Publisher's Statement shows the average qualified circulation, or the number of readers who meet the criteria for getting a free subscription. The publisher decides who is qualified to receive the magazine. For example, to receive a controlled circulation computer magazine, you would have to hold a job as a computer programmer or manage computer programmers. Controlled circulation magazines can also be sent to nonqualified recipients for any of a number of reasons, and that number will also be reported. The BPA statement also includes an occupation breakdown for a specific issue, and publishers report on the source of subscriber names (for example, did the publisher find this subscriber in a directory or did the recipient make a direct request?) and how they are addressed (is the magazine sent to a person by name or by title?) For paid circulation magazines, the BPA statement also provides information on the magazine's renewal rate. ABC will include renewal rate information only if the publisher chooses to report it. Most publishers do not release this information, because renewal rates can fluctuate and a low renewal rate can reflect badly on the magazine.

## THE ROLE OF THE CIRCULATION DIRECTOR

The circulation director in most publishing companies is in charge of all aspects related to the distribution of the magazine, including subscriber acquisition and renewal, single-copy sales, and the fulfillment function. When a magazine's actual circulation falls short of the rate base for a number of months, it is possible that advertisers will expect to receive a rebate of some of their advertising expenditure. More importantly, a magazine that consistently "misses" its rate base is considered to be losing its appeal to readers. It suggests that the magazine is in trouble. Thus rate base management is of the utmost importance. Shoddy rate base management will lead to serious shortfalls in the two primary streams of revenue, advertising and circulation, resulting in serious financial consequences.

The circulation director needs to be knowledgeable in direct mail marketing, finance, and database management and maintenance. The newsstand distribution system demands a keen analytical sense and knowledge of sales and marketing principles.

## CIRCULATION DEPARTMENT ORGANIZATION

Circulation departments may have as few as one or two employees, or as many as a few hundred. For a small-circulation magazine, the circulation department often consists of the circulation director and an assistant, with most functions being performed by outside contractors. Among publishers of multiple magazines, the circulation department can be centralized, decentralized, or a combination of both. Centralized departments offer the flexibility necessary to distribute work during peaks and valleys in the workload and to deal with crisis situations more readily because the director has control over the staff and can assign it to any task based on priorities. The primary disadvantage is that publishers may feel that they have less control over a key element of their magazine operations. Publishers like to feel that the personnel are dedicated to the vision they have for their publication. A way to get some of the best of both worlds is to have a circulation director assigned to each magazine. This person uses the services of the central department to get the job done, but retains responsibility for the circulation process for his or her magazine and reports to the publisher.

Many multiple magazine publishing companies find that centralizing the circulation department increases efficiency and brings acknowledged expertise to bear on all their magazines. A centralized circulation department is likely to have a circulation director, who has each specialist reporting to him or her. This would include a director of single-copy sales, associate subscription promotion managers, a director of planning, and a director of fulfillment. Often, circulation promotion is divided between a specialist in new business promotion and a specialist in billing and renewal promotion. The planning director may have associates specializing in forecast analysis and the fulfillment director will supervise customer service specialists.

## CREATING A PAID SUBSCRIBER BASE

For most magazines the main source for new subscribers is direct mail promotion. The process includes acquisition of a list of potential subscribers, creation and mailing of a solicitation package describing the magazine, and establishing a way for the potential subscriber to respond to the invitation to subscribe. This is a sophisticated and complex process. There are two kinds of basic offers. One asks for payment with order and is called a hard offer. The second provides for the subscriber to be billed later and is called a soft offer. The gross response/return rate is the percentage of orders received to the number of prospects solicited. The net response/return rate is the percentage of those who have ordered and paid for a subscription. Typically, the total number of persons who subscribe and pay for the subscription (the net return rate) will be $1\frac{1}{2}$ to 2 percent of those solicited. And that percentage can only be reached if the circulation director has compiled "responsive" lists (people who are likely to subscribe), set an acceptable price, and created an appealing promotional package. Most direct mail efforts can have a CPM of $400 to $500. In other words, a mailing to 100,000 potential subscribers will cost about $50,000 from start to finish. If the net return rate is at the high end of the scale, say two percent, the magazine will end up with 2,000 subscribers. These 2,000 subscribers cost the magazine $25 each to acquire. If the circulation director has compiled a less efficient list that produces a return of one percent, the cost of acquiring a subscriber is doubled.

You can readily see the importance of small differences when attempting to build a circulation of only 250,000. A net return rate of two percent will require a mailing of 12,500,000 packages at a cost between $5 million and $6.5 million. Direct mail marketing of magazines requires that the circulation director be well versed in how lists of names will behave. No one wants any surprises when the cost of acquiring subscribers is so high. How does the circulation director predict what

**FIGURE 5.3** Circulation department organization.

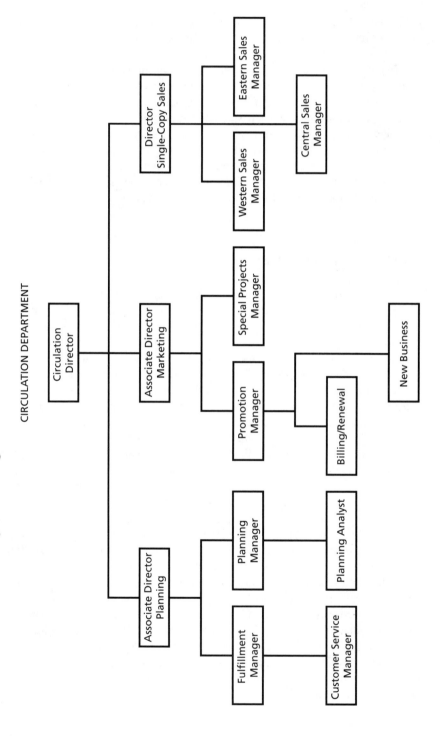

CIRCULATION DEPARTMENT

will happen in the mail? By testing. Testing is essential to the cost-effective development of a magazine subscriber list.

## Testing

Testing is an ongoing process. Every element of the subscription offer including the list of names, the price being offered, and the composition of the promotional package must be tested for efficiency. Most new magazines conduct a test before full-scale publication is undertaken. There are consultants who specialize in the subscriber acquisition process. Because they are exposed to many magazines in the course of their business, they develop expertise in the many vagaries of this effort. Few publishers—especially first-time publishers—feel as competent, so consultants are used frequently at this stage.

For a new magazine, test samples of 5,000 to 10,000 names might be taken from mailing lists that would seem appropriate for reaching the target universe. For instance, to see if a new magazine about nature photography could succeed at a circulation level of 300,000, the publisher might acquire a total of 1,000 names of people who have used their credit card to buy a camera in the past year, 2,500 names of people who took a bird-watching expedition, and 2,000 people who subscribe to *Audubon* magazine. The circulation director and the publisher will agree on two or more subscription price levels to use for the test. Finally, the circulation director commissions two or more promotional packages to be designed. One might be a simple double postcard, describing the new magazine in a paragraph or two; the other might be much more elaborate and expensive, with a full-color brochure, samples of articles, and a four-page letter from the editor. Typically, a magazine's direct mail packages include a letter, a descriptive brochure, a reply card, and an envelope. The package also might feature a fax or toll-free number that potential subscribers can call to request the magazine. The test designer takes all these variables and creates a matrix of cells. Cell A1, for example, might be the recipient from the list of bird-watchers who received the double postcard package offering the magazine at $9.95. Cell B4 might be the *Audubon* subscribers who received the more elaborate package offering the magazine at $12.95. Results are then recorded for each cell and analyzed to determine which offer and combination of variables provides the best gross response and ultimately the best net response.

Here is a simplified example of part of such a matrix:

| | # Pieces Mailed | Package | List | Price | Soft Offer | Hard Offer | Free Issues | Response |
|---|---|---|---|---|---|---|---|---|
| Promotion package 1 | | #1 | A | $19.95 | Yes | | None | |
| Promotion package 2 | | #1 | A | $19.95 | Yes | | 3 | |
| Promotion package 3 | | #1 | A | $24.95 | Yes | | None | |
| Promotion package 4 | | #1 | A | $24.95 | Yes | | 3 | |
| Promotion package 5 | | #1 | A | $14.95 | Yes | | None | |
| Promotion package 6 | | #1 | A | $14.95 | | Yes | 3 | |

The circulation director is testing six separate promotional packages at three pricing levels and a single list. Five packages also test a *soft offer*—that is, subscribers can tell the publisher to bill them; they want the magazine but payment isn't required at the time of the order. A *hard offer* is when the subscriber must send cash or credit card payment to receive the magazine. Most subscription offers are soft offers. Hard offers are seldom used in new subscription promotion. In this example, the publisher is also testing how potential subscribers respond to an offer of free issues as a way to sample the magazine. The results of this test will provide data on which price is most acceptable and whether or not free issues boost response. One can readily see from this small sample the many variables that can be tested. The circulation director will then know which lists are underperforming and can make decisions on the other elements of direct mail marketing for this particular magazine.

Presuming the test has favorable results and a decision is made to launch the magazine, one subscriber solicitation package from the test will emerge as the *control package*. This is the package against which all future subscription efforts will be compared for effectiveness. Over time the control package can change because it is "defeated" by a new promotional package. Yet, many initial control packages have very long lives, consistently outperforming other packages year after year.

The number of responses generated by a subscription promotion is the *gross response* rate. Later, when each respondent is billed and payment is made, the subscriber becomes part of the net return rate. Unfortunately, the *net response* rate can not be accurately determined until after the magazine has been published because the billing effort cannot be precisely measured until after respondents have begun to receive the publication. However, the magazine industry does have historical data that can be used as a reasonable guide. The relationship between the gross and net return rate is important. A cell may produce a very favorable gross response rate but have an unacceptable number of respondents who actually pay the bill. A reasonable gross return rate for most magazines is three percent, four percent or five percent. Rarely will a subscription offer produce a higher return rate. According to Brian Beckwith, president of K-III Special Interest Magazine Group, an acceptable pay-up rate is on the order of 50 percent, so a good net response rate is $1^1/_2$ to $2^1/_2$ percent.

## Who Are the Potential Subscribers?

The editorial mission statement for a magazine will invariably describe the interests of the potential reader. *Time* expects to attract readers who were interested in keeping up with current events, a broad category. *Golf Digest* expects its circulation to be comprised of golfers or would-be golfers. *Organic Gardening* would likely attract gardeners, especially the subcategory of gardeners whose special interest is gardening without chemicals and synthetic ingredients. What makes someone subscribe to a magazine? Not all magazine subscribers purchase the same magazine for the same reason. Take *Architectural Digest*, for example. Some subscribers read it to be entertained, as a form of recreation. Others read to become or stay informed on architectural trends and experts in the design field. Still others subscribe for its educational value. Some subscribe for the "coffee table value" of a magazine. A doctor or lawyer might subscribe for their office waiting rooms. The circulation effort at most magazines is primarily directed toward those who are likely to purchase the magazine for its entertainment, information, or education value. Those who value magazines for the enhancement of their home generally subscribe for one of these reasons, even though they may be less loyal readers. Those who subscribe for a visitor waiting area can be a valuable source of new subscribers, even though the magazine is not bought for their personal use. This latter category is rarely a target for a direct mail promotion.

## List Development

The magazine business doesn't suffer from a shortage of available lists of names. List brokers rent mailing lists compiled from a myriad of sources. Most magazines will rent their mailing lists to other magazines that are not direct competitors. Many associations make their member list available. Numerous directory publishers also rent names from their listings, as well as their own subscriber lists. Credit card companies, catalog sales companies, and other similar organizations have extensive mailing lists for rent. Each issue of *Folio*: has a department entitled "List Activity" that reports on newly available lists and news about improvements in available lists. Standard Rate and Data Service publishes a directory of available direct mail lists. Note that lists are *rented*. They are not sold to the user; ownership remains in the hands of the source. When do you become the owner of a name? Broadly speaking, when a transaction occurs between the list renter and the person on the list, the list renter owns the name.

Publishers need demographic data on their subscribers to sell advertising. As database technology has improved, many publishers and other list managers have compiled extensive data about each person on their list. Thus even very large lists can be made more productive to the buyer and seller by selecting only that part of the list that would be likely subscribers. Testing an entire list of women for a magazine that is aimed at working women would be far less productive than selecting from the larger list only those women who are known to be working.

The challenge is to locate lists that are populated by a large number of potential subscribers. Another important key to a successful list is that the person has previously been a direct mail purchaser. In all but a very few markets, the response rate among those who are direct mail buyers will be significantly higher than among those who have not purchased via direct mail. Magazine subscription solicitations are almost never conducted among persons who have not purchased an item via direct mail.

As we've seen, every list must be tested for effectiveness. It is accepted industry practice to purchase 5,000 to 10,000 names on an "nth" name basis for test purposes. For example, every tenth name from a list of 500,000 would produce 5,000 names. If one were to launch a magazine for those interested in serious photography, lists to consider would be the subscriber lists of other photography magazines, lists maintained by camera and photographic accessory manufacturers (often compiled from warranty registration), and other lists on which the person has indicated an interest in photography. A golf magazine launch might use the lists of other golf magazines, lists compiled by golf club manufacturers, members of golf associations, direct mail buyers of golf paraphernalia, travelers to resort areas, and other lists on which the person has indicated an interest in golf. As mentioned earlier, not all magazines will rent their lists to competitors, but there are numerous exceptions, so it is always worth the effort.

## Price

Many price variations are offered to suggest that the subscriber is getting a bargain—and usually, it *is* a bargain. Direct mail copywriters will aggressively point out how much a subscriber will save on a per copy basis with a subscription. Short-term subscriptions are sometimes offered to promote a low price. For a weekly, an offer may be for the next 20 weeks. For a monthly, one might be for six or nine issues.

Circulation directors often use premiums to entice would-be subscribers. Circulation audit organizations have specific rules on what the value of a premium may be, in order to avoid building a paid circulation on the merits of an expensive gadget—and not the magazine. Premiums usually have a connection with the editorial content of the magazine (in the form of anthologies or videotapes, for example). If a premium is "too good"—that is, more valuable to the recipient than the magazine itself—it can negatively affect the renewal rate.

## The Promotional Package

Assuming that a publisher has a viable list to solicit, the next most important element of the subscription process is the offer. The price, the copy appeal, photography, design, and other elements of the package all contribute mightily to a successful result. This is important enough to provide an attractive business for many consultants who exclusively specialize in the study, analysis, and creation of the complete offering package.

Promotional packages come in all shapes and sizes. Copy on the envelope has proved to be an extremely important part of the package. Getting the prospect to open the package is an obvious first step. A two- or three-page letter is usually included, which publishers don't expect potential subscribers to actually read. Circulation experts have learned that a lengthy letter—even one that is not read, simply scanned—contributes favorably to the response rate. All-important is providing an easy method for the prospect to respond, so most promotions will provide an 800 number (and fax number) as well as a reply card. Credit cards are almost always accepted, and even if payment is not demanded in the offer, the opportunity to use a credit card will be provided.

## When to Mail

Certain months of the year have proved to be best for direct mail response. A magazine that has been in existence for a number of years will have developed a seasonality chart so that mailings are "dropped" (put into the hands of the Postal Service) when the response rate is likely to be highest. Most circulation directors have found that January, September, and October are the best months. No conclusive theory has emerged to determine why these months seem to provide a more accepting frame of mind among prospects. Some experts attribute it to our attitude about a restart that seems to prevail at these times of year. Who has not made a resolution or two to start a new year? At the end of the summer, it's time to get back to work or school and get serious again. A new magazine would be wise to rely on traditional wisdom until their own seasonality data can be accumulated and analyzed.

## Conversions and Renewals

*Conversion* describes those subscribers who have renewed their subscription after their first-time subscription has expired. *Renewal* refers to those who have converted and have renewed their subscription again. Every time a subscriber renews after the conversion, the subscriber is considered a renewal. A reader is a new subscriber and a conversion only once. Thereafter, they are renewals. If Elise Parker is a first-time subscriber to *Vogue* and she renews for another term, she is a conversion. Every extension of Elise's subscription after the conversion is a renewal.

The rate at which subscribers renew is extremely important from a financial point of view. It is far more economical to entice a subscriber to renew as compared to acquiring a new subscriber. Satisfied readers are often renewed by a simple postcard mailing or a wrapper on the magazine or an enclosure with the magazine. We have seen that the cost of a new subscriber can be $25 and more. A renewal can cost less than $1. Usually, the conversion rate is lower than the renewal rate. If new subscribers extend a subscription, it stands to reason that they may enjoy the magazine but might still be uncertain. It is easy to decide to try it for another year. However when they extend their subscription for a second time, it is likely they are clearly pleased with the service performed by the magazine and are likely to become a loyal reader. For most magazines a 50 percent conversion rate is quite acceptable. Many succeed with lower conversion rates. The goal for renewals should be in the

60- to 70-percent range. Besides being an efficient source of subscriptions, the renewal rate is an indication of the acceptance by the reader audience.

Renewal and conversion efforts usually begin no less than three months prior to the subscription expiration date. Many start six months or more ahead. The sooner a subscriber renews, the cheaper the effort. Renewal efforts continue for many months after the expiration date. The number of renewal efforts and the best starting and ending date are determined by careful tracking and analysis of these activities. There is no formula. The success rate depends on the loyalty that can be developed with readers, the price, and the effectiveness of promotional efforts.

The price for a subscription becomes less sensitive with renewals. Some publishers reduce the subscription price at or near the end of a renewal cycle, feeling that there is price sensitivity. Most people do not track what they pay for magazines, and in fact are willing to pay a reasonable amount for a magazine they have come to enjoy or rely upon. Some magazine readers, however, have noticed that the price for some subscriptions gets lower if they do not renew immediately. This must be considered when deciding whether or not to employ this practice. Again, continual testing of all the factors that bear on the success of the renewal effort is a necessary part of the circulation director's job.

## Telemarketing

Infrequently, telemarketing is used for subscription conversion and renewal efforts. It is one of the most expensive methods available. When it is used, telemarketing is generally conducted by an outside vendor. The list is provided by the publisher and the message is carefully scripted, complete with answers to frequently asked questions. Despite the best efforts, telemarketing comes across as an impersonal presentation. The public has become annoyed with the intrusion on its personal time, so besides being costly, the possibility of creating ill will is present. Telemarketing should be near the bottom of the list for subscription activities.

## Other Subscription Sources

*Bind-in cards* are, as the name implies, bound into the magazine. *Blow-in cards* are named for the method used at the printer to place them within the pages of the magazine, but not bound to the spine. While bind-in and blow-in cards do not produce large numbers of new subscribers, both are among the most economical sources for new subscriptions. One might be tempted to limit bind-in and blow-in cards to copies sold through retail outlets. Surprisingly, the number of subscriptions from newsstand copies typically does not overshadow those from subscriber copies. Experts suggest that the card should not be lavishly designed because, in effect, the entire magazine is the promotional package for those who are potential subscribers via bind-in and blow-in cards. An analysis of bind-in and blow-in cards performance by Rodale Press revealed that the more designed the cards were, the worse their performance.[2]

Gift subscriptions are an excellent source of new subscriptions. For current subscribers who enjoy a magazine, holiday shopping can be simplified. An added benefit is that the gift giver is likely to renew the gift (and therefore the subscription) year after year.

Subscription agencies, such as Publishers Clearing House and American Family Publishers, are also a good source for new subscribers. The drawback is that the publication receives little, if any, of the proceeds from the sale of the subscription. The immediate benefit is that the publisher saves the cost of creating and mailing its own promotion package. The longer-term benefit results from successful, and usually less expensive, renewal of subscriptions.

## CREATING A CONTROLLED CIRCULATION SUBSCRIBER BASE

The creation of a controlled subscriber base is infinitely less complex than the creation of a paid subscriber base. Although some trade magazine publishers improve or compile their own lists, all new publications start with rented lists. In some important markets the lists are so precise and well maintained that there is no reason to own the list. The American Medical Association maintains data on all medical doctors in the United States. The AMA franchises the list to a select group of direct mail houses, which in turn rent the list to magazine publishers and others. The mailing house receives updated information weekly from the AMA. This list is considered sufficiently accurate and economical that many, if not most, controlled circulation medical magazines and journals use the portion of the list that is appropriate for their target audience. A magazine directed at cardiologists would select only that group. At the other end of the spectrum are publications that use lists as the basis for compiling their own list. Usually these publishers want a group of individuals for which there is no single list available. If you chose to publish a magazine aimed at engineers, it is likely that you need portions of lists that would pin down the type of engineering in which the individual is engaged, chemical or automotive engineers, for example.

No list is static. People move, get promotions, drop their membership, and make changes in their lives all the time. Constant updating is a never-ending process. Besides additions and deletions there is the need to reverify and requalify readers, to keep the appropriate records for the audit bureau, if the publication is audited, and to satisfy postal service requirements.

## Requalification

Audit bureau regulations generally require that a subscriber be requalified at least every three years. That simply means that the subscriber must explicitly express interest in continuing to receive the magazine. Ideally, it means that the subscriber has signed a document indicating that interest so he or she may be classified as direct request circulation. As mentioned earlier, postal service regulations use direct request circulation to determine if a publisher qualifies for second-class mailing. Competition or advertiser demands may require that this information be updated more often than every three years. Most advertisers would prefer annual updating. Obviously, if your competition meets this demand, you would be wise to do so as well.

Even though the process of updating subscriber information is simpler for a controlled circulation magazine, publishers have found that using the professional methods mentioned above for paid subscription magazines can help reduce the cost of requalification efforts. The promotion package has the same challenge. It most be opened and attractive enough to encourage the recipient to act on the information.

## SINGLE-COPY SALES

Single-copy sales primarily take place in those ubiquitous outlets called newsstands. Every block in an urban business district has one or two. The smallest village will have at least one, usually part of a store that sells newspapers, tobacco products, stationery, and greeting cards. They are located in most airports and train terminals, as well as in most bookstores. Other important retail outlets for magazines include supermarkets and convenience stores. However, there are countless magazines that distribute copies through retail outlets associated with their editorial fare that are known as *affinity outlets*. Photography magazines are likely to be sold in photography shops, for example.

The system for getting copies of magazines to an outlet consists of the publisher, the national distributor, and the wholesaler. The national distributor does not physically handle the magazine. Rather, its role is to assist the publisher in establishing the most efficient number of copies to sell through retail outlets and to supervise the distribution to the outlet by the wholesalers. The national distributor has a sales and service operation that represents the various publishers with the wholesaler. The wholesaler receives shipment of a predetermined number of the magazines from the printer. Wholesalers physically deliver the publications to outlets, invoice, bill, and collect from them; then take back unsold copies of the magazines. Traditionally, wholesalers removed the covers from unsold copies so that they could not be resold. In theory, strips of these covers were returned to the national distributor as evidence that they were, indeed, unsold. Today there is a high degree of faith at play in the system. Wholesalers usually shred unsold copies and the national distributor and publisher accept their counts for sold and unsold copies based on affidavits provided by the wholesaler to the national distributor. Mass paperback books also use this distribution system.

The number of copies a publisher has delivered to wholesalers is known as the *draw*. The number of copies actually sold is known as *sell-through*. A publisher can expect to net 50 percent of the cover price for each copy sold. The balance is used to pay the national distributor, wholesaler, and retailer for the part they play in the distribution system. According to a report released by Vos, Gruppo & Capell, investment advisers, the sell-through margin for 1982 was 67.7 percent and 52.6 percent in 1992.[3] Figure 5.4 shows an example of the result from distribution of 300,000 copies.

There is a special commission called the retail display allowance, usually 10 percent of the cover price, which in theory assures that a magazine will get preferential display. A full-face cover display (in which the entire cover is visible on the newsstand rack) would be an example. In practice, the RDA is paid rather freely by the publishers even though they have little assurance that the retailer will live up to the agreement.

General interest magazines with newsstand clout have found the newsstand an important testing site for new magazines, and the newsstand is an important outlet for seasonal or one-shot publications.

With all this complexity, expense, and uncertainty, why in the world would a magazine bother with newsstand sales? Besides those magazines that are distributed primarily through newsstand circulation, magazines rely on newsstands for

**FIGURE 5.4    Distribution and sell-through**

| | |
|---|---|
| Copies distributed | 300,000 |
| Sell-through rate (50%) | .50 |
| Sell-through copies | 150,000 |
| | |
| Copies distributed | 300,000 |
| Cost to manufacture a copy | $.60 |
| Total manufacturing | $180,000 |
| | |
| Cover price | $4 |
| Distribution cost (50%) | $2 |
| Net to publisher | $2 |
| | |
| Sell-through copies | 150,000 |
| Net per copy | $2 |
| Net on sell-through | $300,000 |
| Less manufacturing | $180,000 |
| Net | $120,000 |

some income, subscribers are obtained through promotional material included in newsstand copies, there is promotional value and, in some cases, it is simply a matter of tradition.

An important retail outlet for some magazines is the food supermarket. Magazines that are primarily sold in single copies find it imperative to be displayed at checkout counters. Examples are *TV Guide, Woman's Day, Family Circle, People, National Enquirer*, and *Star*. Various arrangements have been made to assure display in this prime location. First and foremost, the magazine must be a proven seller at checkout counters. A publisher might offer a guaranteed income per rack from its publication or pay a fee to the supermarket.

Who are newsstand buyers? One magazine authority has written that there are three categories of magazine readers: 25 percent are subscribers, 25 percent are newsstand buyers and 50 percent are both at one time or another.[4] In many instances a newsstand sale is purely an impulse purchase. Someone taking an airplane trip may decide at the last minute that he or she would like to read a magazine in a particular category and not take a chance on what the airline may be providing that day. When supermarket shopping was most often performed by women, one would see *Family Circle, Woman's Day, Mademoiselle,* and other women's magazine in the racks at the checkout counters. Changing times have changed the configuration of magazines displayed at the checkout counter. *GQ, Men's Health*, and other magazines directed primarily toward men can now be found prominently displayed. Cover prices of checkout counter racks can be $1.95, $3.95 and more. One can theorize that even the higher cover prices are quite reasonable in the context of the cost of a grocery order and rather attractive as an impulse buy.

Some readers find they enjoy a magazine but have learned they just don't read every issue of their subscription. The newsstand is perfect for their needs. Others enter the newsstand with a particular category in mind and select from among magazines in the category. And still others are browsers who buy a publication that attracts their attention, usually through the appeal of the cover.

## The Cover as a Newsstand Variable

The variables that can affect the sale of a copy of a magazine are many and include the draw, the cover lines for articles within that issue, cover price, competition from similar magazines on the same display rack, seasonality, issue promotion, and the number of days the publication remains on sale. But no variable is as important as the cover. Unfortunately, designing and creating an attention-getting cover is an inexact science. A cover must be viewed as it might appear on a newsstand, amidst a mass of other magazines of every imaginable design and color.

Today, the public has an insatiable appetite for celebrities and their private lives. With covers being so important to newsstand sales, it is little wonder that celebrities are featured frequently. Each month *Advertising Age* tracks celebrity appearances on the covers of more than 30 of the nation's leading magazines. For the full year 1995, O.J. Simpson led the rankings with 90 appearances. Oprah Winfrey was second with 46 covers and Princess Diana moved up to third place (from tenth in 1994) with 22 cover appearances. Other favorites were George Clooney, Jim Carrey, Kathie Lee Gifford, Whitney Houston, Liz Taylor, Sandra Bullock, Antonio Banderas, and with seven appearances each, Tom Hanks and Nicole Kidman.[5]

There is no assurance that just because a publisher puts a celebrity on the cover of a magazine the magazine will achieve improved sell-through. In 1992, the personal finance magazine *Worth* began experimenting with split run covers. For the magazine's July issue, on those sold west of the Mississippi, the magazine ran a cover story titled "Are Your Parents Robbing You Blind?" examining the perilous state of the Social Security system. For issues east of the Mississippi, the magazine ran a cover photograph of television comedian Jerry Seinfeld. The Social Security cover outperformed Seinfeld two to one. "You haven't seen a celebrity on the cover of *Worth* since," publisher W. Randall Jones told the *New York Times*.[6]

The draw—the physical number of copies distributed on newsstands—is an important element in newsstand sales. The cost of distributing copies for sale on newsstands demands careful analysis of sales data by geographic location, type of outlet, and other variables. If a publisher has a draw of 200,000 and a 50 percent sell-through, the net sale is 100,000 copies. One cannot assume that by establishing a draw of 400,000, 200,000 copies will be sold. The law of diminishing returns clicks in at some point in the process. Most magazines determine the ideal draws through experimentation and analysis of sales results. It is simply too costly to overestimate a draw, when you consider that you are getting roughly half of the cover price and probably 50 percent or fewer copies sold. Because of the complexity of single-copy sales, there are numerous consultants who specialize in this function. Some have their own sales force to help with accurate feedback and analysis. Unless one is steeped in knowledge about this distribution system, it pays to get expert advice.

The cover price is governed by the competition within the category. Testing different cover prices, however, can provide significant guidance. It is safe to say that unless you have a particularly appealing article on the cover, you cannot expect to sell as well at a higher price than your competitor. In early 1994, *American Spectator* published an exposé on President Clinton's alleged womanizing that received heavy press and television coverage throughout the country. That issue sold out immediately, and the cover price of $3.95 was not a deterrent. Under ordinary circumstances one may find a lower cover price to be an advantage.

For some publications, seasonality can be a considerable variable. Wedding magazines sell better in specific months of the year. One might assume that time of the year for some magazines should make no difference. Sales feedback often surprises and indicates that, indeed, there is such a pattern. Thus seasonality must be part of the analysis of historical sales to help determine those months in which the sell-through may benefit from a larger or smaller draw.

Many of the larger general interest publications use point-of-sale racks, billboards, radio, television, newspaper, and magazine advertising to promote their magazine. Midsize and smaller magazines generally use issue-specific promotion, if any at all, and often limit their mass media advertising to those issues they consider of special importance or those that are expected to get attention because of a provocative news report, annual survey, or other editorial feature. Cable television has provided a more affordable buy for special interest magazines. For midsize and smaller magazines, mass media is simply too expensive to be an option.

Days on sale refers to the number of days a magazine remains displayed. This varies depending on the frequency of the publication, the sales rate, and, sometimes, the whim of the individual retailer. Magazines are delivered to retail outlets on a specific day of the week, put on display beginning on a specific day, and stay on display for a specific number of days. Most publishers of monthly magazines would like to remain on sale for 30 days. However, if a magazine is not selling quickly enough, the retailer is likely to move it to the back room to make space for a faster-selling publication.

## MANAGING THE RATE BASE

As we've seen, the rate base of a magazine is the number of copies of the magazine on which the advertising rates are based. For some magazines this may be called the guaranteed rate base, meaning that the publisher promises to deliver no less than the guaranteed rate base for the issue in which one may advertise. In recent years, missing the rate base has become more common, as magazines compete with each other and other media for the attention of a reader. This has led to magazines moving away from the use of the word *guaranteed*. The implication is that they have a rate base that they will do everything possible to attain, but it is not a sure thing. The problem has been acute enough in the last few years that a number of magazines have reduced their rate base. In August of 1995, Hearst announced a bold plan to reduce the rate base of 13 of its monthly magazines. At the same time it planned to increase its advertising rates. This strategy was greeted with an angry reaction from numerous advertisers. Kraft, for one, reacted with the threat of a significant reduction in its ad spending with Hearst. The dynamics of subscriber list maintenance and single-copy sales make the accuracy of a rate base prediction anything but a certainty. Because of this, publishers use a number of methods to keep their rate bases at an acceptable level. Among these are the use of *arrears* and *subscription* agencies.

### Arrears

A circulation director may choose to send copies of a magazine to a subscriber after the term of the subscription has been fulfilled. In other words, a one-year subscription may expire in May. The subscriber is continued on the circulation file in June. That copy is considered to be in arrears. A subscriber in arrears may receive numerous issues of the magazine. Under these circumstances neither the publisher nor the subscriber has created any obligation to the other. The primary purpose of arrears is to help maintain the rate base. The hope, too, is that the subscriber will renew the subscription during the arrears period. During this period the subscriber will be receiving promotional material encouraging renewal. If a subscriber renews the subscription later, the publisher may consider the subscription start date to be the date of expiration of the former subscription , even though that may have been a month or more prior to the current issue. ABC regulations provide that if the issues sent are consecutive within three months of expiration they may be counted as issues in arrears.

## Subscription Agencies

The best-known subscription agencies are Publishers Clearing House and American Family Publishers. Publishers receive little or no portion of the amount paid to these agencies by a subscriber. In effect they receive a subscriber with no attendant income. Why would any publisher give away all this money? For one thing there is no money spent to acquire the subscribers and they can be important to help maintain the rate base. For another, the subscribers represent the opportunity for a long-term relationship if they become loyal readers and renew their subscription. Unfortunately, the renewal rate will almost always be significantly lower than the renewal rate from among subscribers acquired by a carefully tested and executed subscription effort that is totally under the publisher's control.

## CIRCULATION FULFILLMENT AND FILE MAINTENANCE

*Fulfillment* is the word used to describe the maintenance of the subscriber list. This is a complicated process because of the many pieces of information a publisher needs to derive from the fulfillment system. At its simplest, a fulfillment system needs to record the term of the subscription, the amount paid, and the date when a new paid subscription began to be fulfilled. For trade publications that circulate on a controlled basis there is no payment to record; but demographic, job function, and requalification information must be maintained and continually updated. In some instances the circulation of a controlled circulation magazine is small enough (up to 15,000) that a simple database program can handle most of the label production requirements. That's the exception rather than the rule. Most controlled circulation publications, while simpler than paid subscription file maintenance, are sufficiently complex that in-house versus an outside fulfillment house is an important consideration.

The term and start-up date are important because they determine when a subscription expires and when renewal solicitation should begin. The subscription liability can be calculated and the file can be marked to indicate when the publisher should begin to send renewal notices. *Subscription liability* is the term used to describe the amount of money the publisher owes you for issues of the magazine not yet delivered. If, for example, you have paid $24 for a one-year subscription to a monthly publication, the publisher owes you 12 issues of the magazine. If he or she is unable to continue publication, you are entitled to a refund of your money. So, if you have received three copies under your subscription, the publisher's remaining subscription liability is $18. You can see that for a magazine with an average-size circulation, a publisher's subscription liability can be in the millions of dollars. Why is subscription liability important? Obviously, subscription liability contributes to the assessment of the financial picture of a magazine. However, if the magazine continues in business this liability is satisfied by the regular delivery of the magazine. Its importance is magnified when a publication is sold. If a buyer pays $1 million for a magazine, it is essential to the transaction to agree on who assumes the subscription liability. When the $1 million purchase price includes the assumption of another $1 million in subscription liability, the cost of purchasing the magazine is closer to $2 million.

The list of subscribers is a valuable resource for a publisher. The more information that can be added to the file about a subscriber, the more valuable the list. A list of names, or selections from the list, with well-defined demographic characteristics can be readily sold to marketers. The more demographic and psychographic (that is, information on lifestyle and behavior) data contained in the file, the more valuable the list. *Database marketing* is a term used to describe the use of a mailing list to provide a clearly defined market to which other goods can be sold or through which the marketing of a product can be enhanced. Lists of magazine subscribers are important in the realm of database marketing. What better list might there be for a marketer of cooking utensils and implements than the subscription list of a cooking magazine? For books on management and leadership, a list of chief executive officers who receive a magazine might be very fruitful.

An important decision is whether to have subscription fulfillment performed in-house or via a service bureau. Service bureaus exist that are completely dedicated to magazine subscription fulfillment. The complicated functions that are inherent in a paid subscriber magazine subscription list demand special expertise and the use of software and technology that are in a state of constant change. Additionally, the data input requires extensive clerical service. All of this causes most publishers to opt for an outside service. Most in-house management information system personnel are not well versed in the countless nuances and complicating factors in the maintenance of a subscription list and, conversely, most circulation experts are not as expert in the countless nuances and complicating factors inherent in a computer data processing system. Even if a publisher feels that an in-house system would be desirable, it is probably best to begin with an outside service. This could be a means for the different disciplines to have time to acquire the necessary expertise and cross-discipline training to avoid unnecessary risk.

Even if publishers decide to use an outside service, they have several options over how much control to maintain. Publishers may feel that customer service would be of better quality if they had control over the hiring standards. Because data input is prone to error, publishers may decide to handle all or part of the data input function in-house.

The primary advantage of handling circulation fulfillment in-house is that it provides the publisher with complete control over the operation. Another influence on the decision may be that excess computer capacity exists within the company. This might be considered to provide a soft dollar (the cost is already being borne, no additional money needs to be spent) advantage. Rarely, if ever, does an in-house fulfillment operation save hard dollar (out-of-pocket cash) compared to the use of an outside service.

The complete service offered by a fulfillment company consists of billing, receipt of payments, general list maintenance (such as address changes), customer service, mailing label production, services related to subscription promotion (such as generation of renewal notices), and the information necessary for the audit bureau to complete its work in an efficient way. Not all outside services offer all these functions and some may not be able to efficiently handle special needs of the circulation operation.

Among the questions a circulation director will likely ask of the outside fulfillment contractor:

- How frequently will reports be issued?
- What will reports look like?
- What information will be included in the file for each subscriber?
- For issues with regional or split-run advertising, how will a portion of the mailing list be selected?
- What about special handling requirements (oversees subscriptions, bulk subscriptions, or subscriptions requiring special, speedier delivery)?

Most outside services quote their prices in dollars per thousand records, the dollar amount varying by the extent of the service provided on a routine basis.

The vendors must be treated as a partner in terms of how much they know about your circulation policies. They must know how often you want the file data updated and details about your policies regarding billing, renewals, arrears, and the other situations that need special attention, like gift subscriptions. Most important, a circulation director must be assured of the quality of the people and the performance of the outside service, as well as its history in keeping up-to-date with software and hardware technology.

A fulfillment service should be considered an important resource. Most quality vendors have specialists for important functions who can quickly answer your questions about postal regulations, audit bureau regulations, and the like. Sports and Fitness Publishing delivers one of its publications via third-class mail, which requires the use of indicia (that is, the postal service's bar-coded marking substituted for postage). To avoid having the covers of the publication distorted by indicia, the publisher worked with its fulfillment service to generate a mailing label that included the indicia.[7]

Fulfillment services can help avoid complications arising from the design of various elements of the promotion process by assuring that postal regulations are satisfied, the proper space is allotted for computer-generated data, and other details that can produce costly reprinting and delivery. Audit bureaus require data in specific forms to assure that an audit trail is available to complete their work. Many publishers find that they can survive audits more effectively and cost efficiently if they are working with a service that can provide all or most of the data required to complete the audit. In short, a fulfillment service can truly be an interested and useful partner in your circulation effort. Selecting a fulfillment service today can go far beyond the need to maintain a list and produce mailing labels.

## PRINT ORDER PROJECTIONS

The circulation director is responsible for the number of copies of a magazine that are ordered from the printer for each issue. The publisher of a paid circulation magazine will want no fewer than a specific number of paid copies for each issue. They will have been distributed to subscribers via mail and sold to readers via newsstands and other stores. The subscriber file is in a state of continual change, so the circulation director must consider the number of names that are likely to be dropped from the file for this issue. This is composed primarily of those who ordered a subscription but have not paid. Subscriptions from current promotion efforts must also be considered. The newsstand draw is also changing regularly based on reports from the newsstand distributor. Then there are complimentary copies used to promote advertising sales based on a dynamic list of names. In short, numerous details must be considered to construct an accurate number of copies to be printed. Considering the cost of printing, binding, and shipping, an accurate count is essential.

For controlled circulation publications the job of calculating a print order is usually much simpler. The size of the print order does not change significantly from one issue to the next. The qualified circulation goal is affected by removals from the list because of changes in job assignments, but more often than not these are accompanied by an added name from the same company. Methods are used to help maintain the qualified circulation goal, such as keeping new names in a pending file awaiting orders to remove names so that offsetting entries can be made.

# POSTAL REGULATIONS

Inattention to postal regulations can affect the cost and speed of delivery of magazines to subscribers. Most publications aim to be delivered by second-class mail. In order to qualify for second-class mail, a magazine must be paid for or, in the case of controlled circulation, the magazine must have at least 50 percent of its subscribers directly requesting the publication. If the requirements for second-class postal service are not met, the magazine will use third-class service, which is more costly, and delivery is slower. The postal service provides certain discounts to publishers if they make the job easier for the postal service. For example, presorting and bar coding help to speed the magazine through the processing operation; the postal service recognizes this by providing these discounts.

The postal service also regulates what can be mailed with a magazine. Before a publisher decides to ship a magazine in a polybag containing other material, it is essential that the postal regulations be checked to be sure the mailing class is not negatively affected. This is an area in which significant sums of money can be saved or wasted based on knowledge of the postal regulations and system. Smaller publishers that use an outside service for their magazine fulfillment often find that the fulfillment house can provide the expert knowledge they need when a question arises about postal service regulations.

## CASE STUDY
### Ski Country Publishing Company

Bryan Burton was majority owner and president of Ski Country Publishing Company. The company began six years ago, when Burton, who had been a West Coast editor in the San Francisco office of a national magazine, decided it was time to pursue his dream. Burton had grown up in Colorado and spent much of his leisure time on skis. Skiing was a growth industry, so with the help of some private investors he launched a monthly magazine, *Ski Enthusiast*. The magazine took longer than Burton anticipated to turn a profit, but in its third year was profitable, with a paid circulation of more than 200,000.

Realizing that many of *Ski Enthusiast*'s advertisers were interested in promoting their products to ski shops, Burton started a trade magazine, *Ski Trade News*, for ski shops. He compiled a list of shops and launched *Ski Trade News* with seven issues annually and controlled circulation of 25,000. *Ski Trade News* was in the black in its second year.

Ski resorts in most parts of the United States have a short season. The weather also plays an important role in determining whether a season produces a profit or loss. To offset these challenges, many resorts developed golf and tennis facilities to encourage their skiers to return in warmer weather and thus provide year-round income possibilities. Burton started the magazine *Golf and Tennis for Skiers*. The publication was distributed through arrangements with major ski resorts in public lodging rooms in the resort areas. The resorts were extended a free page of advertising in each issue in exchange for their cooperation and endorsement

The early days of Ski Country Publishing Company were a struggle. At times there were serious questions about its viability. Burton had made many personal sacrifices to survive. Now in its sixth year, Ski Country Publishing Company was a thriving company. Burton had made a point of hiring first-rate personnel. As the company grew, the offices and salaries improved. An attraction to many prospective head office employees was the lifestyle associated with living in the foothills of the Rocky Mountains. Burton was able to buy out his initial investors, garnering them a handsome profit on their investment. An East Coast sales office was opened to serve that advertising community, and a full-time editor had been added in Vermont. West Coast and Midwest sales and editorial were covered from the Colorado office. The company had become known for first-rate editorial and effective sales and marketing.

While Burton was building the company he learned much about finance, management, marketing, and distribution the hard way, through his experience. He devoured books and magazine articles about these topics. He subscribed to all the major business magazines.

At the beginning of each year Burton held a meeting with his key managers to discuss the company's progress and explore the future. Now that he had a taste of success, Burton wanted to build on it. As the group discussed the past, Burton commented on his own learning experiences and realized that none of the magazines he read zeroed in on the needs of the entrepreneur who is building a company from nothing or from a small base. Most of the editorial in the publications he had read was directed toward management in larger, more established companies. This led to a lively discussion about the need for a magazine directed to the smaller growing company. As the hours passed the level of enthusiasm grew to a fever pitch. Everyone in attendance thought the idea was a winner. Burton agreed to a quick study of the potential with a task force comprised of Shelagh Dempsey, the vice president of advertising sales, Alan Pierce, the vice president of circulation, and Connor Jachino, chief financial officer. Burton, represented the editorial function. The task force would report back to the management group in 30 days.

At the next meeting Alan Pierce reported that from census data and other sources he had learned that small and midsize growing companies outnumbered large companies by a wide margin. In fact, this preliminary research indicated that the universe was at least 10 million. Additionally, focus groups were conducted and the editorial need was confirmed in each group. Shelagh Dempsey stated that the circulation would need to be at least 300,000 to attract national advertising. Burton suggested that 400,000 circulation be the working number. The management group unanimously agreed that there was a sizable underserved market here and therefore a unique opportunity for the company.

Pierce provided details demonstrating that paid circulation of 400,000 would cost approximately $9 million to acquire (two percent net return rate from 20 million pieces mailed and $450 per thousand for promotional packages and postage). Assuming a $15 subscription price, the income would be $6 million for a net outlay of $3 million. He also provided a report showing that a list of 400,000 could be compiled for under $1 million. With some breaks the list could be as low as $500,000. All these costs were for circulation alone. There would also be the cost of assembling the staff, and printing, binding, and postage.

Jachino provided schedules demonstrating the profit level at various advertising page levels for both paid and controlled circulation. The controlled circulation version showed that profitability could be reached much sooner because of the lower costs. Over a five-year period, paid circulation had a clear edge. Burton admitted that he was attracted to the controlled version because the paid version would be betting the company that the magazine would be a winner.

Dempsey countered that a controlled circulation publication would have the salesforce working with one hand tied behind their backs. The categories of advertising they were targeting did not have a history of accepting magazines with controlled circulation. In fact, just the opposite—they tended not to purchase space in controlled circulation publications.

Burton put forward another option. All were convinced that they could produce an outstanding editorial product. What if they launched the publication on a controlled circulation basis with 400,000 subscribers and at the end of the first year began a process to convert the readers to paid subscribers? This would establish the magazine as one of top editorial service and quality, one that the management of a growing business could not do without. Along the way a stream of revenue would be provided by advertising, helping to keep the investment costs in an area of risk that would be more tenable, should the venture fail. Pierce said there was no precedent for this approach, so the number of subscribers that would convert to paid would be speculative. On the other hand, the company had solid experience with both paid and controlled circulation, so the mechanics of dealing with the program would not be a problem. Dempsey said that while selling advertising in a controlled circulation publication would be challenging, she felt that the salespersons would be capable of working under these conditions provided they did not extend beyond one year.

So the management group is faced with three alternatives. One is to take the lower-risk route via a controlled circulation magazine; another is to take the high-risk route of paid circulation; and the third is to gamble on the company's ability to produce a first-rate product that could be converted successfully from controlled circulation to paid circulation? Which will it be.

## NOTES

[1] Barbara Love, "Circulator: You Can Survive Disasters," *Folio:*, October 1, 1994, 10.

[2] *Folio: Plus*, "Over-Designed Insert Cards Kill Response," November 1, 1994, 10.

[3] Lisa E. Phillips, "Battle for the Newsstand," *Folio:*, March 15, 1994, 67.

[4] Richard M. Koff, *Strategic Planning for Magazine Executives*, 2nd ed. (Stamford, Conn., Folio: Magazine Publishing Corporation, 1987), 101.

[5] Julie A. Johnson, "O.J. Scores Again On '95 Covers," *Advertising Age*, January 1, 1996, 6.

[6] *The New York Times*, May 20, 1995.

[7] Chris Kalamon, "Your Fulfillment Service, Resource Central," *Folio:*, January 1, 1994, 39.

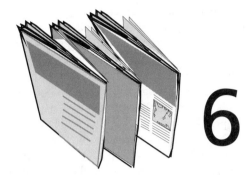

# 6

# Advertising Sales

## THE JOY OF SALES

This past spring, Jane Hocker felt as exhilarated as at any time she could remember. Jane had just completed her first year as account representative for *Attorney at Law,* a monthly magazine. Far more important than that milestone was the receipt of a contract for a spread (two facing pages) in each issue from a top automobile account. This was the first time in its 10-year history that the magazine carried any automotive advertising, and she had been the one to sell the new account. She was basking in glowing praise from her boss, the advertising sales director, and from the publisher himself about her triumph. It took the full year to convince the client and the advertising agency of the merits of advertising their product in *Attorney at Law,* but now it was worth the many weeks of phone calls, personal calls, and the extensive collection of data needed to prepare the numerous presentations she had made. Plus, the commission on the sale would pay the rent for many months. Jane had learned quickly that selling advertising space was a unique experience. She was challenged to know all there was to learn about her magazine, the market it served, and about the marketing challenges faced by her clients and prospects. Her job called for creativity, marketing savvy, and resourcefulness. It was challenging and she loved it.

Very few magazines can survive economically from circulation income alone. Most regard advertising space sales to be the primary source of revenue. In fact, the trade publications that circulate on a controlled basis are entirely dependent on the sale of advertising space. Any magazine selling advertising to outside companies engages in a marketing approach distinct from its marketing to readers. This marketing approach is referred to as advertising sales, and encompasses all efforts to convince manufacturers, service companies, and advertising agencies of the magazine's value as a medium to get an advertising message to a select audience.

Advertising is also the third leg in the three-legged stool on which the magazine's business operations rest. A successful selling effort depends upon the solidity of the other legs of editorial and circulation. The advertising department must be able to make a strong, compelling argument about who their readers are, why they are buying the magazine, and how many of them are buying.

Selling advertising space for a magazine is a complicated, intangible process. Essentially, a publisher is offering a blank page within a magazine, promising that a reasonable number of the readers with specific demographic characteristics will be exposed to the page as they read the publication. The more readers a magazine satisfies and the time a reader spends reading a publication are indications of the chances for exposure of an ad and are essential to advertisers. Many millions of dollars have been and are being spent to attempt to determine the effects of advertising. We know that advertising works, but how much should be spent and where it should be spent are less than an exact science. Any business owner asks such questions about the effect of advertising: If I double my advertising expenditure, will my sales double? If they won't double, how much will they increase? If I spend half as much as I am currently spending on advertising, how much money in sales will I lose? The answers are elusive. And similar questions plague every magazine publisher and advertiser.

Those who make their living in the advertising business are well aware that advertising in magazines works. The Magazine Publishers of America regularly reports on the impact of magazine advertising, and has a developed an advertising campaign of testimonials by people who have seen first-hand the value of magazine advertisements. A 1995 study conducted by Video Storyboard Tests of New York suggested consumers consider print ads more entertaining and less offensive than television advertising. That study showed more consumers considered print ads "artistic," "entertaining" and "enjoyable."[1]

Yet the frustration remains when trying to pin down the precise effect of print advertising. Besides the page or pages on which an ad appears in a magazine there are other variables that can affect the response to advertising in a publication. Do readers need this product? Does it live up to the promise made in the advertising? Is the advertising attractive and compelling enough to capture the attention of the reader? Many of the elements of a successful magazine ad are beyond the influence of the publication. So what does the salesperson sell? A sales staff wants to demonstrate that their magazine—with its unique editorial characteristics—delivers readers who are likely purchasers of a product or service. They want to show that this can be done at a competitive, reasonable cost. This demands using circulation, advertising rate, and readership data to convince advertisers and prospects—at the same time the competition is trying to prove the same thing: that its magazine provides appropriate readers at a good price.

As competition increases, more and more magazine publishers are realizing that they must look upon themselves as important solutions or part of the solutions to a marketer's challenge or problem. Their goal is to be an advertising or marketing partner with the client. This will be discussed more fully later in this chapter.

## ADVERTISING DEPARTMENT ORGANIZATION

The volume of advertising revenue and the number of advertising pages published in a magazine have a direct bearing on the size and organization of the advertising department. In addition to the advertising sales director, magazine sales organizations can include regional managers, category managers, sales representatives, independent sales representatives, a sales promotion director, and, sometimes, a marketing director. At large publications (those with circulation well over one million), the advertising sales director oversees these managers, who, in turn, oversees individual salespeople and representatives.

As we've seen, the vast majority of magazines have revenues under $10 million. Of all the magazines published annually in the United States (a figure that is estimated at 22,000), only 54 sell more than $50 million of advertising space, and overall only 257 enjoy advertising revenue greater than $10 million.[2] Since most consumer and trade publications have advertising revenue of under $10 million, the advertising sales director is often also responsible for the planning and execution of the sales function and execution of the marketing plan.

Smaller publications have an advertising department consisting entirely of sales representatives reporting directly to the advertising sales director. The very small magazines (those with a circulation of 200,000 or less) are likely to have a publisher who doubles as the advertising sales director.

Naturally, exceptions abound. In 1990, Hachette Filipacchi (which publishes 23 magazines and had annual revenues of nearly $800 million) reorganized the corporate sales staff, with salespeople selling their categories of advertising for all the company's magazines. For instance, salespeople for *Car and Driver* and *Road and Track* (with strong contacts and relationships in the automotive industry) would sell automobile ads for the company's noncar titles, such as *Elle, Boating, Yachting,* and *Flying.*[3]

## ADVERTISING SALES DIRECTOR

The head of the department is usually called the advertising sales director, but other titles might also be used: vice president of advertising, associate publisher/advertis-

ADVERTISING SALES DEPARTMENT
SMALL PUBLICATION

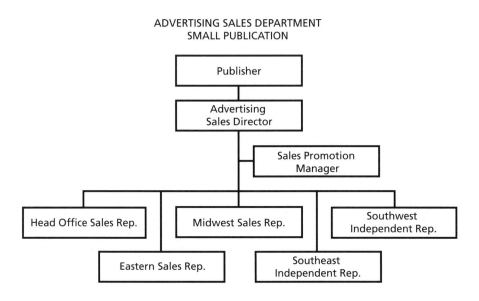

ing director, advertising director, national sales manager, or sales manager. It is a job requiring sophisticated selling skills and personnel management, as well as a thorough understanding of business, publishing, and marketing.

Here's an outline of the advertising sales director's responsibilities:

- Revenue estimates.
- Development of the publication's short-term sales strategy.
- Management oversight of the personal sales operation. This includes the hiring and firing of sales personnel; sales training; sales compensation; relationships with clients and their advertising agencies, particularly where problems exist; contracts and relations with independent sales representatives; and planning and conducting sales meetings.
- Sales promotion. This includes development of major presentations for salespeople; assisting salespeople in the development of special presentations; and development and updating of sales promotion material; planning and coordinating special events; and recommendations for marketing and media research projects.

ADVERTISING SALES DEPARTMENT
LARGE PUBLICATION

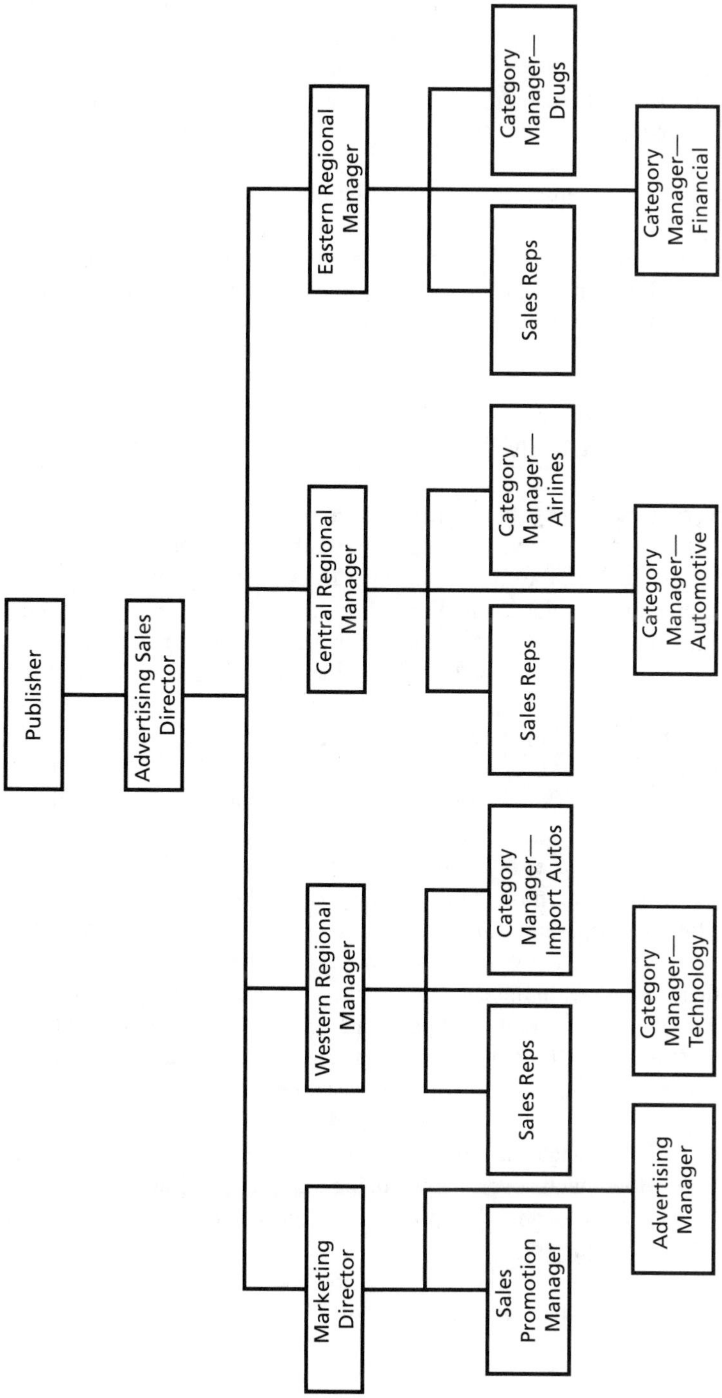

At many publications, the advertising sales director is also responsible for marketing the magazine. That is, he or she directs the effort to enhance awareness of the magazine in the marketplace—the objective being to get advertisers to buy more pages. If so, he or she may be responsible for the following, usually with significant input from the publisher:

- Development of the advertising campaign and placement in appropriate media
- Development of direct marketing campaigns and materials
- Public relations that have an impact on the advertising effort
- Development of market affinity programs
- Oversight of market and media research

## REVENUE ESTIMATES

Every department of a magazine takes part in the annual planning for the coming year and up to five years hence. While the publisher is responsible for the entire plan and budget, the advertising sales director is responsible for accurately estimating the advertising revenue based on his or her projections of the number of ad pages that can be sold for the coming business year. Advertising rates are also reviewed during this process, in conjunction with the publisher. Rate increases and adjustments, if any, are established to arrive at the rates that will be charged in the year ahead. Also, the advertising sales director will develop the expense budget for his or her areas of responsibility. This usually includes sales compensation plans, the cost of sales promotion and presentations, and the cost of attending and exhibiting at trade shows.

The revenue estimate is crucial to the operation because it will influence the level of spending throughout the magazine's departments and, of course, the profit or loss from operations. Advertising sales directors base the revenue estimate on the state of the economy, sales history, current account status, and competition from other magazines in the category and from other media. Each salesperson is expected to produce an estimate of page sales on an account-by-account basis.

It is essential that the advertising sales director have an intimate knowledge of the current circumstances with each account, such as:

- Is the magazine's market a target for their product—or should it be a target?
- How much advertising is being placed with direct and indirect competition?
- Is it reasonable to expect that the magazine can take some pages from direct competitors?
- Are they advertising with us now?
- How buoyant is their business?

- Will they increase or decrease their advertising budget?
- What is the salesperson's track record as an estimator of advertising sales pages?

When projecting advertising sales, salespeople approach the challenge with attitudes ranging from conservative to optimistic. Their compensation is often attached to annual revenue or page quotas. Some salespersons are likely to keep their estimates on the conservative side, anticipating that their quota might be based on their page estimate. Other factors can affect the reliability of salespersons' estimates, such as their level of experience with their accounts. The advertising sales directors need to know the history and status of accounts as well as the salespersons' inclinations so that they can make sensible adjustments to their estimates.

## DEVELOPMENT OF THE SHORT-TERM SALES STRATEGY

The short-term sales strategy for the magazine will be based on the economy, conditions in the advertising category, and competition. The primary objective never changes: to get as many of the advertising dollars as possible. Selling one's magazine as the publication of choice is always a good idea. In good economic times, advertising budgets tend to be larger, and more magazines in a category may enjoy part of a client's business. Convincing clients to put the bulk of their dollars in your magazine would be the goal. In leaner economic times the goal might be to use your magazine exclusively. From this strategy flows the general theme and primary selling proposition that will be featured in advertising, sales promotion, direct mail, and general presentations. There may be subthemes that are targeted at specific categories of advertisers. *National Geographic* sees the travel business as a likely prospect, so it produced ads that ran in 1995 featuring destinations that it covers editorially. The selling message of those advertisements was "We send their minds. Their bodies will soon follow."

## ACCOUNT-BY-ACCOUNT STRATEGY

Most magazines operate according to an 80-20 rule. That is, 80 percent of the business comes from 20 percent of the account and prospect list. Routinely, the advertising sales director must review the status and sales strategy for every account currently running with the magazine and direct competitors. He or she needs to agree with the salesperson on the priorities for managing the sales territory. These questions might include:

- What accounts are the primary and secondary prospects?
- Who is the decision maker and who are the important influencers at each account?
- Who at the account must be called on regularly?
- What is the extent of the advertising agency's influence on media buying?
- Who will respond best to entertainment at lunch, dinner, sports events, or an evening at the theater?

All this information is important to the estimating process but is always subject to change, so it must be reviewed on a regular schedule as part of the management oversight of the sales department.

## MANAGEMENT OVERSIGHT OF THE PERSONAL SALES OPERATION

The advertising sales director is responsible for hiring and maintaining the sales organization at top effectiveness and efficiency, consistent with the hiring policy. To be successful there is no substitute for a well-trained, professional sales organization composed of the following:

### *Sales representatives*

The sales representative is responsible for maximizing the sale of the advertising space potential in his or her territory. Accounts are assigned by geographic area or, in larger markets where there are a number of salespeople, by specific account assignments. These assignments are determined by the advertising sales director. Ideally, salespeople are or become experts in their publication, the market or markets it serves, and advertising and marketing principles. The very best are creative and can give their clients ideas to help solve marketing challenges. They can carry on knowledgeable conversations about advertising and its effects. They know their magazine inside and out. They can talk about the quality of the editorial and why it is effective in serving the reader's needs. The result is, therefore, an outstanding advertising medium. A top-notch salesperson can demonstrate the value of the magazine's audience to an advertising prospect on a moment's notice.

### *Regional managers*

Regional managers will have direct supervision over salespeople in their office. For example, a large Chicago-based magazine is likely to have a regional sales manager directing sales operations out of its New York City, Los Angeles, Dallas, and Atlanta offices, as well as the main office.

### Category managers

Larger-revenue publications have category managers. These managers become expert in particular lines of business. The automotive category is important to most consumer magazines. Thus, an auto category manager will be an important presence in that industry. He or she will attend auto shows and maintain high-level relationships with the client and the advertising agency. In many instances they will be the primary consultant to sales management for sales aids, research programs, and sales promotion program ideas for the market in which they specialize. The results of their efforts are used by other members of the sales staff, who call on auto manufacturers and their advertising agencies.

### Sales promotion director

The sales promotion director is responsible for providing daily and long-term support services for the advertising department. That includes overseeing every message or announcement that an advertiser gets about the magazine through mailings, special events, media kits, special presentations, gifts, contests, and other marketing services.

### Marketing director

Larger consumer magazines often have a marketing director, who is responsible for the advertising and sales promotion efforts. General interest magazines will advertise in trade publications such as *Advertising Age*. However, many can benefit from broader ad programs that will use cable and local TV, drive-time radio, and other publications that are likely to reach their advertising audience. Business publications such as *Business Week* and *Fortune* can reach many in their target audience by sponsoring stock market and other financial reports featured on radio and cable TV. This broader activity demands more experience with general advertising and promotion and, thus, a position and department that go significantly beyond direct mail programs and sales support activities.

## Hiring and Firing

Different magazines have different requirements for hiring. Very few magazine publishers have formal training programs, so, more often than not, they are looking for some experience. Some believe sales representatives should have experience in the particular category. A person from the travel industry might be favored by a magazine for travel agents. Some like the candidate to have advertising sales experience. A few feel that persons with sales experience from a larger marketer can bring the benefits associated with formal sales training that most large companies offer on a regular basis. Rarely is formal education a primary requirement. Persons with limited experience seeking to enter advertising space sales find that trade publications are easier to break into than consumer publications.

For each salesperson there will be a sales target developed in the estimating process described above. The advertising sales director must monitor sales activity, on an account-by-account basis, to be sure sales goals are being reached. If sales are falling short of expectations, the advertising sales director needs to help determine the reason and develop an appropriate strategy.

There are a variety of extenuating circumstances that could be all or part of the reason. Because of a trade dispute, in June 1995 extreme tariffs were imposed by the government on Japanese luxury automobiles. This led to a cessation of advertising for these cars (the trade dispute was eventually settled). Salespeople who had one of these brands on their account list could not be faulted because the advertising target fell short.

Many advertising sales directors use share of market as an important measure of a salesperson's effectiveness. If one or more of the competitive magazines gets more of an advertiser's business and this is not the case with other sales territories, it is likely that there is a problem with the salesperson's effectiveness. A salesperson who is ineffective will usually have difficulty meeting targets in more than one account. It is up to the advertising sales director to help the salesperson improve in areas of weakness. If all efforts to help are for naught, the advertising sales director must terminate the salesperson.

## Sales Training

Sales training can be formal and informal. Formal sales training is often offered as part of a sales meeting, or a salesperson may be enrolled in open seminars offered by outside companies. Informal sales training is a routine part of the advertising sales director's job. Much of his or her time is spent in the field making calls with salespersons.

The advertising sales director will be observing and evaluating:

- The salesperson's rapport with the individuals called on
- Whether the salesperson is gaining access to key decision makers
- The salesperson's knowledge of the account and its advertising goals
- Execution of the account strategy

After each joint call or at day's end the advertising sales director should critique the salesperson on each of these areas and suggest ways the salesperson can improve. With close contact the advertising sales director is best able to judge the value of the salesperson to the sales organization over the long haul.

## Sales Compensation

Sales representatives are compensated with a salary, salary and commission, or salary and bonus. Compensation varies by circulation, frequency of publication, annual ad pages, annual ad revenue, region of the country, and personal experience. The commission—or bonus—is intended to create an incentive to stimulate sales representatives to meet and exceed their goals. Annually, *Folio:* magazine conducts compensation surveys and publishes the results. A sample of the results of the 1995 survey for sales representatives' total compensation is shown in Table 6.1. The survey also reported that the average annual commission was $26,020 overall, $32,296 for consumer magazines and $19,427 for trade publications.[4]

There is no simple formula for the payment of commissions. Some are paid on the number of pages sold, others on ad revenue or share of market, and still others on a combination of factors. If a magazine is second or lower in its category, the advertising sales director might decide that a special commission for new business acquired would help to achieve the sales objective. Some advertising managers are paid a commission on what their sales staff brings in. Commissions are paid on year-over-year increases or on a quota that is established annually. The latter is useful when the economy is down or stagnant and an increase in pages and ad revenue is unlikely. It can provide an incentive even though sales may be lower. On the other hand, sales representatives often feel that it is used by management in good times to put a lid on commission potential. A few magazines pay a bonus in addition to salary. These are based on subjective criteria related to the salesperson's responsibility. It might include factors such as the development of new business, increases in advertising schedules from particular accounts, and general sales skills.

## CLIENT RELATIONSHIPS

Each sales representative is responsible for maintaining and improving client relationships as a fundamental part of his or her job. Nevertheless, the advertising sales director normally has personally established high-level contacts and can be a source of help for newer salespeople. Client relationships are important in every business, but especially so in advertising space sales because of the intangible nature of the

**TABLE 6.1  Sales representatives' salary survey by type of magazine and annual advertising revenue**

| By Annual Ad Revenue | Average | Average Trade | Average Consumer |
|---|---|---|---|
| Up to $999,999 | $53,545 | $65,597 | $42,943 |
| $1 million to $2,999,999 | $52,635 | $68,646 | $42,943 |
| $3 million to $8,999,999 | $75,322 | $80,318 | $66,416 |
| $9 million or more | $99,443 | $103,211 | * |

*Not enough respondents to report accurate results.

Source: *Folio:*

product being sold. Employees at advertising agencies and clients are extremely busy and meetings can be dificult to arrange. A salesperson must establish a reputation for creativity, credibility, and service to be able to make appointments. The advertising sales director needs to encourage sales representatives to call for help when they are having trouble getting to see someone, especially if that person is a decision maker or key influencer.

The advertising sales director will have established relationships at the higher levels of the client and advertising agency. It is not unusual for the advertising sales director to be acquainted with the president of both the company and the advertising agency. These relationships are particularly important when a problem arises at an account. The problem can be as simple as a complaint about the reproduction quality of an ad or as complex as having run an article that is critical of a company or its products. In 1994, Disney discontinued its advertising in all Time Inc. magazines because of advertising that Time Warner had run for Six Flags, Time Warner's own theme parks. Disney maintained that the ads were an insult to their organization. Negotiations to solve a problem of this magnitude would be conducted at very high management levels.

## Independent Sales Representatives

For the majority of magazines, advertisers and potential advertisers are concentrated in geographic areas of the country. The automotive industry is concentrated in Detroit and on the West Coast. The personal computer industry is concentrated on the West Coast, Massachusetts, and Texas. In areas with a smaller, but important, concentration of business a magazine may not be economically able to justify a full-time representative. A full-time salesperson from another company office may be able to spend sufficient time in the location to sell and service accounts. For example, a publication with an important concentration of potential business in Salt Lake City may choose to have a representative from their Chicago or San Francisco office cover the area.

Most magazines will have areas of the country or the world where there is insufficient sales potential to justify a full-time sales representative. This is where independent sales representatives come in. Independent sales representatives may operate alone or as part of any firm. They are experienced professionals who have decided that their contacts in a particular area of the country and in specific markets in that area are substantial enough that they can sell their services to national magazines. They will have contracts with a number of magazines, but none that are competitors. Independent sales representatives are contracted for a specific period of time at an agreed commission rate, which ranges from 10 percent to 20 percent. They pay all of their own expenses but are provided sales promotion materials just as a full-time salesperson would be. Except for the contractual relationship, independent sales representatives are dealt with as though they are company-employed salespersons. Independent sales representatives provide a valuable service. The problem for them comes with success. The more successful they are, the more likely that a full-time salesperson can be justified by the advertising sales director.

## Classified Advertising

Many magazines find a classified advertising section to be another rich source of revenue. This section is usually positioned toward the back of the publication. The charge for a classified ad is by the word or the column inch. This can be a useful service to both readers and small advertisers. The ads are generally appealing to special needs of the readers. For example, in growth markets like the computer industry there are help-wanted ads, and many city magazines find personal ads to be popular. Individual classified ads are not the responsibility of the primary salesforce. There simply is not sufficient revenue per ad to justify their time in this area. Some magazines do not solicit the advertising on a personal basis, instead relying on the attractiveness of the service to bring advertising "over the transom." Others will have a staffer use the phone to solicit and follow up on classified advertising. Some magazines do not accept classified advertising at all on the premise that it cheapens the publication.

## MARKET AFFINITY PROGRAMS

More and more magazine publishers are recognizing the need to position their publication as the core of a broader approach to the market or markets they serve. This means taking advantage of the unique opportunities the publication offers to reach and serve the market beyond simply providing an advertising medium through the pages of the magazine. Meredith Corp. publishes such well-known magazines as *Better Homes and Gardens* and *Ladies' Home Journal*. Bill Kerr, the president of Meredith, was quoted saying, "Much of our industry thinks of derived products as the 4 percent or 5 percent tail you might add on to the basic product. Not us. For every dollar of revenue we generate from *Better Homes and Gardens*, we generate another $1.05 from derived products, whether it's books carrying the *Better Homes and Gardens* name, new magazines for the *Better Homes and Gardens* audience, or licensing deals." [5]

One example of this approach is Cahner's Child Care Group, publisher of *American Baby, Childbirth, First Year of Life,* and *Healthy Kids. American Baby* is a monthly publication directed at expectant and new parents who are first-time parents with children up to two years of age. *Childbirth*, published twice annually, serves expectant mothers who attend childbirth classes. *First Year of Life* is published three times a year as a development guide to the baby's first year of life. *Healthy Kids* is published six times each year to help parents in the healthy development of their child in its early years. The latter is published in collaboration with the American Academy of Pediatricians. These publications represent market segmentation at its finest. Consider the very short window of opportunity advertisers of products specific to a baby's needs have to reach their market. For most products age does not limit the time marketers have to get their product adopted. In this field, however, there is a very brief time span in which to develop a brand and the resulting purchase. The Child Care Group provides the audience precision and time the advertisers need to establish their brand.

Beyond the magazines, the database of names has unusual value to a direct mail marketer. The Child Care Group serves the advertiser's need further by delivering sample packs to new mothers. Advertisers pay for the opportunity to include their product in the sample packs. But the Child Care Group goes even further. Two cable television programs are produced by this group and aired on the Family Channel. This is but one of numerous examples of how publishers are expanding their horizons, looking beyond their basic business and seizing profitable opportunities to be partners with their advertisers.

## PROMOTIONAL GOALS

A rash assumption is that advertisers and ad agencies know your magazine and its market so well that there is little more to say. Magazines and their markets are far more complex than they appear at first glance and therefore one cannot assume anything about an advertiser's familiarity with them. Sales promotion will demonstrate to advertisers the value of the magazine's:

- Audience demographics and psychographics
- Circulation
- Readership
- Editorial
- Market served

### Audience

Reader profiles are important to advertisers to convince and assure them that they are reaching their target audience. Research, either done by an outside firm or conducted by the magazine's research department, will provide demographic and psychographic data for all or part of the audience. Often this data is positioned to demonstrate superiority over the characteristics of a competitor's audience. Advertisers to consumers will want to know the typical reader's age, sex, education, income level, family status, and other characteristics. To add information on lifestyle is a plus. How many cars does he or she own? What kinds and brands of products do they buy? Trade publications will need to provide, in addition to some of the data mentioned above, information about the person's employer or business, length of time he or she has been working, purchasing responsibility, and job function and title. The latter is often useful in determining the level of influence or decision-making capability the person may have relative to the type of product being advertised.

## Circulation

Circulation data are contained in the magazine audit statement, conducted by either the Audit Bureau of Circulations, Inc. or the Business Publications Audit International, Inc. In either case the information collected can result in promotable differences for competing magazines. If a competitor is getting a large number of subscribers because of a premium offer, that might be something to be highlighted or featured in circulation promotion to demonstrate that your publication is more readily accepted by subscribers for its editorial value and does not need to be hyped by premium offers. Thus it can be presented as a superior advertising vehicle.

The number of purchasers of the magazine is a promotable factor. However, more does not necessarily mean better. More important is the demographic profile and additional lifestyle data developed through market research that would convince advertisers that all or a major part of the circulation is a likely prospect for their products. Many publications do very well by demonstrating that although their circulation is lower than a competitor's, the reader demographics are superior for particular categories of products. Conversely, if a magazine about the purchasing function in medium-to-large companies circulates among the purchasing management, it would appear to cover the target audience rather well. A competing publication might well add an engineering function or two on the grounds that they are significant influencers on the product being purchased.

## Readership

Proving the breadth and depth of readership might seem unnecessary for a magazine that circulates on a paid basis. However, circulation data can understate or overstate actual readership. Readers who do not subscribe (pass-along readers) can be as valuable to an advertiser as the buyer of the magazine. Research can uncover the characteristics of pass-along readers, adding to the value of the magazine to an advertiser. Some pass-along readers can be regular readers of a publication. In the consumer area it might be a family member of a subscriber. In the trade market the pass-along reader might be one to whom a publication is routed.

Conversely, there are magazines to which the public subscribes for reasons other than the information that the magazine provides. For example, some publications are considered status symbols. Many intellectual magazines fall into this category. A person may like to have the publication visible in their home but rarely reads it. In this latter situation the circulation statement is overstating the number of actual readers.

Selling points can be developed from other reader behavior, such as:

- A preference for the magazine over competing magazines
- The amount of time a reader spends with each issue, as a measure of the likelihood of exposure to an ad page
- The length of time the reader has been a subscriber or receiver of the publication as a measure of the value of the editorial and of reader loyalty
- Where the magazine is most commonly read as a determinant of the importance the reader places on the publication and the depth of readership
- Requests for reprints and the reader's use of other service activities

Simmons Market Research Bureau (SMRB) and Mediamark Research Inc. (MRI) are two rival companies that conduct measured audience studies for magazine publishers. Both use "through-the-book" methods by which respondents flip through the entire magazine to explain how much they actually read. Advertising agencies and media buying services count heavily on data from Simmons and Mediamark Research Inc. for statistical information on magazine readership. Information is gathered for all the larger consumer magazines and some smaller ones. In all, about 200 magazines are included. By their agreement to participate in the studies, magazines suggest their commitment to the results.

Demographic, purchasing, and magazine reading data is collected from a statistically acceptable sample and projected to the universe (all men and women between ages 18 and 34 is an example of a universe). Both companies use a similar approach. Questionnaires are completed by those in the sample and the answers tabulated. The demographic data includes information such as age, gender, marital status, education, and income. The respondents indicate whether they are regular or occasional users of many categories of products. They also respond regarding their readership of magazines, again indicating whether they are regular, occasional, or nonreaders of the magazines under study, whether they subscribe or purchase the magazine regularly, and how much time they spend reading the publication.

An important measure that is developed in this research is the number of pass-along readers. These are persons who read the magazine but do not purchase it. An example would be a man who subscribes to *Business Week* and whose wife or adult child reads the same copy. It is not unusual for general interest magazines to have two or more pass-along readers.

Magazines that are part of one of the research services base of publications can order a breakdown of special data to satisfy specific situations. If *TV Guide* was soliciting business from a client whose product was targeted toward women between the ages of 18 and 49 who have attended or graduated from college, they would be at a significant disadvantage comparing their total circulation against that of one of the women's magazines like *Family Circle*. What they would do in this case is order a report from the research service with which they participate showing their average audience for this particular group as compared to magazines directed toward women, and any other competitors they might choose.

As with most research of this type, publications are not always happy with the results. They may find their scores lower than expected in a particular category. Such controversy is routine, but the services still manage to maintain their importance. In some instances, publications supplement this research with data they collect on their audience, particularly if the sample for their category is small.

## Editorial

The editorial pages attract readers who are the target for the advertiser's message. The informational, educational, or entertainment value of the publication is fulfilled through the editorial. Numerous parts of the total editorial package can be expanded upon to show why the reader is satisfied and to distinguish the editorial from the competition. A well-read magazine provides greater ad page exposure potential.

Here are some examples:

- Credentials of the editor and staff
- Testimonials and letters to the editor that show reader reliance, involvement and the credibility of the editorial matter
- Superior use of graphics and how data is made easier to grasp for readers
- Awards earned by the editors and art department
- Proof of authenticity, like having editors or articles paraphrased or quoted in publications of national stature

## Market

Advertisers must be convinced that a market consists of likely buyers for their product. Packaged goods, proprietary drugs, and automobiles are purchased by the masses, so advertising in mass circulation publications makes obvious sense. The overwhelming majority of magazines are not mass circulation. In fact the reason d`être for most magazines is that they can offer an advertiser a market with very clearly defined characteristics. Subscribers to *Bon Appetit* are sure to be interested in cooking. Readers of *Advertising Age* are sure to have an interest in advertising and marketing.

Beyond simply being able to demonstrate the viability of a market for an advertiser, many publishers spend large amounts of time and money to get to know their market in great depth and detail. Often a publisher's research will result in enhancing the credibility of the magazine. In some instances, profit-making opportunities are created by the sale of research results or a well-defined mailing list that can be sold to companies that use direct mail marketing. Various characteristics are used to show the value of a market to advertisers, including:

- Demographic and psychographic data
- The rate of growth, both historical and expected
- Buying patterns
- Current product use
- The attitude of the market toward early adoption of new products
- Developing needs

# PROMOTION MEDIA

## Media Kits

A magazine's media kit is a basic collection of information about the magazine presented in an attractive package. Designed and executed correctly, the media kit serves to strengthen the magazine's image, positioning it clearly in the minds of advertisers. When an advertising agency calls for information, usually the first thing it asks for is the media kit. At minimum, the media kit will include the rate card and the latest audit bureau statement. Most magazines seize this opportunity to include information that will demonstrate the strength of the publication. It is not unusual to have some research data demonstrating the superiority of the magazine versus those of competitors. Usually, the media kit and the information it contains are flexible enough so that salespeople can adapt the information for particular categories of advertisers and individual clients.

Here's a partial list of typical media kit elements:

- Rate card
- Editorial mission statement
- Editorial calendar
- Audit bureau statement on circulation
- Readership breakdown, along with information on reader responsiveness
- Information on the size and growth of the market the magazine serves
- Information on merchandising and promotional services

### Sales Presentations

Major advertisers and advertising agencies will subscribe to one or more of the syndicated readership services, such as Simmons and Mediamark Research Inc. An important part of the advertising sales director's job is analyzing and identifying those characteristics of the magazine that are unique. No two direct competitors are the same. The differences can be a demographic or a psychographic characteristic. Usually the differences are based on the editorial approach, encompassing many factors including graphics, types of articles, departments, editorial writing style, and length of articles. Therefore the advertising sales director must know the various characteristics of the publication and the audience to be able to make distinctions that are important to a potential advertiser. Once identifying the unique characteristics, the advertising sales director's challenge is to help the salespeople to develop presentation materials that, with flair and imagination, clearly show how these characteristics will bear on the communication effectiveness an advertiser is seeking. From time to time the internal research or research contracted by the magazine will uncover data that are important to all advertisers and prospects. In such cases it is not unusual to produce a special event (see below) to present the findings.

Presentations come in all shapes and forms—from simple desktop presentations using glassine overlays in a ring binder to presentations using the latest in computer and audio/video technology. Larger magazines will often spend a substantial sum on a presentation for a single client when a contract may be valued at hundreds of thousands of dollars. Small publications' presentations, targeting much lower valued contracts, tend to be less expensively produced.

## Advertising

Advertising space purchased by the magazine to promote itself to potential advertisers is usually confined to print, because television and radio advertising reaches broad audiences that include too much "waste" circulation, meaning persons who are not in a position to influence or decide upon the purchase of advertising space. For example, a gardening publication would be unlikely to advertise in the *Chicago Tribune* because a very small percentage of the readers are likely to be interested in gardening. But some magazines have made successful use of drive-time radio in selected markets, or by buying time on stations that have an advertising or marketing program. The theory regarding drive-time radio is that most listeners are commuters on their way to or from work, among whom are sufficient numbers of persons in the marketing and advertising industry to justify the expenditure.

The smaller the magazine's revenue, the less likely the publication is to use advertising at all. All publications have clearly defined advertising prospects. In most markets there is not a marketing and advertising magazine specific to the category. *Advertising Age* thoroughly covers the field, reaching advertising decision makers in companies across the board. But if you publish a magazine for the health food market and bought advertising space in *Advertising Age* to showcase your title, you would be paying for significant circulation among advertisers and marketers who have little or no interest in the health food market. This is even more the case in most trade markets. An exception is the medical field. *Medical Media and Marketing*, *Pharmaceutical Executive*, and other publications are directed at marketers in this category.

## Direct Mail

All magazines maintain a promotion list of all advertiser and advertising agency personnel that are advertisers or prospects. Most promotion lists number under 2,500 names. Sending promotional material through the mail to these people is an important medium for targeted publications. The reach of the direct mail promotion effort is not a problem; the challenge comes in creating materials that are attractive and appealing enough to make an impression. This demands a consistent direct mail program that imbeds an idea about the magazine in the mind of the recipient. Where budget is a constraint, an advertising sales director is likely to opt for an intense direct mail campaign during the months when marketing, advertising, and media plans are being developed by the client and agency.

## Trade and Professional Meetings

Trade and professional meetings range in type from large conventions of the National Association of Home Builders to small professional meetings such as the American Academy of Anesthesiologists. The former attracts over 100,000 attendees and the latter fewer than 5,000. The meetings include seminars, presentation of research papers, scientific exhibits, and speeches by businesspersons, academics, public figures, and others who have messages of importance to the group in attendance. A source of income to the association is the rental of exhibit space to those who have products or services that are pertinent to the interests of those in attendance. The chief reason these meetings are important to a magazine is that every significant marketer and advertiser who consider the meeting attendees important targets for their products, will be in attendance and, usually, will exhibit at the meeting. In some cases the magazine will rent exhibit space, which is used to promote the publication, conduct some research, and serve as the headquarters for sales personnel. The sales personnel seek the opportunity to renew acquaintances and make new ones among potential advertisers. Often a person with whom it is difficult to get an appointment is readily available for coffee, breakfast, or lunch during a trade or professional meeting.

## Marketing Services

A number of marketing services are offered by magazines. Many have a program whereby an advertiser earns a percentage of its advertising expenditure that can be applied toward marketing services. This is called a merchandising allowance. Still others offer the service without any additional cost. The services are limited only by the creativity of the magazine's personnel. They include use of the publication's mailing list, postcard packs, ad measurement services, point of purchase display cards, reprints of magazine articles, market research, reader panels, and reader services. Normally a magazine sells its mailing list through list brokers or on a direct-to-user basis. The list must be maintained for the subscriber list. Therefore any additional use of the list is relatively cost-free. Although it is a source of revenue, some magazines weigh the value of a sale of the list against the value of an advertising contract and decide there is more to be gained by offering the list as a marketing service based on an advertiser's volume of advertising space.

Postcard packs, like mailing lists, are usually sold to advertisers. These are collections of advertising postcards that invite the receiver to send for more information or to purchase a product. It's a method used to derive more revenue from the magazine's mailing list. The advertiser also benefits from the savings in distribution costs by having the postcards distributed in a single package. For the same reason mentioned above, a publication might opt to offer the service as part of a merchandising allowance program or free as an enticement for a larger advertising schedule.

There are a number of research services that offer ad measurement services. These services are more common among trade publications. Interviews are conducted by mail, phone, or in person to determine whether readers noticed an ad, if they considered the ad believable, if they were already users of the product, and numerous other characteristics. This information is presented to advertisers in an attractive format, showing how they fared against all other ads in the publication, as well as how they rated against advertising in the same product category. Often an award is presented to the advertiser and advertising agency to honor their achievement. In a few cases there is an annual awards dinner honoring the outstanding achievers.

Point of purchase display cards are offered by some consumer publications. These cards will be displayed at the checkout counter of a retailer pointing out that the product was advertised in a particular magazine. The point, of course, is to get some rub-off from the reputation and prestige of the publication.

Some advertisers find that reprints mailed to their clients or for use by their sales personnel are effective. An article in a financial publication rating insurance companies might be attractive to a highly rated insurance company, for example.

Market research, developed by the magazine, can provide useful data that is not available elsewhere. Marketers and advertisers welcome any information that will provide additional insight about their customers. *Medical Economics* magazine conducts an annual survey of physicians' income and expenses. The data is collected and available in the year succeeding the physician's experience. Some of this information is available from government sources but is usually published two to three years after the physician's experience. The *Medical Economics* data also include numerous details that are not available from other sources, like breakdowns by region and medical specialty.

Often a magazine will offer an advertiser the opportunity to cosponsor a contest. In one unique program, *Successful Farming* and one of its regular advertisers, Buctril herbicide, teamed up to sponsor the Great American Farm Dog Contest among the magazine's 480,000 subscribers. Top prize was an original watercolor portrait of the winning dog. Among the judging categories: Favorite Farm Dog Story and Most Heroic Farm Dog Deed. Response was tremendous and enthusiastic. Every recipient of the magazine and contest entrant was exposed to the Buctril herbicide message—truly an added value for this particular advertiser.[6]

Reader or consumer panels are composed of readers of a magazine who have agreed to answer interview questions about a magazine and products advertised in the magazine. The publication uses the power of its relationship with its readers to provide information about a product, including the readers' attitude toward the product, whether or not they are a user, what might make them switch to the brand, and other information that can help the advertiser to direct its advertising message more effectively.

"Reader service" is the terminology used to describe a method whereby an advertiser can encourage a reader to send for additional information. This service is particularly important in some trade markets, in which the introduction of new and improved products is almost routine. The personal computer market would be an example. A reply card (sometimes called a "bingo card") is bound into the magazine and includes numbers that correlate with numbers within an ad and from a list of advertisers in the issue. After the reader sends the card to the magazine, the magazine will provide the advertiser with a mailing label and information about the issue from which the reader responded. Data from reader services is compiled to demonstrate to advertisers that their ad was seen by an involved, responsive audience. Lately, bingo cards are being replaced or supplemented by 800 numbers provided by the publisher. Extension numbers are used for individual advertisers to distinguish one from the other. Consumer magazines also use this form of reader service. The *New Yorker* has a section entitled "R.S.V.P." Readers can get additional information from advertisers through this service by calling 800 numbers.

## Electronic Services

Many publishers are creating electronic services on the Internet or one of the commercial services such as Compuserve, America Online, or Prodigy. On the Internet there is a general location for magazine and other publications called the Electronic Newsstand. Most of the interactivity on these electronic services is used for reader correspondence with editors, for posting parts of the publication, or for circulation solicitation. There is considerable concern within the magazine community as to how these services might be used to provide advertising. The clear answer is yet to come. For now, some publications are selling advertising on a quarterly or annual contract. The advertiser receives a banner or similar figure on the screen that the user can activate to get more detailed information. The problem is to make the advertising sufficiently compelling to attract a reasonable level of activity. The number of persons who use on-line services and who are likely to access a publication's location is vastly smaller than the circulation of the magazines. Thus, this area is considered to be experimental. Nevertheless, there are opportunities to provide access to advertisers as part of the marketing effort and to use data from the service to demonstrate the added value provided to readers from the world of electronic communications.

# PLANNING AND COORDINATING SPECIAL EVENTS

Special events are conducted for internal and external purposes. Internal events are aimed at revving up the sales force. External events are directed at advertisers and their agencies.

### Internal

The primary, and often the only, internal special event is an annual sales meeting. This is distinct from regular sales meetings held by the advertising sales director to keep the sales force abreast of current developments in the magazine operations and to review the status of accounts. The usual purpose of the annual sales meeting is to create enthusiasm about the company and the magazine and to generate a sense of camaraderie among the salespeople. It is usually held at a resort location for at least two days and often up to a week. Timing varies. Some are scheduled to kick off a primary selling season and others to coincide with the beginning of the business' fiscal or calendar year. Companies with multiple magazines will often make the sales meeting a companywide event with salespeople from all magazines in attendance. Even when the meeting is for a single magazine, the brass will be on hand to update the salespeople on the status of the company. If nothing extraordinary is scheduled to be released (such as the results of a new research study or a significant change in circulation), the advertising and promotion program for the coming year is likely to be featured. Often there are one or more speakers from outside the company. The outside speakers may be inspirational and talk about the attitude and characteristics that assure sales success, or they may be experts from within the industry, such as the marketing director of a client company. Overall, the expectation is that those in attendance will return to the job refreshed and excited about themselves, their publication, and their company.

### External

Special events for advertisers and agencies are used to highlight something special or new about a magazine. This would include new findings about readership, reader demographics, the magazine's market, a redesign of the publication, or the introduction of a new editorial section. To create an aura of importance the event might be a breakfast or lunch, with hundreds in attendance, at a well-known hotel or club in a major city. The presentation can be enhanced by the use of experts or nationally known figures. A major presentation is frequently created and set up by companies that specialize in meeting planning. The cities selected for these types of special event would be those that are the headquarters for numerous advertisers and their agencies that are advertisers in and prospects for the magazine. Smaller special events are aimed at advertiser product categories or, in some cases, job function. Information that would be significant for the automotive or telecommunications category would be presented at a special event held for client and advertising personnel in those markets. From time to time a magazine might invite only media planners and buyers to an event. In addition to presenting information such events are designed to forge relationships with those attending.

## PUBLIC RELATIONS

One of the intangible aids to selling more pages of advertising is a positive perception of the magazine in the advertising community and among individual advertising decision makers. Many magazines use classic public relations techniques to improve and enhance that perception. When a magazine is being launched, it's important for the editor and publisher to create "buzz" about the title in the advertising community and generally spread the word that the magazine is hot. Established magazines also want to be perceived by the business community as a leader in their category. Others want everyone to recognize the title as innovative or always ahead of breaking news stories or indispensable to readers. The ways to generate these positive perceptions are limited only by the imagination and energy of the advertising sales director and the publisher. Some publishers and ad directors give speeches that are subsequently covered in the trade and general press. Others make themselves available to reporters for comment and expert observation—both on and off the record—on the state of a particular business. An ad director of a men's magazine who is quoted in the *Wall Street Journal* about how more men are spending more money on casual clothing because of the growth in popularity of "casual Friday" dress at many companies during the summer months will help his or her magazine be seen as the authority on such matters in the marketplace.

When a magazine has news to tell the trade and general press about circulation growth or new advertising rates or a record-breaking issue, the advertising department will often issue a press release. The magazine's special events, parties, receptions, and trade shows are also the occasion for press coverage. Doing good work can also generate good PR. For several years, *GQ* magazine has sponsored a highly successful clothing drive in New York and other cities. Other magazines sponsor auctions, road races, fund-raising events, and other occasions to benefit worthy causes.

Big anniversaries and the results of interesting research can also make headlines for a magazine. In addition, the press attention that a magazine gets for editorial features can be a big boost to the advertising department. *Condé Nast Traveler* magazine's annual Readers' Choice Poll, covering its readers' top preferences in a wide range of travel categories, is well respected in the travel industry. Many travel advertisers include their high scores in this poll in their own advertising—thus attributing to *Condé Nast Traveler* a strong measure of authority in an important advertising market.

# MARKETING AND MEDIA RESEARCH

## Purpose

The absolute relationship between sales produced by a specific advertising campaign in a specific magazine is all but impossible to measure accurately and completely. Therefore any valid research that helps to demonstrate the value of the publication as an advertising medium and the value of the demographics of the market served by the publication to advertisers is helpful in selling advertising space. A publisher needs to ask questions to help direct the research manager or vendor in the design of the study, such as:

- Is the research needed and why?
- Is the research intended to create new knowledge or supplement existing knowledge?
- What question or questions do we expect the research to answer?
- What issues will it address?
- Is the research important enough to merit special attention to the methodology?
- How will the research results be used and presented?

There is no shortage of research among magazines. Too often, however, the work is self-serving. Sales representatives too often attempt to answer the slightest objection of a potential client with quick and dirty research. The most successful magazines are frequently viewed as the primary source of market and media information because they do first-class research. Quality research demands that the methodology follow standards established by the Advertising Research Foundation regarding numerous aspects of the study, with emphasis on the response rate and the quality of the responses that are generated. These factors bear significantly on the level of confidence one can place on the results of the research effort. This is not to say that informal research is useless. Many publications conduct such research to guide their editors. *Medical Economics* magazine conducts a mail reader survey of every issue, designed to produce at least 100 responses solely for editorial staff guidance. The questions include whether the reader spent any time with the particular issue in question, how much time was spent, and specific questions on the level of reading of each article and department in the issue. One hundred responses are too few to establish a reliable level of confidence. Nevertheless, over a period of time reasonable trends can be spotted. For example, if features on recreational travel always scored at the lower level of reader interest, the editor would question how often such articles might run, if at all. Similarly, informal surveys might be useful for other purposes, provided all parties recognize and acknowledge the research limitations.

## Types of Research

Research data is gathered through mail surveys and in telephone and personal interviews. Focus groups are still another research method. Each has its strengths and weaknesses. *Focus groups* represent a qualitative method whereby a small group of individuals is gathered to have a group discussion on a specific topic. A leader will use open-ended questions to engage the discussion. Frequently, interested parties can see the reactions of the group by the use of a one-way mirror. This form of research can be done quickly but is far from representative of a large universe. The method might be used when a magazine launch is planned. The reactions of the group would help to determine if the magazine would serve a useful purpose and if the editorial approach served the purpose in a way that would attract readers with characteristics similar to those taking part in the focus group.

*Mail surveys* are lower in cost than telephone or personal interviews but require a considerably longer time to complete. Long questionnaires and other factors can contribute to an inadequate response rate. This demands additional follow-up and, thus, even more time. The accuracy and credibility has a direct relationship to the response rate. *Telephone surveys* are more efficient than mail and correspondingly more costly. The response rate is easier to control and they take less turn-around time than mail surveys. Most of the calls are made in the evening. People are known to get very annoyed at the number of calls that interrupt their leisure time. So more and more, high response rates are more expensive because of the number of calls required to meet the minimum requirements.

*Personal interviews* are the most costly way to gather data and also suffer from a slow turn-around time. The quality of the interviewer is a variable that needs to be considered because interviews cannot be monitored by a supervisor, as is the case with telephone interviewing. The response rate of personal interviews has a high level of controllability, which is beneficial.

## Use of Research

There are numerous syndicated research companies serving specific markets. These services provide tracking of retail and wholesale sales, product sampling programs, and just about any other measure that would be useful to a marketer. The packaged food and beverage markets are examples. These companies know what is shipped from their plants but that is not a measure of how well the product is selling to the consumer. In the healthcare industry, IMS provides considerable data on the movement of pharmaceuticals from the manufacturer through the wholesaler to retailer chain and, finally, to the user. Additionally, data is gathered on the prescribing profiles of specific physicians.

There are also services to measure elements of an ad or advertising campaign such as awareness, readership (for print ads), and consumer action. As mentioned previously, Simmons and MRI provide magazine demographic and readership data.

Generally, magazine-generated research is intended to supplement syndicated marketing research in markets where these services exist. In other markets a magazine is often the primary source of market data. It is not unusual for a magazine to set a goal to become the key source of market information. This helps to create an aura of credibility for the magazine itself. Magazines do not go so far as to track retail or wholesale sales but will provide data on the market behavior of their readers relative to specific product categories and brands. Magazines for teenage girls, for example, can provide detailed data on the use of acne medication among their audiences.

Readership research is extremely important to establish the value of the magazine as an advertising medium and the personality of the publication. Every magazine cannot be number one in readership in its competitive category. Every magazine can be number one in some parts of its circulation. Selling propositions can be derived from a careful analysis of the details of the studies conducted by syndicated services. From time to time a magazine will undertake research to dispute some of the findings in syndicated readership, but more often the research is supplementary. It is intended to expand on the data available. In most business-to-business markets there is no generally accepted syndicated service, so readership data that is generated by publications is all the more important.

## THE ROLE OF THE ACCOUNT REPRESENTATIVE

As we've seen, the sales representative is responsible for maximizing the sale of the advertising space potential in his or her territory. Accounts are assigned by geographic area or, in larger markets where there are a number of salespersons, by account assignments. These assignments are determined by the advertising sales director. The management of the territory involves:

- Establishing and maintaining relationships with client and advertising agency personnel
- Representing the magazine to these persons
- Establishing the account strategy in conjunction with the advertising sales director
- Closing sales

There probably is no such thing as a typical day for a sales representative. On most days some time will be spent on each of their five basic functions, which are:

- *Sales calls*
  Each sales call—a meeting with an advertiser or potential advertiser—is different, but all should have as an objective strengthening the relationships

with an advertising decision maker and communicating news and information about the magazine. Sales reps will spend time getting to know the people called on and their advertising and marketing goals, as well as brainstorming and kicking around ideas on how the magazine and its services can help market the client's product. Regular calls are important to keep clients who are running ad space sold on the magazine.

- *Telephoning*
  Follow-up calls; seeking the opportunity to be of more service, relationship building, making calls for appointments.

- *Correspondence*
  Thank you letters, often with additional material promised during the sales call, relationship building, confirmation; confirming points agreed on or the scheduling of advertising space.

- *"Fire fighting"*
  Faxing data to a media department from a call asking for information immediately, responding to a complaint about a reproduction quality.

- *Management meetings*
  Sales estimates; updating the sales page estimate for the next issue or for the balance of the business year, account information; reporting good and bad news from calls, help with marketing; discussing marketing services that might be offered to a client in conjunction with an advertising program, such as the use of the mailing list.

When traveling outside a metropolitan area it might be possible to make a call on just one account. In this situation, the sales representative will try to see all the people at the account that would bear on the advertising decision.

The number of people who have some level of influence on the placing of an advertising schedule can range from two or three for a very small account to ten or twenty for a large one. The advertiser is likely to have a director of marketing, a group brand/product supervisor, and a brand or product manager. Larger companies often will have in-house media functions. The advertising agency will have an account supervisor, account executive, director of media, media planner, and media buyer. There will be assistants at all levels for a large advertiser. The sales representative will spend considerable time in the early stages of a relationship determining the hierarchy of influence and decision making. Another important element is the relationship of the client with the agency. In some instances the media schedule will be decided at the client level. In this case the sales representative must use the utmost tact, if he or she is making contact at the client level, to be sure the agency is not left out of the information loop. In trade markets it is common to call on the client.

Personal contact is the principal method for selling advertising space. The challenge is to get to see busy people at both the client and advertising agency. When the sales representative has established himself or herself as a valuable marketing partner, one who can contribute knowledge and ideas, the job becomes easier. The telephone is the most important tool, but actually getting through to talk to the right person can be a challenge. The etiquette and effective use of voice mail is increasingly important. Getting to know administrative assistants is often helpful. They can be an important ally in this most important task. Some sales representatives have found that calling difficult-to-reach people is more successful before or after regular business hours. Under certain circumstances, the sales representative must be prepared to make a presentation over the phone.

Some advertising sales directors demand that a follow-up letter be sent after every call. This is a good habit to develop. Sending a letter or two with some pertinent information between calls helps to establish the sales representative. There is a special skill in writing sales letters. They are really a form of sales promotion, so the letter should be second-person (you) oriented. Too many sales letters accentuate what "we" are doing rather than featuring benefits to the recipient. The sales letter should emphasize benefits to the client and offer reasons to buy.

Once having established a relationship with an advertising client, the sales representative needs to service the contacts on a regular schedule. Advertising contracts can be canceled at will, so a schedule is never permanent. The better sales representatives develop such a large amount of information about their magazine and market that they are never at a loss to be able to make a call that will benefit the person they see. Entertainment plays a role in the maintenance of an account. Breakfast and lunch meetings are almost everyday affairs in the lives of the more successful sales representatives. Many magazines have season tickets to sports or artistic events, which are available for client entertaining. Golf and tennis outings are also valuable entertainment functions.

Account strategy is developed based on knowledge of the needs of the client, the people working on the account, and at the advertising agency. Planning a strategy for at least one year is a good method. The strategy includes whom to call on, how often, and with what information. Those being called on hear from sales representatives from numerous magazines. Delivering information in smaller bites and in the most memorable way possible will help a magazine to stand out from the pack. Sales presentations can be very informal or quite formal. As mentioned previously, they are extremely important and must be carefully planned to provide information and reasons to include your magazine on a schedule. Presentations should be brief, but interesting, if not exciting. Presentations are the end result of the account strategy.

## CASE STUDY
### American News Review

Voorhees Inc., located in southern Indiana, is a manufacturer of air treatment and conditioning equipment. The company's consumer division is well-known because it supplies whole-house air conditioning equipment, as well as window units. The consumer products are distributed through authorized dealers, who receive extensive product information, merchandising plans, and other material from the company to help with the sales effort. Over the years, Voorhees has occasionally advertised its consumer products in newspapers and magazines to draw potential customers to their dealers. The consumer products are advertised under the brand name CoolWave.

Because Voorhees is located in a part of the Midwest that has few potential national advertisers, and because of its inconsistent advertising strategy (the last campaign was three years ago), consumer publication advertising sales representatives rarely call on marketing and advertising personnel at Voorhees. One exception was Mack Graham, account representative for *American News Review*, a leading national newsweekly. Mack had called on Barbara Yandell, the Voorhees marketing director, and Bob Gorton, the CoolWave product manager, two or three times a year. Both said they were very much in favor of a direct-to-the-consumer campaign and, in fact, recommended such a campaign in their plan each year. They believed an ad campaign in late spring and during the heat of summer would be well worth the cost in increased CoolWave sales. However, top management still wasn't convinced. Barbara and Bob indicated that they appreciated the market data and other pertinent media research, provided by Mack, to help them sell their plan to management. Clearly, they were pleased that he took the time to call on them, unlike most other consumer magazine sales representatives. Mack was confident that *American News Review* would get the business, should Bob and Barbara get approval for a consumer ad campaign.

Voorhees' advertising was handled through the E.S. Phipps advertising agency in Chicago. Mack Graham worked out of the Chicago office of *American News Review* so he made regular calls on Phipps for a number of his accounts. He was well-acquainted with the account and media group in charge of CoolWave. Ed Scott, the account supervisor, consistently turned down Mack's requests for appointments. Mack had met him only once and that was a quick introduction when Scott happened to stop by the office of an account executive with whom Mack was meeting. Mack called regularly on Jo Sluyter, Associate Media Director, who was responsible for several accounts including CoolWave.

One day in October, Mack's perseverance appeared to be rewarded. Jo called and told him that Voorhees had approved a national print campaign for CoolWave for the following year. She said that Bob Gorton would be in touch to schedule a presentation at the Voorhees headquarters.

Bob called Mack and thanked him for all the help he had provided. CoolWave would have a limited, but reasonable budget for the campaign. All the advertising would be print. They wanted frequency with this campaign, but could only afford to use one of the national newsweeklies. In early November, management was setting aside a day to receive presentations from each of the national newsweeklies under consideration and *American News Review* was scheduled for 2:00 p.m.

Because of Mack's good relationship with Jo Sluyter, she made numerous helpful suggestions about what might be included and emphasized in the *American News Review* presentation to Voorhees management. She also mentioned that the Voorhees marketing team valued the help that Mack had given them over the years. Buoyed by Jo's comments, Mack nevertheless was somewhat troubled because he continued to be rebuffed in his attempts to get an appointment with Ed Scott. Ed's administrative assistant was very pleasant and courteous, but it was clear that she had instructions not to schedule an appointment with Mack. She insisted that Mr. Scott could not even spare a few minutes. He wondered if the sales reps at his competition were getting to see Scott.

Mack Graham's boss, the *American News Review*'s advertising sales director, accompanied him to Voorhees and was actively involved in the presentation to the company president, Barbara Yandell, Bob Gorton, and a number of assistants. At the conclusion, everyone complimented them on their fine magazine and presentation. They were told the advertising plan would be finalized in six or eight weeks.

The following week, Mack tried once again to get an appointment with Scott. No success. He did have a luncheon meeting with Jo Sluyter who told him the odds favored him and *American News Review*. The marketing management group thought the magazine was the best buy for their campaign and his diligent attention to the Voorhees account would bode well for him and *American News Review*. Jo added that she had recommended *American News Review* before the presentations and would continue to do so. Mack called Bob Gorton at Voorhees to see if he needed any additional information. Bob thanked him and again commented on how favorably the presentation was received by all in attendance.

On the last day of November, Mack Graham stopped by the Phipps agency to drop off material that had been requested by a media planner and happened to pass Jo Sluyter in the corridor. She smiled and said all was well: *American News Review* won the ad sales contract for the CoolWave campaign.

During the first week of December, Mack Graham was at a monthly advertising club luncheon. He sat at a table of ten, directly across from Sheldon Pisani, an advertising representative for a competing newsweekly. Halfway through the lunch he heard the man sitting next to Sheldon congratulate her on winning the CoolWave contract. Mack couldn't wait for the end of the meeting to find out if what he heard was true. He left the table and called his boss with what he had heard. Heart pounding, Mack called Jo Sluyter and was told she could not be reached for a few days. He called Bob Gorton at CoolWave. He was told Gorton was on the road for the rest of the week. Finally, he called Barbara Yandell who took his call. She said that last week the elusive Ed Scott had been instructed to contact all the publications that had made presentations. Mack said he had never heard from Ed Scott but that Jo Sluyter told him, unofficially, that *American News Review* won the ad sales contract for the CoolWave campaign. Barbara sounded annoyed about the situation and said she would call Ed Scott. She suggested that Mack call Scott before the end of the business day. Mack asked if there was any chance to salvage the business. Barbara said that the door was open "maybe an inch."

Just before 5:00 p.m. that day Mack Graham called Ed Scott who immediately took his call. Mack asked for an appointment and was given a date two weeks hence. Despite his plea for an earlier date, Scott insisted that he would be totally tied up for the next two weeks. Mack was crestfallen. If the sale was to be saved he would need to act quickly. Two weeks was simply too long to wait. When he got off the phone, he considered heading over to the agency immediately and knocking on Scott's office door. The receptionist would be gone for the day and since he was well-known around the agency, he could easily enter the office area. What to do?

Overall, Mack Graham felt he had done all the right things a sales representative should do. He was mystified and outraged that, apparently, someone was strongly in the corner of a competitor and that it seemed Jo Sluyter had lied to him. Although the outlook seemed bleak for Mack Graham, he was determined to try to get the business. He was also desperate to find out what happened at either the agency or at Voorhees.

Give him your advice on immediate and subsequent steps to take to deal with his problem.


# NOTES

[1] Kevin Goldman, "Consumers Prefer Print Ads, Study Says," *The Wall Street Journal*, June 5, 1995.

[2] "Top 300 Magazines by Gross Revenue," *Advertising Age,* June 20, 1994, 39–49

[3] Deirdre Carmody, "No Identity Crisis for Hachette Magazines Chief," *The New York Times*, November 28, 1994.

[4] "Ad Sales Salary Survey," *Folio*: Special Sourcebook Issue, 1995, 262–282.

[5] *Forbes,* "The Corn is Green," December 4, 1995, 98.

[6] "Added Value Goes to the Dogs," *Adweek*, January 15, 1994, 37.

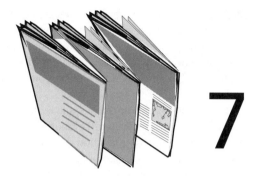

# History of Magazine Production Technologies

## THE MAKING OF MAGAZINES

Nothing takes the measure of creativity, diligence, and teamwork like getting out the next issue of a magazine. At every publication worthy of its audience, each department knows it must achieve a deadline-driven tour de force if that looming on-sale date is to be met. So, editors craft compelling stories under the stern eye of the clock. Art directors labor just as strenuously to enrich the editorial with arresting covers and lucid interior graphics. Advertising sales representatives push persuasiveness to the limit as they coax last-minute insertions from vacillating clients. Circulation managers come to grips with newsstand allotments, database maintenance, postal requirements, and the other intricacies of channeling the finished product into the hands of expectant readers.

Obviously, the "finished product"—the printed and bound magazine the reader ultimately receives—is the physical end result of all of this activity. Nevertheless, the pre-manufacturing nature of these tasks can make it easy to forget that a magazine is as much a product as a box of cereal, or a pair of shoes, or a canister of tennis balls. Like them, a magazine is a mass-produced item consisting of raw materials to which value is added (in this case, in the form of editorial and advertising). It is manufactured by means of specialized equipment according to an equally specialized set of production routines.

At most magazines, seeing that these routines are adhered to is the responsibility of a manufacturing expert known as the production manager or production director. It is a special role. Because production routines influence everything else connected with the operation of a magazine to an extent that other publishing functions do not, no other staff position (with the exception of publisher) has as broad a purview of the process.

Rules laid down by production managers shape decisions about editorial content, issue design, timing of advertising, circulation methods, and all the outcomes that could stem from them. As one production director put it, "About 99 percent of my job is interpretation and communication...For example, if I see that something is late, whether it is an ad or an editorial page, and there's a chance that the quality of the magazine is going to suffer because of it, I am the one who must diplomatically remind the person responsible about the consequences."[1]

Preserving deadline integrity is only one of many ways in which production makes its necessary influence felt. Consider some other kinds of decisions that could not be taken safely without the benefit of the production manager's expertise and experience:

- A publisher hopes to attract more advertising by switching the binding from saddle-stitched to perfect-bound. She knows her advertisers will appreciate the change—but will the anticipated increase in ad revenue cover the increased cost of perfect binding? The publisher, realizing she has only half the answer, will go to her production manager for a quick course in postpress economics.
- An art director envisions a gorgeous spread of four-color with spot color in metallic silver. He isn't sure whether the printer is up to handling the quality-control requirements of a press run this complicated. A meeting with the production manager—the magazine's principal liaison with the printer—will help him decide whether another design approach should be used.
- The magazine's national distributor (a company hired to manage single-copy sales) has advised the circulation director that a different trim size will help the title pick up more "pockets" (i.e., display space) at supermarket checkouts and other high-traffic locations. It sounds promising, but the production manager points out that changing the trim size could also force a change in specifications for advertising film—a major inconvenience for certain advertisers. Now circulation, production, and ad sales know they must find out if acting on the distributor's advice may bring the risk of lost insertions.

These scenarios suggest two conclusions about the proper role of production in magazine publishing. First: Truly efficient production—the kind that improves the performance of every operating department—arises from collaboration, not confrontation. Second: Because production bears upon everything other departments do, production knowledge is a prerequisite for success in every magazine occupation.

While team play is always a praiseworthy goal in itself, today the production partnership is motivated primarily by economics. Once upon a time, many publishers looked on manufacturing expense strictly as an operating cost to be subtracted from revenues yielded by advertising and circulation. But with remarkable new production technologies pointing the way to later ad closings, better-targeted distributions, and other enhancements to profitability, the perception is shifting. Now manufacturing expense can be seen as an income-producing investment. At last, the advantages of production-focused staff teamwork are becoming quantifiable and clear.

"(T)he status of production is definitely changing, in large part because manufacturing is providing potential new revenue sources for publishing," said a manufacturing executive for Time Inc. Magazines. With the change has come a new strategy that emphasizes cooperation for the sake of the bottom line: "We are now getting involved with major publishing and editorial projects on the ground floor...we are trying to show the interconnectedness of all aspects of publishing...That enables us to deliver more value to our readers and makes us more competitive with both traditional and non-traditional sources of news."[2]

Production managers who do the best job of demonstrating the "interconnectedness" are culture crossers who can speak the languages of editorial, art, advertising, circulation, and the other operating departments of their magazines. But the connection will not work if staff members in nonproduction areas lack the technical fluency to make their own contributions to the production dialogue. Editors, designers, sales reps, and circulation hands who study production invariably learn new ways to do their jobs better. Those who ignore production risk errors and oversights that can impede workflow, short-change readers, frustrate advertisers, and hinder careers.

The path to understanding magazine production begins with learning something about the history of its medium, printing. Printing history is a good teacher because the production of magazines, like that of newspapers, has earned printing much of its status as a "mass" medium. We will see that many of the major breakthroughs of modern printing technology were spurred by magazine publishers' common desire for a better-looking, more colorful, more efficiently manufactured product. We will also see that the quest for quality in the closing quarter of the twentieth century has been a ceaseless process of reinventing or rethinking nearly every aspect of production, from our choice of tools to our management of human resources.

A word to the wise: As print and magazines reinvent themselves to compete in the twenty-first century's digital information marketplace, the pressure for innovation and change will intensify to a degree that few people who have fallen behind production's learning curve will be able to withstand. For magazine professionals, there has never been a more advantageous time to gain production knowledge—or a more reckless moment to ignore it.

## FROM ART FORM TO SCIENCE

### Pi Shêng, Gutenberg, Senefelder, Mergenthaler

Printing spans so many centuries, cultures, and individual acts of genius that we tend to think of it as something that must always have been a part of human progress. But the story of what we know as "printing" in the modern sense really began in China at the start of the fifteenth century, when a man named Pi Shêng invented movable, reusable type from molds of clay.[3] Around the middle of the same century, Johann Gensfleisch zum Gutenberg of Mainz, Germany, improved on the concept by developing lead-alloy "foundry" type that could be precision-cast and composed for printing in a systematic way.

This innovation, coupled with a wine press rebuilt as a printing machine, enabled Gutenberg to produce his famous Bible (consisting of 5,600 hand-set characters per spread) at the rate of 200 copies in three years.[4] Although personal craftsmanship would remain the key to the process for the next 500 years, printing had taken its first steps toward becoming a form of manufacturing based upon replication of product through the use of uniform production techniques.

After Gutenberg, printing's evolution was to branch in two directions: *presswork*, the technology whereby inked impressions of type and other images are transferred to a substrate (generally speaking, paper); and *composition*, the process of assembling type into readable units of language. Progress was slow in both branches until the nineteenth century, when new processes better suited to true mass manufacturing began to dethrone the craft-centered methods perfected in the long interval by Gutenberg and his heirs.

One such advance was the imaging technique known as *lithography*, invented by the Bohemian printing pioneer, Alois Senefelder (1771–1834). Until Senefelder's breakthrough, printing had been an almost exclusively mechanical process of pressing sheets of paper against inked type and engravings. Senefelder's experiments showed that images could also be produced from the application of a simple chemical principle: the mutual repellence of greasy printing ink and the other ingredient of his new recipe for reproduction, water. What he discovered was that a picture or manuscript could be sketched on a stone surface treated with a water-based solution for making the non-image areas reject ink. Then paper impressions could be pulled again and again from the flat surface of the stone, transferring all the detail of the original to each succeeding sheet.

Now printing had in its grasp what purely mechanical presswork had failed to give it: the elements of a versatile method for reproducing illustrations in quantity.

Although the fact was not widely recognized in Senefelder's time, lithography also held the promise of becoming a speedier, cheaper form of printing than the methods descended from Gutenberg's retooled wine press. At least one prophecy of lithography's bright future in magazine production appeared in the August 1819 issue of the American periodical *Analectic Magazine*, which reported, "The advantage of expedition in the process is beyond all calculation."[5]

The newspaper industry was the setting for the next great event in printing's march toward mass production. On July 3, 1886, the first fully automatic typesetting machine—called one of the 10 greatest inventions in history—was demonstrated in the composing room of the *New York Tribune*.[6] Ottmar Mergenthaler, the inventor, built his compressed-air powered device around reusable matrices, or letterform molds, that could be filled with hot metal and returned to a holding unit (called, by interesting coincidence, the *magazine*) until strokes from the operator's keyboard signaled that they were needed again.

This amazing machine was dubbed "Linotype" by the *Tribune*'s publisher, who marveled at its ability to produce perfectly spaced "slugs," or lines, of newsprint without composing sticks, "California" job cases, or any of the other paraphernalia of manual typesetting. At last, after four centuries of setting by hand in the manner of Gutenberg's workshop, composition could meet an exploding demand for printed matter that simple human energy could no longer satisfy. True automation had come to printing, and with it the beginnings of our contemporary ideas about production.

It would be a mistake to trace production history strictly from the standpoints of lithography and automated composition. The *gravure* printing process, for example, demands equal treatment for its predominant role in the manufacture of long-run, high-quality magazines and other publications. But developments in lithography and automated composition have the most to tell us about the course of modern magazine production technology as a whole. The eventual marriage of lithography—originally a fine-art process with uncertain potential for mass reproduction—and automated composition—locked for many years into a form fundamentally incompatible with lithographic principles—became the union that now generates the bulk of our routine reading matter, from magazines, newspapers, and books to advertising brochures, mail-order catalogs, and technical literature.

The marriage has seldom been tranquil. It could be consummated only after both partners had defied and defeated predecessor technologies whose reigns seemed perpetually assured. Today, both are being challenged on their own ground by new technologies that will either transform them or plunge them into obsolescence even more rapidly than they did their precursors. Their survival will depend on their traditional ability to draw new power and functionality from parallel technologies, as will be seen from a further examination of their development since the early years of this century.

## THE BIRTH OF MODERN OFFSET LITHOGRAPHY

Lithography is a *planographic* printing method. That means the image and nonimage areas share the same two-dimensional plane of the *image carrier*, or printing plate, much as the dark and light portions of a snapshot blend on the surface of photoprint paper. Viewed edgewise, a lithographic plate reveals none of the *relief* (raised) surfaces that a novice might think necessary for the proper adhesion of ink. The explanation, as Senefelder discovered, is that the distinction between what should and shouldn't print can be maintained chemically in a lithographic image, so that a three-dimensional printing surface isn't needed. [7]

Lithography was originally a pictorial reproduction process in which artisans traced or drew directly on specially prepared lithographing stones, the planographic image carriers of their day. By the middle of the nineteenthth century, hand- and steam-operated lithographic presses could transfer images from stones to paper at a rate approaching the budding mass-production requirements of the time. As the American population grew in numbers and literacy, lithographers found ready markets for decorative prints, sheet music, maps, advertisements, and stock certificates, as well as illustrations for magazines and books. [8]

For all its aesthetic merits, however, direct lithography fell far short of *letterpress* printing in work requiring the efficient reproduction of straight reading matter in bulk. One obstacle, common to all direct-impression methods, was that the process naturally transferred images to paper backward. This obliged lithographers to inscribe text on image carriers in reverse so that the printed result would be right-reading. Direct lithography was also too a fragile process for the long press runs of true mass production. Unlike image carriers for letterpress and gravure, early lithographic plates for direct printing did not stand up well to the abrading effect of contact with printing papers. That drawback, combined with the trickiness of maintaining the chemical conditions that made the process work, kept lithography in a restricted role for most of its first 100 years as a manufacturing method.[9]

An intersection of technological breakthroughs that began in the early years of the twentieth century helped the process to make up for lost time. The introduction of indirect, or *offset*, printing was lithography's primary passport to the broader horizons of modern production. In indirect lithography, a rubber *offset blanket* is interposed between the image carrier and the printing stock. A train of cylinders within the press offsets (transfers) the image from the plate to the blanket, which then transfers the image to paper.

By eliminating direct contact between the primary image carrier and the paper, this arrangement extends plate life and makes the process suitable for a wide variety of papers and other printing surfaces. [10] Another advantage of offset printing is that text and illustrations on lithographic plates do not have to be imaged backward. The double reversal that takes place in transferring the image from plate to blanket to paper yields right-reading print from right-reading text in the litho plate, which is as readable to the eye as its finished product

Other innovations were to take lithography far beyond the production limits of its stone-press days. Steady improvements in the performance of lithographic image carriers made the process desirable for many new kinds of work. So did advances in the design of *dampening systems*—the press components responsible for regulating the crucial ink-water balance during the production run. Underlying lithography's progress was the discovery that it was the natural beneficiary of the image-generating powers of *photomechanics*—a parallel science that would establish lithography as the most cost-efficient and reliable of all the printing processes.

Now lithography was poised to become a universal printing method, equally suited to the reproduction of reading matter and pictures.[11] But there could be room for only one "universal" printing method. Although it was not fully recognized until it was nearly over, the battle for dominance between offset lithography and letterpress had been joined.

## OFFSET LITHOGRAPHY DETHRONES LETTERPRESS

The offset principle was introduced at the right time.[12] Together with photography and photomechanics, it gave lithographic reproduction—which came to be known as *photolithography*—a complete set of mass-manufacturing assets. Nevertheless, seizing the throne held by letterpress would be no lightning coup for the fledgling process. Letterpress, the original method of printing, had existed for more than 500 years by the time offset lithography was ready to mount its challenge. Prior to World War II, lithographers saw their specialty derided as dirty, unreliable, and cheap—wholly inferior in quality to "real" printing by traditional letterpress methods.[13]

Letterpress's long reign rested on the fact that, until the perfection of photomechanics at the end of the nineteenth century, it was the only method capable of printing reading matter in bulk.[14] Also favoring letterpress were the short- and long-run economics of producing reading matter that consisted mostly of print. Thanks to its ability to print directly from type, letterpress was more efficient and more economical for short runs of this kind than any other reproduction procedure. The intrinsic stability of letterpress during the press run made it the process of choice for long runs as well.[15]

But letterpress's advantages had equally intrinsic disadvantages. The typical letterpress image carrier, or *press form*, was not nearly as simple to compose or to handle as the one-piece, lightweight, planographic plates associated with lithography. A press form might comprise slugs and individual pieces of type, wood engravings, photoengravings, and duplicate letterpress plates from a process known as *stereotyping*. Everything was clamped together in a heavy steel frame called a *chase*, which was assembled with positioning hardware known to pressmen of those days as *quoins* and *furniture.*

All of this preparatory work fell into the category of *makeready*—the time-consuming process of preparing the press form so that each of its elements made the correct impression on paper.[16] Positioning the elements was only the first step. For printing on a *flatbed* press, the form had to be built up so that shadow areas, which exerted less pressure on the paper than highlights, would print even and dense. Conversely, the more concentrated pressure of the highlights had to be relieved to keep those parts of the image from puncturing the paper during the run.[17] The same complex adjustments had to be made when running *relief plates* on *rotary* letterpress machines. These were tasks for skilled labor, and they added significantly to the complexity and cost of many letterpress jobs.

During the 1920s and 1930s, practitioners of offset photolithography began to capitalize upon the fact that their method needed no makeready in the letterpress sense. [18] For example, a lithographic plate properly exposed from photographic film could reproduce all the shadow-highlight contrast of the original image without the mechanical assistance required by letterpress image carriers. Artwork could be reduced or enlarged photographically without the need for expensive *photoengravings* (picture blocks etched with acid onto zinc or copper plates). [19] Reduced makeready meant major reductions in prep time for jobs switched from letterpress to the new process—and corresponding savings in total cost of the finished product.

As process improvements after World War II made offset lithography's virtues more and more apparent, many of them were seen to be ideally suited to the production of magazines. One particular advantage of offset over letterpress was that the soft rubber surface of the blanket created a clearer impression on a wider variety of paper surfaces and other substrates with both rough and smooth textures.[20] The engravings used by letterpress to print photographs and other illustrations tended to produce grainy images and sharp breaks in tints on papers that offset could handle with comparative ease. Even when these less expensive stocks were used, offset lithography could be counted on to produce soft, smooth transitions of color and tones that were more faithful to their originals than reproduction by letterpress.[21] That allowed magazine publishers who chose lithography much more latitude in their choice of printing papers, giving them better control over their largest material cost.

Offset lithographic presswork is a complicated subject, but its principal advantages for the production of magazines can be summarized as follows:

- Lithographic image carriers are thin, lightweight plates that can be imaged photographically or, nowadays, directly from digital data. Because the offset process had its origins in photomechanics, it was ideal for the reproduction of photography and photo-composed typography in magazines and other print media.[22] Today, offset lithography is proving to be equally compatible with computerized methods of text-and-image creation.

- The double reversal in the reading direction due to the interposition of the blanket makes it possible to have right-reading plates. Right-reading plates are easier to check than wrong-reading ones. [23]
- The protective action of the offset blanket extends the life of the plate and increases the number of impressions it can deliver. Plate life is one of the keys to longer production runs at higher press speeds. Generally speaking, the closer to its rated top speed that a press can be run, the more cost-efficient its operation will be.
- The smoothness of the offset blanket makes it possible to transfer the fine dot patterns of magazine-quality *halftone* images to rough-surfaced papers with good results. This also applies to the irregular surfaces and textures of *recycled papers,* which many magazines are using or evaluating in their quest for environmentally responsible printing.
- Because the offset ink film is split twice—once between plate and blanket and again between blanket and printing stock—ink coverage in an offset impression is thinner than coverage in direct printing. Thinner ink films give more faithful reproductions of fine or minute detail than thicker ink films, dry faster, and are less prone to smudging and similar problems at the delivery end of the press.[24]

Wartime price controls and materials restrictions held the growth of the lithographic industry somewhat in check until the return of peacetime economy in the early 1950s.[25] Nevertheless, offset lithography continued to outpace tradition-bound letterpress by almost every standard of innovation and production efficiency. As technological advances including presensitized plates, automatic plate processors, and stable lithographic chemistry corrected most of lithography's early shortcomings, interest in its capabilities grew—especially on the part of magazine professionals.

Art directors, dazzled by elaborate, multicolored lithographic effects that letterpress methods could not achieve, came to see the new process as the future of magazine illustration and design. Publishers began to realize its potential for improving the receipt and preparation of advertising material. A magazine printed by letterpress might have to accept illustrated matter for ads in the cumbersome form of engravings or duplicate relief plates. These could come from a variety of sources with varying degrees of quality control. A lithographed periodical, on the other hand, could start with the original artwork. The artwork could then be photographed and converted to film; retouched and color-corrected to meet the magazine's particular quality requirements; *stripped* (assembled) with other pieces of film representing the type; and exposed to make wraparound lithographic image carriers.

However attractive these capabilities might have been to the forward-looking few, they did not cause the magazine publishing industry to abandon letterpress overnight. It was not until the 1950s that developments in lithography had progressed to the point where consistently high-quality lithographic presswork was possible.[26] In the meantime, magazine presses for letterpress held sway as the giants of the letterpress industry. Some could deliver from 32 to 192 pages per cylinder-revolution at speeds up to 2,000 fpm (feet per minute, the rate at which the paper travels through the impression units of the press).[27]

But magazine publishers gradually began to realize that letterpress, after so many years of predominance, had finally reached its limit of perfectibility. Even at its technical and commercial zenith, letterpress fell short of adapting to the changing realities of magazine publishing: increasingly stringent color-quality requirements by advertisers; the demand for more editorial color; shorter-run lengths to suit special-interest publishing for niche markets; and, above all, publishers' ceaseless search for operating economies.

Offset lithography, on the other hand, still had the future ahead of it as a cheaper, more convenient, more creatively flexible method of manufacturing the diversified, colorful, heavily illustrated periodicals that the magazine-reading public now wished to receive. Eventually, industry statistics began to chronicle lithography's rise against the backdrop of letterpress's descent. It was a gradual displacement at first, but the trend accelerated throughout the postwar decades until letterpress had been all but marginalized as an option for magazine manufacturing.

Once it reached technological maturity, offset lithography's fortunes began to skyrocket. The U.S. Department of Commerce, which tracks the annual value of shipments in the major product categories of American industry, put the value of lithographed magazines and periodicals at about $34.2 million in 1954. In 1963, the value was $138.5 million, and in 1967, $296.1 million. [28] Ten years later (1977), the country was producing $1.29 billion worth of magazines and periodicals by offset lithography. It would take only three more years (1980) to break the $2 billion barrier; and by 1988 the value of shipments had doubled again, to $4.2 billion. The following year (1989) saw the next billion-dollar hurdle cleared as the total value of lithographic shipments came in at nearly $5.3 billion.

By the time that magazine lithography entered the billion-dollar range in the Department of Commerce reckoning, magazine letterpress's twilight years were already upon it. In 1977, the value of letterpress magazine and periodical printing was $499.7 million, less than 40 percent of the figure for lithographic shipments. Magazine letterpress would hold more or less steady for the next few years, but with the eighties came the headlong plunge: a nearly 50 percent drop in value of shipments from 1981 to 1982 ($506 million and $267 million, respectively); and a further skid to $161.5 million the following year.

Although the mid-1980s were boom times for many segments of the magazine business, letterpress would never regain its commercial significance in the category. Wholly obsolete by the end of the decade—by which time the entire magazine industry was groping for new production economies in the recessionary aftermath of the 1987 stock market crash—letterpress had ceased to be a practical method for manufacturing contemporary periodical publications. In 1991, letterpress accounted for only a fraction (3.1 percent) of the total value of magazine and periodical printing by all processes. By far the greatest share of this $5.7 billion prize was held by offset lithography (87.7 percent), with gravure claiming the remainder (9.1 percent) in the long-run magazine market.

Department of Commerce data were not the only indicators of letterpress's eclipse by lithography. Within the magazine printing industry itself, the transition was marked by a steadily increasing accumulation of bad news from the letterpress side of the business. For 40 years, recalled one industry veteran, plant mergers, sales, and closures bedeviled letterpress magazine printers while the rest of the industry prospered. By the end of that time, only two of the 20 printing organizations that had dominated magazine printing during the period continued under the same ownership. Only two of the 26 manufacturing plants operated by the leaders were still in existence.[29]

Even so, the passing of letterpress was something that many in the industry refused to acknowledge. Unhappily for them, resistance to change made change no less irresistible. Toward the end, hardly a month passed without word of the demise of some venerable, outwardly prosperous magazine printing establishment. These victims of history, observed the commentator cited above, "stayed with letterpress long after it lost its ability to compete in U.S. magazine production...(they) clung to letterpress and never seemed to make a successful transition to offset with its plate cost and time-saving benefits—so important for the prevailing, shorter run lengths."[30]

Letterpress printing is still used in embossing, stamping, and other special production techniques for magazines and collateral materials. Its principal legacy, however, consists of the lessons it teaches about the inevitable effects of technological change. Those who clung to letterpress made the mistake of assuming that the kinds of magazines they were able to produce were the kinds of magazines that readers and advertisers would continue to accept. In magazine production, however, market requirements dictate manufacturing methods, not the other way around. Because these requirements change constantly, no magazine manufacturing technology—no matter how long-established, how widely praised, or how extensively used—has a perpetual franchise. Once a competing method is recognized to do a better, faster, and cheaper job of producing what the market wants now, the abandonment of the old way becomes a mere matter of time—and probably not much time, given the present pace of development in all branches of magazine manufacturing technology.

Clearly, a sentimental attachment to "traditional" tools can have no useful place in the thinking of magazine production professionals who wish to survive the technological turmoil that always besets their trade. But the recent history of printing shows that even this truism is not as obvious as it may sound. Like the partisans of letterpress, those who stuck fast to time-honored but outmoded methods of composition also learned the hard way that their fidelity had been given in vain. For not only did the specification and setting of type change in response to the transformation of presswork; they also became the gateways for the entry of computerization, the technology by which every aspect of magazine production would be transformed.

## PHOTOCOMPOSITION DETHRONES HOT-METAL TYPESETTING

If the term *user-friendly* had existed in the early days of photocomposition, advocates of the new process would have been among the first to employ it. Because it did not require the molding of three-dimensional letterforms, photocomposition—known then as *cold type*—was cleaner, safer, and easier to generate than the hot-metal type it was destined to replace. Metallic type, cast in intimidating machines built around simmering pots of molten metal, came in pieces almost an inch high. For letterpress makeready, these slugs and letters had to be assembled with other three-dimensional page elements to make a ponderous image carrier that was either placed into the bed of the press or used to mold duplicate relief plates. The process was slow, and it was expensive—not least of all because it demanded the investment of large sums of money in type metal.[31]

Nonmetallic composition, in contrast, was the product of a photographic process that used paper or film as its medium. Type generated in this way did not have relief surfaces, and it could be combined relatively easily with halftones, line art, and other page elements by means of photomechanics. This essentially meant using a camera to create a photographic image of the page, usually in the form of a film negative. Then the image could be transferred from the negative to the printing plate with light and chemistry in a process similar to the developing of the original film.

Eventually the process became the standard method of producing planographic printing plates for offset lithography. Photocomposition, based on identical principles and techniques, came into its own at approximately the same time and was quickly seen as the ideal method of preparing type for lithographic image carriers. Its future now hitched to lithography's rising star, photocomposition could begin to boast of many of the same advantages. Chief among them was its potential for reducing the number of production steps required for page makeup in every major printing process.[32] So broad were the possibilities that some experimenters even devised a way of using letterpress lockups as photographic originals from which offset negatives could be developed.[33]

Like letterpress printing, hot-metal typesetting offered production advantages that kept it the method of choice long after it had been technically surpassed by newer methods. (For instance, until the advent of do-it-yourself typography on the desktop, nothing made it easier for editors to get away with last-minute copy changes to page proofs.) After World War II, however, the publishing industry's growing interest in nonmetallic composition began to highlight the shortcomings of traditional linecasting. One was its unsuitability for offset lithography and gravure, which could not use metal type directly, but needed only type images for reproduction.[34] Another was that even the most highly mechanized hot-metal typesetting systems resisted true automation. Although they could generate type with efficiency and speed, they still required their human operators to make most of the major decisions about the final appearance of the fully composed text.

As computerized composition began to change the nature of typesetting, the continuing difficulty of *hyphenation* and *justification* (h&j) with hot-metal devices became the clearest evidence of their obsolescence. By this time, most linecasting machines had been automated to the point at which they could be controlled by punched tape or cards that carried complex instructions for the proper composition of text. However, if a word had to be divided with a hyphen at the end of a line, that decision fell to the operator punching the tape—just as it would have to a typist forced to break a word at a carriage return. Special-purpose computers designed solely for the efficient preparation of tape eventually would hold decisions about word division to a minimum.[35] But even then, correct hyphenation at the ends of lines remained the overall responsibility of the operator.

Because of this, hot-metal composition retained a link to individual craftsmanship that computerized, nonmetallic composition ultimately would break. The same link to the past characterized hot-metal techniques for justification: the variable spacing of letters and words to produce typeset lines of uniform width (such as the body-copy lines in this textbook). Even though tape-operated linecasting machines preceded high-speed photographic typesetting and computerized composition by about 20 years, the justification of lines on these machines was completely mechanical. From their keyboards, operators used adjustable spacebands to fine-tune the gaps between words until the line approached its full measure (specified width). Near the ends of lines, operators had to determine whether unfilled space could accommodate an additional word or a syllable.

Experienced compositors could make these judgments at a glance.[36] It was well that they could, because their linecasters—rooted in the mechanical design of the nineteenth century—couldn't be taught to do it for them. Photographic composition, on the other hand, offered a more up-to-date combination of optical and mechanical elements. This combination gave film-based systems a flexibility and an efficiency that hot-metal equipment could not match. Photocomposition also had the good fortune to come into being at about the same time as computers and electronics for imaging, when hot-metal equipment had already reached functional maturity. Computers and electronics were to spur the development of several generations of phototypesetting systems, eventually transforming photocomposition into the most technologically advanced segment of the graphic arts. But these new sciences left hot-metal composition essentially unchanged—and, as a result, susceptible to replacement.

Photocomposition's technological break with its predecessor was fundamental. The long-established habit of referring to photocomposition systems as typesetters is misleading in that they set no type in the traditional sense. Instead, they projected images of letters onto light-sensitive paper or graphic arts film. First-generation equipment flashed bursts of light through discs or matrices containing negatives of character sets, one letter at a time. Lenses regulated the size of the images while prisms and mirrors controlled their positioning. So-called full-range equipment could mix fonts, sizes, and styles for both text and display composition.[37] (These units are the ancestors of the page-layout hardware and software systems in general use by periodical publishers today.)

Systems born in succeeding generations imaged letters with beams from cathode ray tubes (CRTs), and, still later, with laser emissions. In the mid-1960s, computerization began to eliminate the need for expert intervention in many functions relating to the composition of text. One of the most significant steps in this direction was the introduction of the noncounting keyboard, which fed a continuous string of characters to a computer programmed to handle all word-spacing calculations and other line-width decisions.[38] This combination of keyboard and controlling computer has come to be known as the front end of a photocomposition system; the back end is where imaging and output take place.

The automation of h&j was only one of many steps in photocomposition's advance to the leading edge of print production. The addition of video display terminals (VDTs) enabled operators to view their input as it was being composed and let them override inappropriate decisions by the computer. VDTs also let them see the effects of changes and error correction prior to imaging. *Area composition* systems displayed text, headline type, and graphics in position for printing—a further foreshadowing of the full-page makeup approach that dominates computerized magazine design today. Improved data storage and transmission methods, from paper tapes and magnetic cards to floppy disks and modems, helped to reduce the number of redundant keystrokes associated with most print jobs. And when personal computers began to duplicate the word-processing and typesetting capabilities that once belonged exclusively to specialized typographic equipment, photocomposition made its most important adaptive adjustment. Systems makers redesigned the units so that they could use PCs as front ends for direct input or accept text composed on PCs for output at the back end.

The desktop publishing revolution of the mid-1980s, covered later in this chapter, merged all of these trends in a way that would end typesetting's status as an independent part of the production sequence. By that point, photocomposition had extended its sway over most of the publishing world, leaving hot-metal methods in use at only a handful of magazines. As with the displacement of letterpress by offset lithography, however, the change was anything but a foregone conclusion. In the late 1960s, when the migration from hot type to cold type began to gather real momentum, the publishing industry's installed base of linecasters outnumbered its complement of full-range photographic composing machines by nearly 200 to 1. Traditional typesetting was especially well entrenched in its birthplace, the newspaper industry, where letterpress printing still reigned and where the text-heavy content of newspaper pages still favored hot-metal composition.[39]

Nevertheless, photocomposition had drawn the publishing industry into an irrevocable break with the past—not just in terms of setting type, but in the entire nature of printing's relationship to new information-processing technologies. In particular, the computerization of typography showed that specialists from other disciplines were starting to redefine many of the production tasks that had once been dictated by the skills and heritage of printing craftsmen. Some astute observers saw an entirely new direction for printing as a result: "For the first time in the more than 550 year history of printing outsiders are in a position to examine printing procedures....Systems analysis is in its beginning in the printing industry, and the composing room has become the first testing ground....Computerized composition is but the first step in a thorough transformation of the whole printing industry."[40]

Once the first step had been taken, there would be no turning back. Today desktop publishing and electronic prepress, the children of photocomposition, are the gateways through which advanced technologies continue to transform printing into a communications medium for the twenty-first century.

## STEADY ADVANCES IN PRODUCTION CAPABILITY

Hindsight tends to depict printing history as a preordained and neatly sequential chain of events that must have been perfectly obvious to everyone as they unfolded. In fact, the evolution of printing technology more closely resembles a gaggle of random lines on a collision course to an unforeseen state of affairs that only hindsight could certify as progress. Production technology is woven of many strands, some of them fundamental and enduring, others incidental and impermanent. Throughout the long time it took offset lithography and automated photocomposition to dominate periodical publishing, many other trends independently fed the stream of mass-production capability for magazine printing. Some were related to the mechanization of presswork (including letterpress); others to the image-generation techniques that gave lithography its advantages as a reproduction process (although lithography was not the only process to benefit).

As these trends converged, they eliminated the abiding dilemma that had restrained the growth of printing and the graphic arts from the middle of the fifteenth century to the last third of the nineteenth. This was the fact that text and pictures were most efficiently reproduced when they were reproduced separately. Printing methods that worked well for bulk reading matter were not suitable for complex images, and vice versa—a conflict that made the idea of profusely illustrated reading material seem as self-contradicting as the horseless carriage or heavier-than-air flight.

The contradiction persisted until graphic arts photography and photomechanics became workable. Photography for the graphic arts aims at producing images that will translate well to the printing press. Photomechanics assists the translation with halftone screens, special films, and other equipment and supplies for re-creating photographic images on printing plates and cylinders. Together, photography and photomechanics completed the mechanization of the printing process.[41] The result was that the traditional division between the reproduction of pictures and that of reading matter was completely overcome.[42] Eventually, most graphic processes became capable of handling both, and illustrations at last became practical and economical to reproduce. Now the stage truly was set for the explosive growth of advertising, periodical, book, and commercial printing.

The development of photomechanics closely paralleled advances in photography.[43] One of the key breakthroughs was the perfection of the process that enabled printing presses to simulate gradations of continuous (unbroken) tones in original images. A press cannot reproduce shadow-and-highlight contrasts by varying the amounts of ink in dark and light portions of the image; the printing plate either accepts ink or it does not. However, photomechanics revealed that if the image was first broken down into a pattern of minute dots on the image carrier, the press could create the illusion of variable tones in solid densities. The earliest known use of this technique, called *halftoning*, took place in 1852 when an Englishman named William Henry Fox Talbot produced the first screened engraving by laying a piece of fine gauze between the coated metal printing plate and a negative of the original picture. By the turn of the century, halftone screening had brought black-and-white photography to the pages of newspapers and magazines, and the technique was also being used to reproduce illustrations in full color. [44]

Printing presses, meanwhile, grew apace with the Industrial Revolution in their potential for mass-production output. Although human-powered presses remained in use throughout the nineteenth century, steam-driven models introduced as early as 1814 began to redefine productive capacity in terms of thousands of impressions per hour. The first American steam press for lithography was available not long after the Civil War, and the offset lithographic press as we know it today by 1906. (Interestingly, the technique of offsetting the image from plate to blanket—the development that more than any other would assure the future of lithography—was discovered more or less by accident in the operation of a traditional lithographic "stone" press. Only after the offset effect was noticed in existing equipment did press manufacturers begin to design new models that could exploit its advantages.[45])

One of the most significant steps in the direction of mass-produced printing was the development of presses fed by *webs*, or continuous rolls, of paper. Ever since Gutenberg's time, many kinds of printing have been done on sheets of paper cut to whatever size best suits the format of the job at hand. Sheetfed printing still accounts for billions of dollars worth of commercial presswork every year, including the production of thousands of short- to medium-run magazines and other periodicals. However, much of the large-scale growth in the lithographic industry can be attributed to the even greater productive capacity of web offset presses, which are used to produce newspapers, large-circulation magazines, business forms, catalogs, direct mail, books, encyclopedias, and a variety of commercial printing.[46]

Web presses have been in operation in America and Britain since the middle of the nineteenth century. Today, as then, their principal advantages over sheetfed equipment are superior printing speed and greater manufacturing capacity. The feeder unit of a sheetfed press has to grasp each sheet individually for transfer to the register unit, a mechanism that positions the sheet for correct travel through the train of impression cylinders. Because a web press feeds from a roll of paper that unwinds at high speed, sheet-handling steps are eliminated and overall operation is much faster. To avoid drying problems associated with high-speed printing, many web presses use hot-air ovens that "set" the ink as the paper completes its trip through the printing units.

Most web offset presses perform additional functions, called *in-line operations*, that add further manufacturing steps to the basic presswork. For example, folding units at the delivery end of the press automatically form printed webs into sections known as *signatures*, which are then cut and fastened together to make finished copies of the publication. Other in-line operations include paste binding, perforating, numbering, rotary sheeting, and slitting.[47]

Modern web offset presses are showcases of manufacturing efficiency. The newest models are operated from computerized consoles that can store ink settings and other production data in digital form, a feature that eliminates repetitive makeready steps when jobs are put back on press. Built-in sensors run diagnostic checks on press functions and monitor the print quality of the run in real time. Other controls automatically adjust web position, tension, and other factors to ensure that images will be properly registered: that is, printed in their correct spatial relationships to one another. Web presses can also detect breaks in paper and splice new rolls to exhausted ones "on the fly," without interrupting the press run.

These assets, combined with the fact that paper in rolls is usually cheaper to use than paper in sheets, have made web offset printing the method of choice for many kinds of periodical publishing. Web offset presses traditionally have been reserved for longer-run publications (50,000 and above) because their cost of makeready tends to exceed that of sheetfed makeready. (Since publication printers recover the cost of makeready by spreading it over the total number of copies manufactured, it would make poor economic sense to put a small-run job on a high-capacity press.) However, "half-web" models and other innovations in web press technology are blurring the boundary between web- and sheetfed manufacturing economies—to web offset's growing advantage in short- to medium-run periodical markets. The heightened competition gives many magazine publishers a broader choice of where, how, and for how much to get their printing done.

# A PORTRAIT OF MAGAZINE GRAVURE

When publication runs are extremely long, or when high-volume color quality requirements are exceptionally stringent, there is little need for debate about the best method to use. Gravure predominates at the top level of contemporary periodical publishing, where (despite some market shrinkage) its hold on the production of the major mass-circulation titles is secure. But there is more to gravure's reputation than page counts. Its distinctive printing characteristics make it the most visually pleasing form of graphic reproduction for magazines, as well as the process yielding the most consistent and predictable results.

Magazine gravure is the most widely used form of *intaglio* printing, the opposite of *relief* printing in terms of the way its image carriers are prepared. Instead of the raised letters and engravings of a relief process like letterpress, an intaglio image carrier for gravure consists of a pattern of sunken cells or wells etched into a copper cylinder or wraparound plate. The unetched portions of the cylinder or plate surface represent the nonprinting areas. The plate cylinder rotates in a bath of ink. The excess is wiped off the surface in squeegee fashion by a flexible steel *doctor blade*. The ink remaining in the thousands of recessed cells transfers the image to the paper as the web passes between the plate cylinder and the impression cylinder.[48]

Rotary intaglio printing from an engraved cylinder is known traditionally as *rotogravure*. The cylinder is usually made of a steel or aluminum core or base, electroplated with copper and then etched or engraved. Etching is done chemically. Modern tools for engraving have included diamond-headed mechanical styluses, laser beams, and, most recently, electron beams. The entire cylinder can be chrome plated to extend the life of the engraving and stabilize image quality over long runs.[49]

Although gravure has been used as a fine-art printing method for nearly as long as letterpress, it came into use as a manufacturing process only at about the same time as offset lithography.[50] The first intaglio plate engraved on metal was used for printing in Germany in 1446, just a handful of years after Gutenberg perfected letterpress printing using raised metal type. Intaglio image carriers were mechanically incompatible with letterpress printing, so books combining type and engravings could not be mass-produced. However, this did not deter Dürer, Rembrandt, Rubens, and many other of Europe's greatest artists from practicing the fine art of engraving, which remained the dominant method of pictorial reproduction until well into the nineteenth century.[51]

Fine-art engraving was a laborious, multistep process that left much to be desired when it came to reproducing accurate gradations of shades and tones. It was not until the middle of the nineteenth century that graphic artists developed simplified photochemical means of transferring gradated images to printing plates. The person who successfully applied these techniques to intaglio imaging was Karel

Klic, who today is recognized as the inventor of modern gravure printing. Klic also pioneered the transition from flat printing plates to printing from a cylinder; developed the doctor blade; and designed a method of printing color on a web press. [52]

Web-fed gravure printing on a *perfecting* press—one capable of printing both surfaces of the paper at once—had been patented in France by 1860. In 1892, Samuel Fawcett, an English engraver, devised a way to reproduce photographic images on gravure image carriers, setting the stage for adoption of the process by the newspaper industry. On April 5, 1914, the first gravure newspaper magazine appeared as a supplement to the *New York Times*.[53] By the 1920s magazines were being printed in full color on multi-unit gravure presses.[54]

Although gravure remains the printing method of choice for many of the nation's most popular long-run magazines, newspaper supplements, and catalogs, publication gravure is the preserve of a small and select industry whose resources were further concentrated by mergers and acquisitions in the late 1980s. Today, gravure plants can be found in only a handful of American cities. In sharp contrast to the thousands of offset lithographers doing publication work, the publication gravure manufacturing base comprised only 6 companies, 26 plants, and 155 gravure presses in 1993.[55]

Despite continuing, gradual declines in the total number of copies printed annually, the combined output of this comparatively tiny segment is enormous. Gravure production of magazines stood at 2.73 billion copies in 1992, representing about 30 major U.S. magazines printed wholly or partially by gravure.[56] (*National Geographic*, for example, prints editorial text and photographs by gravure, while the advertising and cover are printed by offset lithography.[57]) Gravure's share of the total number of pages printed in this group was 69 percent, or 266.8 billion pages. Many of the "top 25" consumer titles are printed by gravure, with the process accounting for 68.4 percent of their total circulation in 1992. Advertising revenues for gravure publications that year came to more than $1.9 billion. Among these household-name circulation and advertising-sales leaders are: *TV Guide* (753,913,732 total copies printed in 1992); *Reader's Digest* (195,101,712); *National Geographic* (116,499,048); *Better Homes & Gardens* (96,031,020); *Good Housekeeping* (61,672,260); and *Playboy* (40,831,560).[58]

Gravure bestrides other publishing markets besides magazines. About 90 percent of the 3.3 billion-copy annual circulation of Sunday magazines, also known as roto sections or Sunday supplements, is produced by gravure. Gravure also has a significant (20.3 percent) share of the catalog and directory printing market and is growing faster than offset lithography in the free-standing newspaper advertising insert market, where it accounts for 11.5 percent of all pieces produced.[59]

Gravure owes its lion's share of large-circulation magazine production to a number of characteristics that make it the ideal process for jobs requiring high quality and extremely long press runs. To begin with, it is the least complex of all printing systems, with the fastest press start-up and the most direct press controls.[60] Mechanically simple compared to other printing presses, a gravure press can be readily combined with converting processes such as laminating, sheeting, folding, creasing, die-cutting, and slitting. [61]

Gravure is also a reliable, predictable process that goes easy on raw materials. A major attraction for budget-conscious magazine publishers who buy their own paper is the fact that gravure has less than half the paper spoilage rate of offset lithography.[62] Offset sometimes requires the running and discarding of numerous test sheets before color and registration can be approved, and even then, unwanted variations can occur during the production run. Unlike offset lithography, gravure does not have to maintain an ink-water balance and is thus spared many problems of keeping color consistent from start to finish. [63]

Steel-cored, copper-and-chrome plated, reusable gravure cylinders are built to stand up to press runs that can last for days. Gravure cylinders routinely yield several million impressions before replating is needed; reports of press runs as high as 20 million impressions from the same cylinder are not uncommon.[64] Some gravure presses, known as variable-cutoff presses, can switch from one cylinder size to another. This feature lets them print a wider range of image sizes than offset presses that operate with fixed-diameter cylinders.

But gravure's hold on mass-circulation magazine publishing stems above all from its reputation for delivering the highest-quality image of the major printing processes.[65] Photography, in particular, reproduces with greater fidelity to the original because gravure imaging produces a "true" halftone effect that lithography cannot duplicate. In a gravure image carrier, the darker areas of the photograph are composed of deep cells that transfer more ink than do shallower cells in the highlight areas. (It will be remembered that shadows and highlights on a lithographic plate are the products of an illusion created by a pattern of variably-sized, two-dimensional halftone dots.) Photographs reproduced by gravure display a greater contrast between light and dark and print with richer, deeper colors from the comparatively heavy film of ink that the process deposits on the paper.[66] Because gravure inks dry quickly, they avoid problems sometimes associated with printing one ink over another while the colors are still wet (as occurs in offset and letterpress).

Gravure's ability to achieve these effects on a wide variety of papers stands out as its biggest single advantage.[67] Because the gravure process prints from plate directly to paper using relatively little pressure, it can run lightweight papers with high ink densities and minimal *dot gain* (the tendency of printing dots to appear larger on paper than they do on the image carrier).[68] Publication gravure presses also obtain good results with stocks ranging in quality from coarse newsprint to expensive coated papers for high-end magazine and catalog work.

As has been the case with offset lithographic presses, the productive capacity of gravure presses has improved steadily over the last several decades. In 1960 the machine considered the world's largest gravure publication press could print 32 magazine pages per revolution at a running speed of about 1,500 feet per minute (fpm).[69] Today many gravure machines can print four times as many comparable pages per revolution at double the 1960 speed. [70] In terms of sheer size, a 125"-wide gravure press operated by Brown Printing Co. (Franklin, Ky.) is now said to be the world's largest.[71] Most frequently encountered are cylinder widths of 70 to 72.5 inches in presses configured with eight printing units. Variable folders have become standard in-line accessories for most publication gravure presses. [72]

Gravure's only major drawback is seen in the time and expense required to prepare the printing cylinder. Modern electronic cylinder-engraving machines are sophisticated precision instruments with high capital-investment and operating costs. Although their engraving heads can cut thousands of cells per second, imaging a typical publication cylinder with this equipment could take hours—an expensive interval in the production cycle of any magazine job. Changes are also costly, because if an error correction or author's alteration is specified after engraving is completed, the cylinder must then be re-engraved (in contrast to the comparatively simpler and cheaper process of remaking lithographic plates from corrected film). The threshold of cost-effectiveness is not absolute, but generally speaking, gravure becomes difficult to justify for press runs of less than 100,000 impressions. The cost of gravure cylinder preparation is so much higher than other prepress processes that some companies refuse jobs of less than one million copies. [73]

Run-length economics may change, thanks to the introduction of *halftone gravure*, a process that permits cylinders to be engraved from screened halftone positives instead of the continuous-tone film required by conventional gravure. The net result is to cut cylinder preparation time approximately in half. Since off-press proofs can be made from the halftone film, corrections can be made to the films before the printing cylinders are engraved.

With halftone gravure, the printing process stays the same—only the prepress procedure is different.[74] Most magazines and Sunday supplements printed by gravure now use the process, and some publishers foresee its eventual adoption by medium-run magazines.

## MAGAZINE PRODUCTION EVOLVES AS A DIGITALLY DRIVEN TECHNOLOGY

For a time, newspapers tended to outpace magazines in their adoption of advanced publishing technologies. This inclination to experiment stemmed from the papers' perennial interest in maximizing the efficiency of production typography, the branch in which most of the principal developments were occurring. By the mid-1960s, for example, nearly 40 newspapers were successfully using digital computers for hyphenated-and-justified typesetting, including at least one paper that planned to use its computer for page makeup.[75]

But magazines were taking their first, tentative steps in the digital direction as well. Among the earliest adopters were publishers of trade magazines, who found the computer a powerful means of composing text-intensive annual suppliers' directories for the industries served by their titles. A pioneering example, the "Merchandise Directory Number" of *Hardware Age*, July, 1965, consisted of 632 pages of three-column type from a conventional typesetter driven by a paper tape that had been punched by a custom program on an RCA 301 computer.[76] By then computers were also being tested as tools for the design of illustrations. The July 1965 issue of *Fortune*, for example, sported a cover photograph of a design generated by a computer on the screen of an oscilloscope. As no conventional graphic design tools had been used, the cover was the first in the magazine's history to have been created entirely by machine. [77]

But the long twilight of traditional production methods demonstrates that not everyone was as quick as the publishers of *Hardware Age* and *Fortune* to grasp the nascent connections between electronic data processing and the creation of the printed page. Even today, when the process has been so thoroughly digitized that we can no longer conceive of publishing anything without at least some help from computers, the trends are seldom easy to follow. To make the point again, "progress" in publishing technology is never linear. Most of the time, it loops, doubles back, and advances one step for every two taken. Because the obsolete and the transitional coexist so closely within its welter of contradictions, even the experts can have a hard time telling them apart.

That is why no decisions in publishing are more problematic than those related to the selection of production systems. The way technology is introduced—to say nothing of the way it is marketed—virtually assures the prospect of a regrettable choice somewhere along the line. Again and again, ostensible "breakthroughs" turn out to be short-lived hybrids of unproved innovations in search of a market and obsolete equipment in need of resuscitation. Vendors sow further disorder in the marketplace by copycatting one another when true technological one-upmanship fails. Systems overlap. Standards are stillborn. Even genuinely groundbreaking technology can go unnoticed until its advantages and applications have been properly defined.

The net result is that the evolution of publishing technology becomes almost as difficult to retrace as it is to predict. A good way to detect a thread in what has happened is to put to the test of time an earlier forecast of what might happen, given the trends and events of the day. One such glimpse of publishing's future was attributed to Dr. N. I. Korman, a research scientist for Radio Corporation of America, in a 1965 article for a printing trade magazine. Once computer-generated type was a reality, Dr. Korman predicted, "Photocopy generation will produce full pages of text, line drawings, and halftones on film, automatically processed and handled. At a later stage of development, the film probably will be by-passed and the plate will be produced by an electron beam, an electronically controlled laser beam, by triggering of a chemical action or in some other way not yet established."[78]

Many events in the 30 years following the publication of this article were to prove how prescient Dr. Korman's forecast was (except, perhaps, in its assumption that fully computerized typesetting systems would be in widespread use by 1970).

Once digitally generated and stored type had become a reality, publishing systems began to incorporate illustrations and photography as well. Soon, tasks that had been restricted to the artist's desk and the stripper's light table would migrate to the video display terminals of systems that let their operators assemble and display entire pages as they would appear in print. Film for platemaking would be imaged, screened, and separated by digital equipment and, eventually, by personal computers. And although graphic arts film remains the key ingredient of most publication prepress work, that dependence is vanishing. As Dr. Korman foresaw, alternative technologies now make it possible to expose printing plates directly from digital page data without using film as an intermediate step.

An "Electronic Publishing Chronology"[79] compiled by Dr. Frank N. Romano of the Rochester Institute of Technology recapitulates this story by charting the most significant developments and product introductions in the field since 1950. Dr. Romano's timeline actually begins in 1926, when the idea of using coded paper tape to drive linecasting machines was first conceived. This concept would lead to the full automation of the typesetting process and paved the way for the transmission of typesetting data (via TeleTypeSetting, or TTS).

The 1950s saw the adoption of first- and second-generation phototypesetters, and with them the first signs of a shift away from traditional hot-metal typography. By the middle of the 1960s, IBM had released the first data processing program for hyphenation and justification on a programmable computer. Hard on the heels of this development was the introduction of the world's first CRT phototypesetter, a costly computer-driven unit with an output speed of 1,000 characters per second.

Price reductions accompanied scientific developments as typesetting—now clearly the technological bellwether for the entire printing industry—led the way into the 1970s. The decade opened with the appearance of video editing terminals and ad makeup systems capable of displaying sizes and positions of type on screen. The first laser platemakers and laser scanners, though ahead of their time in terms of practical marketability, foreshadowed powerful new imaging techniques soon to come. Before the decade was over, Xerox would introduce a publishing device destined to become as ubiquitous and familiar as the photocopier: the laser printer.

With the 1980s came the dawn of the personal computer and the first signs that the day of publishing systems for experts only was waning. A watershed period for print production in every sense, the 1980s ushered in new technologies designed to turn every PC user's "desktop," or digital workspace, into a mini-factory for production tasks that had always lain far beyond the technical reach of nonspecialists. By the end of the decade, many people who were not printers were using deft combinations of hardware and software to compose type, create and place graphic images, assemble pages, and otherwise prepare complete publications for the printing press. These off-the-shelf tools would become instruments not only for democratizing the publishing process but also for demolishing the conventional wisdom that had defined its routines and relationships for centuries.

Nevertheless, initial steps in this radical new direction were tentative. The first personal computers with the ability to display type on screen made little headway because, as Dr. Romano has observed, nobody noticed the typographic metaphor.[80] Typography was still the province of expensive, "high-end" phototypesetting systems operated not by those who originated the text to be typeset, but by specialists hired to turn text into type by means unavailable to the originators. In the specialists' view, no type generated on a desktop computer could provide anything like the typographic quality the professional publishing market was used to obtaining from high-end equipment. And in fact, the primitive quality of the typographic output from the first desktop computers tended to prove the specialists correct.

What the professional typesetting community failed to anticipate was the willingness of publishers, advertisers, and others to put quality into the scales with control—the expanded control of the publishing process that personal computers now promised to give them. The principal components of that control were set in place in 1985, the year we have come to identify with the birth of desktop publishing and the beginning of the digital revolution in publishing. These building-block technologies consisted of:

- *Personal computers* capable of storing digitized type fonts and graphics and displaying them in a form more or less resembling what they would look like in print. Apple's Macintosh was the first machine to offer true desktop publishing capability of this kind.
- *Page layout software* for assembling text and images generated by the computer into complete pages with all type and design elements in place. Aldus Corporation's PageMaker, the vanguard application in 1985, continues in widespread use today, although Quark Inc.'s QuarkXPress is the application of choice for magazine publishing operations.
- *Laser output devices* designed to turn page data into hard-copy proofs or graphic arts film for the ensuing stages of print production. Apple's LaserWriter was the first successful example for low-resolution paper output on the desktop. Camera-ready repro and film for the later stages of production came from high-resolution *imagesetters* introduced by Linotype-Hell, Agfa, and other manufacturers.
- A *page description language*—a set of "invisible" software instructions— enabling output devices to receive and interpret page-layout instructions in a standardized way. Output devices that support a common "PDL" can process page data at whatever resolution (image quality) they are capable of rendering. This being the case, any personal computer able to save type, graphics, and page "geometry" in the format of that PDL is a potential front end for a wide assortment of publishing equipment. Within months of its 1985 debut, Adobe Systems Inc.'s PostScript was recognized as the graphic communication industry's preeminent PDL. Most type manufacturers were quick to reissue their font libraries in PostScript format.

In 1985, a publishing system comprising these tools offered what was then regarded as medium-quality resolution.[81] Type generated at 300 dots per inch on an Apple LaserWriter could appear crude to a trained eye, and many aspects of the fine typographic control afforded by high-end phototypesetting systems were missing. Illustration consisted of line art, black-and-white photographs, and other simple elements; color, if used at all, was limited to "spot" placement.

Nevertheless, even a system with these modest capabilities let its users do the heretofore unimaginable: direct the entire page design and assembly process up to and including the output of a camera-ready original, all without dedicated (special-purpose) production equipment or the services of people trained to operate it. No longer did magazines have to depend on the resources and workflows of outside suppliers. Now publishers could begin to bring typesetting and related functions in-house, where they could be made part of the general scheme of management.

Forward-thinking publishers could see that implications for production scheduling, editorial flexibility, advertising coordination, and cost control were enormous. It was against these powerful attractions that the professionals' arguments for the qualitative superiority of their output began to crumble. Counter-arguments for new concepts such as *acceptable*, *good enough*, and *pleasing* quality were unmistakable signals that once again the publishing marketplace was linking its quality standards to real-world production efficiency, not to ethereal ideals of craftsmanship.

Fortunately for quality, desktop publishing tools kept pushing their own benchmarks as their popularity grew. By the end of the 1980s, given sufficiently powerful personal computers and adequately trained operators, there was no magazine prepress function that could not be carried out, or at least initiated, on the desktop. Applications like Adobe Systems' Illustrator and Photoshop gave publication designers powerful tools not only for creating and manipulating graphic images but also for ensuring their reproduction on press. Color separation—the process of breaking down the colors of original materials into chromatic elements that a printing press can work with—became part of the desktop routine with QuarkXPress, a page-layout program that could output separated images directly from the Macintosh to the imagesetter. In a step that tolled the closing bell for the manual film assembly process known as stripping, imagesetter manufacturers introduced large-format units capable of outputting film with pages automatically "imposed" in place by instructions from software.

Small wonder that by the 1990s, desktop prepress systems had started to replace high-end color systems in magazine production and many other kinds of publication work. A *Folio:* survey of magazine production managers in 1991 found that "desktop page composition has come a long way in a short time. Virtually unheard of five years ago, today it is de rigueur...all but 14.5 percent of our respondents were using personal computers in some form in their electronic prepress operations."[82] Many were working with suites of equipment known as *color electronic prepress systems*, or CEPS. These arrays of computer-controlled input and output devices could perform all the steps from inputting the original copy to exposing the press plate in one system of integrated units. [83] A CEPS might consist entirely of desktop or tabletop components, including comparatively low-cost digital color scanners; or it might have software "links" to older but still productive high-end systems that handled the final stages of processing and output.

As more and more publishers grew convinced of their need to have these tools at their direct disposal, the traditional view of production and its old constants of supply and demand began to fracture. Oversold, in some cases, on the advantages of bringing their prepress workload in-house, publishing companies and advertising agencies for print media invested heavily in desktop prepress systems. Typographers, color separation houses, and other traditional prepress vendors repositioned themselves as desktop specialists or faced commercial extinction by a new breed of trade shop, the all-digital, quick-turnaround "service bureau." Printing plants, hoping to capture more presswork by jockeying for more prep work, became vertically integrated providers of prepress services they once subcontracted to their trade suppliers.

But the digital transformation of magazine manufacturing was by no means over, and as time went on, it was seen to have brought mixed blessings as well as undisputed benefits. Arguments about the sacrifice of quality on the altar of control continued to divide professional opinion, and new technology continued to burst into the marketplace at a rate that bewildered even the savviest production hands. But what most surprised the publishing community was discovering that behind confusion over new equipment lay even deeper uncertainty about the new roles and responsibilities of the people called upon to operate it.

## DIGITAL TECHNOLOGY TRANSFORMS THE TRADITIONAL MAGAZINE PRODUCTION CHAIN

*Production chain* is a blanket term that publishers have often used to refer to the concatenation of equipment, procedures, and skills needed to take a magazine from the raw-copy stage through printing and distribution. In the old days, production was very much like a chain in that it consisted of tightly linked steps occurring in strict order, with little variation from job to job. Each step was a specialty executed on specialized equipment by someone trained to be proficient in that phase of the work, though not necessarily in other phases.

But after the integration of most prepress operations on the desktop in 1985, it grew increasingly difficult to think of production in this segmented and sequential way. Writing in 1991, one production manager observed that new prepress technologies were crisscrossing magazine production's traditionally parallel elements (steps handled as separate operations) with its linear aspects (the necessity of completing one step before proceeding to the next).[84] Now, for example, text could be edited, formatted, and paginated simultaneously, by the same person. Page data could then be passed directly to platemaking without intermediate steps. Production choke points would be eliminated as everything became part of the same electronic workflow.

This was far from being offered as a utopian vision of production's future, however. Just as the emerging trends of 1991 have become the standard operating procedures of today, potential problems glimpsed in them then are predominant concerns for production managers and publishers now. The truth is that desktop computers have hammered the traditional production chain into a production mesh—a matrix of tasks linked in new patterns that have challenged nearly all of the conventional wisdom of production management. As in all such challenges, progress has been achieved at some expense to the comfort levels of those involved. Following are some prominent examples of change and conflict wrought by digital technology:

- The computing power available to every member of the magazine staff has drawn everyone into the production process, causing job functions to overlap. Editors can set type and "flow" copy into page layouts; artists can impose signatures and separate color images. But as editors, artists, and others with new-found production capabilities stray into one another's traditional territories, turf wars and other structural problems are hard to avoid.
- Production timetables based on paper workflows have been replaced with new schedules pegged to the accelerated through-put of digital page data. This has increased publication efficiency by pushing editorial deadlines and ad closings nearer to distribution dates. It has also placed stiffer demands for productivity on systems and personnel.
- Digital publishing technology—automation in its purest form—makes it possible to process more pages with fewer people. Workforce reductions have clear economic benefits for the business side, but they complicate the deployment of staff resources and intensify problems of job overlap and production efficiency.
- Because digital technology changes so rapidly, production competence is no longer the result of perfecting a static body of skills over a period of years. Many digital production skills are ad hoc, with useful lives no greater than those of the systems on which they are practiced. Since most new publishing systems are thought to have about 18 months before obsolescence sets in,[85] continuous retraining in new tools and techniques has become the real key to preserving production efficiency.
- The economics of production management have changed as a consequence of equipment turnover, job realignment, and departmental overlap. In a digital publishing environment, wrote one observer, "(s)hifting areas of responsibility and changing processes cause expenses to shift between cost centers. Bean counters' reports are now apples and oranges."[86] This uncertainty, coupled with the fact that the period for recovering investments in digital

publishing equipment can be brief, makes it difficult for magazines to gauge the profitability of their production operations.

Nevertheless, the magazine publishing industry's rush to embrace digital tools signals its willingness to meet the challenges and opportunities of the new production mesh head-on. For example, a 1994 *Folio:* survey of production executives found that desktop publishing systems were being used in nearly nine out of ten of the design, editorial, and production departments at the respondents' magazines.[87] This abundance of digital resources has brought its share of complications, but it has also given many magazine staff members a greater personal stake in the process by increasing their participation in the manufacture of the finished product. In the long run, say the experts, this is a beneficial trend: "We hear good things about car manufacturers who replace their assembly lines—where each person installs one widget—with teams that build whole cars. The consolidation of prepress functions will have a similar effect, except that the team will create a magazine."[88]

Needless to say, the skills of the production manager are the underpinnings of the entire production team. Today's production manager must be technologist, troubleshooter, trainer, expediter, and mediator in equal measure. But above all, he or she must be a leader. "Like a coach in the NFL," counseled a veteran of the profession, "regardless of how well you know the game, the front office, the ticket sellers, and the players all have to be behind you to bring home a winner."[89] Only by dint of example and inspiration can production managers hope to protect the strength and resilience of the production mesh in the fast-changing digital publishing environment.

## THE DIGITAL DESKTOP PREPRESS REVOLUTION

### Craftsmanship Confronts the Computer

#### *Power to the Originator*

Beginning around the midpoint of this century, print production was transformed first by a revolution and then by a civil war. As we have seen, the revolution was the overthrow of letterpress printing and hot-metal typography, the processes that had dominated the manufacture of printed matter for nearly 500 years. Nevertheless, for many magazine publishers, little had changed. Even though the dethronement of relief printing had transformed the underlying technology of an entire industry, printing's traditional power structure remained serenely intact. Printing continued to be a rigidly defined hierarchy of tasks for experts only. This meant that the tasks were exclusive to the craftsmen who specialized in them. Only typographers set type; nobody but strippers assembled type and images into pages; color separators alone processed color images; and so on throughout the traditional production chain.

As a result, magazine publishers had relatively little hands-on influence over the manufacture of their periodicals. They could, and did, use their purchasing power to obtain top-quality work from the typographers, printers, and other trade service vendors who bid competitively for their business. Even so, most magazine work consisted of out-sourcing arrangements monitored neither in real time nor at the point of production, but after the fact and from a remote location—the publisher's business office. What went on in the type studio or in the printer's prep department did not directly involve the publisher until a proof was delivered, or a change needed approval, or something had gone wrong. Production, for reasons of technology and tradition, lay outside the primary control of the people most urgently concerned with its success.

As business executives with bottom-line accountability, magazine publishers are rarely satisfied with arrangements that fail to give them at least some measure of control over the various facets of publication management. In their early experiments with desktop tools, publishers fired the first shots of a campaign to seize production prerogatives that in their view rightfully belonged to them. The letterpress-to-offset revolution had opened new frontiers of production quality and efficiency. Now the personal computer was at hand as a weapon of insurrection against an entrenched manufacturing system that took its hegemony in the new territory for granted. The civil war between consumers and providers of production services was on.

As magazine publishing enters a new century in which every aspect of production will be based on controlling flows of digital data, it can be reported that partisans of the personal computer have prevailed. Desktop publishing still has bugs and shortcomings, but its essential promise has been fulfilled. Given properly configured personal computers, adequate knowledge of publishing software, and access to peripheral equipment, nonspecialists can set type; lay out pages; add artwork and photography; specify color; make and correct color separations; and output the results for proofing, film and plate making, or even for direct imaging on certain kinds of digital printing presses. The key word here is *nonspecialists*. With some important exceptions and qualifications, it is accurate to say that personal computer users with little or no formal training in the traditional arts and crafts of printing now can execute many production steps they would have been obliged to entrust to experts just a handful of years ago.

Desktop publishing is not a production panacea, nor is it a cheap shortcut to quality for dilettante do-it-yourselfers. Self-taught desktop publishers seldom get the same first-rate results as professionals, particularly with respect to type and publication design. And, as printers know all too well, desktop publishing makes it possible to create many things on a computer screen that are impossible to reproduce on a printing press. Nonetheless, careful and conscientious desktop publishing can achieve acceptable results that will carry through reliably to subsequent stages of production. This means that a reasonable compromise on quality can be traded for increased production control when work is brought in-house by means of desktop technology.

## Changing Economics, Changed Relationships

The prospect of in-house control also gives publishers an economic motive for choosing sides in the desktop civil war. When magazines use personal computers to set type, format pages, and incorporate photographs and artwork, they are performing tasks they once had to pay outsiders to handle for them. As executives responsible for the bottom line, publishers are required to establish as much control over the costs of production as their resources permit. The power of desktop publishing lets them achieve that degree of control and, in the long run, enjoy the savings that result.

This changes the nature of the relationships between publishers and their service providers: the *working* relationship, because now the publishers are doing some of the work themselves; and the *economic* relationship, because publishers no longer need to buy the same kind or quantity of service from their vendors as they once did. The challenge then becomes managing these changed relationships efficiently and profitably. Today's magazine publishers have to choose among all sorts of production options that did not exist for the generation of publishers that preceded them. Obviously, the first thing they need to know is what their options are.

## EQUIPPING FOR DESKTOP PREPRESS

*Desktop publishing* is the popular term, although some of its practitioners prefer to call it *electronic publishing* or *prepublishing*. Whatever the designation, it refers to the use of personal computers, application software, networks, image-capturing devices, and output equipment to accomplish the various tasks of prepress in a magazine publishing environment. (Prepress includes everything that must be done to convert original material into a form that can be reproduced on a printing press.)

The main attraction of desktop publishing is that it gives magazine staff members more temporal control over their portions of the production workflow. With in-house desktop, for example, art directors can output and correct color page proofs in their own offices instead of waiting for a trade shop across town to send them by messenger. Editors can make last-minute copy changes to keep up with late-breaking news. Ad sales staff can offer clients more flexibility on closings. By eliminating delays stemming from dependence on outside services, electronic publishing buys precious extra time for everyone connected with the production of the magazine.

In a professional publishing environment such as a magazine, the degree of control achieved relates directly to the amount of money invested. A basic computer workstation with software for building simple pages with type, spot color, charts, and line art can be assembled for a few thousand dollars. A fully configured electronic publishing network—one that will handle multi-operator, high-volume workloads including color separations and impositions—can run into the high six-figure range. And there are the hidden but high costs of system integration, which means making sure that all the boxes work in harmony; and of operator training, for making sure that users know how to obtain consistently printable results from the publishing equipment placed into their often inexperienced hands.

No matter what their price tags, in-house electronic publishing systems have the same basic components:

- input devices, or scanners;
- publishing platforms—the personal computers or workstations on which pages are designed;
- application software for creating, modifying, and finalizing the digital files of which computerized publications are constructed;
- output devices, which run the gamut from simple black-and-white laser printers to high-resolution film imagesetters;
- digital storage media for archiving editorial material, digitized artwork, and page geometry.

### Scanners

A scanner is a computer-controlled electro-optical input device that looks at text and images and converts them into digital data that can be processed by a desktop publishing system. So-called low-end systems generally use inexpensive flatbed scanners that can capture text, line art, and original color with limited but acceptable detail. Mid-range systems get better quality from desktop drum scanners, which are scaled-down but capable versions of their much more expensive cousins, the high-end scanners. High-end scanners, offering the best color quality for high-volume reproduction, are seldom seen outside printing plants and color trade shops. Although these units maintain their hold on critical color work for magazines, many prepress experts say it is only a matter of time before desktop image-capturing systems will be able to give comparable results at a significantly lower cost per scan.

### Publishing Platforms

So far, Apple Computer's Macintosh line has been the desktop platform of choice among professional publishers. For example, a fall 1994 survey report in *Folio:* noted that Macs were the primary hardware used by the art and production departments at nearly four out of five responding magazines. The Mac's sway is not surprising, given that all of the most powerful desktop publishing applications were originally written to be run on Apple computers. The greatly enhanced processing speed and data-handling capability of Apple's PowerPC series have made the magazine industry's premier publishing tool even more formidable.

Personal computers with operating systems different from Apple's—which desktop publishers commonly call PCs, to distinguish them from Macs—originally lacked the graphical user interface (GUI) architecture that makes page creation on the Mac a relatively straightforward matter of point-and-click. However, Microsoft Corporation's Windows operating system probably will put the PC on a par with the Mac as a desktop publishing option and may even tilt the numbers in favor of the PC. Windows comes fairly close to the Mac operating system for ease of use and ability to handle graphics. Leading desktop applications have been rewritten for Windows, to which the country's installed base of PCs—vastly outnumbering the installed base of Macs—is now rapidly switching.

### Application Software

Desktop publishing software sometimes makes the desktop civil war resemble a popular movement for liberation and empowerment. This is because anyone who acquires a copy of QuarkXPress, PageMaker, Illustrator, and Photoshop can boast of having a complete set of professional production tools at his or her disposal, whether the person is a member of the profession or not. The first two are the leading page layout programs for periodical publishing. Illustrator, an integrated graphic tool kit, is favored by many art directors for editorial and advertising design. Photoshop is an advanced program for manipulating and correcting digitized photographic images.

There are many other competitive and complementary products, but these applications are the most widely used of their kinds. Each is a powerful production studio–in-a-box designed to replace labor- and time-intensive traditional steps with automated techniques that can be rapidly executed on a computer screen. These programs are available both to publishers and the public from thousands of retail and direct-mail sources. Although it can be argued that many more acquire them than learn to use them properly, they have democratized the publishing process by offering lay people the same production opportunities they give professional users.

In most magazine production environments, however, access to these tools may not be quite as democratic. More likely, only those who need to use the programs will be permitted to work with them, according to their roles in the workflow. For example, just because programs like QuarkXPress let editors build fully formatted pages to contain the copy they have written, that does not necessarily mean editors should be doing this part of the work. It may be more efficient for editors to prepare the copy in word processing applications and send the files via local network to an art department that creates pages from predesigned electronic templates. Many workflow scenarios are possible, but the goal of all of them should be to employ desktop publishing software's power in ways that do not become redundant or self-defeating.

### Output Devices

An output device produces hard-copy or hard-dot versions of pages created on the computer screen. If all that is required is a camera-ready printout of text, page layouts, line art, and other simple elements, a black-and-white laser printer will handle the job. If the page has been built in color, and the operator wishes to see approximately what it will look like when it comes off the printing press, he or she will output the page on a color ink-jet printer, on a thermal color proofer, or on an output device that employs a process called dye sublimation transfer.

If the magazine has decided to produce its own fully composed graphic arts film with the halftones screened, the color electronically separated, and the page elements automatically stripped into place, then it must invest in an imagesetter—another expensive piece of equipment limited mostly to professional use. Film output, like high-resolution scanning, is a technically challenging procedure that many publishers are content to leave to their trade service providers.

### Digital Storage Media

In the old days, magazines needed thousands of cubic feet to store mechanicals, original artwork, letterpress "cuts," film, and the other raw materials of production. Magazines still have physical storage requirements, but much of what once had to be packed in boxes and filing cabinets can now be preserved as binary data in much less cumbersome digital storage media. Text, artwork, and page geometry created on computers can be archived in digital form for permanent reference. These files can also be retrieved for "repurposing" as books, special issues, article reprints, and other ancillary products that represent new revenue streams for magazine publishers.

Digital storage systems for publications must be stable: that is, not subject to data loss or deterioration over extended periods of time. Their cost per megabyte of storage should be clearly understood, since the various media have different degrees of cost efficiency. They must make files easy to catalog, manage, and retrieve. They must also have extremely high capacities—in the gigabyte and sometimes the terabyte ranges—if the storage requirement includes color images. Since archives of these sizes would overwhelm the built-in storage of Mac- and PC-based workstations, file servers—networked "hub" computers with multiple arrays of large hard drives—serve the purpose in many production departments. Other storage options include optical cartridges, digital tape, and CD-ROM.

### Limitations and Lessons

Experience strewn with error and disappointment has taught magazine professionals that digital publishing systems, for all their productive power, have significant limitations. For one thing, digital publishing stops when finished page files are sent to the output device. There is still an ink-and-paper magazine to print, bind, and deliver. Even though desktop systems can handle most of the prepress steps leading to high-volume reproduction, that is only the first stage of the publishing process. Publishers still need printers. They also need an understanding of the fundamentals of printing if they are to produce pages on the desktop that stand any chance of running acceptably on the press.

Publishers who ignore or misjudge the relationship of desktop publishing to the rest of the production process will get nothing but bad printing. Despite the fact that anyone can dabble in it, desktop publishing is a skill, and much of that skill consists of knowing how to avoid turning out the kind of job that looks wonderful in proof but mediocre, or worse, in print. Nor is desktop publishing the automatic answer to every production problem. Any magazine production manager worth his or her salt will be the first to observe that, in many cases, the traditional methods of prepress work as well as, if not better than, desktop publishing.

The process limitations of desktop publishing are many. For example, low-end desktop publishing—the kind that most novices do with off-the-shelf hardware and software that they more or less know how to operate—falls far short of perfection when it comes to handling photography. Without professional-level prepress systems, it is hard to do justice to grayscale—the subtle gradation of tones that gives black-and-white photography its clarity and impact. Color photos can be scanned and separated on the desktop with eye-of-the-beholder acceptability—but probably not with quality sufficient to meet the stringent, advertising-driven production requirements of most major publications.

Desktop publishing probably shines brightest as a tool for typography. This was not always the case. In the 1980s, many professional phototypographers dismissed the idea that primitive type from early Macs and 300 dpi laser printers could ever be commercially acceptable. For a brief time, they were right. Their error—fatal for many of them—lay in ignoring the steadily increasing ability of desktop systems to provide the same range of fonts and typographic effects as high-end photocomposition equipment.

But quality is still an issue. Desktop-generated typography has come a long way from the days when it was unable to kern, hyphenate, adjust line leading, or do any of the other things that made commercial typography the only choice for advertising, magazine publishing, annual reports, and other high-quality work. But connoisseurs of typography still argue that setting type on the desktop means accepting compromises in appearance, font scaling, and special typographic effects. Publishers must also remember that if they want to do everything that professionals can do, they must have hundreds if not thousands of digitized fonts on hand. Building font libraries can get expensive, and storing fonts devours memory in already overburdened desktop computers.

### The Quest for Color

Then there is color. At every major printing trade show, the air vibrates with rumors that, this time, color from inexpensive desktop systems will rival the color from high-end laser scanners and CEPS workstations that cost hundreds of dollars an hour to operate. As of this writing, desktop color of that caliber has not appeared yet—at least not at the low end, where most people are likely to get their feet wet in desktop publishing. Low-end hardware and software are good at handling simple things like spot color, tints, and simple color illustrations. But if the job involves full-color illustration and process separations, the desktop publishing options can grow problematic.

The technical issues are extremely complex, but trouble usually arises because one form of color output has made a liar of another form of color output. When it comes to color, what one sees on a color monitor or in a digital proof isn't likely to be an exact match of what one will see on the printed page. The reason: system manufacturers have not completely solved the problems of color calibration  and color management. In other words, they still don't know how to guarantee that the red the artist used in the desktop file will stay the same shade from input to output, much less from the originating system to another system.

There is also the fact that low-end desktop publishing deals with color at correspondingly low levels of resolution. Problems arise when low-resolution color information is subjected to the high-resolution image processing required for high-quality printing. The bottom line is that for the moment—although the moment may be brief—desktop color does represent a trade-off in quality. That is why CEPS manufacturers have come up with linking systems that merge high-resolution color data from high-end equipment with type, page geometry, and line art from the desktop, where these simpler elements can be handled satisfactorily at low levels of resolution. Typically, a linking system gives the desktop operator a temporary set of low-resolution FPO (for position only) color images that can be used for making page layouts. Then, when the finished files are ready for output, the CEPS automatically replaces the low-resolution FPOs with high-resolution color images that have been retouched and color-corrected to publication standards.

### *Preeminence of PostScript*

Many of desktop publishing's limitations are redeemed by PostScript, which is to desktop publishing what French is to the United Nations. PostScript is a programming language, like COBOL or PASCAL or BASIC. It is known as a page description language, or PDL, because it tells many different kinds of desktop publishing software and output hardware how to create and integrate type, line art, photographs, and all the other elements of a computer-designed page.

PostScript lives in the application software used to design pages and in the PostScript-compatible output devices used to print them out. It is a transparent language in the sense that the operator cannot see it at work (unless he or she chooses to do so). But the most important thing about PostScript is the fact that it is device-independent. When text, art, and page layouts have been recorded as PostScript files, they can be imaged on any output device equipped with a PostScript-interpreting device called a RIP (raster image processor). The files can be processed at whatever level of resolution the output unit provides: 600 dpi for a tabletop, black-

and-white laser printer; 2,540 dpi or higher for a high-end imagesetter or film recorder.

This is a vast improvement over the situation that existed in the early days of desktop publishing, when different publishing systems used different, usually incompatible page creation protocols. A document file created in the graphic description language of one system would not look the same on a system speaking another language (if it would run at all). Now desktop publishers can be reasonably certain that, thanks to PostScript, their pages will look good no matter how they are output. There are other page description languages, but PostScript is generally acknowledged as the standard PDL for desktop publishing and its links to high-end production. This means that almost all desktop publishing work will be PostScript-based. It is also why desktop publishing and electronic prepress are commonly referred to as taking place in the PostScript environment.

But even PostScript is not the production cure-all the magazine publishing industry would like it to be. Because PostScript-based desktop systems tend to process data more slowly, and in smaller batches, than proprietary, high-end systems, they may not always be up to the demands of through-putting high volumes of color pages on tight deadlines. Nor do networked desktop systems do as good a job of editorial management as older group-publishing systems such as Atex, which were built to handle the heavy traffic of many editors tinkering with the same material at more or less the same time.

But PostScript systems are developing more production muscle all the time, and many believe it will not be long before there is no publishing challenge that fortified PostScript systems cannot handle. This is strategically advantageous to magazine publishers who invest in these systems, since it lets them plan for increasing physical and budgetary control over the manufacture of their printed products. Therefore the limitations of desktop publishing, while genuine, should not be seen as insurmountable obstacles. Although high-end, professional equipment still represents the peak of excellence in prepress, it is now possible to produce magazines of good and even admirable quality entirely on the desktop. The question is whether it is desirable—meaning economically justifiable—to do so.

### A Variable Investment

The extent to which a magazine makes use of the power of desktop publishing will depend on how deeply involved in prepress its publisher feels it can afford to be. For some magazines, complete in-house prepress capability makes the most economic sense. These publishers have slashed their prepress costs because they had the means to invest not only in equipment but also in the staffing, training, and system maintenance that operating a full-range prepress department entails. Though still an elite group, their numbers are rising: *Folio:*'s annual desktop production survey for 1994 found that the number of respondents producing their own four-color film in-house had doubled from the previous year, to 27 percent from 13 percent. Those processing their own four-color proofs also doubled in number, from 17 percent to 34 percent. [90]

Magazines with slenderer resources will continue to partner with printers, color trade shops, and service bureaus to get their prepress work done. They can increase savings and efficiency by harmonizing their desktop procedures with their vendors' production routines—for example, by "preflighting" their digital files to make certain that all the elements needed to output the job are present and account-ed for. But no matter what the arrangement, every magazine can use desktop-based production tools to speed and smooth its workflow. The fact that publishers responding to *Folio:*'s 1994 desktop survey said they planned to spend an average of more than $30,000 on new hardware is a good indication of the magazine indus-try's commitment to controlling its destiny from the desktop.

## PRODUCTION ECONOMICS/NEW PRESS TECHNIQUES

### Magazine Printing as a Manufacturing Process

#### The New Production Partnership

Computerized publishing's first decade awakened magazine professionals to a reality that many are still struggling to understand and accept. Their discovery was that, ready or not, they had been thrust into positions of unprecedented power over the manufacture of their products. The exercise of this power, they soon would learn, was also a continuous exercise in coping with anxiety driven by radical change. It was stressful to abandon the comforts of production chains and hierar-chies for the uncertainties of a new process that set every task on an even plane. It was personally challenging—sometimes painfully so—to unlearn command-and-control management styles so that free communication could knit together the skills and enthusiasms of cross-functional publishing teams.[91] It was disconcerting, above all, to realize how much make-or-break responsibility for cost control, quality assurance, and production workflow had landed on one's own desk, with no options for buck-passing or blame-fixing should the process go astray.

But if the new obligations were heavy, the perquisites they brought were ample reward. Although the printed and published end product had not changed much, the responsibilities, roles, and relationships behind its creation had been almost entirely rescripted. In simplest terms, the creators of magazines had been empowered to do more,[92] and this empowerment heightened their influence over the process as a whole. Now editors, artists, ad sales reps, and other magazine staff were becoming more closely involved in the production cycle, changing its benchmarks and accel-erating its timetables. They began asking their printers and print-service vendors questions that, once upon a time, would never have occurred to a nonproduction person to ask. Those directly responsible for buying print were the most inquisitive of all. For example, of respondents to a *High Volume Printing* survey of print buyers, better than one-third (36 percent) said they wanted to know specifically which press was used to produce their jobs and what its additional capabilities might be.[93]

Magazine publishers also began to make a practice of keeping close tabs on production from start to finish—a policy tantamount to dictating the success or failure of the cycle.[94] Magazine printers, unwilling to be guilty of lèse-majesté when the customer was king, responded with new methods of accommodating publishers' appetites for continuous information on production status. At many magazine plants, computerized job-tracking systems now generate real-time updates on the whereabouts of any element of a particular issue. These systems use pen-based barcode readers, keypads, or touchscreens to capture job data for storage in a master database. Customer service representatives can then query the database to pinpoint the location of job components or to help the customer reconcile charges on the printing invoice. World Color Press, one of the largest printers of consumer magazines, satisfies its customers' desire for information-on-demand with a dedicated electronic mail system that lets publishers dial up the status of their issues whenever they wish.[95]

## THE PUBLICATION PRODUCTION MANAGER'S ROLE IN COST CONTROL

To be sure, publishers have to work at least as hard as their printers to make worthwhile use of the wealth of production information now available to them. They must also make certain that their internal production capabilities mesh seamlessly and continuously with the ever-advancing technology of their external service providers. The responsibility for maintaining these manufacturing harmonies belongs to the production manager, whose role has changed almost beyond comparison with what it was in the predigital days of magazine publishing.

In those days, it was enough for a production manager to have a broad working knowledge of the various techniques involved in the design and printing of magazines. A production manager who understood the turnaround times and fair-market costs associated with these steps was qualified to do what good production managers were then chiefly expected to do: monitor and certify the work of typesetters, prep houses, and other vendors of magazine manufacturing services. Today, however, much of this work is done either entirely in-house or in computerized partnership with vendors whose services are limited to final output. Now production managers must understand not only the steps of these new workflows but also the digital technology that makes them possible. They must have strategies for matching their computerized production routines to their vendors' requirements so that every issue can be produced on time and within budget. Production managers, in short, now need to possess and leverage much more information than they once did in order to be viewed as competent.[96]

Nevertheless, one performance criterion for production managers that has not changed is skill in controlling production costs. Digital publishing technology may be wonderfully empowering for designers, editors, and other staff members whose creative reach it serves to extend, but that empowerment becomes frivolous when it obstructs the higher goal of getting the magazine printed, bound, and shipped. That is why production managers in computerized publishing environments must be thoroughly skilled at helping staff turn their creativity into digital output that can achieve final, printed form in accordance with the publication's quality standards and budgetary constraints. Because mistakes along these lines can be so costly, the talents that production managers use to head them off are being recognized as never before as essential to the profitability of magazine operations.[97]

Here again, the computer can be seen as both a blessing and a burden for magazine production managers. It always was their task to get their issues produced economically, on schedule, and according to quality requirements. Today, with computerized job-tracking systems keeping the progress and costs of every issue continuously in view, publishers are putting all the more pressure on their production managers to translate this information into permanent cost reductions.[98] As a result, cost control has become the magazine publishing industry's favorite touchstone for success in digital production management. Though publishers rally to the triple slogan of "better, faster, and cheaper," they invariably regard "cheaper" as the precursor and the enabler of the other two.

## Production Cost Components

Candid publishers will admit that "cheaper" is a never-ending uphill struggle. They know, for one thing, that they have only limited control over certain basic costs such as postage and paper. When the U.S. Postal Service and paper-market forces drive the prices of these commodities up, publishers have nowhere to look for savings but in the slate of operating costs they can negotiate or unilaterally rein in. [99] This means that manufacturing expense, which can represent up to 60 percent of a magazine's operating budget,[100] usually rides high on a publisher's list of costs in need of trimming back.

For large, multi-title publishers, the control of production costs has multimillion-dollar implications. For example, in 1994, Meredith Corporation, publisher of *Better Homes and Gardens, Ladies Home Journal*, and other well-known consumer titles, had a total budget of $140 million, of which nearly $70 million was allocated to manufacturing and distribution. For every dollar of revenue taken in by Meredith magazines, 40 percent was spent on getting the magazines printed and into readers' hands. Small wonder that Meredith's production director should have commented, "Cost containment, under present market conditions, is very hot, and will continue to be so."[101]

Manufacturing costs are not the only budgeted items that publishers have to restrain: Some experts say, for example, that the costs of circulation acquisition and maintenance, advertising sales, and editorial are growing even faster.[102] But as long as bottom-line economics continues to demand new options for printing the same magazines—or very nearly the same magazines—for less money, publishers will continue to insist that their manufacturing costs would be smaller if only a little more belt-tightening and ingenuity were being practiced in the editorial office, the prep department, and the pressroom.

Unfortunately, it takes more than just a little creative economizing to save on the consumption of magazine printing's principal raw materials: paper and ink. Paper is the most expensive item in production, often accounting for 50 percent of the total manufacturing cost of the printed product. With many different grades and varieties of publication papers to choose from, a magazine publisher can almost always find a cheaper alternative to the substrate (paper stock) he or she has been using. However, if the bargain substrate is found to have shortcomings that will render the finished printing unacceptable, the economy is a false one. Since defects may not be apparent until after the pages are printed, the economic loss stemming from a poor choice of paper probably will be unrecoverable. Obviously, nothing is saved by pushing thousands of sheets of paper through a press only to find that they are no good.[103]

Years ago, publishers could afford to be casual about the price of printing ink. Many were content to leave ink cost buried in the overall printing price because it generally represented only two to three percent of the total cost. But when oil prices rose sharply in the mid- to late 1970s, the price of ink—a petroleum-based product—shot up beyond 20 percent of the cost of the job.[104] Now the cost is estimated in advance by assigning a percentage of ink coverage that budgets the cost of ink per page. This practice can have a bearing on decisions about design and photography, since the more lavishly illustrated the magazine, the more expensive the ink line on its printing invoice will be.[105]

Likewise, adding pages to an issue adds to the issue's total production cost. Here it is important to understand the economic link between advertising pages and editorial pages. Basically, revenue from the sale of advertising pages underwrites the production of editorial pages, which do not generate revenue (except to the extent that their reader appeal helps to maintain the magazine's paid circulation). This means that the number of editorial pages that can be produced in a given issue is determined, or at least heavily influenced, by the number of advertising pages sold for that issue. Ideally, every editorial page should be supported by an income-producing advertising page. However, since advertising sales results can vary from issue to issue, this ideal ad-edit page ratio is seldom easy for publishers to achieve.

Every magazine has its own formula for basing an issue's *folio*, or total page count, on the number of advertising pages available at closing. These rules of thumb must allow for the fact that magazines are printed not a page at a time, but as *signatures* in multiples of eight. Adding a single page of advertising to a tight issue could force the addition of numerous editorial pages to fill the remainder of the extra signature. Cancellation of an ad, on the other hand, could oblige editors to throw some of their pages out. The formula may also be based on an editorial page minimum below which no issue will go, regardless of the advertising volume. In most cases, however, the editorial page count is triggered by advertising in a way that lets the publisher and the production manager reasonably forecast the issue's total cost to produce.[106]

Understanding the economics of press output and run lengths is another pillar of cost control for magazine production. With operating speeds exceeding 50,000 impressions per hour, modern magazine presses can print signatures for one-third the cost of equivalent work done on predecessor machines that ran half as fast. [107] But capitalizing on these potential savings means using a high-output magazine press only for runs that are worthy of its productive capacity. For example, there is no benefit in knowing that a large press can run a high-quantity job faster than a small press if the quantity is not sufficiently high to begin with. The quantity has to be substantial enough to make setting up the machine cost-efficient for both printer and customer.[108] Otherwise, the production economies will be wasted, and the run will cost more than it needs to.

Today the best advantages of speed, productivity, and automation belong to web offset presses, which are challenging sheetfed equipment in nearly all the categories of magazine work for which sheetfed printing is used. Web offset used to be associated only with high-volume printing, but recent developments in waste control and makeready reduction have made the process competitive even for certain kinds of work in the 10,000- to 20,000-copy range.[109] Although sheetfed printing continues to hold a perceived edge in print quality, web offset printing probably will be accepted as suitable for almost any kind of periodical press run.[110]

Running speed is a matter of choosing one press over another. A magazine's run length, on the other hand, is not a choice but a consequence: the natural outcome of the title's strength or weakness in the market segment in which it competes. In recent years, the fragmentation of the magazine-reading public along special-interest lines has split many of these segments into ever more specialized publishing niches. At the same time, the total size of the readership for all magazines has stayed relatively flat. Predictably, the effect has been to shrink the circulation of many titles, making the economics of run lengths and running speeds that much more difficult for their publishers to calculate. All indications are that the trend toward reader segmentation and shorter press runs will continue as a long-term challenge that press speed and efficiency alone will not be sufficient to overcome.

## Cutting Production Costs

The mere fact that a magazine is printed on the fastest, most efficient equipment does not automatically mean that it is being produced in the most economical way. Publishers know that by the time the next issue is ready for the press, their best opportunities to cut manufacturing costs are already behind them. Cost savings can be planned but seldom improvised, and the later in the production cycle an impromptu economy is attempted, the less worth the effort it probably will be. This is why the most significant cost reductions stem from prior decisions about page size, paper selection and consumption, job setup, closings, and scheduling. These standard operating procedures (which vary, naturally, from magazine to magazine) are the real keys to living within the constraints of today's rigid production budgets.

As already noted, paper selection is often the first cost-cutting opportunity that economy-minded publishers will seize. Switching to lighter-weight stocks that cost less to buy and mail than heavier papers makes sense as long as reproduction quality is not compromised. Lower-grade papers can be used for the black-and-white pages in the back of the magazine, where there are no color requirements to worry about. Once the right papers are chosen, consolidating purchases and buying in larger quantities are musts for controlling the cost of the raw material. [111]

One of the most effective ways to trim paper cost is literally to do it—by trimming the dimensions of the printed page. A magazine's "trim size" is the page size that readers are used to seeing. What they do not see is the waste that has been cut away from the paper on which the impositions, or groups of pages, were printed. The waste occurs because the paper is slightly larger than the trimmed, finished piece, and because the pages have to be cut apart for binding. If the trim size can be reduced without increasing the waste, the savings can be substantial.

The rising costs of paper and postage have prompted many publishers to shrink their trim sizes in hope of achieving these savings. A tour of any magazine rack will reveal that the once-standard $8^{1/2}$" by 11" trim size now shares the slots with 8" by 10 $^{1/2}$" measurements and all sizes in between.[112] It has been estimated that trimming the long dimension of a magazine from 10 $^{7/8}$" to 10 $^{1/2}$" can decrease paper requirements by 4.5 percent. Assuming a $30,000 bill for paper 12 times a year, the $^{3/8}$" reduction in trim size translates into an annual savings of more than $16,000.[113]

For multi-title publishers facing escalating budgets for paper, the economic appeal of trim-size reductions can be irresistible. In 1995, Cahners Publishing Company, the country's largest publisher of trade magazines, dropped the height of 54 of its 91 titles from 10 $^{3/4}$" to 10 $^{1/2}$". Announcing a similar change, Weider Publications said it expected to save five percent on total production costs for its body-building and fitness titles.[114]

Nevertheless, changing trim size is a manufacturing decision as well as an economic one, and doing it successfully is not just a matter of cutting off extra paper at will. Sharply reducing trim size could involve redesigning the book and confronting readers with an unfamiliar, less appealing new layout. It could also mean asking advertisers to bear the inconvenience of complying with altered production specifications.

Moreover, the alteration saves money only if the magazine's print run can be switched from a standard publication press to a "short cutoff" model with cylinder sizes that conform to the sub-8 $^{1/2}$" by 11" trim size desired. Although it is possible to print in smaller sizes than the maximum impression area of a standard press allows, doing so merely wastes sections of paper that the machine was designed to print efficiently. A short-cutoff press, on the other hand, does not need to waste paper in order to use less paper in the final printed piece. It uses less paper to begin with.

During the recessionary days of the early 1990s, the publishing industry's demand for reduced trim sizes grew faster than the printing industry's installed base of short-cutoff publication presses. As a result, publishers often found themselves on waiting lists for press time at the handful of plants then operating the equipment. Today—for publishers who have not already trimmed their editions to the limit— there are around the country a good number of short-cutoff presses capable of delivering pages 10 $1/2$ inches deep.[115]

While it may or may not be possible to change the dimensions of the book, changing the paper the magazine is printed on is a tried-and-true option for cost saving. There are two ways to economize: by switching to a stock with a lighter "basis weight" (pounds per ream in a standard sheet size); or by using a paper of lesser quality. Prudent publishers, always sensitive to the expectations of their readers and advertisers, do not compromise on paper quality too much, because they know that no other production-related decision has as much bearing upon the printability and appearance of their magazines. Heavily illustrated, elaborately designed titles that make extensive use of color have even less latitude: for them, the high-cost papers they use and the high-quality results they get are cause and effect.

Fortunately, the choice of publication papers and the range of paper pricing are so broad that publishers usually can bargain for acceptable substitutes once they have made the decision to switch. Another way publishers can save is to keep an eye on the markups (percentage over basic price) they pay to printers who buy paper for them. Letting the printer buy the paper is a convenience for the publisher, and charging a markup for the service is a legitimate form of compensation for the printer. However, by comparing the paper line in the printer's invoice to quotes on similar quantities from paper brokers, merchants, and mills, publishers can quickly determine whether the convenience is worth the cost.

Multi-title publishing companies usually have the greatest incentive to do their own paper shopping. Volume buying assures them of receiving the best prices and the most preferential treatment from their suppliers. The biggest may order directly from the mills, thereby eliminating all middleman markup.

But even for bulk buyers, leverage can weaken during the tight paper markets that periodically afflict the publishing industry. Tight markets prevail whenever the demand for publication papers surges ahead of the available supply. Paper supplies fluctuate because domestic mills have failed to expand their productive capacity either by installing new papermaking machines or by upgrading current equipment; because shipments of imported paper are down; because print advertising budgets (hence orders for paper) are up; because printers have let their paper inventories dwindle; or because all of these forces are in play at once. In extreme situations, mills and merchants may place publishers on "allocation," restricting the size of their purchases until the market has regained its balance.

Given the perennially high cost of paper and the uncertainty of its supply, publishers and their production managers are well advised to make frugal use of the stocks they have in hand. The most cost-conscious have learned that controlling paper waste—paper used in the magazine manufacturing process but not included in the finished product—is one act of frugality that drops directly to the bottom line. Considering all the possibilities for its occurrence, waste can easily run as high as 22 percent to 25 percent of total paper consumed during the production run. Roll waste, makeready waste, running waste, bindery waste, and trimmer waste all contribute to the inflation of the paper budget.[116]

All waste is controllable, but not all waste is inexcusable. Certain kinds—such as sheets discarded during color adjustments on press—are necessary and predictable elements of the manufacturing process. In fact, printers draw a distinction between this kind of inherent waste and "spoilage," which refers to excess paper consumption from errors or faulty practices that could have been avoided. Magazine publishers battle needless waste by insisting that their printers use spoilage minimization procedures to hold percentages to acceptable levels. A printer who observes self-imposed waste ceilings in his or her magazine work is a publisher's best ally in the war on prodigal paper consumption.

The printer's skill in determining the most economical *imposition* for the job also has a direct effect on production cost. Basically, imposition means arranging magazine pages on press sheets to "read" in the proper sequence once the sheets are folded, cut, and bound. Imposition also involves complex decisions about the size of the press sheet, or form (should the issue be set up as 8, 16, 32, or more pages to the form?); the number of plates to use; and the placement of color pages in ways that minimize the cost of color printing. The general rule for economical impositions is to keep forms as large as possible while paying to print only as many colors in one form as production requirements permit.[117] Production managers and advertising directors should work closely with their printers to assure that the most cost-efficient practical imposition is being used.

Obviously, careful planning is a must for economical magazine production. But even the most carefully worked-out production plan can stray far from its budget if its built-in deadlines are not taken seriously. There are deadlines for everything in magazine production. These deadlines interlock: Missing one production milestone penalizes all subsequent steps. For example, failure to complete page layouts on time could slow the processing of film and plates, leading to the loss of scheduled press time. Deadlines are continuous: Even as one issue is "put to bed" (completed for delivery to the printer), the first stages of production for the next issue will already be in full swing. And, no matter how conscientious the publishing team, no deadline is ever immune to unforeseen delays from late-breaking editorial developments; accommodations for advertising; system or equipment failures; natural disasters; or "acts of God."

Missing deadlines costs money—in some cases, a great deal of money. If an issue slips enough production deadlines, it may be published late (past its promised mailing and distribution dates). A delayed publication date often causes a shortened on-sale period and a loss of profits.[118] Late publication also means a briefer period of exposure for the advertising the issue contains—a situation that could lead to costly quarrels with the clients or agencies that placed the advertising.

The key to deadline-conscious production is accepting the constraints of *lead time*—the days or weeks needed in advance of the publication date to complete the various stages of production. For example, a monthly magazine with a circulation of 500,000 may *close* (require receipt of) editorial and advertising material six to eight weeks before the issue's cover date. If six to eight weeks seems an extravagant amount of lead time, consider what will take place within that time frame: Copy must be edited and typeset; pages must be laid out; the issue must be paginated; the print order must go to the printer; and color material must be sent to the trade shop or service bureau for preparation proofs and final film. In contrast, the manufacture of the magazine—the printing, binding, and mailing—needs only a relatively short amount of lead time, perhaps seven or eight days.[119] Although these latter stages of production usually account for most of the expense, they seldom are the most time-consuming.[120]

Production schedules based on predetermined lead times work well as long as no one attempts to get by with less lead time than a given step requires. An issue's cushion of lead time is shortened whenever a deadline is extended or a production step is undertaken later than planned. The principle of lead time is most often violated in the name of shoehorning more advertising into the issue, no matter how close to the latter stages of production the issue happens to be. Since publishers rarely refuse any opportunity to accommodate income-producing ad pages, late ad closings are a constant challenge to keeping the production schedule on track.

Late insertions cause delays throughout the production sequence, and everyone feels the pressure: in-house design and production departments, trade service shops, printers, and mailing facilities. In magazine work, turning up the pressure on already-airtight production schedules almost always guarantees that errors will go up as well. Moreover, because mistakes are more expensive to correct the later in the production sequence they occur, the cost of fixing a serious mistake in a late ad could exceed the revenue from its sale.[121] Materials supplied in the wrong size, post-deadline copy alterations, changed impositions, and film/plate remakes are potential profit killers lurking in every agreement to extend ad submission deadlines.

Sometimes these added production costs can be passed along to advertisers; sometimes they cannot. To protect themselves, publishers may use late-close forms that spell out both parties' responsibilities when extensions are granted. The best preparation for difficulty, however, is to have a good relationship with the printer on whose shoulders the entire manufacturing burden ultimately rests.[122] More than anything else, having a supportive, responsive printer—one who understands the publication's special needs and knows how to satisfy them even when the odds are against success—makes it possible to endure the crisis-control management style that characterizes so much of the magazine business today.

Choosing a printer is one of the most consequential business decisions a magazine publisher can make. Because manufacturing costs can represent up to 60 percent of a magazine's operating budget, the decision can mean a difference of thousands of dollars to the publication's bottom line.[123] Price is not the only criterion for partnering with a printer. The publisher must also consider the printing company's production capabilities; its track record in magazine manufacturing; and its willingness to make business arrangements that fit the publication's scheduling requirements and budgetary constraints.

Almost any printer with a press of sufficient size can print a magazine, but the best magazine printing comes from plants that specialize in this kind of work. A specialty printer gears the operation to the product by equipping specifically for the manufacture of that product. This makes the operation more efficient and, presumably, more cost-competitive within its niche. So, as with other specialties, the cost of magazine manufacturing should be lower at a magazine printer than at a plant that does not specialize.[124]

A magazine printing plant will almost always be a substantial operation, with equipment, staff, and space sufficient for making and warehousing large amounts of printed product. Many magazine plants also offer addressing and distribution services, including on-site postal facilities. This range of capabilities, combined with expertise in planning and tracking multiple jobs, enables magazine printers to keep their customers' tight production deadlines on schedule. [125]

As far as most publishers are concerned, location counts a great deal less than capability, price, and other factors when it comes to selecting a printer. The reason so many magazines are printed hundreds or even thousands of miles away from their editorial offices is that the best plant for the job is seldom necessarily the closest one. Printing plants are available to the magazine publishing industry in all parts of the country, and most of them compete for work on a national scale. They can do this because, in the case of magazine production, remote manufacturing is frequently the most economical way to go. A printer specializing in periodicals for national markets should be able to bid and produce a magazine job for 30 to 40 percent less than a local printer that does not specialize.[126] With large jobs, the savings may be much greater than the extra costs of doing business at a distance.

To take advantage of these economies, magazine printers and their customers routinely exchange instructions and input materials and proofs over long distances using courier services and, more recently, electronic telecommunications systems. Locally based print sales representatives and brokers also help to expedite traffic between customer and plant. As a result, the need for direct contact is often so limited that the production manager or the art director traveling to the plant for press checks may be the only member of the magazine staff who ever gets a first-hand look at how the issue is printed, bound, and shipped.[127] Although some publishers prefer the up-close-and-personal customer support that only hometown printers can provide, local printing service is seldom critical to the efficient production of a magazine. For titles with national distribution, therefore, plant proximity probably will not be at the top of the list of criteria for selecting a printer.

Better yardsticks are the production runs of the plant's current magazine clientele and the availability of time on its presses. Publishers seeking printers should try to choose plants serving publications with runs comparable to theirs, since the size of a magazine account has a definite bearing on the kind of treatment the printer will give it.[128] Striving to be the smallest magazine on a printer's roster makes scant sense, given that every title the printer handles will be competing for a fixed amount of open press time. Because the plant has to coordinate the overlapping production schedules of multiple titles, press time usually has to be booked well in advance.[129] A small-circ title among giants may have to be content with tail-end time at inconvenient hours, and it probably can expect less accommodation than a bigger account would get in the event of production delays on the publisher's end.

Publishers must also examine prospective printers' other accounts so that they can be certain of buying only the production services they need. Printers, including magazine specialists, install equipment to suit a range of capabilities. They sell time on each machine at different prices, depending on the type of periodical each machine is used to produce. Generally speaking, the most profit comes from maximizing time sold on the plant's most sophisticated or highest-output equipment.

Machinery of this kind is expensive to acquire, operate, staff, and maintain. Because it frequently is purchased with borrowed capital, it has to pay for itself from revenues generated by jobs produced on it. A printer, therefore, has a strong financial incentive to find as much work for the plant's highest-capability equipment as he or she can.[130]

The question the publisher must ask is whether the magazine can be produced economically on the equipment the printer wants to book for the job. Although modern presses can be set up to produce many kinds of periodicals, it probably would be pointless (for example) to print a *Reader's Digest*-size publication on equipment designed for tabloids in the 10 1/2" by 14 1/4" range. Press selection should also be linked to the publication's actual run length and color requirements, not the printer's parameters. At Plant A, a *short-run* press may be one used for jobs under 25,000 copies, while at Plant B, *short-run* could just as easily mean 500,000 copies or less.[131] Obviously, a short-run magazine as defined by Plant A cannot spread its per-copy production costs very effectively on the short-run equipment in use at Plant B. Likewise, if Plant A's two- and five-unit presses can handle the color requirements of a magazine that uses color sparingly, the title has no business being run on the four- and eight-unit equipment that Plant B sets aside for magazines needing heavy color coverage throughout.[132]

Printers like to use their equipment lists as sales tools, and they are always eager to impress prospective customers with news of all the wonderful new production technologies they have invested in. This is good news because, theoretically, the better equipped a printer is, the more cost-efficient his or her operation has the potential to be. Nevertheless, publishers—especially publishers of small-circulation titles—should try to determine just how much of this technology will be applied to the production of their magazines. Because the technology has to be paid for out of operating revenues, the printer's investment cost could be reflected in the invoice for a job whether the equipment was used for that job or not.[133] Only by studying sample copies of the printer's other magazine accounts can a publisher judge how well or poorly the production budget is likely to be served by the plant's complement of printing machinery.

Choosing a printer in this way more or less automatically settles the most basic of all production questions: whether to print the magazine on sheetfed or web equipment. A large-circulation title that finds a good fit in a plant handling other long-run magazines probably will be printed on a high-volume, fast-running web press. For short-run magazines, the decision is a bit more complex. These titles are usually, but not necessarily, printed on sheetfed presses, traditionally the equipment of choice for smaller runs. Today, however, advances in web press design have made it possible for roll-fed equipment to make economical work of print orders in the 10,000-copy range, which qualifies as short-run printing by both sheetfed and web standards. Where sheetfed and web overlap, the choice is based less on run-length economics than on the magazine's quality requirements. Web presses are fine for printing short-run magazines of average quality on lighter, less costly papers. But for top-quality reproduction on expensive stock, sheetfed wins.[134]

No matter what the magazine's specific production requirements, the search for the printer best qualified to fulfill them should begin with a call for bids and end with the signing of a contract. Typically, the publisher and the production manager start the process by prequalifying a list of potential bidders. They can gather information about magazine printers by reading publishing industry trade journals such as *Folio: The Magazine for Magazine Management; High-Volume Printing;* and *MD&P (Magazine Design & Production).* Other publishers can be asked for recommendations, and, of course, there are always printers' sales representatives to talk to.

For very high-volume magazines, and for those requiring gravure or other specialty printing services, the bidders' list will be short. On the other hand, small-to-medium-run magazines probably will discover an abundance of eligible printers wherever they look. As a practical matter, the RFP (request for proposal) list should only be large enough to produce a worthwhile number of finalists after all of the responses have been received and evaluated. For example, sending an RFP to 20 printers may yield a group of three to five hopefuls from among whom the winning bid can be selected.[135]

An old joke in the printing business has to do with the posted notice that customers are rumored to see when they enter certain plants: "PRICE, QUALITY,

SERVICE—PICK ANY TWO." In reality, good-faith negotiations between publishers and bidding printers begin with a clear understanding that the winning bidder will be expected to deliver a well-balanced mixture of all three. Acting in good faith, the publisher should give each bidder identical specifications on which to base proposals and price quotations. Bidders should be prepared to give detailed and candid answers to the publisher's questions about production capabilities, job scheduling and tracking, paper and ink costs, terms of service, observance of trade customs, and many other contractual issues.

In some cases, the bidding and selection process as outlined above can take from 9 to 12 months.[136] In others, a winning bidder can be chosen in considerably less time. Regardless of the time frame, the process should always culminate in the signing of a custom-made printing contract—a business agreement tailored to the specific requirements of the publication.[137] Everything is subject to negotiation; there is no such thing as a one-size-fits-all contract to manufacture magazines.

Because a well-made contract spells out obligations on both sides, it also provides a blame-free framework for resolving problems that may arise while the contract is in effect.[138] More than one publisher has learned the hard way how important it is to have an unambiguous written agreement about who fixes what, under which circumstances, and at what expense to whom when production disasters occur. The moment of a press stoppage or the discovery of a spoiled signature is no time to begin thrashing out questions that should have been anticipated when the contract was first drawn up.

The contract should also indicate in broad terms what the printer will charge the publisher to produce the magazine. In most cases, the estimate or quotation sent in response to the RFP will have placed dollar amounts per issue on the production costs the printer expects to bill. The printer's estimating staff calculates these amounts from the specifications furnished by the publisher in the RFP. The estimators' numbers reflect not only what each issue will cost the printer to produce but also the markup from which the printing company derives its profits.[139]

The contract usually applies these numbers to a year's worth of issues (or to some other contract period that satisfies both parties). Here it is well to remember that a *printer's estimate* is what the term denotes: an informed forecast of production expenses that cannot be tallied precisely until the job is complete or nearly so. Because a magazine is a custom-printed product that can vary in page count, in color coverage, and in many other details from issue to issue, production costs and invoice amounts will also vary from issue to issue. For this reason, the printer will not attempt to provide an individual estimate for each issue (unless, for a given issue, he or she knows in advance that the specifications will differ significantly from the production norms on which the contract estimate was based).

Whenever an invoice exceeds the contract estimate, it is up to the publisher to request a detailed explanation of the extra charges. This task usually falls to the production manager, who routinely audits invoices to make sure that the printer has applied the right prices to the proper amount of work.[140] The most cost-conscious production managers may require a line-by-line breakdown of charges both to pinpoint questionable items and to identify opportunities for future savings. Only when the production manager is satisfied with the breakdown will he or she approve the invoice for payment.

No matter how carefully production managers monitor costs, invoices can still bring disconcerting surprises. The best way to prevent them is to review issue content and mechanical requirements with the printer's sales or customer service representative before production gets under way. The sooner potential cost overruns can be identified, the more time the printer will have to come up with a plan for controlling them. For example, if the printer knows that an issue will contain more editorial color than usual, he or she probably can recommend ways to minimize the additional expenses of separation and makeready.

Because the magazine publishing industry's eagerness to control its production costs has grown so intense, it is easy for some publishers to become obsessed with the expense side of the balance sheet. Sometimes the obsession takes hold during the vendor selection process. Competitive bidding by magazine printers assures magazine publishers of paying competitive prices for printing services, and this is as it should be: Publishers should always strive to make their most advantageous deals with print service vendors. However, *competitive* does not, and should not, mean the lowest price the publisher can extract from the hungriest bidder. *Competitive* means fair—comparable, in other words, to what other printers would reasonably charge for the same work.[141]

Printers are entitled to reasonable profits. Unfortunately, because their industry suffers from a chronic oversupply of productive capacity, many printers have trouble keeping their presses booked unless they cut their prices well below the margins of profit they would prefer to maintain. In unusually competitive times—for example, the early 1990s, when printing markets stagnated almost everywhere—it is possible to buy printing services at prices that virtually eliminate profit to the printer.

However eminently exploitable this situation may appear to the greedy few, it is an unworthy way for ethical magazine publishers to do business. A printer who forsakes profit in a desperate effort to keep a tightfisted customer is a printer with a strangled cash flow and a tenuous lease on life. Publishers who entrust their production schedules to printers whose financial health they have helped to ruin only court poetic justice in the form of a complete production breakdown. Nor is it possible for any publisher to drain blood from a buyer's market indefinitely. Market conditions eventually improve, and when they do, the buyer's advantage wears off. Even in a tight market, if a printer forced by a publisher to cut prices is taken over by another printer, the new owners may have no intention of continuing to tolerate the arrangement. Then the publisher will either have to find another rock-bottom printer or watch his own operating costs soar in response to the truly competitive pricing he is at last being obliged to accept.[142]

# QUALITY CONTROL/QUALITY MANAGEMENT

A far better strategy for protecting the production budget is to join forces with the printer in a just war on quality defects. A quality defect is anything that needs to be changed, corrected, or remanufactured before production can continue. The defect could be a typographical error that a copy editor should have caught in manuscript but didn't; a cracked plate that should not have been delivered to the pressroom but was; or a "ghosted" signature that should have been given extra time to dry properly but wasn't. Printers have long known that the expense of correcting quality defects rises in direct proportion to the time it takes to realize they exist. As an uncorrected defect passes from one stage of manufacturing to the next, its ultimate cost snowballs. According to one formula, a typo that would have cost $.20 to fix at the copy desk will have turned into a $2,000 heart-stopper if it forces a rerun on press.[143] The danger of ten thousand–fold cost increases due to preventable error should be just as obvious to publishers.

No manufacturing process can be error-free, and rare is the magazine that reaches its readers without a production flaw of some kind. Printers and publishers divide quality defects into three categories: *critical* mistakes that render the product unusable; *major* errors that are not critical but are embarrassingly plain to anyone who looks at the magazine; and *minor* imperfections that only a professional eye would be likely to detect. Because each kind of defect can begin to grow at any given stage of production, root causes are sometimes difficult to identify. Electronic publishing magnifies the likelihood of defects because it has eliminated so many of the intermediary steps associated with the predesktop production chain—which, owing to its hierarchical structure, provided more checkpoints for catching errors than today's flattened-out production mesh does.[144]

Printers, knowing they will be asked to answer for defects in the finished product whether the causing was theirs or not, have taken the lead in applying the principles of total quality management (TQM) to magazine production. Some have set up quality control departments staffed by experts in the disciplines of analyzing manufacturing errors. Others, however, are adopting the broader TQM concepts advanced by the school of Dr. W. Edwards Deming, who taught that every employee is a quality-control manager with personal responsibility for quality control every minute of the working day.[145] Deming's approach also encourages each department in a printing plant to think of the next department as its customer, with the same right to a defect-free "product" as the end user of the final printed piece. This means that no work can be passed to the next stage of production unless the passer has performed the quality-control checks that she would have expected her counterpart at the previous stage to perform. When put into practice plantwide, this method supports the goal of detecting quality defects while their causes are still relatively cheap to remove.[146]

Some printers are learning to use the techniques of statistical process control (SPC) to identify and eliminate sources of quality defects. SPC is a method for measuring how much variation takes place within the processes that make up a manufacturing operation. The first step is to take a set of process measurements when the operation is in control: running defect-free, or close to it. These measurements, or statistics, can be used as benchmarks for future operations because they are known to be indicators of a finished product that will meet the end user's quality requirements.

Now the focus can shift to interpreting variations from the benchmark statistics during each stage of manufacturing. Some of these variations will be "normal"—inherent in the process. "Abnormal" variations, on the other hand, point to specific causes of defects that can be eliminated.[147] Various analytical methods—some of them as simple as line-graphing the number of mistakes detected within a given period of time—help SPC practitioners pinpoint where and why process defects are taking place.

SPC techniques can be applied to many facets of the magazine manufacturing process. They let printers and publishers link the subjective, eye-of-the-beholder attributes of a finished piece to a set of physical properties that can be monitored and measured on press. Without SPC, print qualities such as hue, brightness, and contrast tend to provoke open-ended arguments about results that should have been obtained (usually after it is too late to do anything about the results that were obtained). But when press variables such as ink coverage, dot gain, and ink/water balance can be controlled (or at least reliably predicted) by means of SPC, there will be less reason to quarrel over what the customer sees at the end of the run. Since there are more than 100 such variables in four-color printing, the key is to concentrate on the ones that have the most bearing on delivering the kind of quality the customer expects.[148] From the standpoint of SPC, "quality" consists of whatever is measurable whenever the customer is visibly pleased.

A magazine printer with a formal SPC program is a printer with a clear commitment to defect-free publishing. But there are other, more fundamental signs of a printer's concern for the quality of the finished product. Perhaps the most important ones are the printer's plant and equipment maintenance programs.[149] Even a novice can draw useful conclusions about quality from the general condition of a printing plant. As long as magazine presses run on paper, ink, lithographic chemicals, and other raw materials subject to accumulation and waste, magazine manufacturing will never be an immaculate occupation. Nevertheless, one thing that all well-run printing companies have in common is doing everything they can to keep their operations clean, safe, and efficient. Knowing that the eyes of quality-conscious customers are upon them, they have turned their computerized prepress departments—and, increasingly, their pressrooms—into models of industrial hygiene. Pristine or otherwise, appearances do count: A plant that looks dirty and disorganized probably will not succeed in preventing its housekeeping defects from being reflected in the quality of the work it prints.

A quality printing operation will also take justifiable pride in its equipment-maintenance program. Offset lithographic presses are extremely complex pieces of machinery that do not forgive failures to inspect, adjust, and replace their components according to a rigid schedule. As with plant maintenance, looks in the pressroom are more than skin-deep. A grimy, careworn press choked with excess offset spray powder (used to speed drying) probably is as neglected as it appears, and should not be counted upon to give good, consistent results. A thorough maintenance program, on the other hand, can extend the useful life of a press and keep older equipment competitive with newer models, particularly for printing short- to medium-run magazines that do not have the running-speed requirements of large-circulation titles. [150]

Because printers have to vie so strenuously for every kind of job, and because print buyers have grown so demanding in their quality requirements, few plants can afford to be casual about quality management. Modern press technology has also tended to make production quality a given, so that, all else being equal, Printer A probably cannot claim to print better work than Printer B if both have comparable equipment. Assuming that competition has also eliminated significant differences in price, that leaves service as the only arena in which one printer can outdo another. Many publishers have turned this to their advantage by making it known that customer service will be their touchstone for separating the winning bidders from the also-rans.[151]

Popular management theory holds that "customer service" means applying strict standards of behavior to every point of contact between vendor and client, from the receptionist's greeting to the delivery driver's presentation of the manifest. In the high-pressure, crisis-prone world of magazine manufacturing, customer service also means rarely saying "no" to any request for accommodation or support, no matter how late the hour or how difficult the thing requested. That is why printers are taking the concept a step further by making customer education the essence of customer service. As emphasized throughout the chapter, magazine manufacturing has become a partnership that succeeds to the extent that members of the publishing staff grasp their new production responsibilities. The better educated they are, the better their efforts will mesh with work being done at the printing plant. In this way, crisis-mode situations can be kept to a bearable minimum.

Customer education follows a mixed curriculum. One-on-one consultation between publishing staff and the customer service representatives (CSRs) assigned to their magazines is the most basic kind of tutoring. Plant tours, popular for acquainting prospective accounts with the printer's capabilities, can also be used to help current customers better understand what the printing process can and cannot do for them.[152] Some printers use the power of their own medium to educate customers with newsletters that announce the installation of new equipment, explain technical issues, and give guidelines for working more effectively with production staff. Customer education at its best takes the form of free or low-cost seminars sponsored by printing companies, sometimes with the assistance of equipment vendors.

Customer support along educational lines is not a frill or a marketing ploy—it is a value-added benefit that publishers are coming to regard as one proof of a printer's commitment to a quality-focused production partnership. As attitudes change, printers that do not offer these services will find themselves at a considerable disadvantage to competitors that do.

Another way for publishers to measure printers' quality consciousness is to ask whether they observe the various formal quality standards that now apply to graphic arts manufacturing. The broadest of these is promoted by the International Standards Organization (ISO), a standard-making body for the industrial world's scientific and technical communities. ISO 9000, as the group's quality assurance methodology is called, defines a basic system of quality management for all vendors of products and services. To obtain ISO 9000 certification, a vendor must demonstrate that its operating policies and procedures conform to this system.

Originally developed for Europe's Common Market, ISO 9000 is now endorsed by more than 100 countries. Because ISO 9000-certified companies frequently resolve to do business only with other ISO 9000-certified companies, adherence to the standard is becoming a litmus test for vendor selection in many industries, including printing.[153] Soon, noncertified printers may find themselves excluded even from bidding for work from companies that require compliance.[154]

On a more technical level, the magazine industry has developed its own body of standards for assuring the printed quality of the advertising pages that generate the bulk of its revenues. These standards have evolved gradually through intra-industry cooperation, after much deliberation by publishers, printers, and color trade shops (graphics businesses that prepare film and/or digital data for color printing).[155]

The call for standards arose when magazine advertisers began to demand assurances that their advertisements would look the same no matter where they were scheduled to run. The chief difficulty was maintaining the stability of color from one publication to the next. Because magazine printers received their separations from an assortment of trade shops, they frequently found themselves working with films produced to more than one set of specifications. Since it was virtually impossible to satisfy all of the reproduction requirements of a mixed bag of films and proofs in a single press run, individual printers often could not even guarantee the consistency of their own work.[156] Given the equally significant fact that press characteristics and other conditions affecting printed output tended to vary from plant to plant, no one could be certain that an ad appearing in one publication would have the same color qualities as the identical ad in another publication.

As inconsistencies grew, so did advertisers' dissatisfaction with the magazine medium. In the mid-1970s, a coalition of groups representing advertising agencies, magazine publishers, printers, and color trade shops responded to the crisis with the first version of SWOP, the voluntary Specifications for Web Offset Publications.

Formulated with the needs of large-circulation titles in mind, SWOP was an attempt to create standardized technical guidelines for the production of four-color films and proofs. It set up parameters for dot gain, ink coverage, proofing stocks, densitometry, viewing conditions, and many other characteristics and procedures that determine how accurately the printed end-result can be predicted and controlled. Since the parameters were based on production tolerances that most magazine printers could be expected to achieve, it was believed that films and proofs produced according to SWOP guidelines would yield uniform results wherever they were put to use.

Early faith in SWOP's powers of reconciliation was not misplaced. Today, having undergone several revisions with the input and blessing of all the major segments of the magazine publishing industry, SWOP has become the industry's high standard for reproduction quality in web offset lithographic publications. Although compliance is not mandatory, publishers' deference to the many influential advertisers and agencies that endorse SWOP tends to assure that its guidelines will be honored by the magazines to which the guidelines apply. The success of SWOP has inspired similar campaigns for production standards in other segments of periodical publishing: SNAP (Specifications for Non-Heatset Advertising Printing) in the newspaper business; and the GTA (Gravure Technical Association) Series I and V Specifications for publications printed by gravure.

The industry's penchant for standard making also extends to the newest technologies for the production of advertising pages. Given that most pages now begin as or become digitized assemblages of text, line art, halftones, and color, there needs to be an "open" standard by which these data can be moved intact from production system to production system. The evolving standard is known as DDAP, which stands for Digital Distribution of Advertising for Publications.

Like SWOP, DDAP is a pro bono effort by dedicated volunteers from advertising agencies, magazine publishing companies, magazine printers, electronic prepress systems manufacturers, and color prepress houses. DDAP comes under the supervision of a graphic arts technology committee within the American National Standards Institute (ANSI), which has published accredited standards for the transfer and calibration of color digital pages.[157] The graphic arts committee has devised a data file exchange format that could, if adopted by the major prepress system makers, make digital ads as consistent in appearance as conventional ads from SWOP-compliant film.[158]

As digital prepress and production technologies complete the transformation of printing from an art form to a science, standards for the effective use of these powerful new tools will continue to flourish. Of the most practical interest to magazine professionals are the various sets of procedures for the proper submission of digital files. These are designed to help page creators ensure that their files contain everything the printer or trade service vendor will need in order to get the pages into production without difficulty or delay. Examples are the Electronic Mechanical Specifications (EMS) published by the Graphic Communications Association

(GCA), a print industry group; Computer Ready Electronic Files (CREF) from a users' group sponsored by Scitex, a manufacturer of high-end electronic prepress systems; and the "preflight control forms" kit from the National Association of Printers & Lithographers (NAPL). Printers and color trade shops may have their own house rules for digital input. No matter what set of guidelines is used, publisher-vendor communication through the medium of standards is the best way to prevent the kinds of problems that may be impossible to correct without scrapping the run if the first place they are noticed is on a press sheet.

## TRADE CUSTOMS

For the sake of good vendor relations, publishers should also be aware of the printing industry's Graphic Communications Business Practices, a code of voluntary guidelines on technical and business matters for printers and their customers. The guidelines, which are endorsed and periodically updated by the printing industry's principal trade associations, describe the understanding that printers and customers generally have with respect to quotations, orders, ownership of materials, liability, and other aspects of their business relationship. Printers often use these guidelines as the basis of their terms and conditions of sale and may reproduce them on their quotation forms. However, because printers are not obligated to adhere to these business practices, they may modify them to suit the requirements of a particular job or the wishes of individual customers. Since accepting a quote in which the printer's terms are specified represents an agreement to be bound by those terms, wise print buyers always check the fine print before sending the purchase order.

## NOTES

[1]Beth Fein in "Production Managers Talk Back on the Issues" by Teresa Martin and Howard Fenton, *Magazine Design & Production*, May 1992, 32.

[2]David L. Smith in "Production Managers Talk Back on the Issues" by Teresa Martin and Howard Fenton, *Magazine Design & Production*, May 1992, 30.

[3]J. Michael Adams, David D. Faux, and Lloyd J. Rieber, *Printing Technology*, 3rd edit. (Albany: Delmar Publishers Inc., 1988), 2.

[4]Adams, Faux, and Rieber, *Printing Technology*, 20.

[5]Raymond N. Blair, ed., *The Lithographers Manual*, 7th edit. (Pittsburgh: Graphic Arts Technical Foundation, 1983), 1:4.

[6]Adams, Faux, and Rieber, *Printing Technology*, 28.

[7]Michael H. Bruno, ed., *Pocket Pal/A Graphic Arts Production Handbook*, 14th edit. (Memphis: International Paper Company, 1989), 28.

[8]Blair, *The Lithographers Manual*, 1:4.

[9]Victor Strauss, *The Printing Industry: An Introduction to Its Many Branches, Processes and Products* (Washington, D.C.: Printing Industries of America, Inc., 1967), 325–326.

[10]David Bann, *The Print Production Handbook* (Cincinnati: North Light/Writer's Digest Books, 1985), 20.

[11]Strauss, *The Printing Industry*, 37.

[12]Strauss, *The Printing Industry*, 493.

[13]*50 Years/From Pioneers to Leaders* (Teaneck, N.J.: National Association of Printers and Lithographers, 1983), 4.

[14]Strauss, *The Printing Industry*, 277.

[15]Strauss, *The Printing Industry*, 277.

[16]Bruno, *Pocket Pal*, 25.

[17]Bruno, *Pocket Pal*, 131.

[18]Strauss, *The Printing Industry*, 415.

[19]*50 Years/From Pioneers To Leaders*, 13.

[20]Bruno, *Pocket Pal*, 29.

[21]Bruno, *Pocket Pal*, 128.

[22]Bann, *The Print Production Handbook*, 24.

[23]Strauss, *The Printing Industry*, 326.

[24]Bruno, *Pocket Pal*, 132.

[25]*50 Years/From Pioneers To Leaders*, 37–38.

[26]Gary G. Field, *Color and Its Reproduction* (Pittsburgh: Graphic Arts Technical Foundation, 1988), 99.

[27]Strauss, *The Printing Industry*, 282.

[28]Blair, *The Lithographers Manual*, 1:13.

[29]Richard C. Holliday, "Whistling Past the Graveyard/40 Years of Magazine Printing," *High Volume Printing,* April 1994, 34.

[30]Holliday, "Whistling Past the Graveyard," 43.

[31]Bann, *The Print Production Handbook*, 70.

[32]Bruno, *Pocket Pal*, 46.

[33]*50 Years/From Pioneers To Leaders*, 42.

[34]Strauss, *The Printing Industry*, 93.

[35]Strauss, *The Printing Industry*, 79.

[36]Strauss, *The Printing Industry*, 73.

[37]Strauss, *The Printing Industry*, 105.

[38]Bann, *The Print Production Handbook*, 74.

[39]Strauss, *The Printing Industry*, 73.

[40]Strauss, *The Printing Industry*, 147.

[41]Bruno, *Pocket Pal*, 15.

[42]Strauss, *The Printing Industry*, 8.

[43]Bruno, *Pocket Pal*, 16.

[44]Bruno, *Pocket Pal*, 16.

[45]Blair, *The Lithographers Manual*, 1:9–10.

[46]Bruno, *Pocket Pal*, 106.

[47]Bruno, *Pocket Pal*, 133.

[48]Bruno, *Pocket Pal*, 27.

[49]Brett Rutherford, ed., *Gravure: Process and Technology* (Rochester: Gravure Education Foundation and Gravure Association of America, 1991), 6.

[50]Strauss, *The Printing Industry*, 277.

[51]Rutherford, *Gravure: Process and Technology*, 10–13.

[52]Adams, Faux, and Rieber, *Printing Technology,* 452.

[53]Rutherford, *Gravure: Process and Technology*, 19–20; 23.

[54]Adams, Faux, and Rieber, *Printing Technology,* 452.

[55]"The U.S. Gravure Industry Today," *Gravure,* Fall 1994, 18, 30.

[56]"The U.S. Gravure Industry Today," *Gravure,* Fall 1994, 18-21.

[57]Mark Beach, Steve Shepro, and Ken Russon, *Getting It Printed: How to Work With Printers and Graphic Arts Services to Assure Quality, Stay on Schedule, and Control Costs* (Portland, Ore.: Coast to Coast Books, 1986), 143–144.

[58]"The U.S. Gravure Industry Today," *Gravure,* Fall 1994, 18–21.

[59]"The U.S. Gravure Industry Today," *Gravure,* Fall 1994, 20–23.

[60]Adams, Faux, and Rieber, *Printing Technology,* 454.

[61]Rutherford, *Gravure: Process and Technology*, 3.

[62]Adams, Faux, and Rieber, *Printing Technology,* 454.

[63]Bann, *The Print Production Handbook*, 26.

[64]Adams, Faux, and Rieber, *Printing Technology,* 454.

[65]Adams, Faux, and Rieber, *Printing Technology,* 454.

[66]Bann, *The Print Production Handbook*, 25.

[67]Bann, *The Print Production Handbook*, p 27–28.

[68]Mark Beach, *Graphically Speaking: An Illustrated Guide to the Working Language and Design of Printing* (Cincinnati: North Light Books, 1992), 116.

[69]Strauss, *The Printing Industry*, 294.

[70]Bann, *The Print Production Handbook*, 25.

[71]"The U.S. Gravure Industry Today," *Gravure,* Fall 1994, 18.

[72]"The U.S. Gravure Industry Today," *Gravure,* Fall 1994, 30–31.

[73]Adams, Faux, and Rieber, *Printing Technology,* 454–55.

[74]Dean Phillip Lem, *graphics master 4: A Workbook of Planning Aids, Reference Guides, and Graphic Tools for the Design, Estimating, Preparation and Production of Printing, Print Advertising, and Desktop Publishing,* 4th edit. (Los Angeles: Dean Lem Associates, Inc., 1988), 67.

[75]Strauss, *The Printing Industry*, 142.

[76]Strauss, *The Printing Industry*, 144.

[77]Strauss, *The Printing Industry*, 146.

[78]*Printing Production,* June 1965, 78; as excerpted in Strauss, *The Printing Industry*, 134.

[79]Dr. Frank N. Romano, "Electronic Publishing Chronology," © 1994, Dr. Frank N. Romano. Excerpts and commentary used throughout this section appear with his generous permission.

[80]Dr. Frank N. Romano, "Electronic Publishing Chronology."

[81]Barrie Sosinsky, *Beyond the Desktop/Tools and Technology for Computer Publishing* (New York: Bantam Books, 1991), 15

[82]Liz Horton, "Charting the pre-press revolution," *Folio:,* August 1991, 57.

[83]Bruno, *Pocket Pal,* 107.

[84]Lynne Crimando, "Revolution in a Box: How Desktop Production Changes Management Roles," *Folio:*, November 1991, 99.

[85]Patrick Henry, "The Ultimate Question: Can You Really Afford to Have In-House Electronic Prepress?", *CONCEPPTS Connections* (National Association of Printers and Lithographers), May 1993.

[86]Liz Horton, "Charting the pre-press revolution," *Folio:*, August 1991, 59.

[87]Paul McDougall, "Desktop survey: publishers are doing it for themselves," *Folio:*, September 1, 1994, 66ff.

[88]Crimando, "Revolution in a Box," 99.

[89]Robert Jose, "Responsibilities of a Production Coordinator," © 1990, Graphic Communications Association.

[90] Paul McDougall, "Desktop survey: publishers are doing it for themselves," *Folio:*, September 1, 1994, 63

[91]Thad McIlroy and Gord Graham, *Desktop Publishing in Black + White & Color* (San Francisco: The Color Resource, 1992), 116.

[92]Liane Sebastian, *Electronic Design and Publishing: Business Practices* (New York: Allworth Press, 1992), xii.

[93]"Corporate Print Buyers on Service, Capability Expectations," *High Volume Printing*, October 1994, 68.

[94]Gary W. Millet and Ralph G. Rosenberg, *Primer for Graphic Arts Profitability/A Money-Making Formula* (Colorado Springs: Millet Group, Inc., 1992), 13.

[95]Roberta Thomas, "High Tech at the printer/Innovations in printing and binding," *Folio: Special Sourcebook Issue 1995,* 208.

[96]Daniel Dejean and Kurt Klein, "Professional Accreditation for Production Management," *Signature*, January/February 1993, 53.

[97]Dejean and Klein, "Professional Accreditation for Production Management," 53.

[98]Miles Southworth and Donna Southworth, *Quality and Productivity in the Graphic Arts* (Livonia, N.Y.: Graphic Arts Publishing, 1989), 6-1, 6-2.

[99]Michael Garry, "Dollar stretch: Publishers confront the new economic realities," *Folio:*, February 1989, 90.

[100]Janet Mannheimer, "Print bids 101, for publishers," *Folio:*, April 1, 1994, 35.

[101]Bruce Heston, Production Director, Meredith Corporation, quoted in "The Publications Market: What's Important to Today's Publishers?", *Web Offset/The Hard Copy,* Fall 1994, 60.

[102]Garry, "Dollar stretch," *Folio:*, 93

[103]Southworth and Southworth, *Quality and Productivity in the Graphic Arts*, 14-2, 14-3.

[104]Irving Herschbein, "29 ways to reduce production costs," *Folio:*, November 1989, 155.

[105]Alex Brown, "Your Printer's Invoice: Searching for Savings," *Folio:*, March 1990, 101.

[106]Richard M. Koff, *Strategic Planning for Magazine Executives: How to take the guesswork out of magazine publishing decisions* (Stamford: Folio: Magazine Publishing Corporation, 1987), 115.

[107]Jeff Parnau, "A Buyer's Market?", *Magazine Design & Production*, January/February 1992, 73.

[108]Beach, Shepro, and Russon, *Getting It Printed*, 163.

[109]"Web/Sheet Crossover: Are the Lines Blurring?" *Web Offset/The Hard Copy*, Fall 1994, 74.

[110]"The Printer and Publisher Partnership," *Folio: Special Sourcebook Issue 1993*, 200–01.

[111]Garry, "Dollar stretch," *Folio:*, 92

[112]Alex Brown, "Finding the perfect printer," *Folio:*, February 1990, 87.

[113]Herschbein, "29 ways to reduce production costs," 156.

[114]Jenna Schnuer, "Short-cutoff presses grow in popularity," *Folio:*, April 15, 1995, 18.

[115]Brown, "Finding the perfect printer," 87.

[116]Herschbein, "29 ways to reduce production costs," 153.

[117]Mike Cuenca, "5 ways to save money at the printer," *Folio: Special Sourcebook Issue 1995*, 219.

[118]Leonard Mogel, *The Magazine/Everything You Need to Know to Make It in the Magazine Business* (Chester, Conn.: The Globe Pequot Press, 1988), 36.

[119]Mogel, *The Magazine*, 85.

[120]McIlroy and Graham, *Desktop Publishing*, 114.

[121]Mike Cuenca, "Ad sales and production/Ending the deadline wars with a truce," *Folio: Special Sourcebook Issue 1995*, 256.

[122]Barbara Love, "Threats don't pay off at the printer," *Folio: Special Sourcebook Issue 1995*, 194.

[123]Mannheimer, "Print bids 101, for publishers," 35.

[124]Beach, Shepro, and Russon, *Getting It Printed*, 164.

[125]Beach, Shepro, and Russon, *Getting It Printed*, 190.

[126]Beach, Shepro, and Russon, *Getting It Printed*, 167.

[127]Beach, Shepro, and Russon, *Getting It Printed*, 167.

[128]Stan Kaufman, "13 ways to evaluate a printer," *Folio: Sourcebook 1992*, 220.

[129]Beach, Shepro, and Russon, *Getting It Printed*, 162.

[130]Brown, "Finding the perfect printer," 86.

[131]Peter Pallans, "17 surefire ways to trim production costs," *Folio: Special Sourcebook Issue 1994*, 206.

[132]Brown, "Finding the perfect printer," 87.

[133]Kaufman, "13 ways to evaluate a printer," 220.

[134]Kaufman, "13 ways to evaluate a printer," 221.

[135]Stephen W. Frye, "How to analyze printing bids," *Folio: Special Sourcebook Issue 1994*, 202–04

[136]Mannheimer, "Print bids 101, for publishers," 35.

[137]Herschbein, "29 ways to reduce production costs," 156.

[138]Alex Brown, "Negotiating a printing contract," *Folio: Sourcebook 1992*, 222.

[139]Beach, Shepro, and Russon, *Getting It Printed*, 169–70.

[140]Brown, "Your printer's invoice: Searching for savings," 100.

[141]Kaufman, "13 ways to evaluate a printer," 220.

[142]Parnau, "A buyer's market?", 73.

[143]Sebastian, *Electronic Design and Publishing: Business Practices*, 58.

[144]Sebastian, *Electronic Design and Publishing: Business Practices*, 3.

[145]Mike Cuenca, "Quality time with your printer," *Folio:*, March 1, 1994, 39–40.

[146]Southworth and Southworth, *Quality and Productivity in the Graphic Arts* , I-6, I-7.

[147]Miles Southworth and Donna Southworth, *How to Implement Total Quality Management* (Livonia, NY: Graphic Arts Publishing Company, 1992), 57–58.

[148]Southworth and Southworth, *Quality and Productivity in the Graphic Arts* , 5–21.

[149]Brown, "Finding the perfect printer," 89.

[150]Brown, "Finding the perfect printer," 89.

[151]Anon., "The Printer and Publisher Partnership," *Folio: Special Sourcebook Issue 1993,* 200.

[152]Anon., "The Printer and Publisher Partnership," 200–201.

[153]Philip K. Ruggles, *De$ktop Dividend$: Managing Electronic Prepress for Profit* (San Luis Obispo, Calif.: Printing Management Services, 1993), 109.

[154]Ruggles, *De$ktop Dividend$*, 62-63.

[155]The traditional color trade shop—sometimes referred to as the color separator or the photoengraver—is a graphic arts business that supplies the film used by printers for color work. Film-based prepress services such as retouching, stripping, proofing, and platemaking may also be provided. Today, in addition to supplying film, color trade shops offer high-end electronic prepress and desktop publishing support. Establishments known as service bureaus and imaging centers compete with color trade shops for various kinds of digital prepress work.

[156]Field, *Color and Its Reproduction*, 96.

[157]Melene Follert, "DDAP and the World Beyond," *Signature,* April 1993, 36–38.

[158]Rose Blessing and Lea Smith, "Repurposing Content Is a Great Concept, But…How Do We Begin?", *Publishing & Production Executive*, December 1994, 43.

# How Magazines Are Made

## TODAY: THE MAGAZINE PRODUCTION WORKFLOW

To get a sense of the workflow that sustains the production of a magazine, imagine that you and a handful of friends have been given a couple of weeks to organize a black-tie banquet for a large crowd of the most influential people in town. Your kitchen is small, you do not have all of the culinary tools that you would like to have, and there is barely enough time to gather all of the choice ingredients you will need from a long list of specialty-food purveyors. If the start of the banquet is delayed even by a little, or if the dishes aren't uniformly superb, your VIP guests may not come back. This could be most embarrassing for you and your friends, since you are going to be asked to mount a comparable affair for the same haute guest list in another couple of weeks.

As every *chef de cuisine* and production manager knows, the art of fashioning a spectacular repast is the art of making many good things happen at once. While one sous-chef chops, dices, and juliennes, another sees to the sauces. While one production staffer sets up electronic templates for page layout, another works out an imposition to arrange the pages and their color elements in the most mechanically efficient way. When dinner is announced—or when the magazine is ready to enter distribution channels—the result stems not from the completion of any final step in a linear sequence of events but from the simultaneous occurrence of separate events proceeding on parallel time lines. Some of these steps take longer than others and so must begin sooner. Some steps depend on the accuracy of information generated by other steps. The banquet master's task is to synchronize and coordinate the steps so that nothing is still on the stove (or in the production department) when it is time for the feast to be laid before the dinner guests.

Although good production, like good cooking, is often improvisational, most magazines start from a core recipe that is as basic to the process as béchamel is to the great cuisines of France. The rest of this section is a kitchen primer on essential ingredients and preparation techniques.

## THE RAW MATERIAL: EDITORIAL COPY

In a magazine, categorically speaking, everything that is not editorial is advertising, and everything that is not advertising is editorial. Editorial copy consists of news stories, features, columns, departments, readers' letters, sidebars, and photo captions, as well as the journalistic apparatus (tables of contents, callouts, continuation lines, page headers, and so on) that gives cohesiveness to the whole. Editorial matter is either staff-generated—written by people directly employed by the magazine—or submitted by freelance writers, contributing editors, and other outside writers who do not belong to the regular editorial staff.

Editorial matter enters the production workflow as digital files or as hard (paper) copy. Digital files, typically created in word processing applications such as Microsoft Word and WordPerfect, can be input more or less directly into the magazine's computerized publishing system from portable storage media (diskettes, in most instances) and on-line sources. Hard copy, on the other hand, has to be converted to digital form either by scanning or, as a last resort, by rekeying.

Most magazines now begin their production cycles with some form of digital text creation and input. Many different workflow schemes are possible. Members of an in-house editorial staff may work at personal computers connected by a local area network (LAN) to a central file server (a computer with a very high data-storage capacity) that holds their work for routing to other stages of the page-creation sequence. These customized configurations have displaced (but not entirely eliminated) proprietary publishing systems that use dedicated terminals and networking software in contrast to the off-the-shelf components of LAN-based setups. And while networking denotes electronic publishing at its most efficient, it should be remembered that computers without connections can also make up a viable publishing system. Many titles still rely on "sneakernet"—the physical transportation of digital files on magnetic media from one PC to the next—to get their copy processed and their pages built.

However it is configured, an in-house publishing system will always be set up so that everyone is using compatible tools to produce compatible files. For publishing systems built around personal computers, this is principally a matter of favoring one platform operating system (Windows or Macintosh) over another and standardizing word processing, page layout, illustration, and image manipulation chores by using only one application for each of those functions. In other words, if one editor writes her stories in WordPerfect, so do all the other editors; if one page-layout artist uses PageMaker, nobody else in the art department will be using QuarkXPress instead. Apart from its efficiency, this is also the most economical way to invest in publishing software, since it can be done through discounted site-licensing for multiple copies of the selected applications.

It is not nearly as easy to homogenize editorial input from outside sources, and for any magazine that depends on outside sources to fill its pages, file-format compatibility will always be a production issue. Although operating-system improvements and file translation utilities have made resolving conflicts much easier than it used to be, it is still prudent to anticipate extra processing steps, if not outright problems, from any editorial matter created in applications other than the ones used by the in-house publishing system. (Any editor or production person who has experienced the tedium of stripping unwanted hard returns from line-ends in a long manuscript knows what to expect.) Problems can be minimized by giving outside contributors file preparation guidelines that specify preferred formats and warn of manuscript features to be avoided. All guidelines of this kind should require writers to furnish hard copy along with their diskettes, since only by comparing the paper manuscript to what appears on screen can an editor be certain of how the writer intended to format his or her submission.

Magazines still accept hard-copy-only from writers who cannot or will not send diskettes, but with reluctance. Whenever someone has to retype someone else's typing, the work consists of nothing but redundant keystrokes. Each stroke nips at production efficiency and gobbles a bit of cycle time that does not belong to it. Rekeying increases the likelihood of typographical error, and it raises the issue's overall production expense (especially if the rekeying must be done for an added charge by a service bureau or a typographer).

Fortunately, there is an alternative to using hard copy as an excuse for exposing editors and production staff to a heightened risk of carpal-tunnel injury. Today, inexpensive desktop scanners with OCR (optical character recognition) capability can read paper copy and translate it into digital equivalents that most publishing systems can use. OCR scanning is efficient when the original copy is clean, simply formatted, and free of unconventional typefaces or other text features that the OCR software may have difficulty recognizing. Still, there are drawbacks. Faxed copy—a staple of the editorial diet for many magazines—seldom scans well. OCR conversion errors may yield their own crop of needless typos. And while OCR scanning may be fine for capturing a story here or a column there, high-volume usage often demands more processing power and throughput time than the magazine's publishing system and copy deadlines can support. So, although OCR scanning is a handy hedge against rekeying, few magazines will depend on it as a primary means of editorial input.

Everyone knows that the on-line telecommunications explosion has placed extraordinary amounts of information at the fingertips of every person who has access to a modem and a computer. It has also opened an important new channel for editorial input to magazines from outside sources. Now that it is relatively easy for writers to transmit their stories from the same computers on which they compose them, many publications gladly accept submissions delivered via file sharing, E-mail, commercial on-line services, and Internet resources such as anonymous FTP (file transfer protocol). When there is a modem at both ends of the editorial pipeline, and when writer and publication have the right kinds of telecommunications software or on-line access, getting copy into an anxious editor's hands ceases to be the migraine-triggering exercise that freelancers have grown used to accepting as a given of their business.

The beauty of on-line input is its immediacy. As soon as the story is ready, it can be on its way to the editor's screen as fast as data packets can traverse telephone lines. Because transmission is nearly instantaneous, the editorial cycle regains precious time that once had to be set aside for postal mail, overnight express, or personal delivery by the writer. The recovered time can be used to push the editorial deadline even closer to the page-production cutoff so that the issue can carry more late-breaking information. This clearly is a powerful advantage for news magazines and other publications that specialize in time-sensitive material.

Like any method of editorial submission, data telecommunications needs to be managed with understanding, foresight, and care. Editors and production people who use them regularly know that file transmission and E-mail routing are not foolproof. Much happens in cyberspace that can fragment, corrupt, or eradicate a file. Unfamiliar formats ("They sent me a zipfile. Now what do I do?") must be converted, if they can be, into something that the editor's word processor will recognize. And, foolproof or not, the bounties of editorial telecommunications are not free. On-line services and Internet accounts cost money, and so does the telephone connect time that mobilizes them. These expenses, so easy to underestimate, must be carefully forecasted and controlled as part of the overall production budget.

The technicalities of data telecommunications are beyond the scope of this chapter and book. Suffice it to say that the ability to use on-line tools and resources is becoming an essential job skill for everyone who wants to succeed in the magazine publishing business, especially in its editorial and production disciplines.

## THE RAW MATERIAL: ARTWORK

Ever since printing technology first made it feasible to mingle pleasing images with text in the pages of mass-produced periodicals, the look of magazines has been no less important to their appeal than their content. Because computerized publishing has put so many potent creative tools in the hands of today's publication designers, it is difficult to think of a magazine in any category that does not show at least some eye-catching flair for page layout, typography, illustration, photography, or use of color.

Good graphic design has always counted on good print production to transfer its beauty undiminished from the drafting table to the finished page. Nowadays, however, the bywords for the relationship of design arts to production skills have changed from "dependence on" to "identification with." The catalyst in the transformation is digital publishing. At many magazines, designers and production managers are coming to think of their roles in common, exclusively digital terms. In the old days, a designer's work had to be re-created in an entirely different form in the camera room and the stripping department. Today, because pages formatted, typeset, and illustrated on a designer's computer screen furnish data that can be used to drive every subsequent stage of production, the workflow from the art department to the pressroom is becoming an unchanging stream of digital information. This means that designers, no less than their counterparts in production, must work "backward from the press" to ensure that their digital pages are as printable as they are aesthetically appealing.

Nevertheless, although technology now enables any publication to move (or at least think about moving) in the direction of all-digital design and production, conventional methods still have their parts to play in the magazine production workflow. The explanation is that most "digital pages" contain elements that did not come into being that way. For example, as long as photographers use cameras that use film to take pictures, magazines will need ways to deal with photographic prints and transparencies of the pictures they want to reproduce. There is also the fact that many graphic artists and designers—including those who have mastered the computer—continue to execute some of their best magazine work in traditional art media. Advertising agencies, moreover, still favor conventional films and proofs when it comes to preparing their handiwork for production in magazines. Unless a magazine has made the giant leap—as a few have—to fully computer-generated page creation, it must know how to fit nondigital design elements into a workflow that may be digital in some respects but not in every one.

Digital or conventional, the creative building blocks of magazine design are much the same as they ever were. Line art, to begin with, can be rendered with a host of familiar tools from steel-tipped pens to felt-tipped markers. It can also be created in digital form by nearly every high- and low-end software application for desktop publishing (including popular word processors). The most easily reproducible form of illustration, line art consists of black-and-white or monochrome, continuous-tone images that contain no shades of gray and require no halftoning or color separation in order to make them printable.

Line art is widely distributed in "clip-art" collections of all-purpose images that can be used without permission or cost by anyone who is able to copy them. Hard-copy clip art, available in books or as loose sheets, can be readily converted into digital form by scanning. For those without access to scanners, clip art publishers now offer predigitized collections of ready-to-run line art on diskette or CD-ROM.

Graphs, tables, and charts are used to convey statistical information that is too complex to be summarized in editorial prose. Many desktop publishing applications now have modules for graphing and tabling within text documents; some will even calculate the data. Graphs can also be imported into page layouts from popular spreadsheet programs, some of which have sophisticated design and formatting tools. Software features that automatically share updated information among linked applications simplify the task of keeping tabular material current with late editorial changes. Graphs, tables, and charts can either be as simple and straightforward as a report from the accounting department or as visually elaborate as a graphic designer wants to make them.

Artwork more complex than line drawings and simple graphs involves more complex preparation for production. The traditional vehicle for magazine art with multiple design elements and color specifications is the mechanical, also known as a *board* or *keyline*. Assembled by a paste-up artist, this structural collage shows the printer where to position type and images on the page, and how to lay in colors, tints, borders, and other graphic requisites. In preparing mechanicals, artists may use tissue overlays, samples from color swatch books, and FPO (for position only) facsimiles of selected images to make their requirements clear. Carrying out these instructions, printers make individual pieces of graphic arts film for stripping into a larger "flat" that serves as the image carrier for the fully assembled page.

As desktop publishing emerged in the mid-1980s, artists and production people began to use the term *electronic mechanical* to describe the pages they were now assembling as efficiently in software programs as they were accustomed to assembling them on pieces of art board. Much of the artwork for these digital pages came from "draw" and "paint" applications that gave artists powerful new tools for stretching their visual imaginations (in addition to furnishing the digital equivalents of traditional tools). Artwork created in today's illustration programs has the further advantage of being in full harmony with the digital prepress process. As already noted, the data that make up a digital image are the same data that will be used to translate it into a printed image on press. This makes for greater consistency and stability of results from one end of the process to the other. For example, color instructions can be embedded within the digital file that contains the design so that wherever the artwork goes, its precise color requirements will go along with it.

Magazine photography is also branching in new digital directions, but at a more restrained pace, given its historic ties to lithographic printing. Although silver-halide (meaning chemically developed) film is still an important medium for supplying original photographic images to magazines, it is no longer linked as closely to the physics of the prepress process as it once was. Originally, the only way to produce films and plates for offset lithographic printing was to develop them by methods essentially the same as those used to develop photographic prints.

But now that graphic arts films and plates can be imaged directly from digital data, photographic film and its processing methods have moved a step to the rear in the production sequence.

This is because photographic originals (prints and transparencies) have to be converted into digital files before they can be incorporated into a digital workflow. If other page elements can be managed from the outset in digital form, digitizing the photos then represents an extra, preliminary step and an added expense. In contrast, photographic images from filmless sources—for example, digital cameras and video-capture hardware for personal computers—need no such conversion. The unstoppable shift of prepress to all-digital operation, together with the environmental desirability of eliminating the chemical wastes of film processing, spells a shrinking role for conventional photography in the design and manufacture of magazines.

For the moment, however, it is safe to assume that most production workflows will retain their means of dealing with photographic input. The first step, as always, is to transform the continuous tones of the original image into a pattern of halftone dots that can be reproduced on press. In conventional prepress, the original is rephotographed through a patterned piece of film, known as a contact screen, that furnishes the dots. When the original is scanned for digital conversion, scanning algorithms (instructions) in the controlling computer determine the placement, shape, and frequency of the dots to be generated by the imagesetter or film recorder.

In both conventional and digital halftoning, the reproduction quality of the conversion is measured in lines per inch (lpi), a term surviving from the days when originals had to be shot through crosshatched rules etched into pieces of glass. The higher the lpi number, the finer the dot pattern and the better the appearance of the printed image. A quality range of 120 to 150 lpi is standard for most magazine work.

Converting black-and-white photography into halftones is a one-step process. Full-color images, on the other hand, must be "separated" into four distinct patterns of dots that represent the four basic colors from which a printing press is able to re-create the full chromatic range of the original. When these four "process" colors—cyan (a shade of blue), magenta (a shade of red), yellow, and black—are printed over one another in sequence on the press, they form dot clusters called rosettes that essentially trick the eye into seeing what appears to be an unrestricted spectrum of continuous color on the finished page.

The old-fashioned way to make color separations is to expose the original material through a succession of four colored filters that break up the colors of the original into their component process colors. The original can be either transmission copy, through which light passes or reflection copy, from which light is reflected. Transmission copy—colored slides and other photographic positives known as *transparencies* or *chromes*—makes the best separations. The quality of separations made from photographic prints, opaque artwork, and other kinds of reflection copy depends chiefly on the condition and color quality of the input material.

Exposing the original through a red filter yields the negative for cyan; a green filter, the negative for magenta; a blue filter, the negative for yellow; a "modified" filter, the negative for black. These negatives, in turn, serve as the originals for four-color platemaking. Contact screens, added as part of the separation process, have to be set at specific angles to one another so that the halftone rosettes transferred from the negatives to the plates do not create an unwanted visual effect known as *moiré*. Moiré is an underlying pattern of geometric distortion that recalls some of the eye-assaulting op-art productions of the 1960s.

Moiré is unpredictable (although printers of fashion materials know how it can bedevil the halftone reproduction of fabric patterns like tweed and herringbone). Fortunately, a new halftoning process called *stochastic screening* promises to make moiré as much of an anachronism as op art. A scanner using stochastic algorithms generates a random pattern of dots without a line-screen grid. Unlike conventional halftone dots, which vary in diameter according to the lightness or darkness of the areas they occupy, stochastic dots are of uniform size. Producing no rosettes, they fall closer together in shadow areas of the halftone, and farther apart in the mid-tones and the highlights. With no rosettes to be misaligned, a stochastically screened image is much less prone to moiré and misregistration than a convention-ally screened image.

At about the time that the op-art fad was at its height, computer-controlled electronic scanners were starting to replace cameras as the primary tools for mak-ing color separations. Today virtually all color images for commercial reproduction are separated by scanners, and most of these units are fully digital in operation. A digital scanner samples the colors of the original and converts the samples into pix-els (picture elements) that are reconstructed into bitmaps (dot patterns) for generat-ing and color-correcting screened separation film. Data from scanners can also be incorporated into page layouts in both high- and low-resolution formats, depending upon how the page is to be processed.

There are two basic kinds of scanners: drum and flatbed. The heart of a drum scanner is a transparent revolving cylinder (the drum) around which the original copy is wrapped and fastened. As the drum spins, a beam of light traverses the copy in controlled increments. Light reflected from or passing through the origi-nal is analyzed for color separation in a component called the photomultiplier tube (PMT). Instead of a revolving drum, a flatbed scanner has a fixed, horizontal pane of glass that resembles the platen of a photocopying machine. Originals are laid on the glass for illumination by a moving light source. In a flatbed scanner, sensors known as CCDs (charge-coupled devices) do what the PMT does in a drum scanner.

Scanners once were massive, complicated, and costly devices that could be operated only by trained experts at graphics firms specializing in color prep work.

Nowadays there are scanners that will sit snugly on a desktop, respond efficiently to manipulation by amateurs, and fit comfortably within the capital budgets of magazines that decide to purchase them. The decision to bring scanning in-house is usually spurred by management's desire for more control over workflow and production costs. But because not all scanners are created equal in terms of productive capacity and quality of output, the choice of equipment must be made with great care. Some magazines are now happily making their own separations on moderately priced scanners. Many others have concluded that maintaining the status quo of outsourced scanning on high-end equipment is the wisest course to follow, at least for the time being.

## THE RAW MATERIAL: ADVERTISING COPY

There is not much technical difference between editorial pages and advertising pages. Both kinds spring from the same creative tools and techniques and, with exceptions at a few magazines, both kinds are printed the same way on the same equipment. For magazine production managers, the chief difference between them lies in the trafficking: the deadline-sensitive coordination of their movement from source to press. In general, advertising pages are more challenging to traffic because they make more stops along the way.

Most editorial pages originate in publishing offices, where writers and artists can brood them until it is time to send the issue to the printer. Most advertising pages, on the other hand, originate elsewhere: in designs studios, in the creative departments of advertising agencies, and in other places where the publisher does not control the production schedule. If the ad pages must then go to a third-party color trade shop for conversion to film, that represents more time that the publisher must build into the cycle before he can predict when the material will be in his possession. Very often, proofs will have to be sent to the agency or the client for approval—another potential delay.

Looming above everything are the printer's cutoff for receipt of material and the danger of being bumped from prebooked press time if that cutoff is missed. To prevent the unthinkable, a production manager needs three things: a global view of the traffic for every ad the issue contains; a steely-eyed determination to keep the traffic moving by staying in touch with everyone responsible for forwarding the material; and a deal maker's skill in negotiating the inevitable requests for extensions from agency personnel and others who need "just a little more time."

The production specifications in a magazine's *rate card* tell what kinds of advertising pages can be accepted. Display advertising insertions (as distinguished from classified advertising and listings) may be full-page ads or partial-page ads. A full-page ad gets one side of one page to itself; nothing else (including a page number) may be printed in the space that a full-page advertiser has paid for the right to dominate. A facing left- and right-hand page combination, sold as a unit, is called a spread. "Three consecutive pages, opening right" refers to a spread sold with a preceding right-hand page to introduce it. Adding a fourth (left-hand) consecutive page creates a unit that resembles a self-contained, four-page booklet.

Partial-page ads, which cost less to insert and produce than full-page ads because they take up less space, may share their pages with editorial alone or with editorial and other partial-page ads. "Partials" are commonly set up in 7 by 10", one-half, one-third, one-quarter, and one-eighth page configurations, but they can take whatever sizes and shapes a magazine is willing and able to sell. This means that one of the production manager's trickier tasks will be making sure that the issue's mixed bag of partial-page ads can be arrayed to fit neatly into the limited "real estate" they must share with editorial.

The rate card's production specifications give basic information about how display advertising materials should be prepared for submission. Dimensions, line-screen values, and other requirements for halftone films will be specified; so will instructions for *bleed* ads, which have ink coverage that extends beyond the edge of the page (the excess is trimmed off in the bindery). Charges for four-color printing, for "matched" colors specified from a swatch book, and for other standard production services also will be broken out. If an advertiser needs additional assistance to get his or her ad ready for production, these charges will be worked out separately. For example, many publications will design and typeset simple ads for which customers have supplied the written copy. Since furnishing this kind of support can mean an additional production expense to the publisher, a common practice is to bill the customer for the printer's charge plus a reasonable markup.

The main production requirements for classified advertising are entering and placing information for classified listings correctly; making certain that they run when they are supposed to; and making equally certain that they do not run when they are not supposed to. Operating a classified ad department presents traffic-management challenges of a special kind. Magazines that accept classifieds must manage input from several streams at once: telephone, mail, fax, and, lately, on-line sources. Much of this input arrives, or seems to, at five minutes to deadline. Although classified ad managers get some assistance from software that sorts the input, measures the linage, and keeps track of what runs when, in the end it is their personal attention to detail that turns the administrative hell of classified ad-taking into a consistent and dependable profit center.

Most readers think of classified advertising as dense columns of microscopic type in the back of the book where the editorial has petered out, and it is true that a good deal of the classified matter they see conforms to this description. However, as many magazines have discovered, there is no rule against dressing up the classifieds with eye-catching headline type, fancy borders, touches of color, and other adornments for which premium prices gladly will be paid. *Display classifieds* is the hybrid term for listings that wear bits of finery copied from their bigger, more elegant kinfolk, the display-ad pages.

Preprinted advertising inserts need no help with their attire, since they come to the party fully produced. A preprinted insert is a page or a group of pages that is not part of the print run for the issue in which the insert is to be included. Manufactured elsewhere, inserts are delivered to the magazine's printing plant to be bound among the issue's regular signatures as a postpress operation. *Saddle-wired* magazines, which staple their pages together at the center fold, can incorporate inserts by "stitching" them in during the bindery run. *Perfect-bound* magazines, glued at the spine, affix inserts in a gluing procedure called *tipping*. A tipped insert can be either a permanent part of the magazine or a lightly glued pullout section designed as a freestanding advertising piece.

Publishers like preprinted inserts because they come as close to representing pure profit as any kind of magazine advertising can come. Inserts do not have to be shot, scanned, stripped, paginated, or printed, so they involve no production costs other than those connected with binding them into the magazine. The production manager, however, still faces challenges aplenty when it comes to integrating this outside material into the issue's workflow. The primary one is making sure that the inserts will be at the printing plant, in sufficient quantity, when the issue is ready for binding. (This deadline usually will be separate from the cutoff for the receipt of other advertising materials.) Whoever is producing the material must be briefed on trim size, paper weight, and other specifications that govern how successfully the insert will bind in.

Correct placement of the insert is another challenge. For example, binding an insert between certain signatures could make it difficult for the issue to lie flat when closed, so these positions have to be avoided. If the publisher has promised the magazine's display advertisers that inserts will not adjoin or cover their pages, the placement puzzle grows more complicated still. Wherever the insert lands, the production manager must remember to adjust the issue's folio (page) numbers to factor the sides of the insert into the total page count. This adjustment is what causes the page following a two-sided insert tipped to the right of page 40 to be numbered 43, not 41. Since an issue may contain multiple inserts of varying sizes, the numbering may have to be bumped this way in more than one place.

Advertisers sometimes use inserts to achieve production effects that lie far beyond the capabilities of ordinary magazine print runs. The most extreme example, a holiday insert for Absolut vodka, contained an audio chip that played a fragment of a Yuletide melody. Others have engineered inserts with three-dimensional, pop-up models of skyscrapers; heat-sensitive inks that change colors when touched; and "magic" windows through which readers can view hidden graphics. Although few advertisers aspire to extravaganzas like these because of their sky-high design and manufacturing costs, most do expect magazines to provide production support for many less elaborate kinds of preprinted inserts.

## ISSUE DESIGN AND MAKEUP

Just as a building can be designed from subbasement to sundeck long before the first load of concrete is poured, so can an issue of a magazine take shape while there is little or nothing yet in hand to fill its pages. The process of deciding the exact size and content of the book typically starts near the closing dates (or date, if the closings are simultaneous) for advertising and editorial.

Since by this point the production manager will have a good idea of how many and what kinds of pages of advertising the issue will contain, applying the magazine's ad-to-edit ratio will tell her what the total page count probably will be. Now she can make a thumbnail: a planning diagram that represents the issue's pages as a sequence of blank spreads in numerical order. To fill in the thumbnail, she reserves the right-hand pages for full-page ads; full spreads and other combinations for multipage advertisements; space as needed for partials; and, if the magazine carries classifieds, a section for those listings. The positioning of inserts is also indicated on the thumbnail. Whatever is left is for editorial.

The editorial staff, apprised of the number of pages they will have to work with, can begin to fit their lineup of stories to available space. Using their copies of the thumbnail, they work out the order in which the articles will run; the distances to which copy will "jump" (continue from one page to another); the fixed positions that certain departments, columns, and other regularly appearing material must get; and other allocations of the issue's editorial "real estate." Another approach to copyfitting is for the editors to give a story list, with placement recommendations, to the production manager, who then completes the editorial fill-in. Either method works well as long as communications between editorial and production are accurate, timely, and respectful of both departments' obligations to the workflow.

Needless to say, production and editorial should be in continuous consultation with the art director as the issue takes shape. As already discussed, in workflows where the artists who design the issue are also the layout technicians who construct the pages, design requirements will influence production decisions from cover to cover. Maintaining consistency of design also requires a clear understanding between art and editorial with respect to issue theme and emphasis, article length, and choice of illustrations. Confusion about these things can be crippling both to short-term productivity and to long-term staff relationships. The key to keeping confusion from turning into open conflict is to foster effective communications among all parties to the creative process. For example, design-focused brainstorming sessions before writing assignments are made can help to assure that editors and artists have complementary visions of the content of the upcoming issue.

Once the size of the issue has been determined and the principal design decisions have been made, layout can begin. At this point, with the advice of the printer, the production manager can work out a press imposition for the issue: a plan for arranging pages on signatures in a way that puts the pages into proper sequence once the sheets have been folded, cut, and bound to make the finished magazine. Devising good impositions is a skill that aims at maximizing production efficiency and economy: for example, by imposing so that the largest number of pages can be printed on a sheet, or so that all pages requiring color can be printed with the smallest amount of makeready and the fewest number of passes through the press. For example, assume that the issue's ad lineup contains a pair of two-color ads with identical second colors (plus black). If the imposition locates both ads on the same side of the same signature, the press will have to be set up to print the second color only once.

Now the production artists can begin to assemble type, illustrations, photography, and other elements into actual page layouts. Intermediate representations of these layouts are known as proofs, and it is likely that several sets of proofs will be "pulled" for the issue before it is fully approved for release to print. In traditional production, proofs usually are photocopies of boards (layout sheets) onto which galleys (columns of typeset text) and headline type have been pasted. Desktop publishing makes it possible to output near-print quality laser proofs of fully assembled pages. Either kind of proof can be used to check placement of editorial material, the sequence of jumps, and typographic accuracy.

The editorial staff is responsible for line-by-line proofreading through as many sets of proofs as it will take to catch every error that could offend the reader and embarrass the publication. The usual procedure calls for a team of editors to read page proofs in succession, with the first reader's corrections checked in the second set of proofs by the second reader; second-proof corrections verified in third proofs by the third reader; and so on until the chief editor signs his or her approval on a clean set of finals.

Proofreading is not the same as copyediting. Copyediting, with its emphasis on story structure, content, and clarity, is an exercise in critical thinking that should already have been completed to everyone's satisfaction by the time first proofs are handed around. Proofreading, an inspection procedure for quality control, belongs to production. Its purposes are to remove typographical errors; to correct deviations from "house style" (the magazine's body of rules for handling abbreviations, capitalization, punctuation, and the other variables of text formatting); and, when necessary, to amend serious editorial errors and omissions that managed to slip through the copyediting process.

Computerized spelling checkers and grammar assistants offer some help to writers and editors at the manuscript stage, but production proofreading remains an irreplaceably human skill. Because every page proof can be thick with errors both obvious and subtle, proofreaders worthy of the task have to be diligent, scrupulous, and tireless in their pursuit of the flaws. No matter how digitally automated the production of magazines becomes, proofreading is one traditional skill that will always be essential to the process. There is no substitute for proofreading—nor any excuse for slackness in it.

## PREPARATION AND DELIVERY OF INPUT MATERIAL

When advertising and editorial materials are ready for dispatching to the printer, production managers put on their shipping clerks' eyeshades. Now it is time to confirm the formats in which the materials have been prepared and the methods by which they will be sent. With traditional materials, delivery is mostly a matter of efficient freight forwarding. Getting digital input into the printer's hands involves more complicated decisions about ways and means.

In a traditional workflow, mechanicals, films, photographs, original art, and other fragile input materials are packaged securely and shipped for receipt on a date specified by the printer. Many magazine printers provide regular pouch service from their local offices to the main plant; it is also customary for printers' sales representatives to pick up and deliver their magazine clients' materials in person. Other publishers rely on overnight package express or (if the printer is nearby) ordinary messenger services. Whatever the mode of shipment, the printer's deadline for receipt of materials is one that the production manager must take seriously. Since pages can be printed only in groups, and since each group of pages must be composed as a unit, late delivery of even a single page component could compromise the entire production schedule.

As digital creation of magazine pages becomes the norm, printers are seeing less and less in the way of traditional materials. Now printers are learning to deal with input media that do not even physically resemble the pages that have to be extracted from them. When magazines send floppy disks and removable cartridge drives in lieu of mechanicals, they send them without tissue overlays, color chips, or any of the other tangible instructions that once made production requirements so clear. And lately some publishers have even begun to dispense with disks and cartridges, insisting instead that their printers join them in a direct, computer-to-computer exchange of telecommunicated page data. Although these new methods show great promise for overall production efficiency, using them successfully requires close technical coordination between experts on both the publisher's and the printer's end.

The first thing to coordinate is the choice of a magnetic medium for storing and delivering pages in digital form. Ordinary floppy disks can be used, but their limited storage capacity makes them impractical for any but the smallest, least graphically complex publications. The standard device for transporting magazine files is the removable cartridge drive, a compact version of the hard drive found in personal computers. (Because SyQuest Technology Inc. is the leading manufacturer of removable cartridge drives for electronic prepress, the units are often generically but incorrectly referred to as SyQuests.)

The smallest of these drives (at 44 megabytes) can hold 30 times more data than a high-density (1.4 Mb) floppy disk. In their larger configurations, they can handle the many hundreds of megabytes generated by a typical issue's text, page layout, and color files. Data are quickly accessed from removable cartridge drives, and their cost per megabyte of storage is relatively cheap. The only caution to be observed in using them is that their magnetic-disk components do not provide the most stable form of storage. Like floppy disks, removable drives can suffer data loss if they are roughly handled or subjected to harsh ambient conditions. For this reason, highly stable backup storage (for example, on digital tape) is a must for every magazine that entrusts its data to removable cartridge drives.

Magneto-optical drives are another option for high-volume data storage and transportation. Imaged and read by laser equipment, these devices can store up to one gigabyte's worth (1,000 Mb) of page files at less risk of data loss than would be the case with removable cartridge drives. Although magneto-opticals trail removable drives in terms of data access speed and cost-efficiency of storage, their greater capacity and stability have made them the medium of choice in many publishing operations.

But even the most sophisticated data-storage device can travel from publisher to printing plant no more swiftly than an old-fashioned mechanical. Both have to be bundled into a pouch for conveyance by a courier, and both are subject to the same risks of damage, delay, and loss en route. With high-speed data telecommunications, there are no such risks. Any file that can be written to a drive can be transmitted through a telephone line in a fraction of the time required for physical delivery of the drive. Because one publishing system communicates directly with another publishing system, data are moved from point of creation to point of production in the most efficient way.

In theory, data telecommunications is the logical next step for every magazine with a digital workflow and digital production partnerships with its service providers. In reality, it is an evolving technology that makes sense for some publications but not necessarily for others. At its most basic, it consists of an ordinary, two-way modem connection from the publisher's office to the typographer, the service bureau, or the prep department of the printing plant. A modem (*mo*dulator-*dem*odulator) is a simple plug-in device that turns digital data from the sender into analog signals that telephone lines can carry. The receiver's modem changes the analog input back to digital again.

Typically, files are "modemed" from the publisher's desktop computers to the service provider's file server, which routes the publisher's material to the appropriate workstations for processing. The service provider returns files to the client's computer by the same dial-up pathways. Some printers and service bureaus have set up their own bulletin board services (BBS) or file transfer protocol (FTP) sites on the Internet to make the exchange of data more convenient.

Text files usually represent the smallest and most easily transmissible chunks of data that an issue contains, and today's off-the-shelf modems are fast and reliable enough to make telecommunicating most text files a matter of a few minutes' work. Text, however, is only the beginning. The chunks of data that represent page geometry and color are simply too massive for ordinary modems and telephone lines to handle without choking on sheer volume. Some assistance is gained from data compression, a software procedure that rewrites large files in a kind of digital shorthand that can be expanded to original size upon receipt. But even a compressed color file could take hours to transmit, tying up a line and running up the phone bill. Data loss and damage from compression and network "noise" (interference) are other potential drawbacks, particularly with files that have complex images or critical color requirements.

Telecommunications developers have ridden to the rescue with 56 kilobit circuits, T1 channels, Integrated Services Digital Network (ISDN) connections, and other options that offer greater transmission speeds and data safety than conventional home/office telephone hookups. These services, where available, are expensive. They may also require the installation of special equipment at both the publisher's and the service provider's end. Technical staff support—having a troubleshooting expert on call for dealing with inevitable system failures—is another necessity. Telecommunications technology undoubtedly will become cheaper and easier to use, but until it does, relatively few magazines will be able to justify full-scale investment in its benefits. The publications and group-publishing operations that use it successfully now tend to be very high-volume data producers with dedicated or privileged electronic access to their service providers.

Most service providers would agree that the manner in which a file is delivered has far less to do with getting good printed results than the care with which the file has been constructed. It is one thing to cook up an issue of a magazine as a potluck stew of Word, QuarkXPress, Illustrator, and Photoshop. It is another to be certain that nothing has been added to or removed from the recipe in a way that will make the dish inedible. Magazines are served as feasts of words and images, but more than one meal has been spoiled before reaching the table by the sloppiness or inattention of the cook.

The concept of *preflighting* shifts the metaphor from the kitchen to the cockpit. A production manager who preflights digital pages examines them for everything that could cause the file to stall or crash upon takeoff when the service provider attempts to process it. The problem could be a page element that does not belong in the file, or it could be the absence of something needed to ensure that the page can be output intact, the way its designer intended. In the most extreme cases, a file can be so badly flawed that the service provider cannot open it at all. Most of the time, however, an unpreflighted file yields pages with major or critical errors that delay production approval: type in faces other than the ones specified; text that has reflowed out of sequence; marred or missing graphics; unwanted color effects.

Preflighting a digital file can be as simple as completing a written checklist of file components and preparation steps. File-investigation software that analyzes the contents of a file and reports serious errors and omissions automates the procedure. Once the file has been checked, corrected, and approved for delivery to the service provider, the production manager should send along a set of laser-printed page proofs to confirm what the final output is supposed to look like.

The best way to preflight magazine pages is to use whatever tools and techniques the printer or trade shop recommends, and to use them consistently. Preflighting is the customer's responsibility, not the service provider's, and the graphic arts industry's usual practice is to charge for file processing according to the degree of difficulty of the job. In any case, a file done badly is a file that must be done again. That means those who believe they can ignore their obligation to preflight should be prepared for needless expense and frustration with every file they submit.

## FINAL PREPRESS

A magazine enters the home stretch of the prepress workflow when its pages are given final preparation for their transition to image carriers—the lithographic plates or gravure cylinders that transfer their text, pictures, and layouts in inked form to paper during the print run. A key step at this stage is color correction—adjusting the characteristics of color images to ensure the best reproduction on press. In conventional prepress, color was corrected by means of masking, dot etching, and other manual procedures from the realm of photographic processing. As with much else in traditional print production, this was a highly skilled trade craft that depended on the expertise of the individual operator.

Ever since the advent of electronic scanners, most color correction for magazine work has been computerized. Data from scans are delivered to color workstations where technicians use unsharp masking, undercolor removal, gray component replacement, and other techniques to improve contrast and color balance within the digital file. Until recently, electronic color correction was as exclusive in its application as old-time dot etching—only experts with the proper tools and training could do it. Now anyone with a personal computer set up to run QuarkXPress, Photoshop, Live Picture, and comparable image-manipulation software can have a full suite of powerful color correction tools at his or her command.

As page creators in graphic design studios and magazine publishing offices assume more and more responsibility for these challenging chores, the professional service provider's role becomes less about doing prepress work for customers than about making sure that customers have done it properly themselves. But the difference between do-it-yourself image processing and expert prepress service still exists, and it is a distinction that most magazine professionals are happy to acknowledge. For instance, most will honor their service providers' wish to handle trapping—the precise sizing of overprinted areas of color to guard against print defects stemming from misregistration. (Misregistration occurs when overprinted images do not align precisely, leaving visible hairlines of unprinted space around text and other page elements.)

The practice of swapping low- and high-resolution image files within page layouts is another constructive compromise. In this workflow, the service provider gives the customer low-resolution files of scan data for photographs, artwork, and other color elements to be incorporated into the page. These scans do not contain enough data for precise color adjustment, but they are fine for positioning and for generating intermediate proofs. Meanwhile, the service provider color-corrects the high-resolution files to the customer's specifications. When the customer submits the page files, the service provider removes the low-res files from the layouts, replaces them with the color-corrected hi-res files, and makes the final separations.

In order to create the individual pieces of separated film from which the printing plates will be made, there has to be a way to translate data from digital files into a format for imaging the film. By this point, all of the issue's page files will have been encoded in PostScript, and PostScript is a programming language, not a vehicle for graphic imaging per se. PostScript code can, however, be converted into patterns of bitmaps—pixels and dots that describe graphics—for placing halftone screens and other page elements in the appropriate locations on the film.

The transforming agent is the *raster image processor*, or RIP. A RIP can be either a dedicated computer platform or a piece of software that drives a personal computer. In either case, the RIP turns PostScript page files into bitmaps at whatever resolution is offered by the PostScript-compatible output device the data are being "ripped" to. The output device, an imagesetter or film plotter, exposes each piece of separated film at a resolution of 2,450 dots per inch (dpi) or higher. (A desktop laser printer, by comparison, creates images at 300 to 600 dpi.)

After a developing bath in a film processor, the films are ready for plating. To make an offset lithographic plate, the printer places a piece of film into a vacuum frame that holds the film in contact with a blank plate. A powerful light source then strikes the surface of the plate through the film. The plate, presensitized with a photo-receptive chemical coating, now bears the same images of type, photography, and page geometry as the piece of film from which it was exposed. The final step is a trip through a processing unit that develops, washes, and dries the plate for delivery to the press.

On press, the plate's image areas will be ink-receptive and water-rejecting; its nonimage areas will accept water and reject ink. There is, however, a way to maintain the distinction between image- and nonimage areas that eliminates the water altogether. In waterless platemaking and printing, silicone-photopolymer plate coatings and special inks produce the lithographic effect without need of water as a plate dampener. Ink-temperature control units on presses equipped for waterless printing keep the inks within the degree ranges at which they print best. Delivering more consistent color, holding higher line screens, and printing with fewer hazardous air emissions are among the benefits of this increasingly popular process.

Platemaking used to be an entirely manual operation subject to many human and mechanical errors, but now computers give it the efficiency, accuracy, and speed of digital data processing. Automatic step-and-repeat machines can be programmed to make multiple page exposures on large-format plates for high-volume magazine runs. For shorter runs, photosensitive plates can be exposed directly, without film, in the backs of computer-controlled cameras that regulate the placement of images with a high degree of precision. A new generation of plates breaks printing's historic links to photomechanics by accepting laser-imaged page content directly from digital data.

Whatever the nature of the plate, quality control in the platemaking process is one of the true keys to efficiency in the manufacture of magazines. Bad plates with cracks, misregistration, and other defects can halt production during its most costly and time-sensitive phase, the press run. In many instances, the only way to know that a plate is faulty is to discover that it is printing badly, but by then the damage to the issue's production timetable will already have been done. This is why many magazine printing plants make the plate department the focus of their programs to implement statistical process control. Through use of SPC measurement tools, recurring plate problems can be traced to specific pieces of equipment, to particular work shifts, and even to individual operators. Once the causes have been identified and corrected, management can then set numerical targets for a stable platemaking operation based upon an acceptable (meaning minimal) percentage of defects in the finished product.

## PROOFING AND OK TO PRINT

A printer will not start a magazine press run without the publisher's assurance that everything in the issue has been checked for accuracy and printability. That assurance is given through proofing—the publisher's careful examination of a series of intermediate materials that enable reasonably accurate assumptions about what the final printed product will look like. Proofs are not meant to be exact replicas of what eventually will come off the press; there are too many variables in the printing process, and most proofs are produced by methods that only simulate the effects of ink on paper. It is important for publishers and printers to have the same understanding about the limitations and proper uses of proofs, especially with respect to color. Although a policy of signing off on none but the most scrupulously checked proofs cannot guarantee defect-free printing, it is the surest way of keeping unpleasant surprises to a minimum after the start button is pushed.

Editorial proofreading has already been discussed. Thanks to the nearly universal use of desktop publishing for magazine work, most text proofing takes place on fully assembled, laser-printed page layouts generated in the publisher's office. This places 100 percent of the responsibility for the accuracy of text on the publishing staff, since the printer cannot be held accountable for copy he has neither typeset nor even seen before receiving the page files. Text corrections and changes requested by the publisher after delivery of the files fall into the category of author's alterations, or AAs. Printers charge most of their customers for AAs, and the later in the process they are asked to make them, the more they may charge for the service.

Some magazines still use blueprints, also called blueline proofs, as a means of double-checking that page sequences are intact and that everything else in the issue is correctly positioned. Blueprints are exposed from page film onto sheets of photosensitive paper, which the printer trims, folds, and staples into a rough approximation of the finished magazine. If the pages have been imposed correctly—that is, positioned on the film flats in proper order for printing and binding—the blueprint should read correctly as well.

Those checking blueprints should be on the alert for scratches and other film damage that may appear on the pages. Although blueprints are not for proofreading, they may be looked upon as the last chance for catching typos and text errors before page films are sent to the platemaking department. Even if correcting a mistake means making a new piece of film, it is still much cheaper to do it that way than to remake an entire plate.

Blueprints literally are blue—all blue. Monochromatic, they are not much help for representing what full-color printing will look like. Some form of intermediate color proofing is necessary for ads and other color-critical work, because to plate and print straight from untested film would be to gamble on the acceptability of the result. Color proofs provide acceptable targets. Printers use them not to guarantee what final color will look like, but to establish parameters for color reproduction that their presses can be adjusted to work within. In this way, the press run can be controlled so that everyone will have reasonable expectations about how closely the color printed on the press sheets will resemble the color approved in the proof.

Film-based color proofs are prepared by whoever creates the separations—traditionally, the color trade shop. Digital color proofs, on the other hand, can be generated by whoever has a copy of the color data file and a suitable output device. Proofs are submitted for approval to the person responsible for checking color quality: the page designer, the creative director at the ad agency, or the publication production manager. Once approved, proofs go the printer as guides for the press run.

Publishers can choose from among a number of color proofing tools designed to suit different workflows, budgets, and quality requirements. Press proofing, also known as wet proofing, is the most accurate means of forecasting publication color. This is because press proofing, unlike all other forms of proofing, is performed on a special press with the same plates, ink, and paper that will be used in the production run. Separations can be proofed as "progressives" (build-ups to full color in combinations of the process colors) for close inspection of color characteristics. The downsides of press proofing are its slowness and costliness—factors that rule it out as a color-checking option for the average magazine.

Off-press proofs are faster, more economical, and much more widely used. Although their color does not come from printing ink, they can render ink-on-paper halftone dot patterns closely enough to be used as "contract" proofs for final production approval. The leading brands use pigments and proofing stocks that conform to SWOP guidelines for color consistency.

The most popular brands of off-press proofing systems are the laminate types. Laminate proofs are made from a white base stock that has been coated (laminated) with a photopolymer material that becomes sticky upon exposure to light. When the base stock is exposed through separation films laid on its surface, the films' images are transferred to the photopolymer layer. Toners for process and spot colors are applied after each exposure until a full-color image has been built up. DuPont's Cromalin system is the best-known example of this kind of off-press proofing. Other brands, such as 3M's Matchprint and Agfe-Hoechst's Pressmatch, use color-impregnated films instead of toner. The principle, however, is the same as with toner, in that color is transferred to a proofing substrate after the substrate has been exposed through separation film.

Overlay proofs, an older form of off-press proofing, are still sometimes seen. Four pieces of clear acetate film, each bearing a separation of the original image in one of the four process colors, are fastened to a white board representing the proofing stock. The progressive overlay of the acetates causes the four process colors to blend in a full-spectrum rendition of the image. 3M's Color Key product is more or less synonymous with overlay proofing in the publishing industry.

Using any of these film-based proofing options naturally assumes that there will be film to "pull" a proof from. With digital color, there is no such assumption, because digital color can be output by methods that do not depend on film to transfer the image to the proofing medium. Eliminating film from the proofing workflow saves steps, consumable materials, and time. It is also the prelude to an all-digital, computer-to-plate production workflow in which color data, proofed to contract requirements by digital means, can be used to image press plates directly without any need for intermediate film.

The lowest level of digital color proofing is the "soft" proof seen on the color monitor of the PC or workstation on which the image is being created. These screen proofs give a general idea of printed color, and they can be telecommunicated so that people at different locations (advertising agency, service bureau, printer's prep department) can examine them simultaneously. Their colors, however, come from the red, green, and blue emissions of a cathode ray tube, not from the CMYK (cyan-magenta-yellow-black) chromatic model of process color printing. This means that soft proofs should be used for previewing only, not for any serious proofing purposes.

Various digital output devices can be used to generate "hard" proofs that come closer to the real thing. Some ink-jet printers and dye-sublimation units have improved their color fidelity to the point where a few publishers are willing to accept them as contract proofs. But because most digital color printers in this category are low-resolution, continuous-tone devices that cannot simulate halftone dots, their output generally is not suitable for ads and other proofing applications where foreknowledge of halftone characteristics is critical.

Output device manufacturers have started to take digital proofing technology to the next level with digital halftone proofers—units like Kodak's Approval system, which generate color in halftone patterns at resolutions approximating the line-screen values of printed pages. These systems are said to meet the standards of contract proofing, and they can be linked without difficulty to most digital prepress workflows. However, only time will tell whether advertisers and others concerned with magazine color quality can be persuaded to place the same faith in proofs from digital dots as they do in proofs from dots on film.

Once a proof has been generated, it is compared with original materials for fidelity to color and design. Then it is examined for characteristics that will indicate performance on press. Checking color proofs is a skill that requires training, a careful eye, and, when problems are encountered, the ability to ask for corrections in technically correct and unambiguous terms. Tools for checking color proofs include optical magnifiers; ink-measuring densitometers; color bars and control strips printed in the borders of the proof; and an assortment of calibrated devices for inspecting screen angles and other critical measurements. Color should be checked only under standardized viewing conditions, preferably in a specially constructed viewing booth that blocks the perception-distorting effects of ambient light.

## THE PRODUCTION PRESS RUN

Printing a magazine is a form of manufacturing, but it is not like stamping out featureless, endlessly identical pieces of metal or plastic on an automated assembly line. A magazine is as much a product of human skill as of mechanical efficiency. It is neither featureless nor uniform: Each issue is a catalog of special production requirements that test the precision and stability of the magazine manufacturing process to its limits. Good magazine printing, therefore, means controlling an array of production variables more complex than anything known to most other kinds of manufacturing. The most challenging variables present themselves during the final stage of the process, the production press run.

Many variables stem from the condition of the paper on which the magazine is to be printed. When there are papermaking defects or inconsistencies in sheets or roll stock, there are sure to be difficulties in the run. Humidity, temperature, and dirt can also degrade the "runnability" of paper in a nerve-wracking variety of ways. To take just one example, consider what can happen if the moisture content of paper fresh from the warehouse is different from the relative humidity of the pressroom. Edges can warp as the paper suddenly absorbs or loses moisture, leading to misregistration and other problems on press if the paper is used right away. (The preventive step is to condition the paper by holding it in the pressroom until the moisture of the paper matches that of its surroundings.)

Paper is not the only troublemaker. Inks, plates, offset blankets, lithographic chemistry, and mechanical features of the press also have their own special ways of making the process unpredictable. A poorly mixed ink may scratch or rub off. *Scumming*—ink adhesion in nonimage areas—could be the result of a badly made plate. Offset blankets can become *smashed* (damaged) in ways that prevent them from transferring portions of the plate image to paper. High acidity in the fountain solution—the mixture of water and chemicals that dampens the printing plates— can emulsify the ink, turning it into sludge. When ink and dampening rollers are misaligned or improperly adjusted for pressure, image quality also suffers. [1]

Publishers expect their printers to minimize these problems by carefully inspecting incoming materials; by applying SPC and other quality-assurance techniques throughout the premanufacturing phase; and by following a strict routine of equipment maintenance. Other pressroom variables, however, are inherent in the printing process and have to be controlled in more subtle ways.

Dot gain, for example, is a given in even the most carefully controlled printing conditions. Dot gain is the tendency of halftone dots to increase in size as the image proceeds from film and proof to plate and press. Many things can cause dot gain, but the result is always the same: an unwanted intensifying or darkening of color in the printed product that belies the indication of color in the proof. Dot gain is unavoidable, but it can be dealt with at the film stage by reducing the size of the dots by the amount they are expected to grow. Since the graphics arts industry has learned how to predict percentages of dot gain for most kinds of presswork, seeing minimal dot-gain effects has become a routine expectation in magazine printing.

In the final stages of makeready, both the printer and the publisher's representative take steps to certify that variables are under control and that the production run is ready to begin. This procedure is known to publishers as the *press check* or *press OK*. Having mounted the plates and otherwise prepared the press, the press crew runs the first test sheets. These are examined for registration, color quality, and undesirable printing effects such as moiré. Once the press operators have made whatever adjustments are necessary, they should be ready to present the publisher's representative with a press sheet that matches or exceeds the quality of contract color proof. When the publisher's representative signs his or her approval on the OK sheet, it replaces the proof as the color reference for the actual production run.[2]

The magazine's production manager or art director may wish to sign approval on an OK sheet for each signature the issue contains. Now the goal is to make sure that everything at the delivery end of the press will match the initial output that the publisher's representative has approved. The press crew accomplishes this by pulling finished sheets at intervals and comparing them to the OK sheets and proofs. Test strips printed along the edges of the sheets let the operators check for evidence of excessive dot gain, color variation, and other problems that may have to be addressed during the run.

Press OKs produce sheets that do not count toward the total number of impressions specified for the production run. These sheets constitute the run's waste allowance—the number of test impressions the press operators will have to make in order to "come up to color" with an OK sheet that will satisfy the publisher's representative. Waste is always anticipated, because the adjustments needed to bring the press up to color can be made only while the equipment is running. ("Spoilage," on the other hand, is paper unexpectedly discarded because of production errors or poor planning. Waste is excusable; spoilage is not. The cost of spoilage cannot be assessed until after the damage is done.)

How much waste there will be depends on the complexity of the job, the type of paper being used, and the experience of the press operators.[3] It could be equal to six percent of the run length,[4] or it could be higher. Whatever the figure, it represents paper that the publisher must pay for in addition to the cost of paper consumed in producing usable copies of the issue. This extra requirement must be factored into paper purchases, and it should be treated as a cost component that printers will be expected to minimize to the best of their ability.

Publishers should also keep an eye on over- and under-runs: copy counts that exceed or fall short of the number specified in the print order. Like waste, "overs" and "unders" have to be allowed for because of the unpredictability of the production run. The printing industry's trade customs state that over- and under-runs are not to exceed 10 percent of the quantity ordered, and that printers may charge extra or give credit for the difference. These terms are subject to negotiation; for example, some customers take the position that longer runs should have smaller percentages of tolerance.[5] In any event, the actual numbers may matter less than simply knowing that there will be enough extra copies on hand to stuff in media kits, present to advertisers, and ship to trade shows.

## BINDING, FINISHING, AND DISTRIBUTION

The end of the press run is the beginning of the bindery sequence. The finished product racing toward the delivery end of the press is still far from finished, because it still consists of nothing but a stream of uncollected pages that bears little resemblance to the periodical that ultimately will go to mailboxes and newsstands. In magazine production, *finishing* means transforming the raw output of the press into folded, trimmed, and bound magazines that readers will recognize and distribution channels can accept. (*Finishing* has a different meaning in other kinds of printing, where the term refers to specialty processes such as embossing and foil stamping.) Binding and finishing also encompass techniques that powerfully enhance a magazine's ability to compete with other media in the new arena of demographically targeted marketing.

Binding and finishing can take place as a series of *off-line* procedures that are physically removed from the press, or as *in-line* operations that are mechanically linked to the print run. Press sheets for magazines printed on sheetfed equipment will be finished off-line, either in the plant's in-house bindery or at a remote location known as a trade bindery. The flat sheets, given time to dry, are stacked on pallets for removal to the bindery, where guillotine cutters, knife folders, and related units are used to separate and assemble them.

In contrast, magazines produced on web presses usually are candidates for in-line finishing. Web presses equipped for in-line finishing have components or attachments for manipulating the web of paper in various ways after printing is completed. Folding, the most commonly performed in-line operation,[6] involves cutting and creasing the printed web into signatures that can be bound into one another to create the finished product. If certain pages require special finishing steps such as perforating, die cutting, or the application of scent strips and scratch-off panels, these operations also can be executed in-line, saving the delay and extra expense of off-line processing.

Folded signatures, including those for the covers, are then gathered in order for binding; inserted into one another; and fastened with staples or adhesives. (If a magazine's covers and interior pages are printed on the same kind of paper, the bound issue is known as a *self cover*.) The final step is trimming, an operation that slits open the closed edges of folded signatures; adjusts the height and width of the publication to its specified trim size; and separates copies printed as *multiple ups* (connected end to end).[7]

With few exceptions, magazines emerge from the finishing process in either saddle-stitched or perfect bound format. Magazines stapled along the crease of the cover's centerfold are the product of saddle-stitching, so termed for the piece of equipment that inserts the staples by means of a stitcher head fed from a roll of wire. Adhesive-bound magazines, commonly referred to as perfect bound, are assembled from sheets that are roughened along one edge and pressed into a glued strip along the flat spine of the cover's centerfold.

Each method has its merits. Cheap and fast, saddle-stitching is the best way to produce magazines that must lie flat. It is also very well suited to the mechanical requirements of selective binding (discussed below). Perfect binding, on the other hand, creates a more versatile product. Unlike saddle-stitched periodicals, perfect-bound magazines have oblong spines on which titles and other information can be displayed. Perfect binding also makes it easier for a magazine to include papers and other substrates of varying thicknesses and finishes without affecting the binding process.[8] This is a clear advantage for incorporating preprinted inserts, which frequently are produced on heavy stocks that saddle-stitched magazines can place only at certain locations in the folio (or cannot use at all). It is also worth noting that advertisers sometimes make the substantial look and feel of perfect-bound magazines a factor in decisions about where to buy space.

Stapled or glued, a bound and finished magazine witnesses the efficiency of a process that now can be performed almost entirely in-line with high degrees of machine automation and computerized production control. As magazines face unprecedented competition from nonprint media with larger audiences and greater technological dazzle, these manufacturing advantages are becoming as essential to survival as quality editorial and healthy ad page counts. For only by virtue of manufacturing control in the bindery can magazines offer subscribers and advertisers what cable television and other electronic rivals cannot—custom publishing incentives that are based on personalized content and on database-driven, precision-targeted marketing.[9]

Whether readers realize it or not, chances are good that any leading magazine they subscribe to contains pages or sections that are there specifically because of what the publisher has learned about the recipients' backgrounds, interests, and spending habits. Some magazines make their strategy obvious with personalized pages that dangle the one piece of information guaranteed to snare any reader's attention—his or her own name. Once caught, the reader can be drawn into the page—and into the influence of adjacent advertising—with news of local interest or with topical information that targets the reader in some equally specific way.[10]

Pinpointed publishing of this kind owes its existence to the array of manufacturing procedures known as *selective binding*. For magazines, selective binding is most often synonymous with *versioning*[11], the creation of multiple editions of an issue by varying the selection of editorial signatures within each version. Through versioning, an issue can mix local news and features with fixed editorial content in much the same way as a metro newspaper prints neighborhood or suburban sections to supplement its general coverage.

Versioning is not a new technique. Its technology was developed in the 1970s by R.R. Donnelley & Sons Co., the largest U.S. printer, for the agricultural periodical *Farm Journal*. Relying on detailed, constantly updated circulation information, *Farm Journal* had built up what was and is the most information-rich subscriber database in the publishing industry. This database, together with advanced manufacturing techniques, enabled Donnelley to produce literally thousands of individualized versions—as many as 8,896—for a single issue of the magazine.

Catalog producers, not magazine publishers, took the early lead in applying selective binding to targeted consumer publishing.[12] Today, however, selective binding is standard procedure for most nationally circulated and many less widely distributed magazines. Its most important components are automated gathering and computer-controlled ink-jet addressing—technologies that are making it possible for some magazines to have as many versions per issue as other periodicals have subscribers.

Automatic gathering machines contain receptacles, called pockets or hoppers, that hold folded signatures in order for rapid, in-line assembly on a saddle-stitcher or an adhesive-binding unit. The more pockets the gathering machine contains, and the faster it can be made to feed high-speed binding equipment, the more versions the bindery line can create. Ink-jet addressing enables distribution to keep up with production by correctly matching each versioned copy to its designated recipient. Ink-jet printers spray microscopic droplets of electrostatically charged ink onto personalized pages, mailing labels, or blank mailing spaces on covers from a computer-controlled print head. The computer furnishes names, addresses, and other information, one label or field at a time, from the publisher's circulation data banks. The printing of the labels can be made to conform to the categories of information that define the versions—geographic location, household income, reader-survey responses, or whatever other key characteristics the publisher wishes to target.

Editorial versioning is not the only kind of flexibility that selective binding adds to the production process. The same techniques can also be used to enhance a magazine's self-promotion and reader service activities and to add value to advertising. For example, ink-jet messages on cover wraps could welcome new readers or remind current subscribers to renew by paying invoices bound within the issue. The content of ads could be tailored to localities by creating separate ads for split runs defined by zip code. And, of course, nothing would add more value to an ad than a message to the reader by name, courtesy of the publisher's ink-jet personalization capability.[13]

Recent breakthroughs in selective binding technology have given the magazine publishing industry a new vision of how versatile its production runs can be. One such breakthrough, the BLISS software application from ProGraph Management Systems, automatically tells gathering equipment which pockets to activate in order to feed production of a given version.[14] When computer controls such as BLISS are linked to equipment capable of gathering and saddle stitching up to 40,000 magazines per hour, versions can multiply to whatever extent the publisher thinks feasible. With BLISS, for example, the *Ladies Home Journal* expanded its range from about 150 versions to nearly 1,000 in the same print order. *Sports Illustrated* has used the system to run 521 versions.[15]

But even numbers like these probably do not represent anything like the full potential of selective binding. Time Inc. does not think so: In 1993, one of its executives said that *Time*—then already producing 4,000 different versions every week—had a future goal of 100,000 versions.[16] Magazines versioned on this scale would also work at improving production turnarounds with the aim of blunting (if not eliminating) the edge that the electronic media retain over print with respect to timeliness. To accomplish this, a magazine's time-sensitive, versioned sections would have to be bound into waiting, preassembled general editorial sections almost as soon as the versioned signatures cleared the final printing unit of the web press. The publication's speed of distribution would then have to approach that of a newspaper. [17]

Since periodical distribution is largely in the hands of the U.S. Postal Service and a network of private businesses specializing in single-copy sales, there are limits to what publishers can do to improve the efficiency with which their magazines reach the market. The final phase of the production workflow focuses on making sure that the issue, now truly finished, is ready for entry into the postal delivery system (if circulation consists of subscriptions); for shipment to single-copy distributors (if there will be sales through newsstands and other retail outlets); or for distribution through both channels (as is usually the case for consumer magazines).

The magazine's printing plant generally will be where mailing labels are applied and zip-code sorted bundles are prepared. The labels or the data records for ink-jet addressing will come either from the magazine's fulfillment house; from the publisher's circulation department, if the magazine handles its own fulfillment; or from the printer's computers, if the printer offers data management and fulfillment as value-added services. Once copies are labeled, the printer's mailing department bundles them by zip code to comply with postal regulations and to qualify for sortation discounts. Now the bundles can be trucked to the nearest postal facility that accepts bulk entry of magazines. A very high-volume printer of mailed magazines can be designated an entry facility by the postal service, with postal personnel assigned to the plant to supervise the administrative processing.

Single-copy distribution follows an entirely different scheme. Publishers rarely ship product directly to retail outlets, owing to the logistical difficulty and the prohibitive cost of reaching the countless locations where magazines are sold. Instead, publishers rely on a complicated shipping and billing system whereby companies known as national distributors route issues to a network of independent distributors responsible for delivering copies to selected points of sale. About 400 of these *ID wholesalers*, as they are often called, cover retail outlets in major population centers throughout the United States and Canada.

The publisher and the national distributor use sales data from previous issues to set the next issue's draw—the number of copies to be sent to the ID wholesalers. This number, naturally, must be taken into account when determining the size of the press run and the amount of paper to have on hand. On completion of the run, the printer, using labels and manifests supplied by the national distributor, ships the copies to the independent distributor network. The wholesalers then deliver the copies to their retailers and, at a specified date, collect unsold copies for credit so that their retailers' magazine racks will be clear for the next issue. [18]

Criticisms of the efficiency of single-copy distribution are properly made within the context of circulation, not production. However, it must be noted that the system appears far from efficient when measured strictly by sell-through—the number of copies actually sold versus the draw produced for the wholesalers. Because there is no consistently reliable way to forecast draws on the basis of past sales, and because retail magazine outlets vary so widely in terms of sales performance, the present system has to be content with selling only 3 out of every 10 magazines it distributes—a national average sell-through rate of 30 percent or less. [19] Some publishers try to pump more copies of an issue into distribution as a way to boost net sales, but this practice only raises the rate of *prematures*—copies returned by retailers before the issue's on-sale period has expired. [20] It also traps publishers into spending more money on paper that goes straight to trash bins and landfills without ever having stopped in the hands of readers.

It has been said that chronic inefficiencies like these can make the cost of distributing a printed product exceed 25 percent of the total cost of publishing and printing it. [21] Given the single-copy distribution system's obvious influence on production economics, every magazine needs to keep a wary eye on the results its national distributors and ID wholesalers are posting.

On the other hand, it is hard to gainsay the basic soundness of a system that can channel hundreds of millions of magazines to tens of thousands of retail outlets every week, accounting for each sold and unsold copy. Without single-copy distribution, magazines simply would not constitute the mass medium that the present system, for all of its flaws, has made it possible for them to be. Today, publishers are working closely with the national distributor-ID wholesaler network to focus on the most productive retail outlets and to find other ways of improving the network's efficiency.

## NOTES

[1]Examples drawn from Adams, Faux, and Rieber, Chapter 13 ("Offset Press Operation")

[2]Miles Southworth and Donna Southworth, *Pocket Guide to Color Reproduction/Communication and Control* (1994: Bronson Hill Press, Livonia, N.Y.), 101.

[3]Adams, Faux, and Rieber, *Printing Technology*, 381.

[4]Adams, Faux, and Rieber, *Printing Technology,* 381.

[5]Beach, Shepro, and Russon, *Getting It Printed*, 176.

[6]Ralph Lyman, *Binding and Finishing* (Pittsburgh: Graphic Arts Technical Foundation, 1993), 48.

[7]Lyman, *Binding and Finishing* , 57.

[8]Adams, Faux, and Rieber, *Printing Technology*, 551.

[9]Graphic Arts Technical Foundation, *1994 Technology Forecast* (Pittsburgh: 1994), 21.

[10]Graphic Arts Technical Foundation, *1995 Technology Forecast* (Pittsburgh: 1995), 20.

[11]Robert Pfeifer, "Integrated Selective Control System Streamlines Binding, Distribution Operations at Perry, Donnelley," *High Volume Printing,* August 1994, 116.

[12]Pfeifer, "Integrated Selective Control System Streamlines Binding," 116.

[13]Steve Rees, "25 ways to customize your magazine," *Folio: Special Source Book Issue for 1994*, 207–208

[14]Pfeifer, "Integrated Selective Control System Streamlines Binding," 116.

[15]Pfeifer, "Integrated Selective Control System Streamlines Binding," 117.

[16]Graphic Arts Technical Foundation, *1994 Technology Forecast*, 21.

[17]Graphic Arts Technical Foundation, *1995 Technology Forecast*, 20–21.

[18]Mogel, *The Magazine,* 105–106.

[19]Lambeth Hochwald, "High costs force distribution changes," *Folio;,* September 1, 1995, 18.

[20]Mogel, *The Magazine,* 109.

[21]Bruno, *Pocket Pal*, 164.

# The Magazine of the Future—and *Your* Future in Magazines

## THE FUTURE: THE BIRTH OF THE ELECTRONIC PAGE

By the early 1990s, the movement of printed magazines toward alternative forms of publishing had become a self-fulfilling prophecy. The reason: An explosion of electronic communications technologies was creating entirely new markets for information, and prescient publishers wanted their share. The opportunities were simply too rich to pass up. According to *Wired*, a magazine on lifestyles and cultural trends in the digital information age, 100 million personal computers were installed in the United States in 1993. Twenty-nine percent of American homes had computers, and nearly as many were predicted to have fax machines by mid-decade. *Wired* foresaw a $1 trillion market for computer and communications technology of all kinds by 2001.[1] In 1992, publishing industry observers had already reckoned the electronic delivery of information to be a $10.5 billion business spanning on-line, CD-ROM, and fax-based communications systems. [2]

News from the publishing front left little doubt that electronic media were starting to compete seriously with print in segments of publishing that had once belonged exclusively to the printing press. In a few cases, the electronic competition was pushing print out of the picture altogether. In 1992, for example, Christopher Whittle—who once published *Esquire*—announced that Whittle Communications would be focusing most of its resources on electronic properties, which at the time of the announcement accounted for about 70 percent of the company's $230 million in annual revenues. Only four years earlier, print properties had generated 100 percent of Whittle Communications' income.[3]

Understanding that competition from electronic media would not go away, publishers began to look at ink-on-paper magazines as only one of a number of ways in which the information they produced could be delivered. Having learned how to convert their publications' text, images, and color into digital data that could be transmitted on diskettes, over wires, and by satellite—in other words, by whatever means the end users of the data required—they also learned that consumers of information tended to judge information delivery mostly in terms of utility and convenience. If electronic media could do a better job in certain respects than magazines, then those were the media that magazine publishers needed to explore. As the head of a leading information-technology company put it, "Every print publisher has to decide whether to stay in print and lose market share; go into electronic publishing and build up business; or do nothing and go out of business."[4]

Nevertheless, nobody with any true understanding of the trends was suggesting that printing was about to take its place with hieroglyphics as a bygone medium of communication. Because desktop publishing had so thoroughly democratized the publishing process, those with access to a computer might create all the pages they could dream of creating. So even as new technologies pointed the way to alternatives to the traditional printed page, billions of these pages were being generated for the photocopier, the laser printer, and the printing press.

But the fact remained that printed pages were now vying for the public's attention with pages of a radically different kind. The electronic page—an all-digital creation that would never taste ink in a pressroom—was poised to deliver not only text and graphics but also modes of communication beyond the powers of traditional publishing: video, animation, sound, as well as instant links to databases, on-line services, and other documents. Alive with these dynamic elements, the electronic page would be something to interact with, not merely to read. It could be updated almost as soon as its underlying information changed. Its contents could be researched and cross-referenced with all the data-crunching speed and power that a personal computer or a workstation could provide. Producing an electronic page would not be attended by worries about print quantities, color OKs, spoilage, or unsold returns. Unlike the printed page, it was a medium that, theoretically, could never become outdated, over-inventoried, or necessary to recycle.

Theory also suggested that a stack of electronic pages could bound together, digitally speaking, into a periodical of a wholly new kind—the electronic magazine. The new publication would be much more than just a static, on-screen version of the traditional printed product. The electronic magazine would costar with the printed periodical as a separate publishing entity incorporating all of the dazzling techniques and tricks of digital information distribution.

Veteran magazine hands predicted that the appeal of publishing electronic magazines would be irresistible. Writing in 1992, Jerry Borell, then editor in chief of *Macworld,* pointed out that the increasingly "expensive and inefficient" economics of print production had set the stage for a fresh and liberating approach. Environmental concerns—deforestation, pollution from paper manufacturing, toxicity hazards of pressroom inks and chemicals, fears of a waste-disposal crisis linked to old and unsold magazines—were also driving the magazine publishing industry in an all-electronic direction. And what magazine, mused Borell, would not leap at the chance to publish without reliance upon the U.S. Postal Service, which, he wrote, "every year seems a slower and less cost-efficient means of distributing the information that publishers want to rush into their readers' homes and offices."[5]

Concluding that the electronic magazine was destined for success from all the publishing viewpoints that mattered, Borell advised his readers that the advent of the electronic magazine would mean that "the entire realm of how we shape information in today's magazines—and how you use that information—will change." The balance of this chapter will try to assess the nature and the consequences of that change with respect to the competition that printed magazines now face from nonprint alternatives. It will also examine the extent to which postal issues and environmental concerns have reshaped magazine publishing and production strategies. It closes with words on finding production employment in an industry where job descriptions and career opportunities are changing as rapidly as magazines themselves.

## CD-ROM AND ON-LINE: FOR NOW, THE FUTURE

If it is true, as at least one printing industry forecast has declared, that by the year 2000 nearly all information will exist in one digital form or another,[6] the magazine publishing industry will have to determine which of these new media are best suited to repackaging the information it already produces in digital form for prepress applications. By the mid-1990s, the two alternative technologies attracting the most attention and investment in the magazine world were CD-ROM publications and on-line, interactive magazines "circulated" through computer networks. Other forms had fared less well. "Videotex," a hybrid publishing experiment based on television, had a short-lived vogue that did not intersect significantly with magazines. Fax broadcasting and fax-on-demand—electronic publishing variants that accompanied fax machines into millions of offices and homes—were useful for short-form periodicals such as newsletters and newspaper digests. As far as magazines were concerned, however, fax services remained largely ancillary activities that added value to their parent publications without emerging as separate, independent products.

The CD-ROM and on-line versions of magazines, on the other hand, have developed their own editorial styles, cultivated their own audiences, and attracted their own advertisers without aping or undercutting their printed progenitors. Unless one displaces the other—or unless both are eliminated by new nonprint alternatives still over the horizon—they probably represent the magazine of the future to the extent that anyone can predict or define it.

## CD-ROM: PUBLISHING ON SILVER PLATTERS

Digitally engineered, laser-mastered, foil-coated recordings in the format that came to be known as CD-ROM—compact disk, read-only memory—transformed the music business and turned analog recordings into black-vinyl curios almost overnight. Although CD-ROM technology has not changed the landscape of periodical publishing nearly as dramatically, it has added new dimensions of form, content, and interactivity to the concept of what a magazine is. However, there have been no silver spoons or streets paved with gold for magazines launched on the silver platters of CD-ROM. Most CD-ROM titles remain products in search of stable and reliable markets. Lagging consumer acceptance and growing competition from other computer-based media cloud their long-term prospects for success.

Nevertheless, the consensus seems to be that until something significantly better comes along, CD-ROM technology will continue to represent the magazine industry's most versatile option for nonprint publishing. Despite a late start, the industry has learned to use the medium both as a supplement to existing magazine projects and as a vehicle for new publishing ventures that have no counterparts or predecessors in print.

The CD-ROM was born in the early 1980s when the consumer electronics industry reached agreement on recording specifications for a standard, five-inch audio disk. Specifications for recording other kinds of data were developed, leading to the introduction of compact disks that could store more than 600 megabytes of digital information. This is equivalent to 500,000 pages of text—enough to contain the entire listings of all the Yellow Pages directories in the United States, or to present a 21-volume encyclopedia with text, full-color images, animation, video, and sound.[7]

By the mid-1990s, the CD-ROM had won consumer acceptance as a medium not just for recorded music but also for business information and personal entertainment. According to one report, an estimated 15 to 17.5 million CD-ROM drives—five times as many as in the previous year—were sold in 1994.[8] The following year, another estimate held that more than 100 million CD-ROMs were "in print" on the consumer side.[9] By that point, many personal computers were shipping with built-in drives and free assortments of CD-ROM "infotainment" software, further whetting the public's appetite for the diversions of the multimedia compact disk.

Although book publishers had begun developing CD-ROM products in the late 1980s, most magazine publishers played wait-and-see until the 1990s were well along and CD-ROM's consumer base was solidly established.[10] From their vantage point, CD-ROM technology was still too new to permit trustworthy predictions about consumer demand for magazines in CD-ROM form. Knowing the high costs and the chilling mortality rate of new-publication ventures in general, and still smarting from the economic blows it endured in the recessionary opening years of the decade, the magazine industry was in no rush to float unconventional new products before a public that might not be receptive to them. Ironically, though, hesitation helped: The resulting absence of competitive pressure in CD-ROM magazine publishing meant that trial efforts could be safely abandoned if the market's response wasn't favorable. This encouraged publishers to learn the ropes by developing one-shot (onetime) special publications—a safer strategy than launching periodicals, which, if they failed, would have to fail over and over again until the plug was finally pulled.

*Newsweek, Cosmopolitan, Reader's Digest*, and *Audubon* were among the first mainstream consumer magazines to announce plans for multimedia, interactive special issues on CD-ROM disk. A continuing cross-section of one-shots and periodicals would follow. By mid-1995, examples of CD-ROM publications derived from printed magazines included *Newsweek InterActive*; *Playboy*'s 30-year collection of celebrity interviews; *Macworld Interactive*; pro football guides from *The Sporting News*; and *Money in the '90s*, a compendium of three years' worth of issues garnished with video clips and other multimedia enhancements.[11]

Not every CD-ROM magazine is a spin-off of a printed title. Some are published exclusively in CD-ROM format, wholly outside conventional norms of content, production, and distribution. These all-digital periodicals frequently represent CD-ROM publishing's most adventurous uses of interactive elements. For example, Metatec Corporation's *NautilusCD* was designed to entertain its computer-equipped audience of desktop publishing and multimedia enthusiasts with a wealth of "live" features that they could only read about in print: software demonstrations, music samples, and selections from interactive books. At one point, more than 12,000 subscribers were willing to pay the steep price of $9.95 a month (or $119.40 for one year) for the privilege of exploring *NautilusCD* with the help of their CD-ROM drives and computer screens.[12]

A desire to explore the possibilities of CD-ROM technology for general-interest magazine publishing inspired Medio Multimedia Inc. to launch *Medio Magazine,* another CD-ROM-only title, in 1994. It included familiar sections on entertainment, finance, and fashion, but it also offered innovations such as full-motion video clips of upcoming movies; digitized sports photography; and a data bank of thousands of stories and photos from the leading news services. Carrying a "cover price" of $9.95, *Medio Magazine* circulated about 30,000 units within its first 15 months of publication—mostly through single-copy sales in computer stores.[13]

Although the novelty of ventures like these has undeniable appeal in some segments of the magazine marketplace, novelty alone has not been enough to assure CD-ROM's long-term future as a publishing option. For all of its multimedia vibrancy, a CD-ROM publication cannot disguise the limitations of its underlying technology. These limitations can translate into inconvenience for the average reader of CD-ROM magazines, who may then begin to pine for the simplicity and predictability of print.

Nothing more than good light and a comfortable chair is needed for the efficient perusal of a printed magazine. Interacting with a CD-ROM publication, on the other hand, requires fairly sophisticated hardware and a certain amount of technical know-how—commodities that are considerably less widespread among the magazine-buying public than reading lamps and recliners. Even those who own computers may find themselves cut off from the CD-ROM magazine experience if their machines lack sound cards, video capability, or sufficient memory to support the presentation of digital data in interactive formats.

Some of the loudest laments in the litany of limitations for CD-ROM bemoan the medium's sluggish rate of data transfer. The problem, in simplest terms, is that compact disks offer digital information to a computer's central processing unit more slowly than almost any other form of data storage. Faster CD-ROM drives help, but the technology's comparative snail's pace still manifests itself as irritating delays in screen redraws, search procedures, and playback of animation and video. Then there are complaints about the quality of the media that finally do manage to impress the reader of a CD-ROM magazine: video clips that are jumpy and grainy; sound that gives audiophiles waking nightmares; color that looks odd on the old, cheap monitors that many people are still peering into. Small wonder that some have called CD-ROM magazines "the worst of both worlds": inferior in visual quality to print, miles behind on-line services in terms of interactivity and access to current data.[14]

Advances in technology probably will improve the overall quality of CD-ROM magazines, but more than quality will be needed to improve their economic prospects. Although the single-copy price spread between CD-ROM magazines and many conventional periodicals is not enormous, CD-ROM magazines tend to be seen as upscale publishing products that the bulk of the consumer marketplace is not used to paying for.[15] Uncertainty about the mass-market appeal of interactive publishing options like CD-ROM makes it difficult for publishers to know how to plan, price, and promote these risky ventures, at least on the consumer side.[16]

In fact, if CD-ROM magazines do have a long-term outlook, their best prospects probably will be found in nonconsumer publishing applications. Because users of business-to-business directories, trade magazines, and academic periodicals have far less interest in multimedia glitz than they have in high-volume access to practical information—the one aspect of publishing in which CD-ROM technology truly shines—examples of enduringly successful business and professional publications on CD-ROM are not hard to come by. Ziff-Davis's *PC Magazine,* for example, sells 120,000 copies of its quarterly CD-ROM.[17] Byrd Press of Richmond, Virginia, produces CD-ROM versions of *Journal of Bacteriology* for the American Society of Microbiology and *Geophysics* for the Society of Exploration Geophysicists.[18] *The New England Journal of Medicine* has been available both on-line and on CD-ROM since 1984. Each weekly issue goes into the publisher's database for alternative output as soon as it appears in print.[19] It should also be noted that the magazine industry's two primary sources of advertising-related information, the Standard Rate and Data Service (SRDS) and the Audit Bureau of Circulations (ABC), have released searchable, CD-ROM–based compendiums of their vast collections of publishing facts and figures.

The reality may be, as some have predicted, that CD-ROM publishing is merely a "transitory distribution medium"[20] that eventually will be pushed into obsolescence by improved transmission of text and graphics over telephone and cable television lines. According to these forecasts, the high-speed, high-quality data transmission networks of the future will deliver "true" electronic publications offering instant interactivity, continuously updated information, exhibition-quality multimedia, and other features that lie beyond the technical capabilities of CD-ROM.

However, it is also true that these networks do not yet exist. Their predecessors—commercial on-line services and the Internet—are still experimental proving grounds for interactive magazine publishing, with many functional challenges yet to be overcome. This assures CD-ROM magazines of remaining, at least for the time being, the nonprint publishing alternative with the most consistent record of success among audiences who want more excitement or information-crunching power than their printed magazines can give them.

## PUBLISHING IN CYBERSPACE: THE ON-LINE MAGAZINE

Cyberspace is not real space. It is only a metaphor describing the connections that computers establish as they send and receive data across physical space. For a place without physical dimensions, however, cyberspace seems to have plenty of room for magazines. That is fortunate, because indications are strong that many magazines—perhaps most magazines—will soon be looking for addresses in the cyberspace neighborhoods that hundreds (thousands?) of on-line magazines already call home.

The term *on-line magazine* is also a metaphor—a fanciful expression of the concept from which the expression is derived. On-line magazines do not bear much resemblance to other magazines. Like cyberspace itself, they have no physical attributes or components: no page counts, no trim sizes, no ad-to-edit ratios to measure them with; nor any paper, ink, or compact disks to manufacture them from. They are temporary publications, existing only for as long as the reader's computer is turned on and the connection to the publishing site (another computer) is intact. Although they may contain the same general kinds of content as other magazines, that content must be structured, edited, and designed in ways peculiar to the on-line medium. Editing and producing a printed magazine teach relatively little about launching and sustaining its on-line version.

Nevertheless, having found their way into cyberspace either through commercial services such as America Online or by direct connection to the broader horizons of the Internet, periodicals that explore the virtual realm are not likely to turn back. Opportunities to be exploited there promise major advantages in every aspect of magazine publishing:

- **Content.** "Hypertext," color, graphics, sound, animation, and video—all of them updatable as quickly as events or readers' wishes may dictate—endow on-line magazines with breathtaking new powers of communication. For the first time in their history, magazines become two-way media linking editors and audiences in "real time" (or in a time frame very close to "real"). No longer does content become static and obsolescent with the granting of a press OK. Interactivity emerges as the most important benchmark of editorial effectiveness.

- **Production.** When a magazine is published on-line, the need for investment in paper, ink, and presswork becomes academic. Launching a publication in cyberspace costs a fraction of what would have to be spent on printing and distributing the premier issue of a conventional magazine. Money thus saved can then be invested in upgrading content. Production variables affecting product quality vanish: There is no spoilage in cyberspace. No one worries about overruns or underruns, because there are no run lengths to worry about.

- **Circulation.** At a time when printed magazines are believed destined for a future of narrower niches and smaller audiences, on-line publishing opens new vistas of readership in numbers that print can no longer aspire to. Personal connections to all of the various cyberspace locations where on-line magazines can be found are mounting at a rate of millions per month. Access to on-line magazines—for the moment, and for the most part—is free. As a result, the circulation marketplace for on-line magazines is potentially as vast as cyberspace itself. And that vastness awaits without the need to spare a thought for the next round of postal rate increases or for single-copy distributors' demands for increased rack allowances: a circulation manager's dream come true.

- **Advertising.** Circulation in the multimillions implies comparable exposure for the advertising that appears in on-line magazines. On-line publishing's multimedia resources give advertisers new tools for making the presentation unique and the message memorable. Interactivity—the ability of the reader to trade directly with the source by using on-line ads as communication gateways—creates a potential for responsiveness surpassing anything achievable in print.

Some of these advantages carry built-in disadvantages. For example, since there are no cover or subscription prices for on-line publications, one of the most basic yardsticks of any magazine's appeal—the amount of money the reader is willing to pay to receive it—cannot be applied. Measuring response to on-line advertising remains a subject of controversy. It must also be remembered that many on-line periodicals were created as experimental adjuncts to printed magazines, not as replacements for them. Their publishers have learned that in some important respects, the offshoots do not perform nearly as well as the originals.

But despite drawbacks and uncertainties, the magazine industry seems committed to expanding the definition of what it produces to encompass both print and on-line publishing. Ready or not, publishers have embraced on-line telecommunications as the medium that will assure the survival of their magazines in forms that will include, but will not be limited to, the printed products that have held sway until now.[21]

## AN EXPANDING UNIVERSE OF TITLES

As it had done in so many other areas of technology, the newspaper industry broke ground for the rest of publishing in on-line and interactive information services. According to one survey, some 3,200 American newspapers offered on-line news, fax, and other interactive services in 1995, up from 2,700 in 1994, 2,000 in 1993, and 42 in 1989. Newspapers have launched virtual editions on bulletin board networks, commercial on-line services, and the World Wide Web (the portion of the Internet where publishers can add multimedia elements to basic text and images).[22] *The New York Times*, for example, uses America Online as its vehicle for an interactive edition that offers late-breaking news, features and columns, and message boards through which readers can exchange views with *Times* journalists and with one another. *The Mercury-News* of San Jose, California, the first daily newspaper on the World Wide Web, now provides links to newswires as well as a "Newshound" service that delivers "customized" news to recipients' E-mail addresses.[23]

Trade and business magazines have also joined the vanguard of on-line publishing. Business-to-business publishers CMP, Mecklermedia, and IDG Publications have launched interactive editions of various titles on the World Wide Web.[24] Ziff-Davis has put *PC Magazine* and *Interactive Week* on "ZD Net," a Web site that averages 3 million "hits" (requests for access) per month.[25] Penton Publishing is represented in cyberspace by *Industry Week Interactive*; Chilton Publications by *Multichannel News;* Maclean Hunter Publishing by *Progressive Grocer*; and the New York Law Publishing Company by the on-line version of the *National Law Journal.*[26]

In some respects, readers of business publications are the ideal audiences for on-line magazines. Seeking information, not entertainment, from the specialized publications that cross their desks, these executive-level decision makers are always receptive to technologies that promise to bring them more information faster.

Because many of them already use computers, modems, and network connections as everyday tools for information gathering, they soon come to think of browsing an on-line magazine as routine a thing to do as launching a spreadsheet or tapping into a database.

Above all, they value on-line publishing's ability to deliver time-sensitive and accumulative information whenever they need the latest facts and figures to buttress a decision—which is to say continuously, at a moment's notice, with no waiting for printed magazines that may be stuck in the mail or short-stopped in the interoffice pipeline. In fact, when the information that these executives get from on-line publications is detailed, timely, and of clear practical utility, they may be happy to pay extra for it even if they are already receiving controlled-circulation copies of the parent magazines for free.[27]

CMP, a Long Island, New York, publisher of specialized titles for the computer and electronic industries, has capitalized on its readers' natural affinity for high-technology communications with Tech Web, an Internet publishing project launched in November 1994. As its name suggests, Tech Web is a World Wide Web site where everyone—including subscribers, advertisers, and potential members of both groups—can examine the on-line versions of 17 CMP magazines. Long used to competing in overcrowded trade publishing niches, CMP knew that growth in these saturated fields might consist only of whatever circulation and advertising could be snatched from rival magazines in a market that had stopped growing. To be sure, CMP has no intention of abandoning its printed magazines or of ceasing to search for new publishing opportunities in the traditional medium that its readers and advertisers know best. With Tech Web, however, CMP can look beyond the plateau of the print marketplace to an on-line horizon in which it hopes eventually to generate up to 20 percent of its total revenues.[28]

Consumer magazines have an overriding short-term ambition for cyberspace: to be in it. Two household-name examples, *Time* and *People*, have ensconced on-line versions of themselves at the "Pathfinder" Web site operated by parent company Time Inc. Neither *Yankee, Macleans,* nor *Smithsonian* finds cyberspace too new-fangled for its traditional tastes: Each has an interactive edition there. Unconventional titles such as *Mother Jones, Yellow Silk,* and *Out* may be feeling even more at home than the mainstream books as they publish what they like in the freely accessible, uncensored atmosphere of the Web. Needless to say, *Wired,* that inventive monthly chronicler of cyber-culture, also publishes on the Web (as *HotWired,* a no-frills hypertext edition that's easier on the average reader's eyes than the fantastically styled print version of the magazine).

It is not easy to estimate, or even to guesstimate, how many magazines have crossed the line from ink on paper to links in cyberspace. Complicating the census is the fact that there are still no unambiguous standards for defining what an on-line magazine is (and is not). By current conventions, an on-line publication that consists of nothing but straight text has as much right to call itself a magazine as a fully interactive production bursting with graphics, hypertext, links, and multimedia razzle-dazzle. The surest thing that can be said about the universe of on-line magazines is that it is expanding all the time. Here is where a few growth indicators stood when this chapter was researched and written:

- Of the 70 publications offered in the Newsstand area of America Online, most were magazines. CompuServe advertised full-text access to more than 700 publications, including an unspecified number of magazines.
- The Electronic Newsstand, which sells subscriptions to print magazines via the World Wide Web, lets its client publications post excerpts from current issues at its Web site. At the time of writing, 339 magazines were on-line with the Electronic Newsstand in this way.
- Newslink, a clearinghouse for media information on the World Wide Web, was a jumping-off point for connections to 16 magazine publishing companies and to the on-line specimens of about 500 magazines.
- "Yahoo" is a database of Internet resources that is maintained at Stanford University. A search of the magazine's subset of Yahoo's entertainment index listed 34 categories of publications linking to the on-line versions of more than 1,500 titles.

Whatever its precise dimensions, the expanding universe of on-line magazines clearly is a place where editors and publishers believe they can forge a new kind of relationship with audiences whose requirements, until recently, they could satisfy only to the extent that the print medium let them. Now they are counting on two-way, instant communications through interactive pages to give readers direct, personal involvement with the editorial product.[29] They see renewed editorial vitality as the outcome; or, at the very least, they are hoping for more insight than they now get into whether their readers like what they are publishing. Commenting on the launch of a Web site for *Macworld*, the editors wrote that the printed edition of the magazine "receives fewer letters than you might suppose. Without day-to-day feedback from readers, magazine publishing can become an ivory-tower exercise."[30] (But perhaps this should be taken as a case of being careful of what one wishes for. Reader response demands acknowledgment, and as minute-to-minute feedback becomes the order of the day, editorial isolation may come to be viewed with a certain amount of nostalgia.)

Other visionary assumptions have spurred the magazine community's rush to on-line publishing. Gone at last, some say, is the straitjacket of frequency. Now content can updated at low cost whenever the time is right—not just when there are enough ads to pay for the next weekly or monthly issue.[31] Others claim that on-line is a straight line to desirable audiences already out there waiting: for example, Internet-savvy readers of technical and academic magazines; and, of course, people under the age of 30, who make up so much of the citizenry of cyberspace.[32]

Not everyone is willing to call the on-line option a publishing panacea. In 1995, for example, an executive of the Newspaper Association of America claimed that "technophobia" was more widespread than many publishers realized, and that readers did not necessarily believe in their need for information delivery via cyberspace channels.[33] Magazine executives, though generally convinced that on-line publishing is a key to the future, also admit that achieving sustained reader interest in these unfamiliar new products is by no means a foregone conclusion. As competitive pressure induces many of them to rush into launching all-electronic versions of their printed titles, magazine professionals are still searching for publishing formats and editorial formulas that will not fail to capitalize on the on-line medium's unique powers of communication. They are also concerned about the difficulties they will face in building creative and commercial synergies between the printed parent and the interactive offspring.

On-line publishing's pioneers do agree that the quickest way to doom any online magazine is to launch it as a horseless carriage—an unmodified version of the old vehicle hitched to a new form of propulsion that the old vehicle isn't streamlined enough to keep up with. Just dumping text straight from the page-layout workstation into the Web or the network server is no way to leverage the benefits of on-line publishing for readers who want something more from the experience.[34] A printed article repackaged verbatim for on-line distribution is an old wine that may sour the instant its new bottle is uncorked inside the reader's computer. The best on-line content is that designed specifically for a medium bearing only limited resemblance to print in the way it conveys information.[35]

It is an approach much easier to get dogmatic about than to get right, given the fact that creating truly effective interactive materials requires skills and experience that traditional publishing does not necessarily impart.[36] Sometimes the lack of mastery can embarrass even the most prestigious magazines in their attempts to recreate themselves on line. For example, *USA Today* once criticized *Newsweek InterActive* (publishing on the Prodigy commercial network) for failing to adapt its content to the visual realities of the computer: "(T)he heavy audio-video demands slow up transmission. And the large type and small screen capacity work heavily against long stories. It's tough to establish a thought, much less a narrative, when you have to turn a virtual page every three paragraphs."[37] On the other hand, in the same article, *Scientific American* on America Online was praised for giving "added value: some neat things a print mag can't handle, like computer movies and animation relating to stories." It is a lucky thing for beginners that the rapidly reprogrammable nature of on-line magazine publishing makes it possible—even comparatively easy—to undo mistakes and retool false starts.

It is not as easy to interpret the new relationship that has sprung up between the people who publish on-line magazines and the people who read them. This relationship, some observers say, is about shifts in control: specifically, about the readers' new-found power to design a personalized reading experience every time they go on-line.[38] Print magazine publishing cedes no such control. Each of its products is self-contained (defined strictly by what fits between the covers); exclusive (not presented in connection with any other publication); and immutable (subject to no input or alteration by the reader). On-line publishing turns each of these concepts on its head by letting the audience do the key decision making. Readers want on-line magazines to be gateways: not self-sealing stand-alones but open-ended tour guides rich with hypermedia portals to the far corners of cyberspace. Readers also like knowing that when they have established the telecommunication link that lets them access one on-line magazine, they can access all of the other magazines that their on-line service provider supports. And as they browse on-line titles, readers expect to make their presence felt by responding to requests for feedback; down- and uploading many kinds of data; and manipulating the publication in other ways pertinent to their individual needs for information. Publishers who once took an ivory-tower view of their audiences will find that on-line readers not only have minds of their own but are always ready to speak them.[39]

## CHOOSING THE PUBLISHING PATHWAY: COMMERCIAL ON-LINE SERVICES VERSUS THE INTERNET

You are planning a motor trip to a famous resort area where the attractions are first-class and the crowds are the kinds of people you like to rub shoulders with. You may choose one of two ways to get there: Ride a chartered tour bus or use your own car. If you ride the bus, you can relax while someone else does the route planning and the driving, but you have to reserve a seat, observe the timetable, and obey all of the bus company's other rules. You are your own boss if you drive, traveling where and when you want, making up the rules of the trip as you go. Traveling independently, however, means traveling alone: a fact that will be brought back in stark terms in the event of a breakdown or a wrong turn along the way.

For magazines, launching interactive versions through commercial on-line services is riding the bus; self-publishing on the Internet is getting behind the wheel of a privately owned vehicle. Both routes have brought hundreds, if not thousands, of publications on-line, and there is no clear evidence that one works better than the other as a means of bringing interactive magazines to the attention of the reading public. Various censuses and market studies do suggest that magazine publishing on the Internet will eventually surpass magazine publishing through the commercial services. For the moment, however, each method has advantages that will recommend it to publishers seeking to make their on-line debuts as effective as possible.

Commercial services and the Internet are separate galaxies within the same cyberspace universe, although the Internet is many more light-years across. CompuServe, America Online, and Prodigy are the best-known of the commercials. They are discrete networks operated by profit-making enterprises that sell on-line services to their subscribers and "content providers" from centrally located computers. The Internet, contrastingly, is a global entity made up of widely dispersed host computers that operate at minimal cost to users and without obligation to any central authority. Users of commercial networks must pay hourly fees for their access and must, in many cases, add premiums for special services not included in the basic cost of membership. (Charges for telephone connect time are an additional cost component.) Anyone who is able to connect to the Internet can draw upon or contribute to its worldwide stores of information at will, in unlimited amounts, at no cost beyond local telephone charges and a flat rate to the access provider (if access cannot be obtained free). The spirit of the commercial on-line services is pay-as-you-go in an open market; the philosophy of the Internet is that of barter and the commune.

However, as businesses of all kinds learn to exploit the Internet's mercantile possibilities, some of its not-for-profit orientation will vanish, and the differences between it and the commercial on-line services will become harder to discern. Magazine publishers have discovered that the two galaxies already share at least one characteristic: They are growing more crowded and cash-heavy all the time. In 1995 Veronis, Suhler & Associates, a venture-capital firm for media industries, projected 33.4 percent compound annual growth for consumer on-line and Internet-access services, with an estimated 22.5 million American households either subscribing to an on-line service or using an Internet access provider by 1999. These on-line enthusiasts, representing more than 55 percent of all computer-equipped U.S. households, would be spending a combined $6.1 billion for service charges by 1999, according to the Veronis, Suhler forecast.[40]

At mid-decade, some research indicated that direct connections to the Internet were or soon would be generating a larger potential readership for on-line magazines than subscriptions to the commercial services. Veronis, Suhler believed that the total number of direct Internet connections would overtake that of subscriptions to on-line services by 1998, rising to 14 million by 1999. [41] But O'Reilly & Associates, a publisher of computer books and Internet software, claimed that Internet connections had already pulled ahead. Shortly after Veronis, Suhler made its forecast, O'Reilly & Associates released survey results showing Internet connections outnumbering commercial subscriptions by about three to two, with 5.8 million American adults on the Internet and 3.9 million with America Online and its competitors.[42]

As will be seen, both sets of numbers are conservative in comparison with other estimates published at about the same time. But whatever the exact figures may be, they do not imply a simplistic, bigger-is-better choice for would-be publishers of on-line magazines. The commercial services may offer publishers fewer potential readers than the Internet, but at least the commercial services can say how many subscribers they have, who those subscribers are, and what their all-important household demographics are like. The commercial services, in other words, can furnish basic marketing insights that are not readily available to those who publish on the Internet, where quantitative and qualitative information about users often is anyone's guess. Building their business models on a foundation of known facts about their subscriber bases, CompuServe, America Online, and the rest also can offer publishers clearly structured revenue-sharing arrangements of a kind impossible to administer in the terra incognita of the Internet.

Other issues rubbing some of the sparkle off the Internet's superior numbers are its uncertain reputation as a selling tool and worries about its security. Although it was generating $100 million in annual revenues as early as 1993, the Internet still trails the commercial networks as a moneymaker. Consumers have been reluctant to use it as a medium for home shopping, partly because of its unfamiliarity and partly because of its well-publicized vulnerability to criminal hacking and other kinds of fraud. The resulting perception, observed one publishing industry journal, is that "the Internet is great for posting free marketing info and advertising, but not so hot for selling hard goods or content."[43]

Why then would magazine publishers want to venture into cyberspace except in partnership with a comparatively safe, structured, and stable commercial on-line service? To be sure, many publishers have opted for the advantages of affiliation instead of taking to the Internet as independents. By the first quarter of 1995, some of the industry's best-known consumer titles had launched on-line versions through the commercial services, including general-interest leaders *People Weekly* and *Saturday Review*; women's service front-runners *Elle* and *Woman's Day*; and category heavyweights *Scientific American, Golf Digest, Road & Track,* and *Stereo Review*.[44] McGraw-Hill made its view of the matter plain when it created an on-line version of *Business Week* with the help of America Online at the end of 1994. Reportedly, McGraw-Hill chose AOL as its publishing partner because it believed the network's business model was the only one capable of generating revenue.[45]

Growth is still in prospect for the commercial on-line services, with some estimates putting the total number of subscribers at 20 million by the end of 1997.[46] Impossible for publishers to ignore, however, is the fact that the Internet may have already outstripped that figure and is, in any case, expanding at a rate that the commercial services can only dream about. For many in the magazine business, the present size and long-term growth potential of the Internet marketplace more than outweigh its formlessness and its risks. Among the more eye-opening estimates of 1995 were survey results published by Matrix Information and Directory Services, Inc. (MIDS), a research and marketing organization specializing in on-line activities. MIDS reported that as of July of that year, 20 to 30 million people used interactive Internet services including access to the World Wide Web (where the most significant on-line publishing ventures are taking place). By mid-1996, MIDS said, the Internet would be "much bigger."[47] How much bigger remains to be seen, although other estimates put its growth rate at between 10 and 12 percent per month.[48]

The weight of predictions like these has convinced many publishers that the Internet is their path to bigger audiences than the on-line services are likely to deliver. Moreover, publishers who have investigated the revenue-splitting arrangements that on-line services typically impose on magazines and other content providers find they have another reason to prefer the Internet. Whatever its defects as a business model, at least the Internet does not charge content providers the tariffs that the on-line services do.

Publishing a magazine through an on-line service means playing—and paying—according to the on-line service's rules. Basically, the service makes money by leasing space on its network to content providers. Each content provider pays its lease by generating profitable traffic and surrendering most of that revenue to the on-line service.

The content provider's income is based on how much sustained attention, by the on-line service's reckoning, that the content succeeds in attracting, not just to the publisher's site but to the network as a whole. Attention can be measured in terms of the number of times that the service's current subscribers visit the publisher's site; the duration of the visits; the total on-line time logged by new subscribers whom the magazine has persuaded to sign up with the on-line service; the downloading of text and/or software offered by the magazine; and other content-inspired subscriber activities that the network has the means to document.

Royalties to content providers for sustaining these activities consist of percentages of subscribers' monthly fees, hourly rates (including premiums for access to special areas), and download charges. Some of the percentages can be sweetened by building traffic beyond benchmarks set by the on-line service. In no case, however, will the magazine get the lion's share of the money, because that portion will have been swallowed by the network. Some publishers have complained that the lion's leavings are too meager for them to subsist on, with most magazines receiving only 10 to 20 percent of the revenue they generate for CompuServe, America Online, and the other on-line services.[49]

Nor is it just the stingy split of the take that publishers object to. The on-line services' rules for presentation of content can be as rigid and as unaccommodating as their formulas for dividing the pot. Exposure is an issue: Is the content provider's material relatively easy for subscribers to find, or is it sunk in a backwater under a debris of arcane keywords and sub-forum detours? Magazines, which have always charged extra for premium locations in their own folios, may get a taste of the same medicine as they negotiate with the on-line services for acceptable positioning and presence. They may also have to put up with technical restrictions on what and how much they can post, especially with respect to graphics and multimedia elements. No such constraints exist on the World Wide Web, where all the positions are the same and where content is delimited only by the extent of a publisher's ability to design and support richly featured Web pages.

By going directly to the Internet, publishers can be certain of not having to give up any of their creative or economic prerogatives. Nevertheless, the lures of creative control and 100 percent revenue retention do not mean that magazines inevitably will abandon the on-line services for do-it-yourself Net publishing ventures. There are two alternatives to publishing with a commercial service, and each carries a price tag of its own. One is to work with a service provider that arranges access to the World Wide Web and, in some cases, assists with content creation.

The other is to set up a Web site exclusively for the magazine: to become, in other words, part of the loose consortium of host computers that make up the Internet.

The question is how the cost of either alternative compares with what would have to be paid for the relative simplicity of publishing with a commercial on-line network such as America Online. Web-access providers bill publishers according to the volume of content posted and the number of "hits" recorded. Under these terms, the better the magazine fares, the fatter the periodic payments to the service provider will be. Operating a dedicated Web publishing site eliminates payments to outsiders, but the set-up costs and recurring expenses are high. Building a Web site of one's own means investing in a powerful workstation where interactive pages and other data will reside; obtaining the high-speed telephone service whereby readers will access the magazine; and hiring and training staff to maintain the site, input the content, and handle readers' requests. Each activity is an operating expense that will have to be subtracted from the income that the site is expected to produce.

Both the on-line services and the Internet will continue to have their partisans among magazine publishers. As the Internet grows in scope and commercial viability, many publishers will embrace it as the only way to maximize audience size and control both content and income. Others, preferring the structure and convenience of their arrangements with the commercial networks, will tolerate the trade-offs while pushing for the best deals they can get in terms of exposure, service, and revenue-sharing. And others will cover all bets by publishing in both realms, as some, like IDG's *PC World Online*, do now.[50] For the time being, at least, neither seems poised to consume or starve the other. The standoff is probably good for the market in that it gives readers more than one way to access on-line magazines.

## BUILDING CIRCULATION IN CYBERSPACE: UNCERTAIN REWARDS

As far as circulation is concerned, the good news and the bad news for publishers is that in cyberspace, there is no circulation to sell. A magazine's subscriber base is identical with that of its on-line host, and when it comes to broadening the base, the host's good fortune is also the magazine's. Whenever someone signs up with a commercial network or obtains access to the Internet, every magazine published there gets a new potential subscriber without anything like the high cost of acquiring a new subscriber for the printed product. Unfortunately, since little or none of what the subscriber pays in on-line fees goes to the magazine, the economic advantage of building circulation in this way is marginal no matter what the gross numbers are.

Nevertheless, a magazine still bears the expense of supporting its on-line circulation either through splitting revenue with a commercial network or by meeting the costs of self-publishing on the Internet. This would argue that on-line circulation must somehow produce enough revenue to offset the cost of developing and maintaining it. However, despite some interesting experiments, the magazine publishing industry has not yet found the universal key to turning on-line circulation into a significant source of income.

For publishers who distribute interactive magazines through the commercial on-line services, the problem is at least straightforward: lopsided percentages that tend to make circulation building more profitable for the host than for the publication. The difficulty is greater for magazines published on the Internet, which cannot even begin to think in terms of circulation revenue until they have addressed the issue of how readers are to find them in the first place. Anyone wishing to browse preassembled collections of on-line magazines through a commercial service need only click a handy icon or enter a simple keyword. There is no such convenience on the Internet, where most magazines are isolated outposts that readers must track down and access one at a time by using individual URLs, or uniform resource locators (strings of code that are harder to remember than the names of the magazines they refer to).

Some publishers have made access less arduous by grouping their publications at common sites on the World Wide Web. At these sites, readers can browse all of a publisher's offerings with the same point-and-click simplicity offered by the commercial on-line services. Cross-merchandising magazines in this way not only builds exposure, it creates a revenue stream by giving the publisher a chance to promote print subscriptions and ancillary products to as many visitors as the site manages to attract. Time Inc.'s Pathfinder, CMP Publications' Tech Web, and Ziff-Davis's ZD Net sites are examples of proprietary kiosks where traffic-based formulas for generating revenue are producing measurable results.

The Electronic Newsstand, a business venture launched in 1993, broadens the concept by packaging samples of hundreds of magazines in a newsstand-like environment on the World Wide Web. The Electronic Newsstand lets each of its client publications post an editorial mission statement; a table of contents; an invitation to subscribe to the printed version of the magazine; ancillary-product promotions; and plain-text selections from the current issue. The Newsstand also promises to "publicize all articles to the Internet universe and provide customized usage reports." In return, the Newsstand collects $3 to $10 per subscription order requested. It claims an access rate of 200,000 per day, or three million per month.[51]

Even at the Electronic Newsstand, however, the emphasis is on building paid circulation for the parent medium, print. On-line circulation remains an economic question mark, because a "hit" may be merely an expression of no-cost curiosity about a site—not an indication that the visitor considers the visit a privilege worth paying for. The spirit of Internet wayfaring is still one of free and unrestricted access to everything on the Net, a consumer attitude that has kept most publishers reluctant to introduce on-line equivalents of paid circulation as it exists in the world of print. In any case, there are no serious technical obstacles to making access to on-line magazines a paying proposition. A magazine site could easily be set up like a special-interest area in a commercial on-line service, available by password only to paid subscribers. A publisher could also sell decryption keys to issues posted to the Net in encrypted form.[52]

Some publishers will stay resigned to writing off circulation as a source of on-line revenue; others will not. In all likelihood, the opportunity will be strongest in the specialized trade and business segment, where the sale of information in multiple forms is an accepted part of the relationship between these publications and their readers. For example, at the time of this writing, Meredith Corporation had announced plans to charge a subscription fee of $39.95 a month for its first Internet publishing venture, an interactive version of *Successful Farming*. Having determined that nearly 45 percent of the title's 488,000 paying subscribers used PCs for work, 50,000 owned modems, and 13,000 were already on-line, Meredith concluded that the magazine's audience would not object to paying extra for value-added information delivered electronically.[53] Other attempts like Meredith's will follow, and their outcomes will settle the question of whether circulation in cyberspace represents anything that can drop significantly to on-line publishing's bottom line.

## "HITS" AND MISSES FOR ON-LINE ADVERTISING

Printed magazines are physical objects that can be counted at the printing plant, in the post office, and on the newsstand. Their subscribing recipients, for the most part, can be clearly identified. The fact that magazine distribution can be tracked and measured with a fair degree of accuracy also makes it possible to draw reasonable conclusions about the reach and effectiveness of print magazine advertising. The magazine publishing industry uses circulation-auditing and market-research techniques to support its claims. Although advertisers often question publishers' interpretation of the data yielded by these techniques, the validity of the measurements used is generally not in dispute.

Not so in the measurement-defying realm of on-line magazine publishing. Here, almost everything connected with advertising assessment can provoke a shouting match. The confusion begins with the basic unit of measurement, the hit. There is no broad agreement on what this ambiguous indicator really says about the efficiency of an on-line ad or its host magazine. As a result, and to the extreme annoyance of advertisers, on-line ad rate structures tend be based either on guesswork or on pricing models loosely adapted from other media. Small wonder, then, that some advertisers have blasted the on-line medium as a numbers game in which investing a great deal of money buys relatively little in the way of useful exposure or verifiable response.

Economics aside, this harsh judgment fails to acknowledge the flexibility with which on-line advertising space can be packaged. One popular strategy is to let advertisers sponsor the magazine's "home page" or other attention-getting pages in the folio. In this arrangement, the sponsors' logos and messages are prominently displayed on the pages they have paid to support. Built-in hypertext links to advertisers' own home pages can also be offered for sale. A hypertext link takes the reader from any point in the magazine to the advertiser's Web site with a click of the mouse, giving the advertiser's site a traffic-building signpost in cyberspace. On-line ads can also be given to print advertisers as a value-added reward for their business.

But no matter how on-line ads are packaged, the question of reader response always hinges on the debatable significance of the hits they generate. If there is anything like a consensus about hits, it is that even if they are not a very reliable gauge of readership, they are the only form of measurement that advertisers are likely to ask about.[54] Satisfactory answers, unfortunately, are not easy to give, because a hit is not an absolute measurement of anything.

A hit is simply a request to see something posted somewhere on the Internet. When a reader types a magazine's URL into the "go to" line of Netscape or another piece of Web-browsing software, the resulting connection to the magazine's site is logged as a hit. If advertising is present on pages accessed in this way, or if the reader uses hypertext links to access an advertiser's page elsewhere in the magazine or at some other site, the request for access can be recorded as a hit for the advertiser.

There the simplicity and the consensus end. Depending on what is included in the recording of a hit—"embedded" files, pages other than home pages, pages visited more than once—a hit tally compiled by an on-line magazine may represent only a fraction of the kind of hits the advertiser considers worthwhile. In fact, without a clear understanding between publisher and advertiser as to what hits actually stand for, a report of a million hits (or any other number) says virtually nothing about the marketing value of the magazine site's traffic.[55]

With no model to guide them in measuring interactive advertising, publishers have attempted to price their on-line space either by adapting their print rate cards or by working out flat fees with their clients. These strategies, noted one industry newsletter, have been "generally cautious and in the formative stages" as publishers try to determine what kind of rate structure their advertisers will be most receptive to.[56] While the search for standards goes on, on-line ad pricing remains almost completely ad hoc and improvisational: a case of charging, according to the CEO of the Electronic Newsstand, "whatever you can get."[57]

Advertisers, naturally, have their own notions about what the traffic will bear. Some have proposed that publishers be paid for space not according to a fixed schedule of rates but in direct proportion to response—an approach that publishers say would penalize them for creatively weak ads that fail to pull their own weight.[58] One San Francisco–based agency made its position clear with a report claiming that advertisers in on-line magazines were paying about 40 times the cost per thousand (CPM) of they what they would pay for space in the corresponding printed publications.[59] Another agency said that if CPM-based fixed fees were to be used, the rate should fall somewhere between CPMs for magazines and the less expensive CPMs for television.[60]

Other obstacles are slowing progress toward a mutually acceptable formula for pricing on-line advertising. Publishers and advertisers do seem to agree[61] about the technical limitations of on-line ads: They take a long time to find and download; they are easier for readers to avoid or overlook than the much more intrusive ad pages of printed magazines.[62] Publishers are also concerned about the way their magazines are viewed through commercial on-line services that offer access to the World Wide Web. Because of a practice called *caching*, the Web pages that most commercial-service subscribers access are not the originals at their respective sites but replicas stored for convenience in the commercial services' computers. Apart from the copyright questions it raises, caching complicates the tasks of recording hits and reporting the data to advertisers by forcing publishers to wait for update reports from the services doing the caching.[63]

Improved auditing techniques for Web-site usage will be the key to developing marketing data that on-line magazine publishers and their advertisers can use with confidence. At the time of this writing, at least seven media research organizations had released or were testing software claimed capable of monitoring World Wide Web sites for the performance indicators that advertisers are most interested in— number of visits per user, length of visits, and other meaningful criteria.[64] Advertising agencies and their clients ultimately will decide which of these competing solutions is to emerge as the industry standard for measuring the effectiveness of on-line advertising.

Until a such a standard emerges, perhaps the best strategy for publishers will be to use print magazines as promotional vehicles for their on-line counterparts. Doing so will accomplish two things: It will build up a large, loyal, and auditable following for on-line titles; and it will help printed magazines redefine themselves as a mass-communications medium in an all-digital, multimedia age. One lesson learned by magazine publishers that have branched into alternative media is that the alternatives do not have to darken the outlook for the original. Many people, for example, subscribe to all three versions of Ziff-Davis's *PC Magazine*, which is available in print, as *PC Magazine Online*, and on CD-ROM. Ziff clearly is not worried that disseminating *PC Magazine*'s information in nonprint form will cause anyone to abandon the version that comes from the printing press.[65]

Cross-media marketing—defined by one industry analyst as "finding ways to leverage strategic content on as many media as possible, so our customers get more continuity in their marketing and more leveraging of their investment in images and data"[66]—will assure the future of magazines by establishing their rightful place in the new media mix. As publishers shift the task of delivering time-sensitive information to on-line methods, they can concentrate on refashioning their printed magazines into respected vehicles for the kinds of in-depth, feature-oriented journalism that generally do not work well in on-line formats. [67]

This will fundamentally change printed magazines, but it will change them for the better. As Donald D. Kummerfeld, president, Magazine Publishers of America, has noted: "Radio didn't kill print, and television didn't kill radio or print. What new media do is to force each old medium to redefine what it does best."[68]

## THE MEDIUM IS THE MAILBOX: POSTAL ISSUES AND THEIR EFFECTS ON MAGAZINE DISTRIBUTION

It is all very well to speculate about the new roles, readerships, and revenues that magazines may or may not win as they reinvent themselves for the adventures of publishing in cyberspace. But for most publishers, the more immediate concern is managing the familiar difficulties of producing and distributing magazines in the here-and-now of print. The geography of the here-and-now can be traced on any ZIP code map. Sometimes, to hear publishers tell the tale, crossing that mailbox-dotted landscape can be arduous indeed.

Publishers usually are not slow to point out that much of the trouble stems from the industry's obligations to an aging mail distribution system that seems as arcane, expensive, and inflexible as cyberspace appears straightforward, cheap, and accommodating. The U.S. Postal Service (USPS), by nature and tradition a central-ized bureaucracy, replies that the only way it can satisfy its obligations to the frag-mented, highly competitive magazine publishing industry is to impose more rules and higher rates for greater systemwide efficiency. Although the USPS's commit-ment to streamlining its operations is genuine, many publishers are uneasy about entering a new century in lock-step with a system still playing catch-up with the century about to be left behind. Their unease is deepened by the USPS's evident determination to make the industry's mail distribution strategies fit the postal sys-tem's plans for self-overhaul. This carrot-and-stick approach carries economic con-sequences that could recruit more publishers for the private, alternative-distribution networks that have sprung up to challenge the federally protected hegemony of the postal service (to the extent that the rules will let them).

To be fair to the USPS, it does a reasonable and frequently admirable job of conveying better than 80 percent of what the magazine industry produces to hun-dreds of millions of subscribers in America's homes and offices every day. (The other 20 percent of total circulation consists of single-copy sales through news-stands and other retail outlets.) Most magazines that distribute by mail try to take advantage of the postal service's second-class rates for periodicals, a category that is considerably cheaper than first-class rates for letter mail. To qualify for second class, a publication must contain a specified amount of editorial; be able to show that most of its circulation is paid or requested; and file annual circulation state-ments with the USPS.

The magazine industry currently pays about $2.5 billion a year in second-class postage.[69] To the industry's perennial dismay, the figure keeps going up. In three "rate cases" (requests for increases) filed and won by the postal service from 1988 to 1995, second-class rates rose 55 percent.[70] The USPS offers partial rate relief to publishers through *work sharing*, an incentive concept it began promoting in the early 1990s. Work sharing includes presorting magazines to conform as closely as possible to "walk sequence"—the path the mail carrier takes as he or she delivers mail to each address on the route. It also involves making mailing pieces more mechanically compatible with automated mailing equipment at post offices and postal distribution centers. Publishers who are able to assist the USPS in these ways are rewarded with lowered postal costs.[71]

Some second-class mailers have benefited from work sharing, but many others have not. What the postal service regards as efficient sorting may assume that a certain volume of magazines is deliverable to each route—a requirement that many a small-circulation title would be hard put to satisfy. Magazines do not take easily to automated handling, either. They come in too many different sizes and weights; some gum up the works with polybags, *outserts*, and other machine stoppers. As a result, most magazine publishers can do little against cost increases except to protest whatever new rate case happens to be before the Postal Rate Commission (PRC, the body that passes judgment on the request). Scant wonder that in 1995, the executive vice of the Magazine Publishers of America was obliged to conclude that "costs for all magazine publishers, large and small, will continue to rise, disproportionately to costs in other classes, as long as their mail continues to be handled manually and shipped long distances through the postal system."[72]

Nevertheless, the USPS has stuck fast to its notion of work sharing as the quid pro quo for rate relief, at least with respect to presorting. In 1995, it went to the PRC with a proposal to require second-class periodicals to presort at least 90 percent of their copies to three-digit ZIP codes or better, with a minimum density of 24 copies per bundle for each three-digit ZIP code to which the publication is mailed. (The first three digits in a ZIP code pinpoint the neighborhood or district in which the addressee is located; sorting bundles in this way expedites delivery.) This requirement—targeted to take effect in 1997 if approved—would create two new categories within second class: a "publications service" subclass with rates up to 14 percent lower for "highly efficient" mailers able to meet or exceed the 90 percent/24-copy cutoff; and a "regular periodicals" subclass for the less efficient, who could see their rates increase by as much as 17 percent. [73]

In presenting the plan to the PRC, the USPS argued that having two tiers in second class would help the postal system bring rates into line with costs and spread publishers' mailing costs more equitably. The industry, however, fell to arguing over whether the proposal might not merely be an attempt to subsidize big mailers at the expense of small ones. Foreseeing savings from the plan, publishers of mass-circulation titles readily acknowledged its good sense. Many (though not all) smaller publishers denounced it as unjust for imposing requirements that their limited circulations all but guaranteed they could not meet.

For individual and group publishers of small-circulation magazines, no news of postal rate increases can ever be good news. The USPS proposal of 1995, capping a year of publishing cost inflation driven by unprecedented increases in paper prices, seemed gloomy news indeed. Some industry observers predicted that a 17 percent postal rate hike would erode the average small publisher's already-slender profit margin to a point where the likelihood of business failure could not be ruled out.[74] Others reported that most magazines with national subscriber bases under 50,000 could not avoid paying more, since their circulations were spread too thinly to let them meet the density requirement for presorting.[75] Even multi-title houses mailing millions of copies in total found they were vulnerable—a realization that turned them into staunch opponents of the plan.[76] For example, the director of distribution for Cahners Publishing complained of the unfairness of being locked out of the discount subclass because Cahners—America's largest publisher of specialized business-to-business magazines—did not circulate enough copies of most of its titles to qualify it for "publications service" rates.[77]

If the USPS proposal put long faces on potential losers, it also left luckier publishers grinning in anticipation of a savings windfall. Small-circulation regional and city magazines stood to benefit from the fact that they mail most of their copies within tightly defined areas, assuring qualification for the discount subclass.[78] Publishers of high-volume, nationally circulated titles turned gleefully to their spreadsheets to see how much money would drop to their bottom lines by mailing at the publications-service rate. Time Warner Inc. reportedly could savor the prospect of cutting its mailing costs for *Time* and *People* by $16 million a year. The *Wall Street Journal,* which mails 600,000 copies (40 percent of its total circulation) every business day, was said to be looking at a $7 million annual savings as a "highly efficient" mailer of periodicals.[79]

Adopted as proposed, a second-class rate structure that arbitrarily divides the efficient from the not efficient would leave publishers branded as the latter scant hope of dodging a painful rate increase. In theory, a magazine without enough circulation to qualify for the efficient-mailer discount on its own might earn it by comailing with another publication or as part of a group of publications. If the numbers and destinations melded properly, the joint mailing would then have the density needed for sorting as per the 24-copy/90 percent requirement. The comailed issues would have to be identical in size, weight, and shape.[80] Naturally, they would also have to be ready to mail at the same time.

How well would comailing work in practice? Publishers are skeptical, foreseeing unavoidable and possibly insurmountable obstacles to keeping multiple magazines on the same delivery schedule.[81] At most magazines—including the best-managed ones—making a mailing date can be a thing of blood, toil, tears, and sweat even without having to stew over snafus in somebody else's production workflow. Time-sensitive publications—such as news weeklies, or those carrying dated advertising—would find it particularly difficult to justify the risk of gambling on comailing arrangements beyond their complete control. If just one magazine in the pool chokes on its production timetable, everyone else gags on the delay.[82]

As this was being written, the Postal Rate Commission was still considering second-class restructuring and other elements of the rate case then before it on behalf of the USPS. But regardless of its fate, this controversial scheme will have been just another in a continuing series of attempts to make magazine distribution conform to what the USPS sees as its long-term economic and operational imperatives. Outwardly, publishers may chafe at the pressure and dispute the rationale. Realistically, they know that they have no choice but to study the revisions and obey the rules if they want to keep on seeing their magazines delivered to America's mailboxes—where only the USPS may lawfully deposit mail of any kind.

The nation's doorknobs and doorsteps, however, are not off-limits to the delivery of periodicals by carriers other than the USPS. Newspapers and publishers of advertising circulars have distributed their products this way for years. Now magazine publishers, increasingly unhappy with their forcible involvement in the costly complications of postal-service reform, are looking seriously at private or alternative delivery as a means of at least partial escape.

Alternative delivery for magazines is an offshoot of established networks for newspaper home delivery. The two leading private-delivery companies, Alternate Postal Delivery Inc. (APD) and Publishers Express (PubX), use local newspaper delivery services as carriers for their clients' publications. Through signing up additional local carriers, APD expected to be represented in 115 major markets and PubX in 75 markets by the end of 1995.

Because locally owned newspaper delivery services are adept at delivering promotional materials as well as periodicals, they have helped publishers to find new ways of offering value-added services to advertisers. For example, in a private distribution of *Family Circle,* copies of the magazine were packaged in plastic bags along with literature for an airline and a hotel chain (both of which had display advertisements in the issue). The cost of the extra exposure was modest: only 10 cents per promotional piece. [83]

Publishers have found that the cost of alternative delivery can be 10 to 40 percent less than USPS rates for the same service. However, despite its economy and flexibility, alternative delivery has drawbacks. One disadvantage, as already noted, is that private carriers cannot place magazines in mailboxes, which are reserved for delivery by the USPS. Instead, privately distributed magazines must be left to the mercy of the elements on doorsteps and in driveways. And because alternative distribution works best along residential, suburban delivery routes, it is not necessarily a good choice for magazines with other distribution requirements—for example, a high concentration of delivery in urban areas.[84]

Although private delivery shows some promise, it still is struggling to prove itself a viable method of large-scale distribution for magazines. Certainly, the private-delivery industry poses no present threat to the USPS, which dwarfs it in terms of both reach and revenue. But as long as rate-case filings continue, so will publishers' interest in alternative delivery. Its full evolution as a distribution channel will be triggered by the postal rate increase that, come when it finally may, goes a step beyond what the industry believes it should be obliged to endure. The timing of that step, if it is inevitable, belongs to the USPS, not to the magazine publishing industry.

## "SMEARING INK ON DEAD TREES": WHY MAGAZINE PUBLISHERS ARE ENVIRONMENTALLY CHALLENGED, AND HOW THEY GOT THAT WAY

Q: What is this, where is it, and what has it to do with the business of publishing magazines?

Its mass, estimated at 100 million tons, and its volume, estimated at 2.9 billion cubic feet, make it one of the largest man-made structures in North America...[(when shut down)] in the year 2005, [(it)] will have reached a height of 505 feet above sea level, making it the highest geographic feature along a fifteen-hundred-mile stretch of the Atlantic seaboard running north from Florida all the way to Maine...It is 25 times the size of the Great Pyramid of Khufu at Giza...[(its)] volume...is approaching that of the Great Wall of China.[85]

A: It's the Fresh Kills landfill on Staten Island in New York City—a national magazine-publishing center. The awe-inspiring dimensions of Fresh Kills ought to leave magazine publishers everywhere feeling a bit like reluctant pharaohs, because the product they manufacture has had a great deal to do with making Fresh Kills the wonder of the world that it is today.

Paper, claim the authors of the Fresh Kills profile cited above, accounts for more than 40 percent of the contents of the average landfill. Most of the paper waste from periodicals consists of old newspapers. Discarded magazines furnish about 1.2 percent of the recipe for a landfill—a comparatively small amount, but still equal to the recipe's share of fast-food packaging and polystyrene foam combined.[86] If this estimate is correct, then simple arithmetic suggests that 1.2 million tons of what's poking into the sky over Fresh Kills is unrecycled product that the magazine industry has shoehorned into an already overburdened environment.

Paper—buried in landfills, chopped to bits by shredders, tossed by the roadside—is the long-lasting evidence of the uncomfortable part that the magazine industry plays in America's increasingly frustrating waste-disposal scenario. Magazines, like many other paper products, do not break down when consigned to a landfill. Out of sight, but not out of the biosphere, they "mummify"[87] into a permanent volume of refuse that hastens the day when the landfill must be declared packed to capacity and subject to closure. And although fears of a looming landfill crisis are exaggerated, the public still turns a suspicious eye on periodical publishers when informed (for example) that by the year 2003, the country will have only 1,500 of the 20,000 landfills it could blithely truck trash to in 1978.[88]

Magazines are neither the most numerous nor the most voluminous throwaway items now clogging the national waste stream. However, there is no escaping the fact that if Americans read fewer of them, we would be consuming considerably less than the 700 pounds per capita of paper per year that the environmentalists say we consume. Given its necessarily bottomless appetite for paper, the magazine publishing industry finds itself wide open to charges that its profits come from "smearing ink on dead trees" and from other crimes against ecology. Take the following indictment. It came not from a foe of the magazine publishing industry but from the publisher of an environmental magazine:

> Magazine publishing is not what you'd call a very environmentally friendly industry. Considering the paper on which we print, the inks we use, the photographic processes we apply to generate films and plates, the junk mail we send to promote and bill—we're all big-time polluters.... If we were all perfect in our commitment to a clean environment, then in good conscience we would have to stop publishing our magazines. The conventional method of applying ink to paper to produce a product is antithetical to a true green ethic.[89]

This publisher isn't alone in his searing criticism of the manufacturing methods he uses. *Sierra* magazine, which is as committed to safeguarding the environment as it is possible for a periodical to be, reached similar conclusions when it scrutinized the nature of its own raw materials. "At present," wrote the editors, "there are no 100 percent ecologically sound choices for publishers of magazines printed, as ours is, on coated paper—only difficult compromises."[90] For *Sierra,* the "100 percent ecologically sound" option would be to print on recycled paper with at least 30 percent postconsumer content (defined below) that contains totally chlorine-free virgin pulp from second-growth (naturally self-replenishing) forests or plantations. But *Sierra* discovered that a source of supply for paper meeting all of these criteria did not exist in North America.[91]

That is not the only aspect of magazine manufacturing that *Sierra* found disturbing. It also lamented the fact that glossy paper was so heavily used in the four million tons of magazines discarded by U.S. readers every year. Glossy paper, according to *Sierra,* is only about two-thirds paper. The rest consists of clays, fillers, adhesives, and coatings that make magazine pages more printable, better looking, and longer lasting—at the price of making them difficult, if not impossible, to recycle.[92]

By adopting more ecologically sensitive production methods, concerned publications such as *Sierra* have tried to show that magazine manufacturing need not be an unmitigated insult to the environment. In the early 1990s, for example, Rodale Press, the publisher of *Prevention, Men's Health, Backpacker, Bicycling,* and other salubrious special-interest titles, switched all of its magazines to recycled paper with a minimum postconsumer content of 10 percent. Rodale even required its paper suppliers to sign affidavits guaranteeing recycled content and place of origin.[93] *Audubon* began using various recycled papers with the publication of its March/April 1992 issue.[94] Around then, Time Inc. was in the process of switching six of its magazines—*Entertainment Weekly, Parenting, Health, Hippocrates, Sunset*, and the Canadian edition of *Time*—to recycled paper.[95]

Proponents of recycling say that decisions like these have helped the economy as well as the environment. According to Conservatree Paper Co., a dealer of recycled papers, making a ton of new paper from 100 percent wastepaper saves 1,700 trees; enough electricity to power the average home for six months; 60 pounds of air pollutants; three cubic yards of landfill space; and taxes that would have been paid for waste disposal.[96]

Magazine audiences seem to like recycled papers, although it probably is fair to say that they are less interested in the papers per se than in publishers' assurances that only recycled stocks are being used. In any event, Rodale Press received no complaints about print quality from either readers or advertisers when it changed to environmentally friendly grades.[97] *Audubon* asked its readers to comment on trade-offs in reproduction quality that might stem from the changeover to recycled paper; it even alerted them to specific things to look for. Judging from the low level of response, the editors concluded that most readers either did not know or care that anything was different.[98]

Nevertheless, admirable as they are, the policies of *Sierra*, Rodale Press, *Audubon*, and other like-minded publishing operations are only scattered (and, as will be seen in the case of Rodale, temporary) exceptions to the rule. In 1990, only 21 percent of publishers responding to a Magazine Publishers of America survey reported using any recycled paper in their magazines.[99] The situation would not change much as the decade wore on. Today, a true, industry-wide commitment to recycled paper remains an environmentalist's dream—a bright green ideal thwarted by complications of supply-and-demand economics that the magazine publishing industry sees as outside its control. Publishers say that paper manufacturers do not produce enough recycled paper at prices they can afford. The papermakers reply that supplies are down and prices are up because the market is not strong enough to justify their investing in equipment to make more recycled paper. Federal and state lawmakers impose paper-consumption and recycling requirements aimed at creating demand where demand would not otherwise exist. Critics chide everyone for stinginess, timidity, or worse. The nation's landfills, meanwhile, continue to fill up and shut down.

Even the basic terms of the debate are not always clear. To the reading public, for example, "recycling" magazines may simply mean sorting and bundling them for pickup in accordance with local laws. But the recycling of paper or of any other discarded substance is not complete until the sorted, bundled, and collected material has been remanufactured into something that can be sold, and is sold, back to the public.[100] Recycling magazine paper, in other words, is a commercial transaction that cannot benefit the environment unless it makes sense to willing sellers and buyers from the standpoint of profit and loss.

The term *recycled paper* also has more than one dimension. Basically, it is new paper made entirely or partially of already-manufactured paper. But the "old" paper that mills recycle into new paper is of two distinctly different types:

- "postconsumer waste," or paper that has been printed and put to an end use. It includes used corrugated boxes, old newspapers and magazines, discarded copy paper, and other kinds of printed matter commonly found in household and business trash.
- "preconsumer waste," or unprinted, unused paper that never got the chance to be discarded by consumers in the first place. Preconsumer waste includes leftovers from the papermaking process; envelope cuttings; bindery trimmings; butt rolls (partially used rolls of printing stock that do not have enough paper left for another job); rejected stock; and obsolete inventories from paper mills, paper merchants, printers, and converters (for example, envelope manufacturers). [101]

More postconsumer than preconsumer waste goes into landfills. Many environmentally minded consumers who understand the difference between the two believe that any paper wishing to call itself recycled should count only its postconsumer content toward the definition.[102] For these purists, in other words, a paper cannot legitimately be called recycled if its recovered ingredients have preconsumer origins.

Paper manufacturers, in their rush to bring eco-sensitive products to market, seldom drew the same nice distinctions that the purists drew. And rush to market they did: in 1993, for example, the nation's mills produced five times as many different kinds of recycled papers as they had in 1988. The difficulty for environmentalists was that the recycled content of many of those 400 papers consisted mostly of preconsumer scrap.[103] But the mills were doing nothing illegal or even necessarily deceptive: A universally accepted formula for defining recycled papers by their content simply did not exist.

Paper mills, paper users, and paper conservationists are still groping toward a workable definition. Some want the paper industry to adopt an A-B-C self-ranking system that would award the best marks to papers with the highest proportion of recycled content from postconsumer sources.[104] Others say that paper products should be labeled like packaged foods, with their pre- and postconsumer percentages clearly displayed. Others would control the use of the "chasing-arrow" logo that consumers are now used to seeing on paper and paper products claimed to contain recycled ingredients. Critics of the logo point out that it says nothing about the ingredients' pre- versus postconsumer origins. It cannot even guarantee that a given paper contains any recycled material in the first place, since there is no scientific test to prove content.[105]

A cynic might say that one way to settle the question is to pick up a magazine or a piece of direct-mail advertising—you would then be pretty certain of encountering no recycled content at all. In 1990, according to some estimates, less than six percent of printing and writing (P-W) paper had any recycled content. That percentage was predicted to improve to less than 10 percent by 2001. In the meantime, six million tons a year of high-grade P-W paper for magazines and third-class mail—80 percent of the total produced—would be sent straight to the landfill with never a thought of its being recycled into anything. [106]

This is hardly a record to brag about. Why does the magazine industry seem so resistant to recycled papers when the environmental urgency and the social desirability of using them seem so great? What environmentalists often do not see is that publishers cannot avoid basing the decision on price, because paper represents so much of the cost of producing a magazine. The plain fact is that even in the most favorable of paper-market conditions, recycled papers are no bargains. They cost the mills more to produce than virgin stocks, so they cost publishers more to buy— conservatively, six to eight percent more.[107] Their premium pricing makes them especially difficult to cost-justify in tight paper markets, no matter how sincere a publisher's initial determination to switch.

To be sure, some environmentally minded publishers have learned this lesson the hard way. For a time after converting its magazines from virgin to recycled, Rodale Press either broke even or saved a modest amount of money on paper costs.[108] Then came the paper crunch of 1995. That year brought an unusually tight market that sent the prices of all publishing papers soaring—but the prices of recycled papers most of all. Before the year was out, Rodale had announced that five of its leading magazines would be switched back to virgin-fiber paper. Time Inc. also informed its readers that it had been forced to "rethink" plans to print its mass-circulation titles on recycled paper.[109]

It is never easy to square the cost of using recycled papers with the roller-coaster economics of magazine publishing. In recessionary times, when advertising withers and page counts shrink, falling demand for paper of all kinds may cause recycled-paper prices to drop to more competitive levels. In such lean times, however, publishers will be interested in nothing but the best deals for paper they can get—deals that may have nothing to do with recycled papers. In the view from the landfill, economic upturns for the magazine business may be just as unhelpful. As was seen in 1995, when ad page counts began to bounce back, a recovery can trigger surges in demand and price that make recycled papers even less attractive.

The up-and-down behavior of the national economy also complicates matters at the source of supply, which is where publishers say criticism realistically should be focused. To recycle old magazine paper into new, paper mills must first de-ink the printed waste so that its pulp can be recovered for reuse. But installing or upgrading de-inking facilities requires multimillion-dollar, multiyear capital investment projects that papermakers say they are hard put to justify when trends are uncertain and overall demand is low. Often, what de-inked pulp there is goes not to the manufacture of P-W paper but to other markets such as paper tissues and towels.[110] Magazine publishers, therefore, see little reason to believe that ample quantities of competitively priced recycled papers will be available to them anytime soon. Until supplies and prices improve, they contend, their industry should not bear sole blame for paper's contribution to the nation's solid-waste disposal problems.[111]

Except, perhaps, for conscience-driven publications such as *Sierra* and *Audubon,* magazine publishers tend to look at printing on recycled papers as a production-cost issue first and an environmental obligation second. As believers in letting free markets set their own guidelines, most publishers reject the idea of government-imposed standards for the use of recycled papers. But they also have enough political sophistication to know that if they do not move voluntarily in this direction, lawmakers will furnish the impetus in ways they probably will not like. This view is shared even by publishers who have already committed to recycled papers. One such publisher, Rodale Press, has stated that it "would be very unfortunate if the government established recycling percentages and made it impossible for small publishers to comply and stay competitive.... It's incumbent on the publishing industry to...put pressure on the mills and work with them to come up with solutions to the volume question."[112]

Of course, there are sharp and predictable divisions of opinion about how the solutions ought to be worked out. Publishers and paper manufacturers want formulas for setting recycled-content percentages that will let them include fibers recovered from preconsumer materials. Environmental groups, on the other hand, are calling for mandated postconsumer minimums and strict language that would rule out counting certain materials—for example, printed but unsold magazines—toward the definition of postconsumer waste.[113]

All parties to the debate know that the eyes of elected and appointed regulators are upon them. Magazine publishers, suspecting themselves to be "high on many legislative hit lists,"[114] have learned to take the federal government's recycling initiatives seriously. In October 1993, for example, both the magazine publishing and papermaking industries were distressed to learn that the Clinton administration had placed stiff requirements on printing and writing papers procured for federal agencies and the military. The order decreed that by the end of 1994, this paper—some 300,000 tons purchased annually—would have to consist of least 20 percent recycled fiber from postconsumer material, with the volume to rise to 30 percent by the end of 1998. Although the order applied only to uncoated paper, it was, according to one printing industry newsletter, "expected to severely limit the availability of recycled paper for non-government work."[115]

More disturbingly, the order was seen as a model that might further encourage state and local governments to concoct recycled-paper mandates of their own—a trend that was already stitching together "a crazy quilt of regulations that could cause big headaches for national publications."[116] By the mid-1990s, the states' determination to influence the environmental aspects of magazine manufacturing was clear:

- As of January 1, 1994, Minnesota required publishers to use recycled-content paper and inks free of heavy metal and other toxic substances, and to use binding materials that presented "no unreasonable barriers to recycling."
- California required publications labeled as "recycled" to contain at least 10 percent postconsumer material.
- New York State sought regulations to have printing and writing papers contain a minimum of at least 50 percent recovered materials.
- Wisconsin moved to bar magazines, catalogs, and similar materials from state landfills beginning in 1995.[117]

Attitudes toward intervening on behalf of the environment can change, and regulatory zeal at all levels of government waxes and wanes with the national mood. Nevertheless, actions like these should serve to remind every publisher that no matter where magazines are circulated, local lawmakers have the means and frequently the inclination to dictate how much recycled paper magazines should contain. And as if worries about the avenging of "dead trees" were not enough, publishers must also beware of what environmentalists and lawmakers think of the ink they are accused of smearing on the remains. Printing inks, together with coatings and other chemical substances used in print production, draw the magazine publishing industry into the regulatory realm of toxic pollutants—a bureaucratic swamp even harder to cross than the forest of rules pertaining to paper.

Magazines contain or are made with the help of various toxic pollutants—materials that, in certain concentrations, are believed to be harmful to plant and animal life. Organic pollutants such as benzene, carbon tetrachloride, and isopropyl alcohol are used as solvents or in fountain solution as part of the lithographic printing process. Metallic pollutants include the "heavy metals": lead, mercury, silver, and chromium. Many inks contain heavy metals for color and body. Silver is a by-product of litho film processing. All told, about 30 percent of the 126 toxic pollutants listed by the federal Environmental Protection Agency (EPA) can be found in printing and publishing operations. [118]

The chief concern of the EPA and other agencies is determining how these pollutants affect the quality of air emissions from printing operations. Inks, fountain solutions, cleaning solvents, and bindery adhesives are known to generate quantities of volatile organic compounds, or VOCs, through natural evaporation and heat-set drying. VOCs—which are by no means exclusive to printing—contribute to air pollution. But no one knows how much of the VOC content in the average pall of urban smog can be traced to printing. Even the testing methods for measuring VOC emissions are in dispute.

The federal government, wishing to take no chances, made printers subject to its 1990 Clean Air Act Amendments requiring all "major sources" of air pollution to conform to a complex set of operating requirements. Under these rules, every printer deemed capable of emitting at least 10 tons of VOCs per year would have to obtain a permit, report its VOC output, and install antipollution "control technologies" specified by the EPA. Printers in EPA-designated "ozone non-attainment areas"—that is to say, America's most smog-bound cities—faced the most stringent requirements.[119]

States and localities declared air-quality regulations of their own, many of them even tougher than the ones handed down from Washington. Threatened with heavy fines and plant closures for noncompliance, printers everywhere took steps to reduce the real and perceived chemical hazards of their day-to-day operations. With the help of graphic arts film manufacturers, they installed silver-recovery systems to extract that heavy metal from spent photo-processing solutions (which then could be poured safely and lawfully down any drain). They switched to alcohol-free fountain solutions and to press washes that substituted natural citrus essences for harmful solvents. They experimented with low-VOC inks in which the "vehicle"— the oil that carries the pigment—was derived not from petroleum but from soybeans and other vegetables.

Each of these steps has had its effect upon the quality, efficiency, and economics of magazine production. A detailed discussion of the effects is beyond the scope of the present work, but the message to both current and future production specialists should be clear. Magazine readers and the officials who represent them want magazines to be more "environmentally responsible" according to rules that they, not the magazine industry, will lay down. This means that every magazine should be ready with a plan for its "next incarnation" as a product designed specifically for recycling.[120] Recycling-oriented design and production may dictate considerable change in the industry's choice of raw materials and manufacturing methods; but the change, when it comes, will have to be faced. "Smearing ink on dead trees" is not a joke for publishers to laugh off. It is an undercurrent of unhappiness that only publishers can keep from turning into a mass of outrage as overwhelming as the mountains of trash they are helping to build not just at Great Kills but wherever people are discarding their old magazines to make room for the next issue.

## CAREER PATHS: HAVING AND GETTING
## WHAT IT TAKES TO BE EMPLOYED IN MAGAZINES

As mass-communications media go, magazine publishing is neither an especially large employer nor a runaway engine of job growth. At the beginning of 1995, employment in the periodicals industry—including magazines, comics, journals, and television guides—stood at about 130,200, or roughly the same as it had been four years earlier.[121] Given the small size of the total labor pool, few magazines will face much risk of being criticized for overstaffing. In other words, jobs are hard to come by and there's much competition for both entry level positions and promotion in the editorial, advertising, circulation, production, and general management ranks.

What distinguishes the role models from the misfits in this industry? Certainly, professional competence—mastery of the tools and techniques surveyed in this book—is a foundation of success. But other skills are just as important. We've seen that editors need to have a passion for writing and ideas; publishers must be inspiring leaders, production specialists must be wizards from the desktop to the pressroom, advertising pros need to have enthusiasm, stamina, and expertise in a variety of marketing techniques. In fact, those who have succeeded in magazine publishing are rightly admired for their ability to:

- Stay abreast of changing technologies through personal initiative and continuous self-improvement.
- Understand and support the other publishing functions. Editors should understand production techniques; production directors must understand the pressures attendant on circulation and advertising directors.
- Grasp and apply the principles of financial management cost reduction. No one—not art directors, salespeople, circulation directors, or editors—can hope to succeed without understanding the importance of budgeting.
- Manage people both in their own departments and in others with tact, diplomacy, and firmness. The importance of "people" skills should never be underestimated in magazine publishing. This is a communications business. Publishers, production directors, circulation directors, editors, and advertising directors will all be called on at one time or another to play the ombudsperson's or mediator's role.

Developing talents like these is the work of a lifetime, and most of your professional development will take place on the job, not in the lecture room. Nevertheless, there are ways in which students of magazines can begin building their skills even before employment enters the picture. Here is a short course of self-help steps and information resources; any beginner can profit from following these seven steps.

1. **Study magazines—and the magazine-reading public.** Spend time browsing at the newsstand. Watch what other people are reading on trains and what they're buying at the grocery store. Really get to know your favorite magazines. Study the mix of articles, design, and advertising. Become familiar with writers and their style. Look carefully at the paper quality and reproduction. Even take a few extra minutes to examine the direct-mail solicitations from magazines that arrive in your mailbox.

2. **Find ways to do what you love.** If you want to be a production director and you've never flowed text into a QuarkXPress template or savored the aroma of fresh ink in a pressroom; if you want to work in advertising sales and you've never experienced the thrill of closing a sale; if you want to be an editor and you haven't personally gone through the process of seeing your idea for a story appear in print, your education still has a long, long way to go. As you probably have come to suspect from plowing your way through these chapters, just reading what somebody else has written about advertising, editorial, circulation, or production is not enough. Reading is important—it furnishes the underlying concepts and keeps you abreast of changes in the field. But in order to grasp how magazines work as an interconnected sequence of steps and events, you have to see a magazine in operation. You don't need to wait until you've landed your first paying job in publishing to begin acquiring this valuable experience. Take an internship or an apprenticeship—with or without pay—at a newspaper, a magazine, a printing plant, or another establishment where you can get hands-on lessons. Join the staff of a campus or community publication and be the person willing to put in late nights. Find out if your house of worship publishes a newsletter or bulletin, and volunteer to sell advertising for it. Don't worry if your preemployment training doesn't appear to match the kind of magazine work that you would eventually like to do. The practical insights you will gain into deadline pressure, workflow management, quality control, and other publishing necessities will serve you well no matter where your career in magazine publishing takes you.

3. **Own and operate a computer equipped for desktop publishing.** The sooner you familiarize yourself with the basics of word processing, page layout, and publication graphics, the sooner your career will start to take shape. A personal computer is not a small investment, but for students of

publishing it is a necessary one. There simply is no substitute for having a machine of your own to practice on or undertake "real" assignments with whenever the opportunity should arise. Read the popular computing magazines to learn what kinds of hardware and software you will need. If you are already working in publishing or graphic arts production, ask if your employer will subsidize your purchase of a home computer either by rebating some of the cost or by making an interest-free loan to cover your cash outlay. Alternatively, your company may be able to arrange a discount on your purchase from the computer dealer it buys its own publishing equipment from. Because Macintoshes remain the platforms of choice for professional magazine production, buying a Mac to acquire Mac skills makes sense in the long run. But bear in mind that other models can do what Macs do, and that non-Mac platforms dominate the business side of many publishing operations. Let your budget be your guide. The important thing is to waste no time in getting comfortable with the tool that you will not put down for as long as you remain in magazine production. When it comes to computers, your comfort level is your employment edge.

4. **Consider your options for education.**
*Editorial*
Usually, the big decision a person with editorial aspirations must make when it comes to education is whether to study in a liberal arts environment, a specific field, or go to journalism school. For editorial work, it's essential to possess a firm command of language and have exceptional skill in writing and editing. Either a strong liberal arts education or journalism training can provide this. Some successful editors and writers have majored in English literature or history or economics or the classics. Some have gone on to get a graduate degree in a field of interest to them—or in journalism. Others have an undergraduate journalism degree. Still others have no particular academic training. Just as important as a good grounding in writing and journalism is a variety of experiences. Travel. Read widely. Expose yourself to different cultural perspectives. Cultivate a broad worldview. An inquisitive mind and a willingness to explore are most valuable to people who traffic in ideas. If you're out of college or in mid-career, writing and editing workshops or classes can help you hone your skills, develop your interests, and learn what it is to work with someone who is critiquing your writing and style. Continuing-education classes in these areas are usually offered at local colleges and universities. Many communities also have writing workshops of varying size and intensity—and writing classes are often most valuable because they force you to set aside time for writing, which can sometimes be difficult in busy, overscheduled lives. As we've seen, the educational path of professionals in magazine editorial departments takes many different directions. If you want to be an editor specializing in a part of the

world or in a specific cultural or technical field, you'll need to attain appropriate experience and knowledge in that area. This also applies to people starting out in entry level jobs. Fact checkers who speak more than one language are especially valued in research departments.

*Advertising*

Advertising sales jobs at magazines can be very lucrative as well as exciting. A strict business education or advanced course work in advertising or marketing is not required but is helpful. Prospective sales people should have a facility with numbers and be familiar with marketing principles. Because this part of the business involves a high level of personal contact and negotiating skills, an education in psychology doesn't hurt, either. Advertising directors at magazines prize salespeople with strong presentation skills—people who can argue persuasively and articulately, who can capture the attention of a roomful of people, who have a pleasing telephone manner—all tend to move quickly up the ladder in magazine sales. To work in sales at a specialized magazine (such as a medical journal or computer publication) you might do well to study further in the area in which you'll concentrate. You'll be meeting and entertaining clients who have made this field their lifework, and you should be able to converse with them intelligently and knowledgeably.

*Circulation*

Like their colleagues in advertising, circulation executives don't require a specialized course of study but should have a facility with computers, budgeting programs, and direct marketing concepts. Many circulation professionals have advanced degrees in business. Another good way to be exposed to the actual work that an advertising or circulation executive engages in is to enroll in one of the intensive, hands-on magazine publishing programs that are offered around the country. In many of these programs, which can take place full time over the summer or part-time over the course of a couple of years, students get practical experience in producing a magazine from editorial concept through circulation marketing to selling advertising. Working professionals lecture, lead workshops, and evaluate students' work. Many also become valuable professional contacts for those who are job hunting. Among the courses available are the Radcliffe Publishing Course (Cambridge, Mass.), Stanford Publishing Course (Stanford, Calif.), Rice University Publishing Course (Houston, Tex.), and the publishing programs offered through the schools of continuing education at New York University and the University of Chicago.

*Production*

For centuries—and the closing years of the present one are no exception—the teaching of production skills has favored the master-to-apprentice model, with newcomers to the trade gaining most of their expertise from one-on-one, on-the-job instruction by veterans. For this reason, the disciplines of the graphic arts are not as widely represented in the academic world as other bodies of occupational knowledge. However, accredited and respected training in print production is available from a number of colleges and universities, including Rochester Institute of Technology's School of Printing Management and Sciences (Rochester, N.Y.); New York University's Center for Graphic Communications Management & Technology (New York, N.Y.); Drexel University (Philadelphia, Pa.); Carnegie-Mellon University (Pittsburgh, Pa.); and California Polytechnic State University (San Luis Obispo, Calif.). Community colleges frequently offer structured programs of study in the graphic arts, accompanied by local job-placement services.

Wherever your interests lie, get as much advance information about an educational program as you can. Read college catalogs and talk with educational counselors. Ask friends and acquaintances in publishing where they received their training. Most printing and publishing trade associations are deeply involved in professional education; staff members at these organizations should be able to offer helpful suggestions. Look for programs taught by instructors who are working professionals—people whose primary employment in publishing, editing, writing, advertising, circulation, or the graphic arts keeps them in constant touch with industry trends and technological change. Be certain, also, that the school has enough up-to-date equipment to do a proper job of imparting the skills it claims to teach.

Not everyone who is successful in magazine publishing studied it in school. Nevertheless, the right kind of academic training can be a tremendous asset to a budding career. It should figure, now or later, in your own plans.

5. **Start reading.** No matter how or where you acquire your knowledge of magazines, no one is going to spoon-feed you—least of all when the information you picked up last year (or last month) starts to change. Excuses have no place: Your employers and your co-workers will simply expect you to know what is going on if it has anything to do with improving or economizing the operation. Career-wise, staying ahead of the technological curve is a responsibility to take seriously. One of the best ways to outrun personal obsolescence is to keep pace with the professional literature of your industry—its business publications. These include: *Folio:*, *Media Week*, *Advertising Age*, *Inside Media*, *Adweek*, *Magazine and Bookseller*. Many articles from these "magazines about magazines" have been cited in the preparation of these chapters. The same is true for the media coverage in daily newspapers. Both the *Wall Street Journal* and *New York Times* have extensive news coverage and commentary on media, publishing, and advertising—and should be required reading for you. All these publications are, and will continue to be, the publishing industry's leading sources of infor-

mation about new technologies and management methods. The time to begin a career-long habit of following them is now.

Of course, getting your hands on trade publications isn't easy if you're not working in the business, and subscription fees can be hefty. Check your library. Ask friends or colleagues working in the field if you can borrow their copies. If it's in your budget, a subscription can be a wise investment. You can start building a publishing bookshelf with any of the titles cited as source material for these chapters, but special mention must be given to *Pocket Pal/A Graphic Arts Production Handbook*. Published in 16 editions since 1934 by International Paper Company, the *Pocket Pal* probably has demystified printing technology for more people than all other books on the subject combined. This concise, illustrated, and inexpensive guide—continually updated to include new trends and developments—outlines every important aspect of print production in thorough but nontechnical style. It is highly recommended for anyone who designs, produces, buys, sells, or studies printing. For information about ordering, call (800) 854-3212.

6. **Ask the associations**. When Alexis de Tocqueville wrote about the natural tendency of Americans to form commercial societies and other common-interest groups, was he thinking prophetically about America's printers and publishers? Today, many of the nation's printing companies and magazine publishing houses are interlaced in a network of national and local trade associations—private, not-for-profit, voluntary groups chartered to advance the professional and business interests of the people and companies that belong to them. Because these organizations exist primarily to serve their memberships, the assistance they have to offer nonmembers is limited. However, they are good places to go for general information about the industry segments that support them, and they often conduct activities of interest to students and others pursuing careers in the printing and publishing fields.

Trade associations conduct their affairs from national headquarters; through affiliated regional associations (if they have any); or on both the national and local fronts. Their activities may include educational events such as evening schools; technical conferences; trade shows; career outreach programs; employment referral services; and visits to printing plants, paper mills, and other production facilities. Some groups publish newsletters and bulletins or operate mail-order bookstores carrying titles on production that are not easily obtainable elsewhere.

All of these services cost money, but some associations may offer discounts or other kinds of help to students and careerists. Groups to contact include:

**Magazine Publishers of America,** 919 Third Avenue, New York, N.Y. 10022; (212) 872-3700. MPA is the industry association for consumer magazines. It serves as an advocacy group for member publishers and is the leading source of statistical information about the magazine publishing industry. Along with the American Society of Magazine Editors, it sponsors the prestigious National Magazine Awards—the "Oscars" of the industry. Those with Internet access can see what the MPA offers by visiting its World Wide Web site at http://www.magazine.org

**City and Regional Magazine Association,** 58-20 Wilshire Blvd., Suite 500, Los Angeles, Calif. 90036; (213) 937-5514. CRMA is smaller than MPA but can help with questions about this special niche of magazines.

**Business Press Educational Foundation Inc./American Business Press,** 675 Third Avenue, New York, N.Y. 10017-5704; (212) 682-4410. BPEF was created by business magazine publishers to encourage careers in the specialized business press. Publications, teaching aids, and other resources for students and instructors are available.

**Printing Industries of America,** 100 Daingerfield Road, Alexandria, Va. 22314-2804; (703) 519-8100. PIA, the largest printing trade association, pursues an extensive agenda of educational, legislative, economic, and technical objectives from its national headquarters near Washington, D.C. PIA also has about two dozen regional affiliates across the country, each of which offers its own selection of member services. Ask which one serves your region.

**National Association of Printers and Lithographers,** 780 Palisade Avenue, Teaneck, N.J., 07666; (201) 342-0700. NAPL specializes in management training and development for printing and publishing operations of all kinds. It has an excellent selection of periodicals, mail-order books, audiovisual resources, and computer products. It also conducts production-focused seminars and conferences in various parts of the country throughout the year. NAPL's World Wide Web site is http://www.napl.org

**The International Association of Printing House Craftsmen,** 7042 Brooklyn Boulevard, Minneapolis, Minn. 55429-1370; (800) 466-4274, (612) 560-1620. IAPHC is the central headquarters for the Craftsmen "movement," a chain of local Craftsmen clubs in most major metropolitan areas. The men and women of the Craftsmen clubs uphold their motto, "Share Your Knowledge," through educational programs and other fraternal activities. Contact IAPHC for more information, or see its Web site at http://www.iaphc.org

**Graphic Arts Technical Foundation,** 4615 Forbes Avenue, Pittsburgh, Pa. 15213; (412) 621-6941. GATF is the graphic communications industry's premier source of information about the applied sciences of imaging, reproduction, and quality control. Textbooks published by GATF are the standards in their fields. GATF is also the host organization for the National Scholarship Trust Fund, an industry-supported program that dispenses college scholarships and graduate-fellowship assistance to those pursuing their careers in graphic communications. GATF's Web site, at http://www.gatf.lm.com, has all the details.

7. **Show potential employers and managers that you have the right stuff.** It sounds like basic, Job Hunting 101 advice—but it bears repeating. Make sure the people who make hiring and promotion decisions *know* you have the skills for the job you want. All too often a lapse in proofreading a résumé has cost someone a job. Yours should be 100 percent error-free, particularly if you are applying for an editorial position.

   Be sure to demonstrate that your experience can meet an employer's needs and solve his or her problems. The magazine industry thrives on punctuality, meeting deadlines, attention to detail, and creative ideas. It's not too early to start practicing these skills in your job hunting.

Use all these resources—now and throughout your career. Achievement in the magazine profession, as in any professional endeavor, is the product of thorough training, hard work, and good luck. If you prepare yourself for achievement by supplying the first two, the third is assured, because luck is what happens when preparation meets opportunity.[122]

May every professional success and personal satisfaction in magazines be yours!

## NOTES

[1]Statistics from *Wired* quoted by Peter Kupfer in "The New Generation of Cyberzines," *Folio:*, March 1, 1993, 60.

[2]Kevin Fogarty, "Publishing Firms Move Toward Future With Electronic Media," *Magazine Week,* March 23, 1992, 29.

[3]Lisa I. Fried, "Hundreds Laid Off As Whittle Focuses on Electronic Media," *Magazine Week,* May 25, 1992, 1.

[4]Dr. Bernard J. Luskin, Philips Interactive Media of North America, quoted by Sean Callahan in "New Media Dilemma," *Folio:*, March 1, 1993, 69.

[5]Jerry Borrell, "Electronic Magazines: Will You Read One?", *Magazine Week,* June 22, 1992, 102.

[6]*One Source: The Banta Resource Handbook/A Review of Current Imaging Technologies Affecting Major Print Markets* (Menasha, Wisc.: Banta Corporation, 1995), 52.

[7]Steve Bosak and Jeffrey Sloman, *The CD-ROM Book* (Indianapolis: Que Corporation, 1993), 10.

[8]*Seybold Special Report: Seybold San Francisco '94, Part I*, October 10, 1994, 10.

[9]*One Source: The Banta Resource Handbook*, 52.

[10]Todd Harris, "CD-ROMP," *Folio:*, February 15, 1995, 41.

[11]Lorne Manly, "The CD-ROM imperative," *Folio:*, March 15, 1994, 53–55.

[12]Lorne Manly, "CD-ROM-only titles gain momentum," *Folio:*, February 1, 1991, 16.

[13]Tim Bogardus, "CD-ROM category expands in scope," *Folio:* August 1, 1994, 24.

[14]Lorne Manly, "CD-ROM titles fail to catch fire," *Folio:*, August 1, 1995, 26.

[15]Manly, "CD-ROM titles fail to catch fire," 26.

[16]Donald D. Kummerfeld, "New media and magazines: Where do we go from here?", *Folio: Special Sourcebook Issue for 1995*, 241.

[17]Lorne Manly, "CD-ROM titles fail to catch fire," 26.

[18]Manly, "The CD-ROM imperative," 54.

[19]Kevin Fogarty, "Electronic Publishing Raises Questions, Doubts & Passions," *Magazine Week,* February 3, 1992, 11.

[20]Jerry Borell, "Electronic Magazines: Will You Read One?", *Magazine Week*, June 22, 1992, 102.

[21]Paul Ferguson, "On the Cyber Racks," *Internet World*, September 1995, 37.

[22]Reid Goldsborough, "News Paperless," *Internet World,* September 1995, 40.

[23]Bob Powell and Karen Wickre, *Atlas to the World Wide Web* (Emeryville, Calif.: Ziff-Davis Press, 1995), 164.

[24]Lorne Manly, "Weaving the world wide web," *Folio:*, February 15, 1995, 64.

[25]"Sponsoring Cyberspace: What's Its Cost?", *InterAd Monthly,* July 1995, 6.

[26]Lorne Manly, "Trades take to the I-way," *Folio:*, February 1, 1995, 20.

[27]Manly, "Trades take to the I-way," 20.

[28]"Pubs Making Move to the Web," *Seybold Special Report: Seybold Seminars Boston '95, Part I,* April 21, 1995, 11.

[29]Kummerfeld, "New Media and Magazines: Where Do We Go From Here?", 240.

[30]"Macworld Web Launch," *Macworld*, September 1995, 43.

[31]"Pubs Making Move to the Web," *Seybold Special Report*, 11.

[32]Manly, "Weaving the World Wide Web," 65.

[33]"HVP Forecast: 1995 Industry Economic Outlook," *High Volume Printing*, February 1995, 14–15.

[34]Barbara Love, "Online Advantage: Strong brand and a loyal customer base," *Folio:*, September 1, 1995, 10.

[35]Stefan Sharansky, "Unleash your magazine on the Internet," *Folio:*, February 15, 1995, 61.

[36]Kummerfeld, "New Media and Magazines: Where Do We Go From Here?", 241.

[37]Bruce Schwartz, "On-line Browsing Through Magazines," *USA Today,* November 10, 1994, 40.

[38]"Pubs Making Move to the Web," *Seybold Special Report*, 11-12.

[39]William F. Allman, "The 10 commandments of cyberspace," *Folio:*, September 15, 1995, 68.

[40]Veronis, Suhler & Associates, Inc., "Veronis, Suhler 9th Annual Communications Industry Forecast/Fact Sheet: Interactive Digital Media 1995–1999," August 3, 1995.

[41]Press release: "Veronis, Suhler 9th Annual Communications Industry Forecast/Fact Sheet," Veronis, Suhler & Associates Inc., New York, N.Y., August 3, 1995.

[42]Steve Lohr, "Who Uses Internet? 5.8 Million Are Said to Be Linked in U.S.," *The New York Times,* September 27, 1995.

[43]*Seybold Special Report: Seybold San Francisco '94, Part I,* October 10, 1994, 8.

[44]Steve Wilson, "Launch lag," *Folio:,* January 15, 1995, 44.

[45]"Pubs Making Move to the Web," *Seybold Special Report,* 12.

[46]Mark Nollinger, "America, Online!", *Wired,* September 1995, 160. (The figure of 20 million includes presumed users of the Microsoft Network, an on-line service bundled with Microsoft Corp.'s Windows 95, the best-selling operating system for personal computers.)

[47]Press release: "Finally, 20 to 30 Million Users on the Internet," Matrix Information & Directory Services, Austin, Tex., August 25, 1995.

[48]"How Big is the Internet?", *InterAd Monthly,* July 1995, 3.

[49]Lorraine Sileo, "Interchange Frustrates, But Is a Web-Only Strategy Much Better?", *Online Tactics,* October 1995, 11.

[50]"PC World Online Finds the Right Formula for Making Money," *Online Tactics,* October 1995, 7.

[51]All citations are from FAQs (frequently asked questions) and other information posted by The Electronic Newsstand, http://www.enews.com, September 10, 1995.

[52]Adam C. Engst and William Dickson, *Internet Explorer Kit for Macintosh* (Indianapolis: Hayden Books, 1994), 354.

[53]"Meredith sows cyberseeds," *Folio:,* August 1, 1995, 18.

[54]"Pubs Making Move to the Web," *Seybold Special Report,* 11.

[55]"Online Primer: Hits vs. Hype: The Lowdown on Site Traffic Stats," *InterAd Monthly,* July 1995, 9.

[56]"Consumer Publishing Online: New Markets or Money Losers?", *Online Tactics,* October 1995, 1.

[57]Lorne Manly, "Online ad pricing keeps publishers guessing," *Folio:,* May 15, 1995, 18.

[58]Manly, "Online ad pricing keeps publishers guessing," 18.

[59]Lorne Manly, "Web-site pricing draws criticism," *Folio:,* August 1, 1995, 20.

[60]Manly, "Online ad pricing keeps publishers guessing," 18.

[61]Kummerfeld, "New Media and Magazines: Where Do We Go From Here?", 241.

[62]Manly, "Web-site pricing draws criticism," 20.

[63]Lorne Manly, "Web issue worries publishers," *Folio:,* September 15, 1995, 27

[64]Lorne Manly, "Online auditing attracts many contenders," *Folio:,* September 15, 1995, 34.

[65]Barbara Love, "New media won't kill magazines," *Folio:,* December 15, 1994, 9.

[66]Jeff Martin, "What Will the Information Superhighway Mean to You?", *Vue/Point: The Hard Copy,* Summer 1994, 108.

[67]Robert Sentinery, "Your magazine's future is in print," *Folio:,* August 1, 1995, 96.

[68]Kummerfeld, "New media and magazines: Where do we go from here?", 240.

[69]Edmund L. Andrews, "A Publishers' Slugfest Over Postal Rates," *The New York Times,* November 13, 1995, 1.

[70]George Gross, "Reclassification will raise all boats, *Folio:,* July 1, 1995, 36.

[71]Constance J. Sidles, "Pleasing Mr. Postman," *Adobe Magazine,* January/February 1995, 49–50.

[72]Gross, "Reclassification will raise all boats," 36.

[73]Tim Bogardus, "Reclassification splits industry," *Folio:,* May 1, 1995, 24.

[74]John Emery, "Volume subclass will torpedo value," *Folio:,* July 1, 1995, 37.

[75]Tim Bogardus, "Publishers weigh co-mailing options," *Folio:,* June 15, 1995, 31.

[76]Andrews, "A Publishers' Slugfest Over Postal Rates," 3.

[77]Bogardus, "Reclassification splits industry," 24.

[78]Bogardus, "Reclassification splits industry," 24–25.

[79]Andrews, "A Publishers' Slugfest Over Postal Rates," 3.

[80]Sidles, "Pleasing Mr. Postman," 50.

[81]John Emery, "Volume subclass will torpedo value," 37.

[82]Bogardus, "Publishers weigh co-mailing options," 31.

[83]Len Egol, "Alternate Delivery Reaches for America's Doorknobs," *Printing Manager,* September/October 1993, 5.

[84]Tim Bogardus, "Private mailers offer united front against USPS," *Folio:,* June 15, 1995, 18.

[85]William L. Rathje and Cullen Murphy, *Rubbish!: The Archaeology of Garbage* (New York: HarperCollins, 1992), 3–4.

[86]Rathje and Murphy, *Rubbish!* 103–104.

[87]Rathje and Murphy, *Rubbish!* 105.

[88]Carolyn Hurlbert, "Giving It Back/Recycling in the '90's," *Graphic Arts Journal,* May/June 1993, 17.

[89]Joseph E. Daniel, "Good trash versus seriously bad trash," *Folio:,* June 1, 1993, 112.

[90]John Byrne Barry, "Mea Pulpa," *Sierra,* January/February 1994, 60.

[91]Barry, "Mea Pulpa," 63.

[92]Barry, "Mea Pulpa," 152.

[93]Benjamin J. Wallace, "The Green Dilemma: Earth or Profits First?", *Magazine Week,* May 24, 1993, 18.

[94]Lorraine Calvacca, *"Audubon*'s paper chase," *Folio:,* May 1, 1993, 19.

[95]Benjamin J. Wallace, "The Green Dilemma: Earth or Profits First?", *Magazine Week,* May 24, 1993, 19.

[96]Ron Hendricks, "Make It Again, Sam," *Graphic Arts Journal,* May/June 1993, 13.

[97]Esther Barbara D'Amico, "How Soon Will You Print on Recycled Paper?", *Folio:,* May 15, 1993, 94.

[98]Calvacca, *"Audubon*'s paper chase," 19.

[99]Wallace, "The Green Dilemma: Earth or Profits First?", 21.

[100]Rathje and Murphy, *Rubbish!,* 203.

[101]Ron Hendricks, "Make It Again, Sam," *Graphic Arts Journal,* May/June 1993, 13.

[102]Dana F. Arnold and Judith Usherson, "A Printer's Primer on Recycled Paper," Special Report S441, National Association of Printers and Lithographers, December 1991.

[103]Claudia Thompson, "Evaluating the Press Performance of Recycled Papers," Special Report S274, National Association of Printers & Lithographers, June 1993.

[104]Esther Barbara D'Amico, "Paper firm ups recycling heat," *Folio:,* April 15, 1993, 17.

[105]Arnold and Usherson, "A Printer's Primer on Recycled Paper."

[106]D'Amico, "How Soon Will You Print on Recycled Paper?", 56.

[107]Hendricks, "Make It Again, Sam," 13.

[108]Wallace, "The Green Dilemma: Earth or Profits First?", 18.

[109]Tim Bogardus, "Recycled paper gets the ax," *Folio:*, November 1, 1995, 28.

[110]D'Amico, "How Soon Will You Print on Recycled Paper?", 94.

[111]Paul McDougall, "Eco Responsibility/How Much Is Too Much?", *Folio:,* February 1, 1994, 85.

[112]Lambeth Hochwald, "Recycled: Forcing the issue," *Folio:,* April 15, 1993, 52.

[113]Paul McDougall, "Debate over recycled paper intensifies," *Folio:,* September 15, 1993, 20.

[114]McDougall, "Eco Responsibility/How Much Is Too Much?", 42–43.

[115]Monica McCabe, "Executive Order Defines Recycled Paper Properties," *Environmental Advisor,* National Association of Printers & Lithographers, December 1993.

[116]McDougall, "Eco Responsibility/How Much Is Too Much?", 43.

[117]All examples: Monica McCabe, "Agencies Cast Their Nets Wider, Target Publishers," *Environmental Advisor,* National Association of Printers and Lithographers, March 1994.

[118]Dr. Albert R. Materazzi, "Water Quality Regulations and Their Effect on Printers," Special Report S439, National Association of Printers & Lithographers, August 1989.

[119]Glen Macri, "Grime & Punishment: Limiting Liability Through Environmental Compliance," Special Report S443, National Association of Printers and Lithographers, August 1993.

[120]Barry, "Mea Pulpa," *Sierra,* January/February 1994, 152.

[121]"Periodicals employment grows slowly," *Folio:*, January 15, 1995, 16.

[122]This proverb is the wisdom of Robin Williams, author of *The Little Mac Book* (Peachpit Press) and other indispensable guides for desktop publishing and graphic design.

# Glossary of Magazine Publishing Terms

*ABC*   Audit Bureau of Circulations, Inc.  The independent, nonprofit organization that provides verified audits of magazines' circulations.  Most consumer magazines that sell advertising to outside companies pay to be audited by ABC.  The organization is directed by advertisers, agencies, and publishers.

*Added value*   See merchandising.

*Affinity outlets*   Retail outlets for single-copy sales that are associated with the editorial offerings of an individual magazine.  For instance, an affinity outlet for a cooking magazine might be a high-end gourmet food store.

*Arrears*   Issues of a magazine sent to a subscriber by the publisher after the term of subscription has officially expired.

*Audit report*   Annual official findings of an audit bureau as a result of its examination of the magazine's records.

*Average net paid circulation*   Average paid circulation per issue arrived at by dividing total circulation of all issues during an audit period by the number of issues for the audit period.

*Average paid circulation*   Average circulation, qualified as paid circulation, of all the issues arrived at by dividing the total of all the paid copies during the period by the total number of issues.

*BPA* Business Publications Audit, Inc.  The auditing body that oversees and audits the circulations of business or trade publications.  Like ABC, this independent, nonprofit organization is composed of advertisers, agencies, and publishers.

*BRE* Business reply envelope   In magazine publishing, the device provided by a publisher in a direct mail package to enable a subscriber to send in a check or order for a magazine. Postage is usually supplied by the publisher to facilitate payment.

*Bad debt* Accounting term. When a subscriber or advertiser doesn't pay the magazine what's owed.

*Bimonthly* Published every other month.

*Bingo card* A reader response device sponsored and managed by the magazine and designed as an added value for the magazine's advertisers. Readers indicate items they wish to receive or obtain information about and return it to the magazine. The magazine passes along these "sales leads" to the participating advertisers.

*Biweekly* Published every other week—or twice a month.

*Bleed* An image printed on a page all the way to the edge of the paper. The image is said to bleed off the page.

*Bluelines, blueprint, blues* A kind of proof (q.v.) made up in a printed, folded, and bound format that approximates what the finished magazine will look like; so called because all the colors are represented as a single shade of blue. (Other kinds of proofs are used for checking color.) Production managers examine bluelines, which are developed from fully composed or final film, to check the positions of pages and page elements and to catch typographical errors not corrected in editorial copyediting. Since the films from which the blueline is "pulled" also are the films from which the printing plates will be processed, any change requested after the blueline is approved could require plate remake —a costly and time-consuming procedure.

*Book* Industry slang for a magazine.

*Bulk sales* (1.) Definitions applicable to Audit Bureau of Circulations (q.v.): all copies or subscriptions purchased in quantities of five or more that promote the business or professional interest of the purchaser; single-copy sales in bulk sales of a single issue of a publication in quantities of five or more to one purchaser; term subscriptions in bulk subscriptions for two or more consecutive issues of a publication sold in quantities of five or more to one purchaser. (2.) Definition applicable to Business Publications Audit (q.v.): two or more copies of publication (whether or not individually wrapped or addressed) sent to a single addressee.

*Business-to-business magazine* See trade magazine.

*CPM* Cost per thousand   The standard measure publishers and advertisers use to gauge the efficiency of a medium. It is simply the cost of reaching an audience of 1,000. A page of advertising that costs $5,000 in a magazine with a circulation of 500,000 has a CPM of $10. Advertising rates for magazines with differing circulations are compared by figuring their CPM. Circulation directors can also judge the efficiency of one direct mail package compared to another by comparing their respective CPMs—the cost of reaching 1,000 potential subscribers.

*Card deck*    Postcards purchased by advertisers and mailed to subscribers of a magazine. Magazine publishers organize and sponsor the distribution of card decks, which are usually limited to a specific demographic segment of the magazine's total subscriber file.

*Cash discount*    Reduction in cost of advertising space for cash payment, usually two percent of the net cost.

*Center spread*    The two facing center pages of a publication.

*Charter subscription*    Sale of a magazine to a purchaser when the publication is started or on special terms with a guarantee that the subscription price will not be increased provided the purchaser renews regularly at expiration.

*Checking copy*    Copy of the magazine sent to an advertiser or agency to verify that the advertisement appeared.

*Church and state*    A metaphor for the division between the creative side (editorial) and the commercial side (advertising) that may exist at a magazine. At many magazines, either a formal or informal structure is established to prevent the church from being influenced by the commercial interests of the state. At one end of the spectrum was Harold Ross and his decision to relegate the advertising staff and editorial staff to different floors at *The New Yorker*. Most magazines that wish to maintain editorial integrity and the respect of both their advertisers and their readers will make every effort to keep commercial concerns from dictating editorial decisions.

*Classified advertising*    A form of advertising in a magazine that is arranged (or classified) in distinctive headings or categories of interest to the readers of the magazine. Individuals and small companies usually buy classified advertising space in magazines to announce employment opportunities (help wanted) or to sell a single item or service, but not mass product promotion. Usually classified advertisements have special rates for insertion and are in uniform and specific type. (When size varies, it's called display classified.) In most cases, the solicitation and maintenance of classified advertising is done by telephone and does not require the personal selling that other advertising does.

*Closing or close*    The production deadline for completion or receipt of material intended for the next issue of the magazine. Advertising closings usually take place later in the production cycle than editorial closings. Depending on the printer's requirements, the production manager may specify separate closings for certain kinds of artwork.

*Color electronic prepress systems (CEPS)*    Sophisticated, expensive, computer-controlled equipment for acquiring, digitizing, manipulating, correcting, and outputting page images in color. Sometimes called *proprietary* or *high-end* systems in order to distinguish their specialized architectures from the off-the-shelf components of desktop publishing, CEPS are designed for the kinds of high-throughput, data-intensive prepress work that personal computers are not robust enough to handle. (Also see OPI.)

*Commission*    The amount of money—or bonus—a publishing company pays to an advertising representative when he or she brings in a sale or achieves a sales objective in terms of revenue or number of pages sold. There's no set formula for a commission: Some magazines pay advertising sales representatives a percentage of the revenues brought in; others might opt for a more complicated formula related to advances in share of market.

*Comp list, complimentary copy*    The complimentary subscription list maintained by a magazine. The people on this list are the men and women who the publisher has determined need to get the magazine on a regular basis free of charge. The comp list usually consists of advertising decision makers, members of the press, and government officials or other VIPs who should be aware of the magazine.

*Contributing editor*    An editor or writer not on the staff of a magazine, who provides journalistic advice, editorial contributions, or other special editorial services.

*Control package*    In circulation jargon, the direct mail package that has generated the most responses from potential subscribers. Once the control package is determined, all other variations on the package are compared to this winning package.

*Controlled circulation*    Circulation that is limited to people whose job title or job description is appropriate to editorial content. The publisher of a controlled circulation magazine determines who is eligible to receive the magazine free.

*Conversion*    When a subscriber renews a subscription for the first time. Following this first-time conversion of a new subscriber, the subscriber becomes a renewal. Magazine conversion rates are usually much lower than renewal rates.

*Copy*    The editorial material (articles, stories, etc.) that will be published in a magazine.

*Copy editor*    Staff position at a magazine. The copy editor is responsible for style, grammar, and spelling.

*Copyright*    The ownership of a creative work. To register a work or for more information, contact The Copyright Office, Information and Publication Section LM 455, Library of Congress, Washington, D.C. 20559.

*Custom publishing*    When a company publishes its own magazine for a targeted group of customers. Sometimes, a magazine company will serve as a custom publisher for one of its advertisers.

*Cylinder*    A rotary unit inside a printing press for mounting a plate or an offset blanket that transfers images to paper. (The cylinder that delivers the paper is known as the impression cylinder.) The term also refers to the engraved image carrier for gravure printing (q.v.).

*Defamation*  Damage to reputation. Defamation can either take place in writing, in which case it is known as libel (q.v.), or by spoken word, in which case the defamation is called slander.

*Desktop publishing*  The use of personal computers and popular software to design and produce magazines (and virtually every other kind of printed matter). Nearly all professionally produced magazines use some element of desktop publishing, and many are created entirely on the desktop without need for the prepress (q.v.) services that once only printers and graphic arts trade shops could provide.

*Direct mail*  The highly sophisticated process by which magazine publishers mail invitations and solicitations to subscribe to individuals they suspect are likely subscribers.

*Direct-to-plate or computer-to-plate*  Imaging printing plates directly from digital data without using film (q.v.) as an intermediate image carrier. Plates can be imaged while they are mounted on press, or they can be imaged off press in stand-alone digital plate processors. The elimination of film from the platemaking sequence promises considerable savings in time and expense, and a number of magazines have already taken the filmless route. Further improvements in digital color proofing systems will accelerate the acceptance of the direct-to-plate workflow.

*Display advertising*  As opposed to classified advertising (q.v.), display advertising in a magazine is usually the result of work by advertising agencies and other marketers. Display advertising in magazines can either be black-and-white or full color. Usually, the advertiser will supply all the finished artwork and film (q.v.).

*Draw*  The number of copies a magazine publisher delivers to a wholesaler (q.v.) for distribution to individual retailers.

*Editorial board*  A group of experts assembled to consult with a magazine's editorial staff, providing direction and strategy. The editorial board may also set editorial policy.

*Editorial inventory*  Articles a magazine has purchased but not yet published. Editors and publishers want to ensure that the inventory has strong material for possible future use—but not *too* much material, because a huge shelf of unpublished articles can be a liability for a young magazine.

*Fact checker*  Editorial staff position. A fact checker is charged with confirming all statements of fact in an article before it is published.

*Fair use*  When a printed work is free to be copied and distributed without permission from or payment to the copyright holder.

*Film*  Until the mid-1980s, the unchallenged medium for image transmission in the graphic arts. Film dominated typography (q.v.) until typesetting via desktop publishing replaced typesetting via photocomposition. Film demanded the manual assembly of images until page-layout programs and computerized imposition (q.v.) equipment began phasing out the need for "stripping" (using razor blades, tape, "Rubylith," and "goldenrod" to cobble together pages from separate pieces of film). Film is still the most widely used means of transferring halftone (q.v.) dot patterns to lithographic printing plates. But even that sway is being challenged by computer-to-plate systems that put dots onto plates straight from digital data, without any need for film as a go-between. Some magazines are now produced entirely without film; in the future, many more will be.

*Folio* (1) A large sheet of paper folded once in the middle, making two leaves or four pages of a book or manuscript. (2) A book or manuscript of the largest common size, usually about 15 inches in height, consisting of such folded sheets. (3) A page number. (4) To consecutively number the pages of (a book or magazine). (5) The number of pages. (6) The name of a popular magazine for the magazine industry.

*Four-color or process-color* Sequentially printing the colors known as the *subtractive primaries*—yellow, cyan, and magenta—plus black to create the illusion of a full spectrum of color in the finished image. With process-color printing, only four inks are needed to reproduce images that appear to consist of an infinite range of colors. To reproduce full-color artwork in this way, the original image must be converted into four *separations*—individually extracted subimages representing each process-color component of the original. The halftone (q.v.) dot pattern of each separation is then transferred to its own image carrier (plate or gravure cylinder) for mounting on press. As the paper passes through the press, each image carrier deposits its process color and the appearance of a full-spectrum image is built up. A four-color press is any press set up for printing the four process colors in a single pass. (See also multicolor printing.)

*Freelancer or freelance writer* Writer whose work is published in a magazine, but who is not employed as a regular staff member by the business.

*Frequency* (1) Number of advertising insertions bought during a set period (usually a year), sometimes a basis for reduced rates. (2) The number of times during a set period of time a publication is issued.

*Fulfillment* The maintenance of the subscriber file—that is, all the data on subscribers including new subscribers, renewals, address changes, cancellations. The file is used to generate the correct labels for mailing each issue.

*Gatefold* A four-page sheet, creased and folded approximately halfway of its width so as to bind one end and to open (like a gate) to double-page size.

*Gravure* The printing method of choice for long-run periodical and catalog work. Gravure presses print from cylinders engraved with millions of recessed ink cells. Because gravure transfers large quantities of ink directly to the paper, it yields greater depth and richness of color than any other process. Some magazines are printed partly by gravure and partly by offset lithography, with gravure reserved for the sections wherein reproduction quality is critical.

*Halftone*  A photographic image converted to a pattern of dots reproducible by offset lithography (which cannot print the continuous-tone appearance of the original). Halftones used to be made by reshooting the original photo through pieces of glass etched with a "screen" of crosshatched lines or rules. The finer the line screen, the more detail in the printed image. Today scanners and digital computers furnish the dots for most halftones, but the terminology of screen rulings continues to be used. For instance, the "mechanical specifications" section of many magazine rate cards requires screen values of 133 to 150 lpi (lines per inch) for photo images in advertising films and other input materials. (Also see stochastic screening.)

*Hard offer*  When a publisher requires that a new subscriber pay for the order before any issues are delivered.

*Heatset printing*  In web offset (q.v.) presswork, using a hot-air oven or another heat source to "set" the ink as the paper moves from the printing units to the delivery end of the press. Heatset drying is mandatory for printing magazines on coated papers, which are not absorbent enough to permit drying by evaporation at web offset's high running speeds. An alternative to heatset drying is "curing" by ultraviolet light or electron-beam radiation; results can be excellent, but specially formulated inks must be used. (Also see non-heatset printing.)

*House organ*  A publication issued periodically by a business concern to further its own interest among its employees and its salespeople or among outlets, suppliers, and the public and sometimes among all these classes. Also called a company magazine.

*ISSN.*  International Standard Serials Number. This is the internationally accepted, concise, unique, unambiguous code of identification of serial publications. It is assigned to periodicals, including magazines, and used primarily for ordering and billing information. For more information contact: ISSN International Centre; 20, rue Bachaumont; 75002 Paris. Or, in the United States: National Serials Data Program, Library of Congress, Washington, D.C. 20540.

*Imagesetter*  An output device for prepress (q.v.) that uses a laser to transfer digitized page images to film or photosensitive paper. Imagesetters are driven by hardware or software controllers known as RIPs (raster image processors). RIPs (pronounced "rips") turn digital page data from the desktop publishing computer or CEPS into "bitmaps" reproducible on the film or the paper.

*Imposition*  During prepress (q.v.), arranging pages in proper order for efficient production in the press run. Pages must be set up so that they will print as signatures (q.v.) from which the magazine can be assembled. Good imposition also makes the most economical use of films, plates, and presswork.

*Indicia*  (1) A page in a publication that contains the name of the publication, date of issue, frequency, serial number, publication office, subscription price, and notice of entry to appear within first five pages of the issue. (2) Markings on bulk mail that take the place of postage stamps, cancellation, and postmarks.

*In-line finishing*   Bindery steps performed as part of presswork. For example, some web-fed presses (q.v.) have folding units that cut and fold the web of paper into signatures (q.v.) that are then delivered to the bindery.

*Ink-jet printing*   A computer-controlled, database-driven imprinting technique for the targeted marketing of magazines. With ink-jet printing, publishers can personalize issues by displaying individual subscribers' names in prominent positions, and label special editions for delivery according to zip-code breakdown and other criteria. Ink-jet printing goes hand-in-hand with selective binding (q.v.) for the "versioning" of magazines.

*Insert*   Extra printed matter bound inside a magazine: advertising supplements, response cards, pull-out sections, etc. Not part of the publication press run, inserts are prepared elsewhere and are delivered to the bindery fully printed. They may be "tipped" (glued) into the issue or saddle-stitched (q.v.) in place. Saddle-stitched inserts consisting of a single sheet may need an additional "lip" of paper to be properly affixed. (Also see outsert.)

*Insertion order*   Formal instruction from the advertiser or advertising agency for the publisher to run a specified advertisement at a certain time.

*Kill fee*   Compensation to a writer whose work was contracted by the magazine but is not accepted for publication.

*Layout*   Building a magazine page or a series of linked pages from body type, headlines, sidebars, tables, charts, artwork, photography, ads, column rules, folio numbers, jump notations ("continued on/from page 00"), headers and footers, etc. Editors and production staff used to make layouts by pasting or taping replicas of these page elements in position on paper templates known as "dummies." Artists then re-created the dummies as "mechanicals" that could be photographed to make graphic arts film for platemaking. Nowadays, because so many magazines use page-creation software such as QuarkXPress and PageMaker to do this work, dummying is all but dead and the electronic mechanical is the standard vehicle for nearly all publication layout.

*Letterpress*   A centuries-old printing process built around metal type, photoengravings, and other time-honored but cumbersome graphical elements. Letterpress was synonymous with printing from Gutenberg's day until about the middle of the twentieth century, when it was all but eclipsed by offset lithography. Letterpress survives as an art form, but it is little used for magazine manufacturing.

*Libel*   Damage to a person's reputation that appears in print.

*Line screen*   See halftone.

*Lithography*   A printing process based on the phenomenon that causes oil-based inks and water-based dampeners to repel each other on the planographic (flat) surface of the lithographic printing plate. The plate's image areas—the sections containing type, illustrations, and photography—attract ink and repel water. Dampening solution in the nonimage areas repels ink. In this way, only the page elements intended for reproduction are transferred to the paper. (Also see offset lithography and waterless printing.)

*Logo or logotype*   Two or more letters or a whole word or distinctive setting of a name, cast as a single piece of metal. A standardized pattern as for the advertiser's name or trademark.

*Makeready*   Preparing the printing press for the production run. Makeready includes mounting the plates, adjusting the ink settings, and "getting the press up to color"—producing test sheets that match the proofs (q.v.) approved by the customer. Fast, trouble-free makeready is the key to cost-efficient press operation.

*Masthead*   Summary of a publication's identification and ownership, usually including the names and titles of the magazine's staff.

*Media kit*   A package of information about a magazine, including circulation, ad rate, and editorial data, issued by the magazine and used by potential advertisers to assess the magazine's appropriateness for advertising.

*Merchandising*   Any activity that makes advertising or other promotion more effective, especially by calling it to the attention of buyers that might otherwise overlook it.

*Merchandising allowance (or added value)*   The amount of money a magazine sets aside to develop promotional programs for advertisers. These programs are designed to increase the effectiveness of advertising by translating it into advantages for dealers, retailers, and salespeople and by projecting the advertiser's message beyond the publication's usual circulation channels. Includes the use of advertising point-of-sales displays, direct mail, reprints of advertisements, enlargements, providing lists of dealers, etc.

*Mission statement*   The editorial explanation for a magazine's existence.

*Multicolor printing*   Printing that consists of two or more colors other than the process colors (see four-color or process-color printing). Multicolor printing cannot achieve the same "realistic" full-spectrum effects as four-color printing.

*Negative*   Graphic arts film that reverses the light and shadow values of the original image so that solids are white or clear and clear portions are black or opaque. (Also see *positive*.)

*Net*   The amount paid to the magazine by the advertising agency after deducting the agency commission.

*Non-heatset printing*   Printing on paper that does not need help from heat in order to dry properly. Web presses set up to run publications on uncoated paper do not have to be equipped for heatset operations, because uncoated papers are ink-absorbent and dry readily. Sheetfed printing is by its nature a non-heatset process, although a pressroom aid known as anti-offset spray powder is often used to speed the drying of printed sheets.

*Offset lithography*   The standard method of lithography for reproduction in quantity. An offset lithographic press transfers print images from the plate to a rubber blanket mounted on a cylinder that rotates against the surface of the impression cylinder bearing the paper. The image is said to be "offset" from the plate to the blanket to the paper. Among the advantages of the process are its good reproduction of photographs; its suitability for a broad range of printing papers; and its versatility. Offset lithography dominates the production of short- to medium-run magazines. It is also the most widely used process for advertising materials and other kinds of commercial printing.

*OPI (open prepress interface)*    Various hardware and software links that enable high-end color electronic prepress systems (q.v.), or CEPS, equipment and desktop publishing computers to be part of the same digital workflow. One of the most important OPI functions is image "swapping," whereby less powerful desktop computers work with low-resolution images that are automatically replaced with high-resolution versions when the pages are ready for final processing at the CEPS.

*Open rate or one-time rate*    The advertising charge for a single insertion; a rate subject to no discounts.

*Outsert*    Preprinted material attached to the exterior of a magazine. Examples: cover wraps, used for time-to-renew-your-subscription reminders and for tear-off, mail-back reader surveys; and issue-encircling "belly bands" carrying advertising. Some publishers also refer to loose items in polybags (q.v.) as outserts.

*Paid circulation*    The number of copies of a magazine that have been paid for by a purchaser—either a subscription, a newsstand sale, or another audit bureau–approved source.

*Pass-along circulation*    Copies of a publication that come to the attention of others besides the subscriber, who makes them available to nonsubscribers.

*Perfect binding*    Making folded and cut sheets into a magazine by gluing them into the cover fold. Advantages: creates a flat spine on which copy can be printed; convenient for inserts (q.v.). Disadvantages: open magazine won't lie flat; more expensive than saddle-stitching (q.v.).

*Pink sheet*    The publisher's statement (printed on pink paper) of circulation over a six-month period issued by a magazine under the auspices of the Audit Bureau of Circulations, Inc. (q.v.).

*Plate*    An image carrier for various kinds of presses. Plates are flexible and curved to fit around plate cylinders (q.v.) that revolve against other press cylinders bearing offset blankets or paper. Plates may be made from metal, photopolymer (plastic), rubber, or paper. Lithographic magazine work uses photosensitive metal plates exposed from film.

*Polybagging*    Delivering an issue of a magazine together with free-standing supplements—catalogs, diskettes, other publications—in a durable plastic bag. As a means of providing "bonus" distribution for advertising materials, polybagging can be an important source of ancillary income for magazine publishers.

*Positive*    Film made from a negative that reproduces light and shade as in the original subject.

*Postpress*  The magazine assembly steps that take place in the bindery after the printing of signatures is complete: principally folding, cutting, trimming, collating, gathering, and binding. (Also see in-line finishing.)

*Premium*  (1) Free gift offered by the magazine publisher as an incentive to order a subscription to the magazine. (2) "Premium position" refers to a special advertising placement in the magazine generally sold at a higher rate.

*Prepress*  All of the preparatory steps that take place from receipt of original copy and art to the initial phase of presswork known as makeready (q.v.). The general objective of prepress is, or should be, to "work from the press backward" —that is, to create only the kinds of page images that will reproduce successfully during the production run. Prepress encompasses typography; page layout; incorporation of photography and illustration; image enhancement and color correction; the preparation of image carriers (chiefly lithographic plates and gravure cylinders); and preproduction proofing. Prepress once was a highly specialized, photomechanical process based entirely on photocomposition, "stripping," and other film-based techniques. Today prepress is performed largely on the desktop with personal computers or by means of high-end color electronic prepress systems (q.v.).

*Press check or press OK*  The process whereby the production manager or art director certifies that the magazine is ready to print; this usually take place at the printing plant. Once the magazine's representative has reviewed bluelines and off-press color proofs (q.v.), the press operators make proof sheets for the final stage of inspection. The press sheets that the magazine's representative approves are the ones that the press crew will attempt to match throughout the production run.

*Print order*  The number of copies of a magazine that are ordered from the printer for each issue. Because of the expense of printing, it's important that an accurate count be determined. One of the primary jobs of the circulation director.

*Privilege*  Constitutional protection from libel or slander afforded public officials or people testifying in a legal or otherwise official gathering.

*Proof*  A facsimile or sample of a page or a publication that gives a reasonably accurate idea of what the final printed product will look like. Because there are so many things to check before approval to print can be given, the most important kinds are: (1) blueline or blueprint (q.v.) proofs, for checking position; (2) off-press proofs, for simulating press color without printing. Taking images from separated film, off-press proofs use dyes, laminates, and colored transparent film to represent the colors of press ink; (3) press proofs, consisting of ink-on-paper test sheets "pulled" from the press on which the job will be printed or from a special proofing press. Because press proofs come from the same plates (q.v.) that will be used for the actual production run, press proofing is the most reliable way to foresee the end result. (It is also the most expensive method of proofing.); (4) digital proofs, or direct digital color proofs (DDCP)—filmless impressions made from digital page data by means of ink-jet printers, thermal printers, dye-sublimation units, and other computer-controlled color output devices. (A digital image of a page displayed on a color monitor is known as a "soft proof.") Digital proofing is not yet widely accepted for color approval in magazine work, but eventually will be.

*Proofreader*   Editorial staff member who is responsible for reading proofs—the final step before printing—to ensure accuracy, flow, etc.

*Publisher's statement*   Certified statement of circulation and distribution data for a six-month period made by a publisher and issued unaudited but subject to audit.

*Pull quote*   A short excerpt from a magazine story set in larger type and used both as a design element and a way to attract the reader's attention to a story. Also know as a "callout."

*Qualified circulation*   Circulation of a magazine (either paid or nonpaid) for which the mailing address, recipient eligibility, and the correct business and/or occupational classifications are verified by auditable documentary evidence dated within 36 months. Qualified recipients must receive every issue of the publication.

*Query*   The formal proposal made by a freelance writer to report and/or write an article for a magazine. Usually the query includes a sense of why the story is important, why it's appropriate for the specific magazine, and an outline of how the writer proposes to approach the subject. Used also as a verb, as in "Why don't you query me on that story idea?"

*RDA* Retail display allowance.   The amount of money a publisher pays to a retailer or to the agent of a retailer to guarantee that the magazine gets preferential, prominent placement in the retail outlet.

*Rate base*   The number of buyers of a magazine that the publisher projects. Publishers use this number of "guaranteed" circulation on which to base their rates.

*Rate card*   A card, folder, or brochure listing of advertising rates by frequency, size of advertisement, and color. Also gives data on mechanical requirements and closing dates.

*Recycled paper*   Paper stock made wholly or partially from fibers recovered from other paper. A recycled stock's postconsumer content comes from paper that entered the "consumer waste stream" by being put to the home or business use for which it was manufactured. Preconsumer content comes from paper that, for one reason or another, never left the paper mill or the printing plant. Many advocates of printing magazines on recycled paper say that only postconsumer content should be counted when determining how "green" a recycled paper really is.

*Renewal*   When a subscriber agrees to buy another subscription to a magazine he or she has been receiving. The first time a subscriber extends the subscription, it is a conversion (q.v.); the second time, and all subsequent times, it is a renewal.

*R.O.P.* Run of paper or run of press. Any location or position for advertising in a publication that's convenient for the publisher. Distinguished from specific preferred position.

*Saddle-stitching*  Assembling magazines with wire staples at the center fold; so called because of the "saddle bar" that the signatures (q.v.) ride as they move toward the stitching unit. Advantages: makes magazines that lie flat; less expensive than perfect binding. Disadvantages: restrictions on how and in what positions inserts can be bound in.

*Selective binding*  Creating special editions for special interests by varying the signatures (q.v.) that make up a given issue of a magazine. An issue that consists of fixed content as well as signatures targeted to selected groups of recipients is said to be versioned: each targeted group gets an edition with a special section that no other readers see (although all recipients share the fixed content). In postpress operations, computer-controlled collating equipment and ink-jet addressing units are what make selective binding possible.

*Sell-through*  The number of copies of an issue of a magazine distributed to retail outlets that are actually sold. Usually expressed as a percentage, as in "The November issue had a sell-through of 60 percent."

*Separation*  See four-color or process-color printing.

*Sheetfed printing*  Printing on sheets of paper precut to standard publication sizes. In some respects, sheetfed presses deliver better print quality than web-fed (q.v.) presses, and their cost of makeready is smaller. These advantages recommend sheetfed printing to publishers of short- to medium-run magazines.

*Signature*  In magazine work, a printed and folded press sheet consisting of pages in multiples of eight. The pages are so arranged that when the signature is cut and gathered for binding with other signatures making up the magazine, all the pages are in proper numerical order. (Also see imposition.)

*Single-copy sales*  Copies of a magazine sold individually, i.e., not by subscription. Single-copy sales outlets include newsstands, grocery store checkouts, and other specialty stores and retail outlets.

*Soft offer*  The "send-no-money-now" offer to enter a subscription to a magazine. (See hard offer.)

*Spoilage*  Paper consumed and discarded because of makeready errors, press problems, last-minute changes by customers, and other costly events that might have been prevented by better planning or greater attention to quality control. Spoilage is not excusable, nor is it identical to waste (q.v.).

*Stochastic screening*  A halftone dot-generation technique that places very small but uniformly sized dots at varying distances from one another on films and plates. (Conventional halftoning, in contrast, creates differently sized dots at regular intervals determined by the lines-per-inch measurement of the screen ruling.) Stochastic screening, also known as FM or frequency modulated screening, produces images comparable in appearance to their continuous-tone originals. The combination of stochastic screening and waterless printing (q.v.) is said to deliver the highest reproduction quality currently available.

*Trade magazine*    A magazine published for a targeted professional, business, technical, scientific, or trade audience. Also called "business to business" or "specialized business magazine." See business-to-business magazine.

*Typography*    The art and technology of creating orderly, pleasing, and readable arrangements of letterforms on the pages of magazines and other publications. Typography, once the sole preserve of a class of graphic arts professionals known as typographers, was one of the first popular conquests of the desktop publishing revolution. Typographers to the magazine trade still exist, but it is uncommon today to find a publication that does not use personal computers to store, specify, and set its own collection of digital fonts.

*VOC, or volatile organic compound*    An air pollutant said to be a by-product of the evaporation of the inks used in magazine printing and other kinds of printing production.

*Waste*    Paper consumed and discarded as part of normal operations during press makeready. Printers try to limit waste to a specific percentage of the total paper to be used in the production run. Waste is an acceptable cost component; spoilage (q.v.) is not.

*Waterless printing*    Also known as waterless offset. A variant of lithography that keeps image and nonimage areas separate by means of special plates, inks, and temperature controls instead of dampeners. Waterless printing can reproduce fine details and deliver exceptionally high color quality.

*Web-fed printing*    Printing on a continuous web or roll of paper. Thanks to economies of scale in paper buying, long-run publications find high-speed, web-fed printing a more cost-efficient way to produce magazines than sheetfed printing (q.v.).

*White mail*    Inquiries about subscribing to a magazine that cannot be traced to an identifiable source. By far, most people subscribe to a magazine because they have received a direct mail piece or seen a television commercial with a toll-free number. Sometimes, though, a new subscriber will enter the magazine's rolls after hearing a friend talk about an issue or seeing news coverage of the magazine.

*Wholesaler*    Person or company whose job is to assess the number of retail outlets in a region and determine how many copies of the magazine he or she should order for display.

*'Zines*    The independently produced, small circulation, mostly literary magazines that burst onto the publishing scene in the 1990s with the advances in desktop publishing.

# Bibliography

## ADVERTISING MANAGEMENT

Albion, Mark S., and Paul W. Farris. *The Advertising Controversy: Evidence on the Economic Effects of Advertising*. Boston: Auburn, 1981.

Alwitt, Linda F., and Andrew A. Mitchell. *Psychological Processes and Advertising Effects: Theory, Research, and Applications*. Hillsdale, N.J.: Lawrence Erlbaum Associates, 1985.

Association of Business Publishers. *Top Management's Role in Directing, Budgeting, and Evaluating Advertising Programs*. New York: ABP, no date.

_____. *The ARF/ABP Study: The Impact of Business Publication Advertising on Sales and Profits*. New York: ABP, 1987.

Brown, Paul B. *Marketing Masters: Lessons in the Art of Marketing*. New York: Harper & Row, 1988.

Carmody, Deirdre, "Where to Draw the Line When Helping Advertisers," *The New York Times*, 1 July 1991.

Crimp, Margaret. *The Marketing Research Process*. Englewood Cliffs, N.J.: Prentice-Hall, 1985.

Drucker, Peter. *Management: Tasks, Responsibilities, Practices*. New York: Harper & Row, 1974.

_____. *The Effective Executive*. New York, Harper & Row, 1967.

_____. *The New Realities*. New York: Harper & Row, 1989.

Duke, Judith S. *The Technical, Scientific, and Medical Publishing Market*. White Plains, N.Y.: Knowledge Industry Publications, 1985.

Ewen, Stuart. *Captains of Consciousness: Advertising and the Social Roots of the Consumer Culture.* New York: McGraw-Hill, 1976.

Fueroghne, Dean Keith. *"But the People in Legal Said...": A Guide to Current Legal Issues in Advertising.* Homewood, Ill.: Dow Jones-Irwin, 1989.

Gale Research, *The Gale Directory of Publications.* Detroit: Gale Research, 1995.

Greco, Albert N. *Business Journalism: Management Notes and Cases.* New York: New York University Press, 1988.

Horowitz, Irving Louis. *Communicating Ideas: The Crisis of Publishing in a Post-Industrial Society.* New York: Oxford University Press, 1986.

Kanter, Rosabeth Moss. *When Giants Learn to Dance: Mastering the Challenges of Strategy, Management, and Careers in the 1990s.* New York: Simon & Schuster, 1989.

Kotler, Philip, and Eduardo L. Roberto. *Social Marketing: Strategies for Changing Public Behavior.* New York: The Free Press, 1989.

Meyers, William. *The Image-Makers: Power and Persuasion on Madison Avenue.* New York: Times Books, 1984.

Ogilvy, David. *Confessions of an Advertising Man.* New York: Atheneum, 1981.

_____. *On Advertising.* New York: Vintage, 1985.

Roman, Kenneth and Jane Maav. *How to Advertise.* New York: St. Martin's Press, 1976.

Standard Rate and Data Service. *Business Publications Rates and Data, Part I.* Wilmette, Ill.: Standard Rate and Data Service, February 1996.

Theberge, P., "Musician Magazines in the 1980s, the Creation of a Community and Consumer Market," *Cultural Studies,* October 1991, 5(3): 270–293.

# EMPLOYMENT/BUSINESS FORECASTS

"HVP Forecast: 1995 Industry Economic Outlook," *High Volume Printing,* February 1995.

"Periodicals Employment Grows Slowly," *Folio:,* 15 January 1995.

U.S. Department of Commerce, Bureau of the Census. *1982 Census of Manufacturers: Newspapers, Periodicals, Books, and Miscellaneous Publishing.* Washington, D.C.: GPO, 1985, 27A-6 through 27A-11.

U.S. Department of Commerce, Bureau of the Census. *1987 Census of Manufacturers: Newspapers, Periodicals, Books, and Miscellaneous Publishing.* Washington, D.C.: GPO, 1990, 27A-6 through 27A-11.

U.S. Department of Commerce, International Trade Administration. *1989 U.S. Industrial Outlook.* Washington, D.C.: GPO, 1989, 17–20.

U.S. Department of Labor. *Employment Projections For 1995: Data And Methods.* Washington, D.C.: GPO, 1986, 39, 41–5.

U.S. Department of Labor. *Occupational Employment in Manufacturing Industries.* Washington, D.C.: GPO, 1985, 45–50.

Wendt, Lloyd. The Wall Street Journal: *The Story of Dow Jones and the Nation's Business Newspaper.* New York: Rand McNally, 1982.

## CIRCULATION

Carmody, Deirdre, "On the Annual Scoreboard of New Magazines, It's Sports 67, Sex 44," *The New York Times*, 12 June 1995.

*Folio: 500*, Folio, 1 July 1995.

*Folio: Plus*, "Over-Designed Insert Cards Kill Response," 1 November 1994,

Johnson, Julie A., "O.J. Scores Again on '95 Covers," *Advertising Age*, 1 January 1996.

Kalamon, Chris, "Your Fulfillment Service:  Resource Central," *Folio:*, 1 October 1994.

Kelly, Keith J., "Newsstand Decline Deepens for Magazines," *Advertising Age*, 20 February 1995.

Love, Barbara. "Circulators: You Can Survive Disasters," *Folio:*, 1 October 1994.

"Circulation Leaders," *Folio: Special Sourcebook Issue 1996*, November 1995.

## EDITORIAL

Click, J. William, and Russell N. Baird. *Magazine Editing and Production*, 5th edit. Dubuque: William C. Brown Publishers, 1990.

Diamond, Edwin, "Can You Change a Magazine's DNA?" New York Magazine, 20 July 1992.

"Editorial Salary Survey," *Folio:*, 1 August 1995, 59, 64–70.

Gross, David M., "Zine Dreams," *The New York Times Sunday Magazine*, 17 December 1995, 72–74.

Halcrow, Alan, "Extending Your Reach With Editorial Boards," *Folio:*, July 1992, 67–70.

Landler, Mark, "Time Warner, Under Its Own Spotlight," *The New York Times*, 12 June 1995.

Mann, Jim, *Magazine Editing: Its Art and Practice*. Folio Magazine Publishing Corp., 1985.

McCracken, Ellen. *Decoding Women's Magazines*, New York: St. Martin's 1993.

"Tina's Turn,"*New York Magazine*, 2 July 1992.

Taft, William H. *American Magazines for the 1980s*. New York: Hastings House Publishers. 1982.

## FINANCE

Craig, Peter M., ed., *Financial and Accounting Management for Magazine Publishing*, 2nd edit. Stamford: Cowles Business Media, 1993.

# LEGAL

*A.P Stylebook and Libel Manual*
*Media & the Law,* Stamford, Conn: Simba Information Inc.
Alderman, Ellen, and Caroline Kennedy, *The Right of Privacy.* New York:
HarperCollins, 1995.
Carmody, Deirdre, "Writers Fight for Electronic Rights," *The New York Times,* 7
November 1994.
"Times Mirror Unit Pays Freelancers for E-Rights," *Folio: First Day,* 13 November
1995.
Gillmore, Donald M. *Power, Publicity, and the Abuse of Libel Law.* New York: Oxford
University Press. 1992.
Lury, Celia. *Cultural Rights: Technology, Legality and Personality.* New York:
Routledge, 1993.
Patterson, L. Ray and Stanley Lindberg. *The Nature of Copyright: A Law of Users'
Rights.* Athens, Georgia: University of Georgia Press, 1991.
Rohrer, Daniel Morgan, ed. *Mass Media, Freedom of Speech, and Advertising.*
Dubuque: Kendall/Hunt, 1979.


# MAGAZINE PUBLISHING MANAGEMENT

Brooks, John. *The Takeover Game.* New York: E. P. Dutton, 1987.
Bruck, Connie. *Master of the Game.* Simon & Schuster, 1994.
Carmody, Deirdre, "Sensing a Trend Toward Renovation and Remodeling, Home
Magazines Are Adding Up," *The New York Times,* 8 June 1995.
_____, "A Rejuvenated Life Magazine Bounces Back," *The New York Times,*
26 September 1994.
Hochwald, Lambeth, "Have Database, Will Publish," *Folio:,* 15 November 95, 69.
Koff, Richard M., *Strategic Planning for Magazine Executives.* Folio Magazine
Publishing Corporation, Stamford CT, 1981, 1987.
Marino, Sal. *Business Magazine Publishing: Creative Ideas on Management, Editorial,
Selling Space, Promotion... and Boosting Profits.* NTC Business Books, 1993.
Mogel, Leonard. *The Magazine: Everything You Need to Know to Make It in the
Magazine Business.* Globe Pequot Press, 1988.
Rankin, W. Parkman and E. S. Waggaman, *Business Management of General Consumer
Magazines* New York:Praeger, 1984.


# INTERNATIONAL PUBLISHING

Butler, Sir Michael. *Europe: More Than A Continent.* London: Heinemann, 1988.
Carmody, Deirdre, "Magazines Find Green Pastures Abroad," *The New York Times,* 20
March 1995.

Douglas, Susan P. and C. Samuel Craig. *International Marketing Research*. Englewood Cliffs, N.J.: Prentice-Hall, 1983.

Kennedy, Gavin. *Doing Business Abroad*. New York: Simon & Schuster, 1985.

Levitt, Theodore. *The Marketing Imagination*. New York: The Free Press, 1983.

Reilly, Patrick, "Pitfalls of Exporting Magazine Formulas," *The Wall Street Journal*, 24 July 1995.

Wall Street Journal, "German Forbes Falls Victim to Differences Over Its Direction," 5 May 1995

## MASS COMMUNICATIONS

Agee, Warren K. *Maincurrents in Mass Communications*. New York: Harper & Row, 1986.

Altschull, J. Herbert. *Agents of Power: The Role of the News Media In Human Events*. White Plains, N.Y.: Longman, 1984.

Bagdikian, Ben H., *The Media Monopoly*. Boston: Beacon Press, 1992.

Hill, George H. *Black Media in America: A Resource Guide*. Boston: G. K. Hall, 1984.

Katzen, May. "A National Information Network." *Scholarly Publishing* (July 1988): 210–216.

Mitchell, Craig. *Media Promotion*. Chicago: Crain Books, 1985.

Smith, Anthony. *The Politics of Information: Problems of Policy in Modern Media*. London: Macmillan, 1979.

Wimmer, Roger, and Joseph R. Dominick. *Mass Media Research*. Belmont, Calif.: Wadsworth, 1983.

## HISTORY

Byron, Christopher. *The Fanciest Dive*. New York: Norton, 1984.

Clurman, Richard, *To the End of Time*, New York: Simon & Schuster, 1992.

Draper, Robert. *Rolling Stone Magazine: The Uncensored History*. New York: Doubleday.

Elfenbein, Julius. *Business Journalism*. New York: Harper & Row, 1960.

Forsyth, David. *The Business Press in America: 1750-1865*. Philadelphia: Chilton, 1964.

Friedrich, Otto. *Decline and Fall*. New York: Harper & Row, 1969.

Gill, Brendan, *Here at the New Yorker*. New York: Random House, 1975.

Heidendry, John. *Theirs Was the Kingdom: Lila and DeWitt Wallace and the Story of Reader's Digest*. New York: W. W. Norton, 1993.

Janello, Amy, and Brennon Jones for Magazine Publishers of America. *The American Magazine: 1741–1991*. New York: Harry Abram, 1991.

Lemay, J. A. Leo, ed. *Benjamin Franklin: Writings*. New York: The Library of America, 1987.

*Los Angeles Times,* 30 March 1994.

Mahon, Gigi. *Last Days of the New Yorker*. New York: McGraw Hill, 1988.

Mott, Frank Luther. *A History of American Magazines, vol. I: 1741–1850.* Cambridge, Mass.: Harvard University Press, 1966.

_____. *A History of American Magazines vol. II: 1850–1865.* Cambridge, Mass.: Harvard University Press, 1957.

_____. *A History of American Magazines vol. III: 1865–1885.* Cambridge, Mass.: Harvard University Press, 1967.

_____. *A History of American Magazines vol. IV: 1885–1905.* Cambridge, Mass.: Harvard University Press, 1957.

_____. *A History of American Magazines vol. V: 1905–1930.* Cambridge, Mass.: Harvard University Press, 1968.

Ohman, Richard. *Selling Culture: Magazines, Markets and Class at the Turn of the Century.* New York: Verso, 1996.

Peterson, Theodore. *Magazines in the Twentieth Century.* Urbana, Ill.: University of Illinois Press, 1964.

Posgrova, Carol, *It Wasn't Pretty, Folks, But Didn't We Have Fun? Esquire in the Sixties.* New York: W. W. Norton, 1995.

Powell, Walter W. *Getting into Print.* Chicago: University of Chicago Press, 1985.

Richard, Lyon N. *A History of Early American Magazines: 1741–1789.* New York: Thomas Nelson, 1931.

Sedgwick, Ellery. *A History of the Atlantic Monthly: 1741–1980.* New York: Oxford University Press, 1991.

Server, Lee. *Danger is My Business: An Illustrated History of the Fabulous Pulp Magazines, 1896–1953.* San Francisco: Chronicle Books, 1993.

Swanberg, W. A., *Luce and His Empire.* New York, Scribners, 1972.

Tebble, John. *George Horace Lorimer and the Saturday Evening Post: The Biography of a Great Editor.* New York: Doubleday, 1948.

_____ and M. Zuckerman, *The Magazine in America: 1741–1990* New York: Oxford University Press, 1991.

Thurber, James. *The Years with Ross* New York: Grosset & Dunlap, 1959.

Wainwright, Loudon. *The Great American Magazine: An Inside History of Life.* New York: Knopf, 1986.

## NEW MEDIA TECHNOLOGY

"Consumer Publishing Online: New Markets or Money Losers?", *Online Tactics,* October 1995.

"FAQs (frequently asked questions)," *The Electronic Newsstand, http://ww.enews.com,* 10 September 1995.

"Finally, 20 to 30 Million Users on the Internet," Matrix Information & Directory Services, Austin, Tex., 25 August 1995.

"How Big Is the Internet?", *InterAd Monthly,* July 1995.

"Macworld Web Launch," *Macword,* September 1995.

"Meredith Sows Cyberseeds," *Folio:* 1 August 1995.

"Online Primer: Hits vs. Hype: The Lowdown on Site Traffic Stats," *InterAd Monthly,* July 1995.

"PC World Online Finds the Right Formula For Making Money," *Online Tactics,* October 1995.

"Pubs Making Move to the Web," *Seybold Special Report:* Seybold Seminars Boston '95, Part I, 21 April 1995.

"Sponsoring Cyberspace: What's Its Cost?", *InterAd Monthly,* July 1995.

Allman, William F., "The 10 Commandments of Cyberspace," *Folio:,* 15 September 1995.

Blessing, Rose, and Lea Smith. "Repurposing Content is a Great Concept, But... How Do We Begin?", *Publishing and Production Executive,* December 1994.

Bogardus, Tim, "CD-ROM Category expands in scope," *Folio:,* 1 August 1994.

Borrell, Jerry, "Electronic Magazines: Will You Read One?", *Magazine Week,* 22 June 1992.

Bosak, Steve, and Jeffrey Sloman. *The CD-ROM Book.* Indianapolis: Que Corporation, 1993.

Callahan, Sean, "New Media Dilemma," *Folio:,* 1 March 1993.

Engst, Adam C., and William Dickson. *Internet Explorer Kit for Macintosh.* Indianapolis: Hayden Books, 1994.

Ferguson, Paul, "On the Cyber Racks," *Internet World,* September 1995.

Fogarty, Kevin, "Electronic Publishing Raises Questions, Doubts & Passions," *Magazine Week,* 3 February 1992.

"Publishing Firms Move Toward Future With Electronic Media," *Magazine Week,* 23 March 1992.

Fried, Lisa I. "Hundreds Laid off as Whittle Focuses on Electronic Media," *Magazine Week,* 25 May 1992.

Goldsborough, Reid, "News Paperless," *Internet World,* September 1995.

Harris, Todd, "CD-ROMP," *Folio:,* 15 February 1995.

Kummerfeld, Donald D., "New Media and Magazines: Where Do We Go From Here?", *Folio: Special Sourcebook Issue for 1995.*

Kupfer, Peter, "The New Generation of Cyberzines," *Folio:,* 1 March 1993.

Lohr, Steve, "Who Uses Internet? 5.8 Million Are Said to Be Linked in U.S.," *The New York Times,* 27 September 1995.

Love, Barbara, "New media won't kill magazines," *Folio:,* 15 December 1994.

_____. "Online Advantage: Strong brand and a loyal customer base," Folio:, September 1, 1995.

Manly, Lorne. "CD-ROM titles fail to catch fire," *Folio:,* 1 August 1995.

_____. "CD-ROM-only titles gain momentum," *Folio:,* 1 February 1991

_____. "Online ad pricing keeps publishers guessing," *Folio:* 15 May 1995.

_____. "Online auditing attracts many contenders," *Folio:,* 15 September 1995.

_____. "The CD-ROM imperative," *Folio:,* 15 March 1994.

_____. "Trades take to the I-way," *Folio:,* 1 February 1995.

_____. "Weaving the world wide web," *Folio:,* 15 February 1995.

_____. "Web issue worries publishers," *Folio:,* 15September 1995.

_____. "Web-site pricing draws criticism," *Folio:,* 1 August 1995.

Martin, Jeff. "What Will the Information Superhighway Mean to You?" *Vue/Point: The Hard Copy,* Summer 1994.

Nollinger, Mark. "America, Online!", *Wired,* September 1995.

Powell, Bob, and Karen Wickre. *Atlas to the World Wide Web.* Emeryville, Calif.: Ziff-Davis Press, 1995.

Schwartz, Bruce. "On-Line Browsing Through Magazines," *USA Today,* 10 November 1994.

Sharansky, Stefan. "Unleash your magazine on the Internet," *Folio:,* 15 February 1995.

Sileo, Lorraine. "Interchange Frustrates, But Is a Web-Only Strategy Much Better?" *Online Tactics,* October 1995.

## PUBLIC RELATIONS/PUBLICITY

Klein, Ted, and Fred Danzig. *Publicity: How to Make the Media Work for You.* New York: Scribner's, 1985.

## ENVIRONMENTAL CONCERNS

Arnold, Dana F., and Judith Usherson, "A Printer's Primer on Recycled Paper," *Special Report S441,* National Association of Printers and Lithographers, December 1991.

Barry, John Byrne, "Mea Pulpa," *Sierra,* January/February 1994.

Bogardus, Tim, "Recycled paper gets the ax," *Folio:,* 1 November 1995.

Calvacca, Lorraine, "Audubon's paper chase," *Folio:,* 1 May 1993.

D'Amico, Esther Barbara, "How Soon Will You Print on Recycled Paper?" *Folio:,* 15 May 1993.

"Paper firm ups recycling heat," *Folio:,* 15 April 1993.

Daniel, Joseph E., "Good trash versus seriously bad trash," Folio:, June 1, 1993.

Hochwald, Lambeth, "Recycled: Forcing the issue," *Folio:,* 15 April 1993.

Hurlbert, Carolyn. "Giving It Back/Recycling in the 90s," *Graphic Arts Journal,* May/June 1993.

Macri, Glen, "Grime & Punishment: Limiting Liability Through Environmental Compliance," *Special Report S443,* National Association of Printers and Lithographers, August 1993.

Materazzi, Albert R, "Water Quality Regulations and Their Effect on Printers," *Special Report S439,* National Association of Printers & Lithographers, August 1989.

McCabe, Monica, "Executive Order Defines Recycled Paper Properties," *Environmental Advisor,* National Association of Printers & Lithographers, December 1993.

McDougall, Paul, "Debate over recycled paper intensifies," *Folio:,* 15 September 1993.

"Eco Responsibility/How Much Is Too Much?", *Folio:,* 1 February 1994.

Rathje, William L., and Murphy Cullen. R*ubbish!: The Archaeology of Garbage.* New York: HarperCollins Publishers, 1992.

Thompson, Claudia, "Evaluating the Press Performance of Recycled Papers," *Special Report S274,* National Association of Printers & Lithographers, June 1993.

Wallace, Benjamin J., "The Green Dilemma: Earth or Profits First?", *Magazine Week,* 24 May 1993.

# PRODUCTION/MANUFACTURING

"Corporate Print Buyers on Service, Capability Expectations," *High Volume Printing*, October 1994.

*One Source: The Banta Resource Handbook/A Review of Current Imaging Technologies Affecting Major Printer Markets.* Menasha, Wisc.: Banta Corporation, 1995

"The Printer and Publisher Partnership," *Folio: Special Sourcebook Issue 1993.*

"The U.S. Gravure Indstury Today," *Gravure*, Fall 1994.

"Web/Sheet Crossover: Are the Lines Blurring?" *Web Offset/The Hard Copy*, Fall 1994.

*50 Years/From Pioneers to Leaders.* Teaneck, N.J.: National Association of Printers and Lithographers, 1983.

1994 Technology Forecast. Graphic Arts Technical Foundation, Pittsburgh, Pa., 1994.

1995 Technology Forecast. Graphic Arts Technical Foundation, Pittsburgh, Pa., 1995.

Adams, Michael J., David D. Faux, and Lloyd J. Rieber. *Printing Technology*, 3rd Edit. Albany: Delmar Publishers, 1988.

Andrews, Edmund L, "A Publishers' Slugfest Over Postal Rates," *The New York Times*, 13 November 1995.

Bann, David. *The Print Production Handbook*. Cincinnati: North Light/Writer's Digest Books, 1985.

Beach, Mark. *Graphically Speaking: An Illustrated Guide to the Working Language and Design of Printing*. Cincinnati: North Light Books, 1992.

Beach, Mark, Steve Shepro, and Ken Russon. *Getting It Printed: How To Work With Printers and Graphic Arts Services to Assure Quality, Stay on Schedule, and Control Costs*. Portland, Ore.: Coast to Coast Books, 1986.

Blair, Raymond N., ed. *The Lithographers Manual*, 7th edit. Pittsburgh: Graphic Arts Technical Foundation, 1983.

Bogardus, Tim, "Private mailers offer united front against USPS," *Folio:*, 15 June 1995.

_____. "Publishers weight co-mailing options," Folio:, June 15, 1995.

_____. "Reclassification splits industry," Folio:, May 1, 1995.

Brown, Alex, "Finding the perfect printer," *Folio:*, February 1990.

_____. "Negotiating a printing contract," *Folio: Sourcebook 1992.*

_____. "Your printer's invoice: searching for savings," *Folio:*, March 1990.

Bruno, Michael H., ed. *Pocket Pal/A Graphic Arts Production Handbook, 14th ed.* Memphis: International Paper Company, 1989.

Crimando, Lynne, "Revolution In a Box: How Desktop Production Changes Management Roles," *Folio:*, November 1991.

Cuenca, Mike, "5 ways to save money at the printer," *Folio:, Special Sourcebook Issue 1995.*

_____. "Ad sales and production/Ending the deadline wars with a truce," *Folio: Special Sourcebook issue 1995.*

_____. "Quality time with your printer," *Folio:*, 1 March 1994.

Dejean, Daniel, and Kurt Klein, "Professional Accreditation for Production Management," *Signature*, January/February 1993.

Egol, Len, "Alternative Delivery Reaches for America's Doorknobs," *Printing Manager,* September/October 1993.

Emery, John, "Volume subclass will torpedo value," *Folio:*, 1 July 1995.

Field, Gary G. *Color and Its Reproduction.* Pittsburgh: Graphic Arts Technical Foundation, 1988.

Follert, Melene, "DDAP and the World Beyond," *Signature,* April 1993.

Frye, Stephen W, "How to analyze printing bids," *Folio: Special Sourcebook Issue 1994.*

Garry, Michael, "Dollar stretch: Publishers confront the new economic realities," Folio:, February 1989.

Gross, George, "Reclassification will raise all boats," *Folio:,* 1 July 1995.

Hendricks, Ron, "Make It Again, Sam," *Graphic Arts Journal,* May/June 1993.

Henry, Patrick, "The Ultimate Question: Can You Really Afford to Have In-house Electronic Prepress?", *CONCEPPTS Connections* (National Association of Printers and Lithographers), May 1993.

Herschbein, Irving. "29 ways to reduce production costs," *Folio:,* November 1989.

Heston, Bruce. Quoted in "The Publications Market: What's Important to Today's Publishers?", *Web Offset/The Hard Copy,* Fall 1994.

Holliday, Richard C., "Whistling Past the Graveyard: 40 Years of Magazine Printing." *High Volume Printing,* April 1994.

Horton, Liz. "Charting the pre-press revolution," *Folio:,* August 1991.

Jose, Robert. "Responsibilities of a Production Coordinator," © 1990, Graphic Communications Association.

Kaufman, Stan. "13 ways to evaluate a printer," *Folio: Sourcebook 1992.*

Koff, Richard M. *Strategic Planning for Magazine Executives: How to Take the Guesswork Out of Magazine Publishing Decisions.* Stamford: Folio: Magazine Publishing, 1987.

Lem, Dean Phillip. *graphics master 4: A Workbook of Planning Aids, Reference Guides, and Graphic Tools for the Design, Estimating, Preparation and Production of Printing, Print Advertising, and Desktop Publishing, 4tht edit.* Los Angeles: Dean Lem Associates, 1988.

Love, Barbara, "Threats don't pay off at the printer," *Folio: Special Sourcebook Issue 1995.*

Lyman, Ralph. *Binding and Finishing.* Pittsburgh: Graphic Arts Technical Foudnation, 1993.

Mannheimer, Janet. "Print bids 101, for publishers," *Folio:,* April 1, 1994.

Martin, Teresa and Howard Fenton "Production Managers Talk Back on the Issues," *Magazine Design & Production,* May 1992.

McCabe, Monica, "Agencies Cast Their Nets Wider, Target Publishers," *Environmental Advisor,* National Association of Printers and Lithographers, March 1994.

McDougall, Paul, "Desktop survey: Publishers are doing it for themselves," *Folio:,* 1 September 1994.

McIlroy, Thad, and Gord Graham, *Desktop Publishing in Black + White & Color.* San Francisco: The Color Resource, 1992.

Millet, Gary W., and Ralph G. Rosenberg, *Primer for Graphic Arts Profitability/A Money-Making Formula.* Colorado Springs: Millet Group, Inc., 1992.

Mogel, Leonard. *The Magazine/Everything You Need to Know to Make It in the Magazine Business.* Chester, Conn.: The Globe Pequot Press, 1988.

Pallans, Peter, "17 surefire ways to trim production costs," *Folio: Special Sourcebook Issue 1994.*

Parmau, Jeff. "A boxer's market?", *Magazine Design & Production*, January/February 1992

Pfeifer, Robert, "Integrated Selective Control System Streamlines Binding, Distribution Operations at Perry, Donnelley," *High Volume Printing*, August 1994.

Rees, Steve, "25 ways to customize your magazine," *Folio: Special Source Book Issue for 1994.*

Romano, Dr. Frank, "Electronic Publishing Chronology," © 1994, Frank N. Romano.

Ruggles, Philip K. *De$ktop Dividend$: Managing Electronic Prepress for Profit.* San Luis Obispo, Calif.: Printing Management Services, 1993.

Rutherford, Brett, ed., *Gravure: Process and Technology.* Rochester: Gravure Education Foundation and Gravure Association of America, 1991.

Schnuer, Jenna, "Short-cutoff presses grow in popularity," *Folio:*, 15 April 1995.

Sebastian, Liane. *Electronic Design and Publishing: Business Practices.* New York: Allworth Press, 1992.

Sentinery, Robert, "Your magazine's future is in print," *Folio:*, 1 August 1995

Seybold Special Report: Seybold San Francisco '94, Park I, October 10, 1994.

Sidels, Constance J., "Pleasing Mr. Postman," *Adobe Magazine*, January/February 1995.

Silber, Tony. "Production salary survey/The upward trend continues," *Folio: Special Sourcebook Issue 1996.*

Sosinsky, Barrie. *Beyond the Desktop/Tools and Technology for Computer Publishing.* New York: Bantam Books, 1991.

Southworth, Miles, and Donna Southworth, *How to Implement Total Quality Management.* Livonia, N.Y.: Graphic Arts Publishing,, 1992.

_____. *Pocket Guide to Color Reproduction/Communication and Control.* Livonia, N.Y.: Bronson Hill Press, 1994.

_____. *Quality and Productivity in the Graphic Arts.* Livonia, N.Y.: Graphic Arts Publishing, 1989.

Thomas, Roberta. "High tech at the printer/Innovations in printing and binding," *Folio: Special Sourcebook Issue 1995.*

Veronis, Suhler & Associates, Inc., "Veronis Suhler 9th Annual Communications Industry Forecast/Fact Sheet: Interactive Digital Media 1995–1999," 3 August 1995.

Wilson, Steve, "Launch lag," *Folio:*, 15 January 1995.

# Index*

*Boldface numbers indicate illustrations.